Entry
and Market Contestability

𝕭

Entry
and Market Contestability

An International Comparison

Edited by
P.A. Geroski and J. Schwalbach

BLACKWELL
Oxford UK & Cambridge USA

Copyright © Basil Blackwell 1991

First published 1991

Basil Blackwell Ltd
108 Cowley Road, Oxford, OX4 1JF, UK

Basil Blackwell, Inc.
3 Cambridge Center
Cambridge, Massachusetts 02142, USA

Library of Congress Cataloging in Publication Data

Entry and market contestability : an international comparison / edited by P.A. Geroski and J. Schwalbach.
    p.   cm.
Includes bibliographical references and index.
ISBN 0-631-17401-X
    1. Export marketing—Econometric models.   2. Competition, International—Econometric models.   I. Geroski, Paul.
II. Schwalbach, Joachim.
HF1416.E58   1991
382—dc20   90–1094
                                    CIP

British Library Cataloguing in Publication Data

A CIP catalogue record for this book is available from the British Library.

Typeset in 10 on 12 pt California
by Colset Private Limited, Singapore
Printed in Great Britain by T.J. Press Ltd, Padstow, Cornwall

Contents

Preface   vii

Acknowledgments   x

Contributors   xi

1   Entry, Exit, and the Competitive Process   1
D.C. Mueller

2   Entry and Market Contestability: The Evidence from the
United States   23
I.N. Kessides

3   Sunk Costs and Entry by Small and Large Plants   49
J. Mata

4   Domestic and Foreign Entry in the United Kingdom:
1983–1984   63
P.A. Geroski

5   Domestic Entry in Norwegian Manufacturing Industries   89
N.-H. Mørch von der Fehr

6   Entry and Exit in Belgian Manufacturing   111
L. Sleuwaegen and W. Dehandschutter

7   Entry, Exit, Concentration, and Market Contestability   121
J. Schwalbach

8   Entry during Explosive Growth: Korea during Take-off   143
K.-Y. Jeong and R.T. Masson

9   The Effects of Business Conditions on Net Entry: Evidence
from Japan   168
H. Yamawaki

10   Variation in Producer Turnover Across US Manufacturing
     Industries   187
     T. Dunne and M.J. Roberts

11   Patterns of Entry, Exit, and Merger in Yugoslavia   204
     S. Estrin and T. Petrin

12   Innovation as a Means of Entry: an Overview   222
     D.B. Audretsch and Z.J. Acs

13   Entry, Exit, and Productivity Growth   244
     J.R. Baldwin and P.K. Gorecki

14   International Comparisons of Entry and Exit   257
     J. Cable and J. Schwalbach

15   Some Data-Driven Reflections on the Entry Process   282
     P.A. Geroski

Index   297

Preface

The entry of new competitors into markets is both an interesting and an important phenomenon. The process of entry is interesting to observe because, amongst other things, it is a selection process in which the market chooses between established and entrant firms as well as between different types of entrant. The precise method by which selection occurs in any period affects not only the range and prices of goods offered on the market in that period, but also the number and types of firms willing to compete for a place in that market at some future date. Entry is important because the performance of a market depends on how well the range and prices of goods it produces for sale mesh with consumer needs and resource scarcities, as well as on how fast it takes the market to respond to changes in those needs or resource scarcities. Economists are fond of thinking of competitive markets using the analogy of natural selection, and often have a deeply held belief that whatever emerges from "economic natural selection" in the way of a market outcome is likely to be fairly efficient. Entry is interesting and important because it is the most visible manifestation of this selection process.

The papers published in this volume are the result of a project designed to encourage the development of more empirical work on the nature of the entry process. The goal of the project was twofold: first, we wished to stimulate the collection of new data on entry; second, we wished to stimulate the development of a range of models to explore the causes and consequences of the observed entry flows recorded in that data. The whole exercise developed over a period of about three years. Starting from a small core of scholars who had access to relatively high quality large-scale data bases on entry across a wide range of industries, we gradually identified a number of other scholars who were interested in the area and willing to dig out further data. The group as it stood in 1988 met in Berlin at the end of that year for a two-day working conference attended by about 30 people, insiders and outsiders. A range of models and associated results were presented by those whose work was sufficiently advanced, and an active discussion was initiated around the research proposals advanced by those still busy digging out their data. A second meeting a year later, attended by about 50 insiders and outsiders, discussed the work that had been done since the first meeting plus the contributions of one or two further scholars who had come on board at a late stage.

This project is, in fact, the third in a series sponsored by the Social Science Research Center Berlin (WZB). The two earlier projects – work on mergers and on the persistence of profits, both directed by Dennis Mueller and published in volumes edited by him – shared with this third project a firm commitment to encourage the development of work in as wide a range of countries as possible. Economists have rather limited settings in which to observe the "experiments" that generate the data needed to test their theories, and most of the interesting problems in empirical work involve evaluating the process by which the data were generated and trying to control for a whole variety of extraneous factors. Cross-agent comparisons and comparisons of the same agent over time are two of the most commonly used methods of testing hypotheses, each being a way of holding constant (rather different) extraneous factors. Less well developed as a methodology are cross-national comparisons, and the goal of all three WZB projects has been to encourage the development of such work.

Cross-national comparisons have the major virtue of enabling one to take account of the ways in which deep-seated institutional structures and different types of national economic policy affect certain phenomena of interest. In the case of entry processes, it seems more than reasonable to believe that centrally managed economies will generate rather different types of entrants in rather different numbers than advanced Western economies, that newly developing high growth economies will differ from less dynamic less advanced economies, and so on. These are conjectures that are interesting to pursue, and, to do so, one requires an experimental design that allows for variations in the deep-seated institutional structures that characterize different national economies. However, international comparisons also have their hazards, and these come in two forms. First, data sources are rarely standardized across national economies, and this makes it difficult to be sure that one is always comparing like with like. Second, and more subtly, the role that entry plays in markets may depend in part on the deep-seated institutional factors that help to define the characteristics that markets have in different economies. Models of the causes and consequences of entry must remain alert to these differences, and it is by no means obvious that model structures ought to be standardized across the different countries, even if the data happen to have been standardized.

Thus the project was designed to encourage the development of comparable new data on entry in a wide variety of countries, and to stimulate the application of a range of similar models to that data. In the event, we have been only partially successful on both counts. Most – but not all – of the data that have been generated tabulate gross entry flows that are measured by comparing annual Censuses of Production, and most cover several years in the early 1980s. However, some come from three-digit industries, some from four-digit industries, and some from five-digit industries, and this makes a comparison of the raw totals difficult. Similarly, many of the models in this volume are designed to explain the determinants of entry and share a similar rather simple structure. Only two of the papers report work with more elaborate models of the determinants of entry, and only a few are rather more concerned with the consequences than with the causes of entry. While this no doubt reflects the state of work in the area, a better balanced collection might have reported more work that explored the determinants of survival and turnover amongst entrants, and the several types of effects that entry can have on markets. Taken together, the papers have as much of the flavor of a pastiche as of a systematic international comparison.

As with all projects, this one ended up with a long future research agenda composed of topics that were thrown up by the work done on the project. Perhaps the strongest feeling shared by all the participants of both conferences is that entry is but a part of a much broader more important dynamic phenomenon. Entrants are a small part of the producer population of most markets, and their penetration into these markets is only the first step in a longer process of growth and decline that afflicts most firms. Much of the recent excitement generated by the proposition that potential competition may be a perfect substitute for actual competition, and much of the interest stimulated by the new theories of strategic competition actually obscure the point that much of the competitive pressure faced by market leaders originates within the set of established firms in the market. These forces can often lead to a good deal of intra-industry market share mobility, and to considerable turnover at the top of the market and, indeed, throughout the size ranking of firms. Entry is only the tip of a much larger iceberg, one that may prove to be rather more interesting and important than entry itself.

P.A. Geroski
J. Schwalbach

Acknowledgments

The papers published in this volume were presented and extensively discussed at two conferences held in Berlin in November 1988 and November 1989. We should like to thank Manfred Fleischer and Brigitte Erlinghagen for the superb job they did in organizing and running these two meetings, and the Social Science Research Centre Berlin (WZB), the Thyssen Foundation, the VW Foundation, and the German Marshall Fund for their generous financial support. Both conferences were immensely enriched by the active role played by all the participants, and we should like to thank Hans-Gerd Bannasch, Tito Boeri, Ronald Clapham, Bill Commanor, Ulrich Cramer, Steve Davies, Raymond de Bondt, Jean-Pierre De Laet, Rainer Feuerstack, Manfred Fleischer, Finn Forsund, Jurgen Franke, Bernhard Gahlen, Gerhard Gobel, Knud Hansen, Einar Hope, Kirsty Hughes, Yoshinari Inagaki, Bruce Lyons, Talat Mahmood, Dalia Marin, Steve Martin, Andreas Menidiatis, Jurgen Muller, Manfred Neumann, Louis Phlips, Thorsten Posselt, Danny Shapiro, Mark Schankerman, Horst-Manfred Schellhaass, Ingo Schmidt, Frank Schohl, Manfred Stadler, Thomas von Ungern-Sternberg, Reinhilde Veugelars, Mike Waterson, and Jurgen Wolters for their many helpful comments.

The Authors

Contributors

Zoltan J. Acs: Wissenschaftszentrum Berlin für Sozialforschung, FRG
David B. Audretsch: Merrick School of Business, University of Baltimore, USA
John R. Baldwin: Queen's University, Ontario, Canada
John Cable: The University College of Wales, Aberystwyth, UK
Wim Dehandschutter: Catholic University of Leuven, Belgium
Timothy Dunne: US Census Bureau, USA
Saul Estrin: London School of Economics, UK
Paul K. Gorecki: Economic Council of Canada, Ontario, Canada
Kap-Young Jeong: Yonsei University, Seoul, Korea
Ioannis N. Kessides: University of Maryland, USA
Robert T. Masson: Cornell University, USA
José Mata: Universidade do Minho, Portugal
Nils-Henrik Mørch von der Fehr: University of Oslo, Norway
Dennis C. Mueller: University of Maryland, USA
Tea Petrin: University of Ljubljana, Yugoslavia
Mark J. Roberts: Pennsylvania State University, USA
Leo Sleuwaegen: Catholic University of Leuven, Belgium
Hideki Yamawaki: Wissenschaftszentrum Berlin, FRG

1

Entry, Exit, and the Competitive Process

Dennis C. Mueller

Much modeling of markets in industrial organization takes the number of sellers as fixed. Homogeneous products are also often assumed. Many important insights regarding the competitive process have been drawn from these models: (a) the relationship between the number of sellers and industry price (Cournot, 1838); (b) the relationship between firm conjectures regarding the behavior of other firms and industry price (Bresnahan, 1981; Kamien and Schwartz, 1983); (c) the relationship between changes in market shares and industry price (Stigler, 1964). Although the focus of this literature has been on oligopolistic *inter-actions*, the analysis has been almost entirely static. Nevertheless, the lament heard for so many years, that economics lacked a theory of oligopoly (Rothschild, 1947), is no longer valid. Indeed, if any complaint is justified now it is that too many theories exist. The researcher has a plethora of assumptions and equilibrium concepts from which to choose when trying to explain a particular constellation of industry price and quantities.[1]

To describe the salient characteristics of the competitive process, two important modifications of the standard Cournot-type model must be introduced. Allowance must be made for both product differentiation and the entry and exit of firms. Both modifications move one toward the kind of modeling of competition as a dynamic process that is associated with Schumpeter (1934) and Clark (1962).

The pioneering analyses of product differentiation were of course those of Robinson (1932) and Chamberlain (1933). They were also entirely static, however. Much of the subsequent literature, both theoretical and empirical, follows in the same vein. Product differentiation is treated as a state, as a characteristic of an industry.[2] The *act* of differentiating one's product is not studied.

Helpful comments were received from Paul Geroski.

The study of entry and exit, on the other hand, has often employed dynamic models of the competitive process. Bain's (1949) pioneering "note" on limit pricing was a static analysis. But it was Gaskins' (1971) dynamic model that illuminated the relevant issues involved when price is used as a strategic variable to limit entry, and launched its own stream of research on the topic. Empirical studies of entry and exit, beginning with that of Orr (1974), have of necessity been dynamic in nature. It is interesting in this regard to note, however, that the most influential body of work in the last decade on the consequences of entry and exit for market performance has been the contestable market literature (Baumol et al., 1982). This work, like the original contributions by Bain (1949, 1956), is entirely static. It examines the *conditions* of entry and exit that lead to the existence of market equilibria, and the characteristics of these equilibria when they do exist.

In contrast with this work and much other work on market structure and performance, the essays in this volume are concerned with the dynamic modeling of market behavior and performance. Although it is customary to close a presidential address or a survey of almost any branch of economics with a plea for more dynamic modeling of the economic process, the need for such modeling must arise out of the failure of existing static models, and the empirical research based upon them, to describe accurately the economic phenomena they purport to explain. By way of an introduction to these essays, I shall suggest in the following pages that such a need exists. I shall also indicate some important and related topics on which further research is warranted.

1 Static Oligopoly Models and Empirical Research

The empirical literature testing the predictions of oligopoly theory can be divided into three categories: (a) structure–performance studies linking profitability and concentration; (b) experimental studies of situations that resemble oligopolistic markets; (c) estimations of behavioral parameters in structural oligopoly models. I shall briefly review all three.

The most venerable hypothesis in the oligopoly literature is Cournot's (1838) prediction of an inverse relationship between the price in a market and the number of sellers. If all firms in the market are identical, the product is homogenous, and each firm is a quantity setter who anticipates no reaction to its change in quantity from all other sellers, then the Cournot equilibrium satisfies the following equation:

$$\frac{p - c}{P} = \frac{1}{n\eta} = \frac{H}{\eta} \qquad (1.1)$$

where P is the price of the product, c is the marginal cost of a representative firm, n is the number of firms in the market, H is the Herfindahl index of concentration, and η is the price elasticity of the market's demand schedule (Stigler, 1964; Cowling and Waterson, 1976). Equation (1.1) can be regarded as the theoretical justification for the many studies that have regressed some measure of firm or industry profitability on some measure of concentration. Confidence in the prediction that price–cost margins or profitability are positively correlated is further buttressed by the assumption that collusive behavior is more likely in concentrated markets, and thus that positive errors to (1.1) will themselves be positively correlated with concentration (Marvel, 1980).

The findings of the voluminous literature testing for a positive correlation between concentration and profitability can be roughly divided into two groups. The studies appearing prior to the early 1970s generally found a positive correlation between concentration and profitability and other evidence that they interpreted as supporting a Cournot-collusion-oligopoly hypothesis; the studies appearing since the early 1970s have generally found no positive correlation, and frequently even a negative correlation.[3] Although there are reasons to believe that the methodologies of some of the more recent studies are biased against finding concentration and profitability to be positively correlated,[4] the consensus among industrial organization specialists today must certainly be that the correlation between industry concentration and either firm or industry profitability, if positive, is surely weak, and might very well be nonexistent or even negative.

A similar picture regarding the robustness of collusive behavior is evidenced in the experimental literature. Experiments in market-like situations in which participants choose prices or quantities and can keep any additional profits that they can earn indicate that market outcomes are quite sensitive to the number of sellers. When more than two or maybe three sellers exist in a market, collusive outcomes are difficult to establish or sustain, and they do not always emerge even when there are just two sellers. Nash equilibria abound.[5]

The third relevant literature attempts to determine the nature of oligopolistic interactions from observed price and quantity data within an industry. This literature can in turn be subdivided into two parts according to whether it utilizes cross-sectional data analyses or time series analyses.

If one makes the more general assumption that a given firm i

conjectures that the other firms in the market will respond to a change of one unit in its quantity by changing their outputs by λ_i, then profits maximization by all firms in the industry leads to an equilibrium at which the following equation is satisfied:

$$\frac{P_i - c_i}{P_i} = \frac{H(1 + \lambda_i)}{\eta} \qquad (1.2)$$

where firm marginal costs are now also allowed to vary.[6] Marginal costs can be estimated from available firm-level data; demand elasticity can be estimated using industry-level time series data; price and concentration, H, are observables. Thus, the behavioral variable λ_i can be estimated as essentially a residual to equation (1.1) from observed price–cost margins and the other estimated parameters.

While elements of noncompetitive behavior have been observed in these studies, the major findings often suggest that this behavior is not characteristic of most firms in most markets.[7] For example, at least three studies have tested models of this type on data for 52 coffee roasting firms in the United States. For all but the two, or perhaps five (Geroski, 1982), leading firms in the industry the hypothesis that they were price-takers could not be rejected. Although this finding resembles what one would expect to observe from the dominant-firm model, this model was also rejected by the data in at least one of the studies (Roberts, 1984). Since the leading two firms in this market account for a larger fraction of industry sales than their counterparts in most other industries (55 percent), one suspects that other industries must be characterized by even more competitive behavior. Moreover, without some significant cost advantage on the part of the industry leaders, one expects the price-taking behavior of the substantial competitive fringe in this market to expand over time, further encroaching upon the market power of the leaders (Worcester, 1957).

Bresnahan (1987) does observe cooperative behavior in the US automobile industry in two of the three years 1954, 1955, and 1956. But this cooperation is observed only in the price–cost margin data, when two or three sellers confront one another in the same, rather narrow, segment of the market – the kind of market structure in which the experimental literature also suggests that cooperation may be possible. But what then are we to expect the behavior of firms to be in those markets in which more than two or three effective competitors are present?

Robert Porter (1983, 1985) examined the pattern of prices of a railroad cartel based in Chicago over the period 1880–6 to test for the existence of cooperative behavior. The hypothesis put forward was that the cartel members would price at the joint-profit-maximizing level until some firm was suspected of cheating on the cartel, and then revert to noncooperative behavior to punish the firm suspected of cheating (Friedman, 1983; Green and Porter, 1984). Thus, rather abrupt shifts in prices over time between those predicted by the cooperative and noncooperative solutions to the game are expected. Porter did indeed observe the predicted pattern of changes, but at considerably lower levels than the theory implies. The best that the cartel could accomplish was the set of prices that one would expect to observe if the market was in a noncooperative Cournot equilibrium. When "cooperation" broke down prices fell considerably below this level, although not all the way to the perfectly competitive Bertrand equilibrium. And this behavior was observed in a market with from three to five firms that were openly engaged in running a cartel! Margaret Slade (1987) also found that the pricing behavior in the market for gasoline in Vancouver, BC, was closer (but not equal) to what one would expect in a competitive market than to what one would expect under the assumption of perfect collusion.

Also interesting in this regard is the study of cereals pricing in the United States by J. Nellie Liang (1989). As in Bresnahan's (1987) study of the automobile market, Liang divided the cereals market into sub-markets of closely related products to test for cooperative behavior. She did find evidence of cooperative interactions in pricing behavior in those markets in which two or three firms sold very close substitutes, although she consistently rejected the hypothesis of perfect collusion. On the other hand the most profitable products in the cereals industry were those with no close substitutes, and for which the Cournot behavioral assumption was most appropriate. They ignored other sellers because they were essentially monopolists in their particular submarket, and priced and earned profits accordingly.

It is difficult to escape the conclusion when reviewing this literature that large price–cost margins or profit rates, if they exist, are not the result of tacit or overt collusion among sellers in most markets. In some cases, like particular segments of the automobile market in the United States in 1954 and 1956, or cornflakes today, the number of sellers may be so small that effective coordination of prices to restrain output is possible. But in most markets the number of effective competitors is going to be too large to make this feasible. The "monopoly problem," if there is one, is not one of several firms producing the same product and conspiring overtly or otherwise to raise prices. But before concerning ourselves with the question of what the monopoly problem is, we must determine whether or not there is one.

2 Prices, Profits, and Monopoly

When one looks at aggregated data on price–cost margins, the answer to the above question appears to be no. The average price–cost margin for a US manufacturing firm is small, suggesting that the typical US firm does not possess much monopoly power, or, if it does, it chooses not to exercise it. At least this was the conclusion reached by William W. Alberts (1984). He observed that only about 17 percent of the 777 large firms he examined had rates of return on equity capital 5 percentage points or more above his estimate of the competitive return (0.13), (Alberts, 1984, p. 628). In my own work some 82 of the 551 companies I studied had projected returns on total assets of 50 percent or more above the average return on assets, where the average return was estimated to be some 4–20 percent above the competitive return (Mueller, 1986, pp. 33–9). These 82 companies, 15 percent of the sample, had mean long-run projected returns of more than double the average for the entire sample.

Whether one views these percentages and averages as large or small may be somewhat of a matter of taste. But in either case it is clear that some firms would appear to have and take advantage of significant market power. There are two ways in which one can view this fact. First, one can think of the entire competitive process as being highly stochastic. Some firms inevitably get lucky, and these are the fortunate recipients of above normal profits. Others are unlucky and they are found at the bottom of the distribution. Although there is a seductive simplicity to this stochastic description of the process of competition, it does not wholly accord with the facts. The stochastic view of competition would seem to suggest considerable flux in the distribution of company profits over time. Today firm X is lucky, tomorrow Y. But when one observes the identities of the companies at the top of the distribution, one finds considerable stability. The projections indicating that 15 percent of the sample would earn double the average return of the sample were based on a 23 year time series, and were projections into the indefinite future. A substantial fraction of the companies at the top of the distribution of profit rates appear there year in year out (Mueller, 1986).

Of course some stability in the identities of the most profitable firms would be expected even in a completely stochastic environment. Some firms will experience a "string of good luck" and be found at the top of the distribution for several years (Mancke, 1974). There are two difficulties with this interpretation of the profits data, however. First, the

Bernoullian view of the competitive process does not accord well with many of its attributes that we observe. The management of Kellogg's does not reach into a bag of products each year and just happen to be lucky enough to come up with cornflakes and the other highly profitable products that it sells every time. Even if luck was partly involved in Kellogg's original development of these products, its continued dominance of the cereals market over the last 100 years is not simply a matter of a continual "luck of the draw." Second, the fraction of the most profitable firms at any one point in time that remain persistently profitable is too large to be attributed merely to chance.[8]

If chance cannot explain all the observed pattern of profitability differences across firms, we are left with the more traditional deterministic explanation. Some firms possess and consciously exploit persistent market power advantages. Instances of monopoly power do exist, and they account for the above normal profits observed.

This conclusion is buttressed by the strong relationship between profitability and market shares observed in recent studies.[9] This correlation could occur because the larger firms have lower costs, charge lower prices, and thus capture a larger fraction of the market (Demsetz, 1973, 1974). But the little empirical work that exists relating market shares to prices suggests that the correlation is positive.[10]

My results relating long-run profits to market shares are also consistent with a price-raising interpretation of this relationship. The positive correlation between profits and market share was significant only in the presence of product differentiation, a result one expects to find if the correlation stems from a more inelastic demand for the larger firm's product rather than lower costs (Mueller, 1986, chs 4, 5). Ravenscraft (1983) reports similar findings using different data for the United States, as does Odagiri (1988) for Japan.

The conclusion that the positive profitability–market share correlation reflects the price-raising capacity associated with market power is further strengthened when one examines the identities of the firms that are persistently profitable in the United States. This list includes Black and Decker, Campbell Soup, Coca-Cola, Corning Glass, Du Pont, Kodak, Gerber, Gillette, Hershey, Heublin, Hoover, IBM, Kellogg, Maytag, 3M, Polaroid, Proctor and Gamble, and Wrigley. All these, and many other less familiar names of the list, obtain their above normal profits not by continually undercutting the prices of their competitors, but by being able to sell at prices that are *above* those of their competitors.[11]

Thus we conclude that the phenomenon of some firms earning above normal profits, and some industries having several firms earning above normal profits so that the industry's profits are above the average, does not seem to be so much a manifestation of oligopoly power, the capacity of firms acting in consort to raise prices, but of monopoly power in its classic sense. The products of some firms are sufficiently differentiated in the eyes of buyers from those of other firms in the "same industry" that the former are able to charge prices that are persistently above those of their rivals.

3 Monopoly, Entry, and Exit

The essence of monopoly power is the ability to set price above costs. But the exercise of this market power should in turn attract other firms to enter the monopolist's market and undercut its price at a profit. What prevents other firms from entering the markets in which firms with market power select high price–cost margins?

A long list of answers have been given to this question. One of the first, and best known, is that of Joe Bain (1949): the monopolist sets the price so low that it is unprofitable to enter. But this strategy can be effective only if the monopolist has a cost advantage over the potential entrant, and even then his optimal strategy is more likely to entail allowing some entry over time and a gradual erosion of his monopoly position (Gaskins, 1971; Kamien and Schwartz, 1971). Neither set of arguments seems to be an adequate explanation for why some firms can earn persistently above normal profits by charging higher prices than their rivals.

A more profitable strategy for deterring entry than to set the price so low as to limit entry is to set quantity so high that the residual demand schedule faced by the potential entrant does not provide profitable price–output combinations (Sylos-Labini, 1957; Modigliani, 1958). This strategy is generally dominated, however, by one of building sufficient capacity to deter entry, if fully utilized, but then pricing to maximize profits, thereby allowing some capacity to go unused (Spence, 1977). Although this strategy seems potentially descriptive of some industries like steel, other heavy metals, and chemicals, it does not seem to be a very accurate characterization of many of the markets in which market power appears to be particularly strong, as evidenced by profit margins.[12] Kodak does not remain dominant in the film and film developing markets because it maintains excess capacity in these markets and threatens to flood them with film and developing services should entry take place. "Entry" has already taken place, or at least close substitutes exist, and yet Kodak is able to maintain both its large market shares and higher prices in these markets. What little empirical evidence there is on the matter also does not suggest that the strategy is often used. Managers answering Smiley's (1988) questionnaire survey placed creating excess capacity at the bottom of their list of entry-deterring strategies. Neither Hilke (1984) nor Lieberman (1987) were able to uncover statistical evidence that the strategy is used to a significant degree.

Perhaps in implicit recognition of the inapplicability of the excess capacity argument in some markets, Spence (1977, p. 543) speculates at the close of his original paper that advertising may play a similar entry-deterring role as excess capacity. But the analogy seems strained. Excess capacity can be an entry deterrent because the potential entrant realizes that the incumbent firm can quickly expand output and drive price down to levels at which the entrant cannot survive. But heavy advertising does not in and of itself connote a capacity to expand output and lower price. What is the threat implied by heavy advertising?

If advertising is an investment creating an intangible stock, then past outlays can constitute a sunk cost that generates an asymmetry between incumbent and potentially entering firms, an asymmetry that does impede entry. Considerable evidence exists suggesting that advertising does play this entry-deterring role (Comanor and Wilson, 1967, 1974; Porter, 1974; Kessides, 1986; chapters 2, 6 and 8 in this volume).

Many of the persistently most profitable firms in the United States are companies which came into existence along with the products with which they are most closely associated, e.g. Kodak, Gillette, Kellogg's, Gerber, Campbell Soup, Polaroid, Coca-Cola, Wrigley, and Hoover. This symbiosis between company and product in turn suggests first-mover advantages of one sort or another. But what are these first-mover advantages, and why are they so powerful in some markets like canned soups, and so weak in others like canned fruits and vegetables?

Lieberman and Montgomery (1988) have recently surveyed the literature on first-mover advantages and identified three major categories: (a) technological leadership, (b) preemption of assets, and (c) buyer switching costs. Learning-by-doing cost reductions and patent-protected technological leadership are examples of the first. Xerox, Polaroid, and General Electric (light bulbs) are companies that illustrate this kind of technological leadership.

The purchase of rights to ore reserves is an obvious, although fairly rare, example of first-mover preemption through the purchase of scarce assets. Occupying choice locations in physical or product characteristics space is another example. The case brought by the Federal Trade Commission (FTC) against breakfast cereals firms attempted to press this argument (Schmalensee, 1978; Scherer, 1982).

Richard Schmalensee's (1982) model of first-mover advantage fits into the third category. He demonstrates that buyer uncertainty over the quality of a new product will lead some buyers to continue to purchase a pioneering brand whose quality is known to them, even when a second brand of unknown but equal quality is available at a lower price. Firms following a pioneer brand are at a competitive disadvantage even when they have costs and quality equal to that of the pioneer, simply because the quality of their product is unknown.

Schmalensee's first-mover hypothesis would seem to fit some products better than others. It is difficult to imagine that any individual in the United States who drinks many soft drinks can reach the age of maturity without having tried not only Coca-Cola and Pepsi Cola, but also RC Cola, supermarket brands of cola, and numerous other noncola soft drinks. The continued dominance of the cola soft drink market by the Coca Cola and Pepsi Cola companies and their high profitability cannot be plausibly attributed to buyer uncertainty over the quality of substitute brands.

The purchase of a car is a sufficiently large and infrequent occurrence that it is reasonable to assume that most buyers have not tried all other brands. But, given the magnitude of the purchase, one would expect buyers to engage in information gathering about product quality before buying a car. Buyer uncertainty does not seem like a plausible explanation for the persistent profitability of Mercedes Benz in the luxury car market, or, for an analogous reason, IBM in office machinery and computers.

Markets that might fit Schmalensee's hypothesis well are film and film developing. Assuming that the amateur photographer takes only a few rolls of film per year, she may deem the extra cost she pays for Kodak film and developing, a small premium to pay for the extra assurance she perceives the Kodak name provides to her that the pictures she takes will be of high quality.

Although examples of companies that fit each category of first-mover advantage can be found (e.g. Polaroid, International Nickel, Kodak), others do not seem to fit any category well (Campbell Soup, Coca-Cola, 3M (Scotch Tape)). The inherent nature of first-mover advantages remains somewhat of a mystery.

Few if any areas in industrial organization have yielded a larger and richer set of hypotheses than has the theoretical literature on entry and entry deterrence over the last two decades. That no single hypothesis seems likely to account for most of the instances of persistent market power and high profitability that are observed should not be surprising. Answers to our questions must lie in some weighted average of all existing hypotheses and some yet to be formulated. To go beyond this tautological statement we must delve below the rarified pinnacles of theoretical analysis. We must examine the empirical literature, a literature that often appears as a muddy quagmire alongside the elegant beauty of the theoretical work from which it derives.

4 Empirical Evidence on Entry and Exit

Despite the theoretical importance of entry and exit in the process of competition, they have been the subject of empirical research in only the last 15 years. Although the tempo of this area of investigation has quickened in recent years, many questions about the nature and effects of this process remain unanswered.

If what we mean by entry is that a firm which did not manufacture a product in a given four-digit industry last year does so this year, and employ the symmetric definition for exit, then two facts about entry and exit stand out. On average there is a lot of both going on, and there is considerable heterogeneity in the amount of entry and exit across industries. On average in four-digit US manufacturing industries the number of new entrants over any 5-year census interval equals roughly half the total number of firms in an industry. The number of exits tends to be slightly less than the number of entrants (Dunne et al., 1989). The range of entry rates is from zero to nearly 100 percent (Dunne et al., 1989, table 5).

Several studies have also noted the considerable heterogeneity that exists in the characteristics of the firms that enter. At least five distinctions have been found to be important: (a) entry by a newly created firm; (b) entry by an existing firm that builds a new plant in the industry; (c) entry by an existing firm that buys a plant (firm) already in the industry; (d) entry by an existing firm that alters the product mix in an existing plant; (e) entry by a foreign-owned firm in one of the above ways as opposed to a domestic firm (Baldwin and Gorecki, 1987; Dunne et al., 1989a, 1989b; Geroski, 1989). Entry by newly created firms, the type of entry that perhaps comes to mind first, tends to be on a smaller scale than the other forms of entry and to have a significantly lower probability of survival.

The latter fact largely explains another salient feature of entry and exit; they are highly correlated across industries. Indeed, today's new entrant is likely to be tomorrow's exit statistic (Shapiro and Khemani, 1987; Dunne et al., 1989a, 1989b). Insight as to why this is so is contained in the study by Ralph Biggadike (1976). He examined the histories of 40 market entries by a sample of large diversified firms. Despite their size (all but one was in the Fortune 500), the average entrant suffered substantial losses during the first few years of operation and required 8 years to just break even. Presumably, new or small firm entrants would fare even worse.

These observations in turn largely explain another. Despite the seemingly large amounts of entry and exit that occur in most industries, neither has much of a measurable effect on their basic structural characteristics (Geroski et al., 1987; Dunne et al., 1989a, 1989b). The leading firms in most industries stand calmly in the center, as if in the eye of a tornado, while myriad smaller challengers whirl in and out along the periphery (but see chapter 13 in this volume).

The latter fact helps account for our final empirical generalization. Industry price–cost margins and profit rates do not appear to be greatly affected by entry and exit.[13] With respect to normative issues concerning the process of competition, this final observation is the most important of all. The economic model of the entry–exit process has each of these responding to industry profit levels, and industry profit levels in turn responding to entry and exit.[14] Some, but not overwhelming, support for the first half of the model does exist in the literature.[15] Empirical support for the second half of the two-way causal relationship is very weak.[16] Both industry market structures and the profits of leading firms do not seem to be greatly disturbed by the coming and going of entering firms and products.

Insight as to why this is true can be obtained from the history of the ready-to-eat cereal industry in the United States. This industry has been dominated by six firms. Four-firm concentration ratios since the Second World War have been around 90 percent. Profit rates have been considerably above average (Scherer, 1982). Between 1950 and 1973 84 new brands were introduced into the market (Scherer, 1982, p. 199). Yet despite this onslaught of competition, the list of leading brands remained remarkably stable. In 1965, for example, six of the seven leading brands had been on the market since well before the Second World War (Nelson, 1966). The one newcomer was Kellogg's Sugar Frosted Flakes, a sugar-coated version of its cornflake, the perennial leading selling brand. How can so much entry and innovative activity produce so little effect on the product structure and profitability of an industry? The answer is that the typical new product never captured more than a couple of percent of the cereals' market, nor lasted for more than a few years on supermarket shelves. The new products displaced one another, and left the market positions and profitability of the leading brands unperturbed (Schmalensee, 1978, pp. 317–18; Scherer, 1982, p. 198).

The histories of most industries follow a similar pattern.[17] An industry is born with the invention of a new product or on occasion a new production technique. In the beginning a competition for the best product design and/or production technique ensues. Many firms enter this competition; many fail to pick a winner. Rapid entry is followed by rapid exit. A small subset of product designs and production techniques are selected for survival. The winners of this competition go on to become the industry leaders, the first movers, whose product images and learning-by-doing efficiencies are nearly impossible to duplicate. These companies remain on top of the industry year in and year out. Their eclipse often comes only when tastes or technology change so as to displace the entire industry.

This sketch of an industry's history helps to explain the often weak statistical performance of entry and exit models when estimated using cross-sectional data. In any cross section industries will be captured in different stages of their life cycle. The current profits of a young industry may be low, but entry and exit rates are high as new competitors strive for the leadership positions that will some day earn them high profits. Profits in a mature industry may be high, but entry rates low (Biggadike, 1976, pp. 205–6), with entry largely limited to the industry's periphery and the leaders protected by their product images, knowledge, and other first-mover advantages. Given these inter-industry differences, a poor correlation between entry and profit rates is less surprising.

The above historical sketch and the models of entry and exit extant both in the literature and in this volume envisage entry into a domestic industry by a domestic firm. It is entry of this type, once an industry has reached a given level of maturity, that generally has little impact on the profitability of incumbents.

But there is a second form of entry that can have quite a different effect, namely that of an international competitor. A domestic entrant must hire labor from the same labor market as an incumbent, purchase capital and materials in the same markets, and draw upon the same knowledge base (if not a narrower one). Factor price and technology differences across countries may be so substantial, however, as to allow a foreign firm to enter a domestic market and significantly underprice the domestic firms or offer a far superior product. The foreign entrant, although a newcomer in the domestic market, may be a well-established company in its home and other foreign markets. It will not suffer from many of the start-up cost problems a domestic entrant faces, and therefore may be a much more formidable competitor. Thus, although domestic entry seems to have a modest effect on the profitability of incumbent firms, import competition can have a substantial effect, as one industry after another in the United States and Western Europe has borne witness in recent years. This process of entry and exit is different from the one described in the existing literature and in the papers of this volume (but see chapter 4).

5 Implications for Future Research

Although much empirical work exists on the causes of firm and industry differences in profitability, studies of entry and exit and their relationship to profitability remain relatively rare. The papers in this volume are thus a welcome addition to the subject. Beyond their contribution a couple of topics requiring yet further research remain in view.

When this observer purviews the literature on profitability, entry, and exit, one characteristic stands out – heterogeneity. Heterogeneity appears in the studies of profitability in the important role that product differentiation plays as an explanation for or correlate of profitability. It is typically differentiated product industries like pharmaceuticals, cosmetics, cereals, distilled beverages, photographic equipment, cigarettes – industries in which advertising, research and development (R & D), and patent protection are important – that stand at the top of the profitability list. Within these industries it is the handful of companies that has succeeded in differentiating their products from those of their rivals *in the same industry* – the Mercks, Kelloggs, and Kodaks – that earn the highest profit rates.

Heterogeneity is also apparent in the entry and exit process. It is apparent in the great differences that exist across industries in the amounts of entry and exit taking place. It is apparent in the differing characteristics of the firms entering. The importance of these heterogeneities in the statistics on profitability, entry, and exit suggests the need for more research of both an analytical and an empirical kind.

One of the most basic and least edifying tasks in industrial economics is defining an industry. All empirical work simply takes as given the definitions of industries made by the government agency that gathers the data, with perhaps some adjustments being made by combining a few industries or disaggregating the data geographically. Government statistics offices invariably base their definitions on a combination of considerations of substitution in consumption and substitution in production.

Only an empirical nihilist can take serious exception to these practices, since no academic researcher has the resources or legal backing to try and duplicate the efforts of government statistical censuses using alternative definitions. Nevertheless, one must recognize that within the boundaries of many "industries" as defined in empirical work, not all firms compete directly with one another, nor will all new entrants have a symmetric impact on incumbent firms.

In much modeling of the entry process, new entry is treated as a viscous substance that is poured into an industry at varying flow velocities. Upon entering, this substance combines with that already present in the industry to form a homogeneous blend. Post-entry all firms are and behave alike. But, as the preceding discussion and examples should have made clear, this model does not accurately describe all industries, and perhaps not any. Maintaining the liquid analogy, we are usually more accurate in thinking of entrants as flowing into small puddles and ponds that remain separate from the large lakes in which the major incumbents are found. Occasionally entry may be so fast that it spills over the banks of the small ponds and into the larger bodies. But they never (seldom) merge into one giant body of liquid.

To pursue this perspective further requires that we adopt a more micro-oriented approach, and go inside the conventionally defined boundaries of industries and examine the various subindustries and submarkets of which it is composed. Such an approach might very well have to take the form of industry case studies. Beginnings in this direction exist in the work on intra-industry mobility barriers (Caves and Porter, 1977), and in models of entry and structure–performance that allow firms to occupy separate niches[18] (Kessides, 1986; chapter 2 of this volume). But models of this type simplify the complexity of the problem greatly, and are a distinct minority in the empirical literature.

To understand the impact of the entrance of Polaroid into the photographic equipment "industry," one must recognize that the instant development camera that Polaroid first marketed was not a close substitute for the conventional commercial development cameras then in the market. Polaroid created a new submarket within "photographic equipment and supplies," and although it undoubtedly took some sales away from Kodak, it also created new customers for its products. To understand how and why Polaroid entered this industry, one must not only concern oneself with market definitions but must also learn something about Edwin H. Land, the innovator who founded the Polaroid company (see chapter 12 of this volume).

When neoclassical economics was first spawned at the end of the nineteenth century and the beginning of the twentieth, the entrepreneur was the focal point of much writing by economists. Of course there was considerable relevance to this topic, for this was the era in which great trusts often arose out of the individual efforts of their founders.

The monopolistic competition revolution in the 1930s reawakened interest in just what it was that the entrepreneur in the firm did to justify his claim to a part of the revenues of the firm. But in recent years the topic has been essentially dead in both the industrial organization literature and in economics more generally. A quick check of the indexes of six of the leading industrial organization textbooks reveals that the subject heading "entrepreneur" is absent from all of them. This neglect is understandable, since the entrepreneur is difficult to identify in the modern large corporation, and concern with principal–agent problems and the like is more appropriate.

But when attention is given to the process of entry and exit, and Schumpeterian competition more generally, the role of the entrepreneur comes once again to the fore. Those individuals who choose to found new firms and bring out new products differ greatly in their educational backgrounds, their access to capital, and still other factors that may figure importantly in the potential success of their undertaking (Bates, 1989). A good deal of the heterogeneity of the entry–exit process stems from the heterogeneities in the companies themselves, and these in turn are often directly related to the backgrounds and personalities of the individuals who run them. A full understanding of the processes of entry, exit, and innovation in the evolution of capitalist industrial structures still requires that some attention be given to the study of the entrepreneurial role in these processes, and of the environment that fosters entrepreneurial activity. Here again normal more aggregate analyses may have to be supplemented by case studies to gain a full understanding of what is going on.

Notes

1 See Ulph (1983) and the survey by Shapiro (1989).
2 See, for example, the way in which Kamien and Schwartz (1983) treat product differentiation as an industry parameter in their analysis of oligopolistic interactions, and the similar treatment in my empirical study (Mueller, 1986).
3 For a survey of the early literature, see Weiss (1974). For a survey that includes the more recent work, see Schmalensee (1989).
4 Ravenscraft (1983) and Haid and Neumann (1988) discuss econometric problems that arise when concentration and market share are included in the

same equation as is the practice in the recent literature, but reach opposite conclusions on the matter.

5 See the surveys by Plott (1989) and Geroski et al. (1985).

6 The pioneering reference here is Cowling and Waterson (1976). For a discussion of various permutations on this equation see Clarke and Davies (1982).

7 See again the surveys of Geroski et al. (1985) and Shapiro (1989).

8 For evidence from the United States, see Mueller (1977, 1986); for the FRG see Schohl (1990).

9 See, for example, Shepherd (1972, 1975), Martin (1983), Ravenscraft (1983), and Mueller (1986).

10 See Marion et al. (1979, ch. 4), Curry (1981), Osborne and Wendel (1981), and Nelson and Siegfried (1989). Berger and Hannan (1989) find a price-reducing effect, however. For evidence linking prices positively to industry concentration, see Weiss (1989).

11 Frederick deB. Harris (1986) cautions that a positive market share–profit relationship in industries with product differentiation could come from either the price-raising or cost-reducing effects of market share. His argument is valid, but I still suspect that the much stronger positive correlation between market share and profitability in the presence of product differentiation than in its absence suggests that cost-reducing effects are not dominating.

12 When the strategic interactions between incumbent and potential entrant are modeled, the incumbent often chooses to deter entry by a Stackelberg-like quantity–capacity choice. No excess capacity is observed (Dixit, 1979, 1980; Eaton and Lipsey, 1981). Such strategic choices again rely on the incumbent firm supplying greater output and thus lower prices that it would as a simple monopolist. It is not clear, therefore, how descriptive they are of the many markets one observes in which close substitutes seem to exist already, and yet the leading firm enjoys a large market share, and charges higher prices and has higher profits than its closest rivals.

13 See the discussion of the literature in Geroski and Masson (1987), the results in Geroski (1988), and chapters 4 and 8 in this volume.

14 The pioneering empirical effort of this type was by Orr (1974).

15 On the support side see, in particular, Masson and Shaanan (1982), Khemani and Shapiro (1986), Highfield and Smiley (1987), Shapiro and Khemani (1987), Kessides (1990), and chapters 2, 4, 6, 8, and 11 in this volume. For further discussion and references to the negative findings, see Geroski and Masson (1987).

16 Ibid.

17 For further discussion and references to the literature, see Mueller (1987) and chapter 12 of this volume.

18 Somehow the word "niche," so commonly used now to describe intra-industry heterogeneity, does not seem to capture well one's image of the positions of an IBM or a Kodak in their respective "industries."

18   *D.C. Mueller*

References

Alberts, W.W. (1984) Do oligopolists earn "noncompetitive" rates of return? *American Economic Review* 74, 624–33.

Bain, J.S. (1949) A note on pricing in monopoly and oligopoly, *American Economic Review* 39, 448–64.

Bain, J.S. (1956) *Barriers to New Competition*. Cambridge, MA: Harvard University Press.

Baldwin, J.R. and Gorecki, P.K. (1987) Plant creation versus plant acquisition: the entry process in Canadian manufacturing. *International Journal of Industrial Organization* 5, 27–41.

Bates, T. (1989) Entrepreneur factor inputs and small business longevity, Paper CES 89-4, Center for Economic Studies. Washington, DC.

Baumol, W.J., Panzer, J.C. and Willig, R.D. (1982) *Contestable Markets and the Theory of Industry Structure*. New York: Harcourt Brace Jovanovich.

Berger, A.N. and Hannan, T.H. (1989) The price–concentration relationship in banking. *Review of Economics and Statistics* 71, 291–9.

Biggadike, E.R. (1976) *Corporate Diversification: Entry, Strategy and Performance*. Cambridge, MA: Harvard University Press.

Bresnahan, T.F. (1981) Duopoly models with consistent conjectures. *American Economic Review* 71, 934–45.

Bresnahan, T.F. (1987) Competition and collusion in the American automobile industry: the 1955 price war. *Journal of Industrial Economics* 35, 457–82.

Caves, R. and Porter, M. (1977) From entry to mobility barriers. *Quarterly Journal of Economics* 91, 241–61.

Chamberlain, E.H. (1933) *The Theory of Monopolistic Competition*. Cambridge, MA: Harvard University Press.

Clark J.M. (1962) *Competition as a Dynamic Process*. Washington, DC: Brookings Institution.

Clarke, R. and Davies, S.W. (1982) Market structure and price–cost margins. *Economica* 49, 277–87.

Comanor, W. and Wilson, T. (1967) Advertising, market structure and performance. *Review of Economics and Statistics* 49, 423–40.

Comanor, W.S. and Wilson, T.A. (1974) *Advertising and Market Power*. Cambridge, MA: Harvard University Press.

Cournot, A.A. (1927) *Researches into the Mathematical Principles of the Theory of Wealth*. New York: Macmillan (original publication 1838).

Cowling, K. and Waterson, M. (1976) Price–cost margins and market structure. *Economica* 43, 267–74.

Curry, T.J. (1981) The pre-acquisition characteristics of banks acquired by multibank holding companies, *Journal of Bank Research* 12, 82–9.

Demsetz, H. (1973) Industry structure, market rivalry, and public policy. *Journal of Law and Economics* 16, 1–9.

Demsetz, H. (1974) Two systems of belief about monopoly. In H.J. Goldschmid,

H.M. Mann and J.F. Weston (eds), *Industrial Concentration: The New Learning*. Boston, MA: Little, Brown, pp. 164–84.

Dixit, A. (1979) A model of duopoly suggesting a theory of entry barriers. *Bell Journal of Economics* 10, 20–32.

Dixit, A. (1980) The role of investment in entry deterrence. *Economic Journal* 90, 95–106.

Dunne, T., Roberts, M.J. and Samuelson, L. (1988) The growth and failure of U.S. manufacturing plants. *Quarterly Journal of Economics*, 104, 671–98.

Dunne, T., Roberts, M.J. and Samuelson, L. (1989b) Firm entry and post-entry performance in the U.S. chemical industries. Working Paper CES 89-6, Center for Economic Studies, Washington, DC.

Eaton, B.C. and Lipsey, R.G. (1981) Capital commitment and entry equilibrium. *Bell Journal of Economics* 12, 593–604.

Friedman, J. (1983) *Oligopoly Theory*. Cambridge: Cambridge University Press.

Gaskins, D.W., Jr (1971) Dynamic limit pricing: optimal pricing under threat of entry. *Journal of Economic Theory* 3, 306–22.

Geroski, P.A. (1982) The empirical analysis of conjectural variations in oligopoly. Mimeo, London Business School.

Geroski, P.A. (1988) The effect of entry on profit margins in the short and long run. Mimeo, London Business School.

Geroski, P.A. (1989) Entry, innovation and productivity growth. Mimeo, London Business School.

Geroski, P.A. and Masson, R.T. (1987) Dynamic market models in industrial organization. *International Journal of Industrial Organization* 5, 1–13.

Geroski, P.A., Masson, R.T. and Shaanan, J. (1987) The dynamics of market structure. *International Journal of Industrial Organization* 5, 93–100.

Geroski, P.A., Philips, L. and Ulph, A. (1985) Oligopoly, competition, and welfare: some recent developments, *Journal of Industrial Economics* 33, 369–86.

Green, E.J. and Porter, R.H. (1984) Noncooperative collusion under imperfect price information. *Econometrica* 52, 87–100.

Haid, A. and Neumann M. (1988) Market share and concentration in the structure–performance paradigm and the new learning. Mimeo, University of Erlangen-Nuernberg.

Harris F.H. deB. (1986) Market structure and price–cost performance under endogenous profit risk. *Journal of Industrial Economics* 35, 35–59.

Highfield, R. and Smiley, R. (1987) New business starts and economic activity: an empirical investigation. *International Journal of Industrial Organization* 5, 51–66.

Hilke, J.C. (1984) Excess capacity and entry: some empirical evidence, *Journal of Industrial Economics* 33, 233–41.

Kamien, M.I. and Schwartz, N.L. (1971) Limit pricing and uncertain entry. *Econometrica* 39, 441–54.

Kamien, M.I. and Schwartz, N.L. (1983) Conjectural variations. *Canadian Journal of Economics* 16, 191–211.

Kessides, I.N. (1986) Advertising, sunk costs, and barriers to entry. *Review of Economics and Statistics* 68, 84–96.

Kessides, I.N. (1990) Toward a testable model of entry: a study of the U.S. manufacturing industries. *Economica* 57, 219–38.

Khemani, R.S. and Shapiro, D. (1986) The determinants of new plant entry in Canada. *Applied Economics* 18, 1243–57.

Liang, J.N. (1989) Price reaction functions anc conjectural variations: an application to the breakfast cereal industry. *Review of Industrial Organization* 4, 31–58.

Lieberman, M.B. (1987) Excess capacity as a barrier to entry: an empirical appraisal. *Journal of Industrial Economics* 35, 607–27.

Lieberman, M.B. and Montgomery, D.B. (1988) First-mover advantages. *Strategic Management Journal* 9, 41–58.

Mancke, R.B. (1974) Causes of interfirm profitability differences: a new interpretation of the evidence. *Quarterly Journal of Economics* 88, 181–93.

Marion, B.W., Mueller, W.F., Cotterill, R.W., Geithman, F.E. and Schmelzer, J.R. (1979) *The Food Retailing Industry*. New York: Praeger.

Martin, S. (1983) *Market, Firm and Economic Performance: An Empirical Analysis*. New York: Salomon Brothers Center.

Marvel, H.P. (1980) Collusion and the pattern of rates of return. *Southern Economic Journal* 47, 375–87.

Masson, R. and Shaanan, J. (1982) Stochastic dynamic limit pricing: an empirical test. *Review of Economics and Statistics* 64, 413–22.

Modigliani, F. (1958) New developments on the oligopoly front. *Journal of Political Economy* 66, 215–32.

Mueller, D.C. (1977) The persistence of profits above the norm. *Economica* 44, 369–80.

Mueller, D.C. (1986) *Profits in the Long Run*. Cambridge: Cambridge University Press.

Mueller, D.C. (1987) *The Corporation: Growth, Diversification and Mergers*. Chur: Harwood Academic Publishers.

Nelson, P. and Siegfried, J. (1989) A simultaneous equations model of coffee brand pricing and advertising. Mimeo, Vanderbilt University.

Nelson, R.C. (1966) Cereals snap, crackle, sometimes lay bombs. *Printer's Ink* 19ff.

Odagiri, H. (1988) Inferring changing modes of oligopolistic relationship from the Japanese studies on market share–profitability association. University of Tsukuba, Japan.

Orr, D. (1974) The determinants of entry: a study of the Canadian manufacturing industries. *Review of Economics and Statistics* 56, 58–66.

Osborne, D. and Wendel, J. (1981) A note on concentration and checking account prices. *Journal of Finance* 36, 181–6.

Plott, C.R. (1989) An updated review of industrial organization: applications of experimental methods. In R. Schmalensee and R.D. Willig (eds), *Handbook of Industrial Organization II*, Amsterdam: North-Holland, pp. 1109–76.

Porter, M.E. (1974) Consumer behavior, retailer power and market performance in consumer goods industries. *Review of Economics and Statistics* 56, 419–36.

Porter, R.H. (1983) A study of cartel stability: the joint executive committee, 1880–1886. *Bell Journal of Economics* 14, 301–14.

Porter, R.H. (1985) On the incidence and duration of price wars. *Journal of Industrial Economics* 33, 415–26.

Ravenscraft, D.J. (1983) Structure–profit relationships at the line of business and industry level. *Review of Economics and Statistics* 65, 22–31.

Roberts, M.J. (1984) Testing oligopolistic behavior. *International Journal of Industrial Organization* 2, 367–83.

Robinson, J. (1932) *The Economics of Imperfect Competition*. London: Macmillan.

Rothschild, K.W. (1947) Price theory and oligopoly. *Economic Journal* 57, 299–320. Reprinted in G.J. Stigler and K.E. Boulding (eds), *Readings in Price Theory*, Chicago, IL: Irwin, 1952, pp. 440–64.

Scherer, F.M. (1982) The breakfast cereal industry. In W. Adams (ed.), *The Structure of American Industry*, 6th edn, New York: Macmillan pp. 191–217.

Schmalensee, R. (1978) Entry deferrence in the ready-to-eat breakfast cereal industry. *Bell Journal of Economics* 9, 305–27.

Schmalensee, R. (1982) Product differentiation advantages of pioneering brands. *American Economic Review* 72, 349–66.

Schmalensee, R. (1989) Inter-industry studies of structure and performance. In R. Schmalensee and R.D. Willig (eds), *Handbook of Industrial Organization II*, Amsterdam: North-Holland. pp. 951–1009.

Schohl, F. (1990) Persistence of profits in the long run: a critical extension of some recent findings. *International Journal of Industrial Organization*, 8, 385–403.

Schumpeter, J.A. (1934) *The Theory of Economic Development*. Cambridge, MA: Harvard University Press.

Shapiro, C. (1989) Theories of oligopoly behavior. In R. Schmalensee and R. D. Willig (eds), *Handbook of Industrial Organization II*, Amsterdam: North-Holland, pp. 329–414.

Shapiro, D. and Khemani, R.S. (1987) The determinants of entry and exit reconsidered. *International Journal of Industrial Organization* 5, 15–26.

Shepherd, W.G. (1972) The elements of market structure. *Review of Economics and Statistics* 54, 25–37.

Shepherd, W.G. (1975) *The Treatment of Market Power*. New York: Columbia University Press.

Slade, M.E. (1987) Interfirm rivalry in a repeated game: an empirical test of tacit collusion. *Journal of Industrial Economics* 35, 499–516.

Smiley, R. (1988) Empirical evidence on strategic entry deterrence. *International Journal of Industrial Organization* 6, 167–80.

Spence, A.M. (1977) Entry, capacity, investment and oligopolistic pricing. *Bell Journal of Economics* 8, 534–44.

Stigler, G. (1964) A theory of oligopoly. *Journal of Political Economy* 72, 44–61.

Sylos-Labini, P. (1957) *Oligopolio e Progresso Tecnico*. Milan: Giuffre.

Ulph, D. (1983) Rational conjectures in the theory of oligopoly. *International Journal of Industrial Organization* 1, 131–54.

Weiss, L.W. (1974) The concentration–profits relationship and antitrust. In H.J. Goldschmid, H.M. Mann, and J.F. Weston (eds), *Industrial Concentration: The New Learning*, Boston, MA: Little, Brown.

Weiss, L.W. (1989) *Concentration and Price* Cambridge, MA: MIT Press.

Worcester, D.A. (1957) Why "dominant firms" decline. *Journal of Political Economy* 65, 338–47.

2

Entry and Market Contestability: The Evidence from the United States

Ioannis N. Kessides

1 Introduction

The goal of this paper is to construct a simple but carefully specified and testable model of entry behavior which describes the factors that influence the entry decisions of firms and makes precise the critical role of sunk costs in the process of entry deterrence. We seek to evaluate the costs of entry and exit and the magnitude of unavoidable sunk costs, and thus to provide a first step toward determining the degree of contestability of markets. In addition, we attempt to provide a direct test of the hypothesis that advertising serves as a barrier to new competition.

We note that, although the important influence of entry on economic performance has long been recognized by economic theory, direct and systematic statistical evidence of factors that affect entry is sparse (Geroski (1983) provides an excellent survey of the relevant literature).[1] Formal models of entry suffer from their lack of testable implications, while much of the empirical work is based on loosely specified models that do not permit precise hypothesis testing. We attempt to make a partial correction of this imbalance between model building and model testing, with a model which is admittedly simple in comparison with the theoretical state of the art. Nevertheless, this simple model generates useful economic insights, permits the testing of economically meaningful hypotheses, and provides guidance for the design of public policy aimed at improving market performance.

The model leads to an estimable equation that relates the (net) number of entrants over a period to the pre-entry profit level of incumbents, the minimum efficient scale of entry, the rate of demand growth, the elasticity of demand, and the magnitude of sunk costs. The equation is estimated using census data on four-digit US manufacturing industries.

The model predicts that the rate of entry increases with the profit level of incumbents, holding fixed the irrecoverable costs of entry. It shows that the presence of these sunk costs diminishes the rate at which entry responds to positive incumbent profits and the empirical testing establishes their significance as an important barrier to entry. In addition, it is found that entrants perceive a greater likelihood of an aggressive incumbent response when such incumbents are both profitable and concentrated.

The mechanism through which advertising affects entry is also clarified. Advertising plays two roles: it adds to the sunk costs required for entry, and it affects the risk of entry as perceived by potential entrants. Our empirical results reveal that advertising does act as a sunk cost, one more important to the total entry barrier than tangible sunk costs. However, the perceived probability of unsuccessful entry is lower the greater are industry advertising expenditures.

2 The Model

We present a model whose simplistic structure permits us to highlight the role of sunk costs as a barrier to entry. Sunk costs are, by definition, a multi-period phenomenon. Entry must also be viewed as an inter-temporal process. Thus the model presented is given at least a modicum of dynamic structure. Initially, at time zero, n_0 firms operate within an industry supplying Q_0 units of output and receiving a price p_0. With no loss of generality, we assume that $n_e - 1$ firms have instantaneously completed their entry at time zero. In analyzing the entry decision of the n_eth potential entrant, we divide time into three periods: (a) the past, which lasts until time zero, the beginning of period 1; (b) period 1, of length T; (c) the future, which starts at time T, the beginning of period 2. We propose two possible outcomes following entry.

1   With probability α, a passive noncooperative incumbent response, with the entrant staying in and receiving during period 1 the posted price p_e at the beginning of period 1 (i.e. the incumbents, because of capacity constraints, lack of information, regulation, etc., are unable to adjust their prices in response to entry during period 1). Under this outcome the entrant realizes profits in period 2 with a present value (discounted to the beginning of period 2) of π_e^f.

2   With probability $1 - \alpha$, the incumbents react aggressively and

force the entrant to exit. In this case, the entrant suffers the lost of sunk costs.

Assume that the $n_e - 1$ firms that have entered the industry since time zero supplied Q_e additional units of output. If the incumbents maintain their output levels and there is no growth in demand for the industry's product, then the price that the n_eth entrant should receive is given by

$$p_e = p(Q_0 + Q_e + \tilde{q}_e)$$

$$\approx p(Q_0) + (Q_e + \tilde{q}_e) \left. \frac{\partial p}{\partial q} \right|_{q = Q_0}$$

$$\approx p_0 \left(1 - \frac{Q_e + \tilde{q}_e}{Q_0} \epsilon \right) = p_0 \left(1 - n_e \frac{q_e}{Q_0} \epsilon \right) \tag{2.1}$$

where

$$p_0 = p(Q_0), \; \epsilon = - \frac{Q_0}{p_0} \left. \frac{\partial p}{\partial q} \right|_{q = Q_0}$$

$\tilde{q}_e$ is the output supplied by the n_eth entrant, and q_e/Q_0 is the industry-specific mean scale of entry to be defined later. For the above approximation to be globally valid we make the strong assumption that demand is nearly linear. However, the curvature of the demand curve certainly varies across industries, and the validity of the linearity assumption is an empirical question.

If the demand–price relationship for the industry's product remains constant, then equation (2.1) simply indicates that the amount by which price falls following entry depends on the excess of the post-entry output over the pre-entry output and the relevant elasticity of demand. Assume now, however, that there has been a growth in demand for the industry's product given by g, and that the n_eth entrant expects such growth to continue following its entry.[2] Then it is easy to compute the price change induced by the additional output supplied by the entrants since $t = 0$. For this we write the demand equation as

$$Q_0 + \Delta q_e = (1 + g) f (p_0 + \Delta p_t + \Delta p_e) = (1 + g) f (p_0 + \Delta p) \tag{2.2}$$

where $\Delta q_e = Q_e + \tilde{q}_e$ represents the entry output, Δp_t is the change in price due to the demand shift, Δp_e is the change in price due to entry, $\Delta p = \Delta p_t + \Delta p_e$, and $Q_0 = f(p_0)$ represents the demand for the industry's product at $t = 0$.

We write (2.2) in the approximate form (again assuming a nearly linear demand)

$$Q_0 + \Delta q_e \approx (1 + g)\left[f(p_0) + \Delta p \left.\frac{\partial f}{\partial p}\right|_{p=p_0}\right] \tag{2.3}$$

Rearranging and solving for Δp yields

$$\Delta p = \frac{\Delta q_e - g Q_0}{(1 + g)(\partial f/\partial p)|_{p=p_0}} = p_0 \frac{n_e(q_e/Q_0) - g}{(1 + g)(-\epsilon_p)} \tag{2.4}$$

where

$$\epsilon_p = -\left.\frac{p_0}{Q_0}\frac{\partial f}{\partial p}\right|_{p=p_0}$$

is the price elasticity of demand for the industry's product.

We now relax the assumption that the established firms maintain their output at the pre-entry levels. Thus, we assume that incumbents will expand by $\tilde{g}$ (on a percentage basis) and (2.4) is modified as follows:

$$\Delta p = p_0 \frac{n_e(q_e/Q_0) - (g - \tilde{g})}{(1 + g)(-\epsilon_p)} \tag{2.5}$$

Therefore in the case of anticipated growth of demand and output expansion by incumbents, the price that the n_eth entrant should expect is given by

$$p_e = p_0\left[1 - \frac{n_e(q_e/Q_0) - (g - \tilde{g})}{(1 + g)\epsilon_p}\right] \tag{2.6}$$

The discounted present value of the flow of profits expected by the n_eth entrant can be written as

$$E(\Pi_e) = \alpha\left(\left\{p_0\left[1 - \frac{n_e(q_e/Q_0) - (g - \tilde{g})}{(1 + g)\epsilon_p}\right] - AC\right\}\tilde{q}_e\gamma_T + \pi_e^f e^{-rT}\right)$$
$$- (1 - \alpha)\, SU_e \tag{2.7}$$

where AC is the average cost of production including capital costs (i.e. depreciation and user cost), $\gamma_T = \int_0^T e^{-rt}dt$, where r is the discount rate, and SU_e is the portion of the entry investment that is sunk. Clearly, the entrant's future profits π_e^f depend on the detailed characteristics of the post-entry equilibrium in period 2. However, the nature of this post-entry equilibrium is intentionally not prespecified, since we wish to abstract from the complex issues which arise with regard to specific theories of incumbent–entrant interaction.

While we impose no restrictions on the nature of the post-entry market equilibrium in period 2, it may be reasonable to assume that the present value of the furture profits of the entrant is a function of the state variables of the system at the beginning of period 2 (Baumol and Willig, 1981). Thus we assume that future profits are proportional to period 1 profits. Let ψ denote the constant of proportionality.

We assume that entry continues until the value of entry is driven to zero. Thus, setting (2.7) equal to zero and solving for n_e yields the following expression for the number of new entrants:

$$n_e = \frac{g - \bar{g}}{q_e/Q_0} + \frac{1 + g}{q_e/Q_0} \, \epsilon_p \Pi_0 \left[1 - \frac{1}{\gamma_T(1 + \psi)\Pi_0} \frac{1 - \alpha}{\alpha} \frac{\mathrm{SU}_e}{S_e} \right] \quad (2.8)$$

where $\Pi_0 = (p_0 - \mathrm{AC})/p_0$ is the pre-entry price–cost margin of the incumbents and $S_e = p_0 \bar{q}_e$.

2.1 Factors Affecting the Probability of Successful Entry

For analytic simplicity we neglect entry through product variation and assume that the uncertainty and risk of failure facing the potential entrant are primarily determined by the behavior of the incumbent firms in the market. Thus we neglect the effect of demand uncertainty and abstract from the risk of failure that may also arise when the entrant is introducing a product with new and untested attributes and therefore is facing the possibility of a low buyer's valuation.

The behavior of the incumbents is determined by the incentives that they face and the market form of the industry. This market form in turn is a function of the number and resources of the established competitors, the physical nature of the market, and the legal and informational environment of the industry (Shubik and Levitan, 1980). Our basic conjecture is that these variables limit the post-entry strategies that are available to established sellers in their efforts to thwart entry. Thus economic structure may constrain the course of action adopted by the incumbents regardless of their attitude towards fighting entrants, i.e. the strategies available to the incumbents are structurally constrained.

By investing in deterrence technology, the established seller can inflict costs upon the potential competitor if it attempts entry. However, such investment activity also causes the incumbent's own net profits to decline. If we assume that capital markets are imperfect, it may then be plausibly argued that incumbents with surplus funds at their disposal (secured from past profitable operations) are in general more able to engage in aggressive behavior than incumbents who might have a similar attitude toward fighting but possess no financial slack. Established sellers may also be more protective of, and defend more vigorously, profitable market positions. Clearly, the advantage of a "deep pocket" might be minimized if firms can freely tap outside capital. However, it is not clear that outside financing can be secured as speedily as internal funds. In addition, capital sources are likely to perceive investment in deterrence activities to be a risky venture (perhaps even more risky than the incumbent perceives them to be). Then, such external capital comes at a higher effective cost.

We do not seek to provide an exhaustive analysis of investment in deterrence technology by incumbents. The optimal level, effectiveness, and type of such activity certainly also depends on the resources available to the potential entrant, whether the entrant chooses to burn his bridges by deliberately sinking substantial costs upon entry, and so on. These issues have been debated extensively in the literature. Our limited objective here is to provide a formal characterization of the differences in incumbent responses to entry where incumbents have profitable market positions to protect and where they do not.

In an unconcentrated market with a large number of sellers, the initiation of retaliatory measures against an entrant is subject to free-rider problems. In a concentrated market, however, the fortunes of the firms are strategically interlinked and incumbent sellers might find it easier to engage in collusive punitive actions against newcomers.

Given the assumption that the probability of successful entry is determined primarily by incumbent behavior, and the conjectured relationship between this behavior and economic structure, we propose to test the following hypotheses.[3]

The threat of an aggressive post-entry reaction (such as output expansion) is more credible when:

Hypothesis 1   Incumbents have positive profits to protect and are able to cover transitory losses; thus

$$\frac{\partial}{\partial \Pi_0} \left(\frac{1 - \alpha}{\alpha} \right) > 0$$

Hypothesis 2   The free-rider effect in driving the entrant out is smaller; thus,

$$\frac{\partial}{\partial C_0} \left(\frac{1 - \alpha}{\alpha} \right) > 0$$

where C_0 is a measure of industry concentration.

We proceed now with the formulation of additional hypotheses in the context of our model.

2.2 The Effect of Sunk Costs

Sunk costs impose an asymmetry in the incremental cost and risk faced by an entrant and an incumbent. For the entrant, the act of entry requires the conversion of liquid assets into frozen physical capital, only part of which is recoverable through disinvestment. For the incumbent, however, these commitments have either already been made (initial capital investment) or they constitute a normal cost of doing business (advertising). Thus the entrant's incremental cost includes the full amount of the sunk costs which are largely bygone to the incumbent. In addition, the entrant's perceived risk of failure is apt to be larger than the risk already accepted by the incumbent because, as Willig (1982) notes, "the entrant knows that competition with the incumbent is inevitable, while the incumbent may have enjoyed a less competitive environment and may have discounted the possibility of later competitive encroachment." The entrant's incremental cost and risk require a compensating profit differential. It is in this sense that sunk costs constitute an entry barrier.[4]

From equation (2.8) we define the effective unit cost of entry (i.e. cost per dollar of sales) as

$$EC_e = \frac{1 - \alpha}{\alpha} \frac{SU_e}{S_e}. \qquad (2.9)$$

If all the entrant's capital investment can be resold at no loss, i.e. $SU_e = 0$, then the effective cost of entry is zero and there is no barrier to entry. Also, if sunk costs are zero, then the possibility that the incumbents might retaliate (affecting α) does not deter entry. Deterrence activities raise the effective cost of entry and thus are a source of barriers only in the presence of sunk costs.

It is important to emphasize here the basic distinction between sunk and fixed costs in their effect on entry. Fixed costs do not give rise to entry barriers unless they also happen to be sunk. for example, if capital is perfectly mobile and fungible, then, as we shall see below, all entry investments are perfectly reversible and sunk costs are zero. In that case, the asymmetry just described (and consequently the corresponding entry cost) is eliminated regardless of the magnitude of the capitalization that the entrant must incur in order to enter the industry.

Hypothesis 3   The entry cost EC_e constitutes a barrier to entry. The height of this barrier increases with the proportion of the original investment which is unrecoverable in the event of exit.

2.3 The Effect of the Price-Cost Margin

Equation (2.8) implies that entry is an increasing function of the pre-entry margin of the incumbents. High margins signal profitable opportunities and thus provide an incentive for entry. According to hypothesis 1, however, the ability and incentive of the incumbents to retaliate is also an increasing function of their margin. The threat of such rataliatory action, as equation (2.9) indicates, raises the effective entry cost and thus the height of the entry barrier.

Our model suggests, therefore, the presence of two countervailing forces due to the margin which can balance either way. In industries with high sunk costs, entry and the margin could move in opposite directions (i.e. the perceived threat of retaliation signified by a higher margin might outweigh the corresponding incentive).

Hypothesis 4   The price–cost margin gives rise to conflicting forces in its effect on entry: high price–cost margins signal profitable opportunities and provide an incentive for entry; on the other hand, incumbents are more likely to react aggressively when they are profitable, thus increasing the risk due to sunk costs and lowering the expected profitability of entry.

2.4 The Effect of Growth in Demand

If $\tilde{g} \leq g$, i.e. if incumbents expand at a slower rate than industry demand grows, then the term $(g - \tilde{g})/(q_e/Q_0)$ $(= (g - \tilde{g})Q_0/q_e)$ in equation (2.8) indicates the number of additional firms that could fit within the industry without depressing price and without reducing incumbents' sales – again assuming an industry-specific mean scale of entry. Thus growth permits industry size (i.e. the number of established firms) to increase without a reduction in the profits accruing to each operating firm.[5]

A specialized feature of our model is the manner in which it is assumed that growth affects demand, as indicated by equation (2.2). In the case of linear demand, for example, it pivots the demand curve through its vertical intercept. This effect is captured by the $1 + g$ factor of the second term in equation (2.8). It expresses the fact that, because of the growth in demand, any additional output supplied to the market will depress price at a slower rate.

Hypothesis 5   Growth in the demand for the industry's product exerts a positive influence on entry, because it implies that any additional output supplied to the market will depress price at a slower rate and that the number of firms operating within the industry can increase without lowering the profits accruing to each such firm.

In addition to being conducive to entry, growth also encourages expansion by the existing firms. It the established sellers fully anticipate the increases in demand and are prepared to supply it with new capacity already in place, then $\bar{g} = g$. When the incumbents fully exploit every new sales opportunity and expand at the same rate as industry demand grows, then the first term in equation (2.8) is obviated, but not the factor $1 + g$ of the second term. It should be noted that this result is dependent upon our special assumption regarding the manner in which growth affects demand.

Conjecture 1   Incumbents expand at the same rate as industry demand.

2.5 *The Effect of Advertising*

If we assume that advertising has a long-lasting effect on sales then it has to be considered as an investment in a capital asset. For the prospective entrant, the act of entry requires the conversion of liquid assets into advertising capital, a large portion of which is likely to be non-salvageable if the entrant is forced to exit. This need to sink money into advertising imposes as asymmetry between the incremental cost and incremental risk faced by a potential entrant and those faced by the incumbent firms in the same manner as the need to sink money into machines.

It is in this sense that advertising constitutes a barrier to entry. We should note that economies of scale in advertising or the possibility that the new entrant might have to advertise more than the incumbents (per unit of sales) to overcome consumer inertia are not necessary conditions for advertising to constitute an entry barrier. Even if there were no economies of scale or consumer inertia, advertising would still give rise to an entry barrier because of the above-mentioned asymmetry in the costs and risks to a new entrant and the incumbents. Notwithstanding this, the existence of economies of scale and consumer brand loyalty would certainly accentuate this asymmetry.

Hypothesis 6 For the potential entrant, the required investment in advertising leads to an entry cost that is irrecoverable in the event of exit – thus, advertising creates a sunk cost barrier to entry.

According to equation (2.8), the height of the barrier that sunk costs are hypothesized to erect depends on the risk to which they expose the entrant – the effective cost of entry is a function of $(1 - \alpha)/\alpha$, the relative probability of failure as perceived by the entrant. A major factor contributing to such risk is brand loyalty resulting from the experience of buyers with the established products.

According to the "advertising = market power" school, advertising is an instrument of persuasion. It increases brand loyalty, reduces the perceived number of product substitutes by enhancing differentiability, and ultimately lowers the cross-price elasticity of demand. The "advertising = competition" school, however, maintains that advertising is an attention-getting device. It informs buyers about the attributes and prices of products, thereby reducing their search costs and decreasing their inertia. It acts as a substitute for experience and thus is a means of overcoming loyalty.

This paper is based on the premise that, in an actual market, advertising includes elements of both persuasion and information. Any monopolistic potential that might be created by enhanced product differentiation and loyalty is counterbalanced by the competitive pressure resulting from different sellers attempting to concentrate demand upon their own brands. Which of these two forces is more powerful is a question that can be answered only by looking at the empirical evidence.

Thus, we propose to discriminate between the following two alternative hypotheses.[6]

Hypothesis 7a (advertising = persuasion school) Potential entrants perceive a greater risk of failure in markets with high advertising intensity; thus

$$\frac{\partial}{\partial(A/S)} \frac{1 - \alpha}{\alpha} > 0$$

Hypothesis 7b (advertising = information school) Potential entrants perceive a greater likelihood of success in markets where advertising is important; thus

$$\frac{\partial}{\partial(A/S)} \frac{1 - \alpha}{\alpha} < 0$$

A/S is the advertising intensity (advertising-to-sales ratio) in a given market.

3 Data and Measurement Problems

We test the hypotheses generated by the model using the cross-section sample of all four-digit US manufacturing industries which experienced net entry between the census years 1972 and 1977. To test for stability of coefficients, we re-estimate the model's basic equation using the corresponding cross-section sample of industries which experienced net entry between 1977 and 1982.

Definitions of, and sources for, the variables used in this paper are provided in the appendix. We restrict our attention to those variables which entail measurement and definitional difficulties.

3.1 A Measure of Entry

Our underlying analysis deals with an equilibrium model of entry. The computed limit quantity of entry output determines the number of new firms that in the long run could profitably fit into a given industry. Our model therefore predicts the long-run net addition to the number of firms as the industry reaches its equilibrium structure. In (2.8), n_e represents the net number of entrants over the period during which such an equilibrium is reached.

The number of firms in each of the four-digit US manufacturing industries is reported during the census years. We thus measure net entry between the census years. By choosing the years 1972 and 1977 as our base we construct for a given industry the variable representing net entry as

$$n_e = N_{77} - N_{72} \qquad (2.10)$$

where N_{72} and N_{77} are the number of firms in the industry in 1972 and 1977 respectively.

Implicit in the above definition is the assumption that the time interval between the census years is sufficiently long so that this measure of entry captures the basic features of our equilibrium model. It is not claimed that such an equilibrium is actually reached, but rather that each industry is in a path toward its equilibrium configuration. Thus we assume that $n_e = \zeta n_e^*$ where n_e^* is the predicted net number of entrants, n_e is the measured net entry, and ζ is an industry-specific parameter.

3.2 Tangible Sunk Costs: Measurement and Correlates

We introduce here a commonly accepted distinction between two
forms of physical assets – buildings and structures, and machines and
equipment – as to their relative degree of fungibility. It can be reasonably assumed that buildings and structures are in large part fungible, in
that with certain modifications they can be converted for a different use.
Machines and equipment, however, being in general task-specific, are
not amenable to such conversion.

The above distinction between machines and buildings should not be
exaggerated, in that machines can be sold to other firms within the same
industry. For a cost to be truly sunk for the entrant, it must be firm
specific and not just industry-specific. Machines are in general more
industry-specific than buildings and (though to a lesser degree) they are
probably also more firm-specific. Thus we conjecture that machines are
more sunk than buildings.

Conjecture 2   The required investment in machines and equipment
comprises a component of entry cost that is irrecoverable in the event of
exit, while this is not the case for buildings and structures.

Lack of detailed data on the availability of resale markets for durable
inputs precludes a precise evaluation of the unavoidable sunk costs
facing an entrant. Such measurement is further complicated by the fact
that fixed costs that are firm-specific are in general more sunk than those
that are just industry-specific. Still, readily available measures which
theory suggests are pertinent permit us to construct upper bounds and
meaningful proxies for these costs.

Let B_i and M_i represent the fixed depreciable assets in the form
of buildings and machines in industry i. Also, let DCB_i and DCM_i
denote the depreciation charges made during the year against these
assets. Then, under the assumption that entry takes place at a scale
$MES_e^i = (q_e^i/Q_0^i)$ and that entrants have the same capital-to-sales ratio
as the incumbents, the expressions

$$SUB_e^i = (1 - DCB_i)B_i MES_e^i \qquad (2.11)$$
$$SUM_e^i = (1 - DCM_i)M_i MES_e^i$$

provide upper bound measures of the entry investment in buildings
and machines, respectively, that might be irrecoverable in the event of
exit.[7] The logic for these proxies is that if exit occurs after a depreciation of k percent, then that depreciation is a normal cost of doing

business in the industry already captured in the user cost of capital (a cost also borne by the incumbents and reflected in their pre-entry computed rate of profit). In contrast, the remaining $1 - k$ per cent of the original investment undergoing resale will produce a sunk cost.

Assume now that the entrant can rent a portion of its entry capital. The availability of a rental market significantly reduces or completely eliminates the sunk costs facing the entrant to the extent that it augments the mobility and fungibility of durable inputs among their alternative uses and eliminates the financial commitment which the entrant would be normally required to make. Assume further that the entrant's capital has approximately the same composition as that of the industry. Let RB_i and RM_i denote the rental payments made for the use of buildings and equipment in industry i. Then, to take into account the potential effect of the rental market, we modify our upper-bound measures of sunk costs as follows:[8]

$$\text{SURB}_e^i = \left(1 - \frac{RB_i}{B_i}\right)(1 - DCB_i)B_i\text{MES}_e^i$$

$$\text{SURM}_e^i = \left(1 - \frac{RM_i}{M_i}\right)(1 - DCM_i)M_i\text{MES}_e^i$$

(2.12)

3.3 Advertising Sunk Costs

Let A_0^i and λ_A^i denote the level of advertising and the rate at which such advertising depreciates in industry i. Then the expression

$$\text{SUA}_e^i = (1 - \lambda_A^i)A_0^i\text{MES}_e^i \qquad (2.13)$$

provides a measure of the portion of the original investment in advertising that might be irrecoverable in the event of exit.

While some estimates of the depreciation rates for advertising do exist in the literature, they are not available for a large diverse sample of four-digit industries – they are not of sufficient detail for the purposes of this study. Thus we are forced to restrict the depreciation rate for advertising to being the same across industries.

3.4 Scale of Entry

We again face a problem of measurement since there are no available data on the actual output size at which newcomers enter a given industry. For each industry, however, we do have information on the distribution of plants according to employment size. Let n_i represent the number of plants in the jth size group and S_j the total sales of the plants in the group, and let m be the number of group sizes. Within each size group it is meaningful to define the average plant size

$$\tilde{S}_j = S_j/n_j \qquad j = 1, 2, \ldots, m \tag{2.14}$$

as representative, considering that the size groups as defined are too narrow to permit much intra-group variation. If *a priori* we have no strong basis for assigning probabilities of entry into each of the size groups, then an appropriate measure of the size of entry would be the simple average of the representative plants in each group:

$$\tilde{S}_e = \frac{1}{m} \sum_{j=1}^{m} \tilde{S}_j \tag{2.15}$$

Thus our scale of entry proxy is $\text{MES}_e = \tilde{S}_e/S_0$ where $S_0 = \sum_{j=1}^{m} S_j$ is total industry sales.

4 Specification and Estimation Issues

The structural characteristics of the model suggest that cross-industry inference is appropriate. We therefore propose to test whether the observed inter-industry differences in net entry can be explained by differences in the pre-entry price–cost margin Π_0, the scale of entry MES_e, the rate g of demand growth, the sunk costs SU_e/S_e that the entrant must commit per dollar of revenues generated, and the price elasticity of demand ϵ_p. It is important to note that the model makes precise predictions with respect to the sign and magnitude of the elasticities of these terms. One possible way of testing the model is to estimate a relationship of the form

$$n_e = \beta_0 \frac{(g - \tilde{g})^{\beta_1}}{\text{MES}_e^{\beta_2}} + \beta_3 \frac{(1 + g)^{\beta_4}}{\text{MES}_e^{\beta_5}} \Pi_0^{\beta_6} \epsilon_p^{\beta_7} \left[1 - \frac{1}{\gamma_T(1 + \psi)\Pi_0} \frac{1 - \alpha}{\alpha} \frac{\text{SU}_e}{S_e} \right] + u_1 \tag{2.16}$$

where β_0, β_1, β_2, β_3, β_4, β_5, β_6, and β_7 are parameters to be estimated, u_1 is the disturbance which is assumed to be normal and homoskedastic, and the relative probability of exit $(1 - \alpha)/\alpha$ and the perceived magnitude of sunk costs SU_e are specified so as to permit the testing of hypotheses 1, 2, 3, and 4 and conjecture 2. We implicitly assume that $\tilde{g} = \mu g$, i.e. the incumbents will expand and capture a portion μ of the additional industry demand, and then we test the hypothesis that $\mu = 1$ (conjecture 1). We also assume that ζ, γ_T, and ψ are equal across industries. The theoretical predictions of parameter values, i.e. that $\beta_0 = 0$ (conjecture 1), $\beta_1 = 1$, $\beta_2 = 1$, $\beta_3 = 1$, $\beta_4 = 1$, $\beta_5 = 1$, $\beta_6 = 1$, and $\beta_7 = 1$, are then formally tested.

To test the hypothesis that incumbents are more likely to react aggressively when they are profitable (hypothesis 1), we need an appropriate specification for the relative probability of failure $(1 - \alpha)/\alpha$ as perceived by potential entrants. We note that the logistic function provides a convenient basis for such a specification. Thus we propose the following log-linear relationship to describe the odds of entry failure:

$$\ln\left(\frac{1 - \alpha}{\alpha}\right) = \delta_0 + \delta_1 \ln \Pi_0 \qquad (2.17)$$

In addition, to test the conjecture that the machine and equipment costs of entry are significantly more sunk than building and structure costs (conjecture 2), we impose on the costs of entry the functional form

$$\text{SU}_e = z_1\text{SUM}_e + z_2\text{SUB}_e \qquad z_1 \leqslant 1,\ z_2 \leqslant 1 \qquad (2.18)$$

where, as defined earlier, SUM_e and SUB_e provide an upper-bound measure of the original investment in machines and buildings that might be irrecoverable in the event of exit.

However, we begin first by testing the conjecture that incumbents expand at the same rate as industry demand. For this we need to assess the significance of the first term $(g - \bar{g})/\text{MES}_e$ in explaining the observed variance in n_e. Thus we need to estimate the two nested nonlinear models

$$n_e = \beta_0 \frac{(g - \bar{g})^{\beta_1}}{\text{MES}_e^{\beta_2}} + \beta_3 \frac{(1 + g)^{\beta_4}}{\text{MES}_e^{\beta_5}} \Pi_0^{\beta_6} \epsilon_p^{\beta_7}\left(1 - \lambda_1 \frac{\text{SU}_e}{S_e} \Pi_0^{\lambda_2}\right) + u_1$$

$$(2.19\text{a})$$

$$n_e = \xi_0 \frac{(1 + g)^{\xi_1}}{\text{MES}_e^{\xi_2}} \Pi_0^{\xi_3} \epsilon_p^{\xi_4}\left(1 - \lambda_1 \frac{\text{SU}_e}{S_e} \Pi_0^{\lambda_2}\right) + u_2 \qquad (2.19\text{b})$$

A comparison of equations (2.17), (2.19a), and (2.19b) indicates the following relationship between the estimated coefficients and the parameters of the model:[9]

$$\hat{\lambda}_1 = \frac{1}{\gamma_T(1 + \psi)} \exp(\delta_0) \qquad \hat{\lambda}_2 = \delta_1 - 1$$

The significance of the first term is determined by an F-test for the reduction in the error sum of squares between the restricted (2.19b) and unrestricted (2.19a) models (Gallant, 1975).

Given that the contribution of the first term is not significant (i.e. the approximate model in (2.19b) is statistically acceptable), we then estimate the nonlinear equation[10]

$$\ln n_e = a_0 + a_1 \ln(1 + g) + a_2 \ln \text{MES}_e + a_3 \ln \Pi_0$$

$$+ a_4 \ln\left[1 - \left(a_5 \frac{\text{SUM}_e}{S_e} + a_6 \frac{\text{SUB}_e}{S_e}\right) \Pi_0^{a_7}\right] + \epsilon_1 \qquad (2.20)$$

We should recognize the precise prediction that our model makes with respect to the size and magnitude of the coefficients in equation (2.20). A comparison of equations (2.8), (2.19b), and (2.20) indicates that the hypothesis of interest is a test of[11]

$$H_0 : \theta = \theta_0 \text{ against } H_1 : \theta \neq \theta_0$$

where $\theta = (a_0, a_1, a_2, a_3, a_4)$ and $\theta_0 = (0, 1, -1, 1, 1)$. Also, a comparison of equations (2.17), (2.18), (2.19b), and (2.20) indicates further the following relationship between the estimated coefficients and the parameters of the model:

$$\hat{a}_5 = \frac{z_1}{\gamma_T(1 + \psi)} \exp(\delta_0) \quad \hat{a}_6 = \frac{z_2}{\gamma_T(1 + \psi)} \exp(\delta_0) \quad \hat{a}_7 = \delta_1 - 1$$

Thus hypothesis 1 is supported if $\hat{a}_7 > -1$, while conjecture 2 will not be rejected if $\hat{a}_5$ is significantly positive and $\hat{a}_6$ is close to zero.

As stated in hypothesis 2, the threat of an aggressive post-entry reaction by incumbents is more credible in concentrated industries where the free-rider effect in driving the entrant out is smaller. To test hypothesis 2 (in addition to hypothesis 1), we impose on the relative probability of exit the functional form

$$\ln\left(\frac{1 - \alpha}{\alpha}\right) = \delta_0 + \delta_1 \ln \Pi_0 + \delta_2 \ln C_0 \qquad (2.21)$$

and then estimate the nonlinear equation

$$\ln n_e = a_0 + a_1 \ln(1 + g) + a_2 \ln \text{MES}_e + a_3 \ln \Pi_0$$

$$+ a_4 \ln\left[1 - \left(a_5 \frac{\text{SUM}_e}{S_e} + a_6 \frac{\text{SUB}_e}{S_e}\right) \Pi_0^{a_7} C_0^{a_8}\right] + \epsilon_2 \qquad (2.22)$$

Hypothesis 2 is confirmed if $\hat{a}_8$ is significantly positive.

Next, we test the conjecture that the availability of a rental market facilitates entry by reducing sunk costs. To access this potential effect of the rental market, we estimate the equation

$$\ln n_e = a_0 + a_1 \ln(1 + g) + a_2 \ln \text{MES}_e + a_3 \ln \Pi_0$$

$$+ a_4 \ln\left[1 - \left(a_5 \frac{\text{SURM}_e}{S_e} + a_6 \frac{\text{SURB}_e}{S_e}\right) \Pi_0^{a_7}\right] + \epsilon_3 \quad (2.23)$$

where, as previously defined, SURM_e and SURB_e are sunk cost measures, adjusted to take into account the intensity of the rental market. We use an extension of the Cox likelihood ratio test, the N test, to discriminate between the two competing nonnested model (2.20) and (2.23).[12] The significance of the sunk-cost-reducing effect of the rental market is established if we find that (2.23) rejects (2.20).

Finally, to test hypothesis 6, we rewrite equation (2.18) as

$$\text{SU}_e = z_1 \text{SUM}_e + z_2 \text{SUB}_e + z_3 \text{SUA}_e \qquad z_1 \leqslant 1, z_2 \leqslant 1, z_3 \leqslant 1 \quad (2.24)$$

where, as before, SUA_e is a measure of the entry investment in advertising that is sunk in the event of exit. To discriminate between hypotheses 7a and 7b, we modify equation (2.21), defining the relative probability of exit as

$$\ln\left(\frac{1 - \alpha}{\alpha}\right) = \delta_0 + \delta_1 \ln \Pi_0 + \delta_2 \ln C_0 + \delta_3 \ln\left(\frac{A_0}{S_0}\right) \quad (2.25)$$

where A_0/S_0 is the industry's pre-entry level of advertising intensity. We then estimate the equation

$$\ln n_e = a_0 + a_1 \ln(1 + g) + a_2 \ln \text{MES}_e + a_3 \ln \Pi_0$$

$$+ \ln\left[1 - \left(a_4 \frac{\text{SUM}_e}{S_e} + a_5 \frac{\text{SUB}_e}{S_e} + a_6 \frac{\text{SUA}_e}{S_e}\right) \Pi_0^{a_7} C_0^{a_8} \left(\frac{A_0}{S_0}\right)^{a_9}\right] + \epsilon_4$$

$$(2.26)$$

5 The Empirical Results

The likelihood ratio test supports the conjecture that past growth in demand for the industry's product encourages future expansion by the incumbent firms. In fact, the hypothesis that incumbents expand at the same rate as industry demand is not rejected at conventional levels.[13] Thus, conjecture 1 is confirmed, and our focus on the approximate model (2.19b) is appropriate.

Table 2.1 summarizes the results of nonlinear least squares estimation of equation (2.19b).[14] The tests of the separate hypotheses that $a_0 = 0$,

Table 2.1

Equation (2.20): 1972–7

$$\ln n_e = a_0 + a_1 \ln(1+g) + a_2 \ln MES_e + a_3 \ln \Pi_0 + a_4 \ln\left[1 - \left(a_5\frac{SUM_e}{S_e} + a_6\frac{SUB_e}{S_e}\right)\Pi_0^{a_7}\right] + \epsilon_1$$

Parameters	a_0	a_1	a_2	a_3	a_4	a_5	a_6	a_7
Estimates	0.113	0.847	-1.021	0.830	1.663	1.520	0.384	0.837
	(0.107)	(0.096)	(0.020)	(0.044)	(0.376)	(0.052)	(0.715)	(0.060)

Equation (2.22): 1972–7

$$\ln n_e = a_0 + a_1 \ln(1+g) + a_2 \ln MES_e + a_3 \ln \Pi_0 + a_4 \ln\left[1 - \left(a_5\frac{SUM_e}{S_e} + a_6\frac{SUB_e}{S_e}\right)\Pi_0^{a_7}C_0^{a_8}\right] + \epsilon_2$$

Parameters	a_0	a_1	a_2	a_3	a_4	a_5	a_6	a_7	a_8
Estimates	0.851	0.825	-0.870	0.779	34.24	0.195	0.050	0.509	1.048
	(0.099)	(0.096)	(0.013)	(0.040)	(4.76)	(0.023)	(0.136)	(0.042)	(0.193)

Equation (2.26): 1972–7

$$\ln n_e = a_0 + a_1 \ln(1+g) + a_2 \ln MES_e + a_3 \ln \Pi_0 + \ln\left[1 - \left(a_4\frac{SUM_e}{S_e} + a_5\frac{SUB_e}{S_e} + a_6\frac{SUA_e}{S_e}\right)\Pi_0^{a_7}C_0^{a_8}\left(\frac{A_0}{S_0}\right)^{a_9}\right] + \epsilon_4$$

Parameters	a_0	a_1	a_2	a_3	a_4	a_5	a_6	a_7	a_8	a_9
Estimates	0.164	0.850	-0.939	0.582	0.040	0.025	5.667	1.659	1.112	-0.689
	(0.220)	(0.244)	(0.069)	(0.193)	(0.014)	(0.034)	(2.528)	(0.170)	(0.144)	(0.032)

Standard errors in parentheses.
Number of observations, 264.
Annual depreciation rate of advertising $\lambda_A = 0.5$.

$a_1 = 1$, $a_2 = -1$, $a_4 = 1$, $a_5 > 0$, $a_6 = 0$, and $a_7 > -1$ signal rejection at P levels equal to 29.2, 11.2, 29.5, 7.9, 99.9, 59.2, and 99.9 percent respectively. The null hypothesis that $a_3 = 1$, however, can be rejected at the 0.01 percent level. In addition, we find that the test of the joint hypothesis $H_0: \theta = \theta_0$ signals rejection at the 3.4 percent level. Overall, these results provide a measure of support for the proposed theoretical model.[15]

The estimated coefficients $\hat{a}_1$, $\hat{a}_2$, and $\hat{a}_3$ indicate that the rate of entry increases with the profit level Π_0 of incumbents and the rate of growth g of industry demand, while it varies inversely with the required scale of entry MES_e, holding fixed the expected losses from the possibility of exit. Indeed, the significance of the estimated coefficients suggests that the profit level of incumbents and past growth of industry demand are very strong incentives to entry.[16] This is in agreement with the conventional wisdom that these variables can be taken as a signal by the potential entrant of the opportunities open to him. Thus, both hypothesis 4 (effect of Π_0) and hypothesis 5 (effect of g) are strongly supported. Also, the highly significant coefficient of MES_e confirms the importance of the supply effect.

Our finding that $\hat{a}_5$, the estimated coefficient of SUM, is positive and highly significant, while $\hat{a}_6$ for SUB is close to zero and statistically insignificant, provides strong support for conjecture 2 – that the required investment in machines and equipment comprises a component of entry cost that is irrecoverable in the event of exit, but that this is not the case for buildings and structures. This is consistent with the prevailing view that, in general, machines are more sunk than buildings. These results also show that sunk costs have a significant negative impact on entry and that their presence diminishes the rate at which entry responds to positive incumbent profits. It is important to note the implication that the required capital investment is a barrier to entry only to the extent that it is a sunk cost – the required investment in machines and equipment impedes entry, but the required investment in buildings and structures does not. Thus hypothesis 3 is also confirmed.

Next, we focus on the estimated relationship between the probability of an aggressive post-entry incumbent response $(1 - \alpha)/\alpha$ and economic structure. The 95 percent confidence interval for $\hat{a}_7$ is given by

$$\hat{a}_7: (0.719, 0.955)$$

This estimate indicates that incumbents are significantly more likely to react aggressively when they are profitable. Indeed, the implied functional form for the probability of an aggressive incumbent response is[17]

$$\frac{1 - \alpha}{\alpha} \sim \Pi_0^{1.837}$$

which clearly demonstrates that the likelihood of such an aggressive post-entry reaction increases with the profit level of incumbents. Thus, hypothesis 1 is confirmed.

In addition, these results indicate the presence of two countervailing forces due to the profit margin of incumbents. The estimated relationship between net entry and the profit margin (holding other factors fixed) is

$$n_e \sim \Pi_0^{0.830} \left[1 - \Pi_0^{0.837} \left(1.520 \, \frac{SUM_e}{S_e} \right) \right]$$

Thus, entry increases with the profit level of incumbents but at a decreasing rate. In fact, entry and the margin will move in opposite directions beyond the critical level[18]

$$\Pi_0^* = \frac{0.255}{(SUM_e/S_e)^{1.280}}$$

which, for industries with high sunk costs, is within the observed range of Π_0. In such industries, the threat of an aggressive reaction signified by a higher margin, and thus the risk of incurring a sizeable loss of sunk costs, outweighs the incentive to enter.[19]

The estimates of the parameters in equation (2.22), also reported in table 2.1, provide strong support for hypothesis 2 (in addition to hypothesis 1) – that the threat of an aggressive post-entry reaction by incumbents is more credible in concentrated industries where the free-rider effect in driving the entrant out is smaller. Concentration, then, deters entry to the extent that potential entrants perceive a higher probability of an aggressive response in concentrated industries, which, according to equation (2.9), raises the effective cost of entry.[20] The presence of this deterrent effect could partly explain why existing firms in concentrated industries may command supranormal profits that persist over time.

The differential impact on entry of the two forms of capital investment (machines versus buildings) permits us to distinguish effectively the "capital is a sunk cost" argument from the old "capital *qua* capital is a barrier to entry" story. This interpretation is further strengthened by our finding that the availability of a rental market reduces the extent to which such capital investment is an impediment to entry. If we take equation (2.20) as our maintained hypothesis, the N ratio which is asymptotically distributed as $N(0,1)$ takes the value of -6.49 against equation (2.23). This evidence suggests that we should reject equation (2.20) in favor of equation (2.23). It appears, therefore, that the availability of a rental market reduces sunk costs and may facilitate entry.

In addition we should note that, according to equation (2.7), the expression

$$\Pi^* = \frac{1}{\gamma_T(1 + \psi)} \; \frac{1 - \alpha}{\alpha} \; \frac{SU_e}{S_e}$$

represents the industry-specific "limit profit" that is sustainable against any entry even in the long run. Our estimates imply an average value of 0.05 for the limit profit in the US manufacturing industries compared with an average value of 0.21 for the pre-entry profit.

The estimates of the parameters in equation (2.26), reported in table 2.1, support hypothesis 6 (sunk cost effect of advertising) and decisively reject hypothesis 7a ("advertising = persuasion" school) in favor of hypothesis 7b ("advertising = information" school).

Finally, to assess the sensitivity of our results with respect to the time period chosen, we assembled data on US manufacturing industries that experienced net entry between the census years 1977 and 1982. We then re-estimated our basic equation (2.5). The results of this estimation are presented in table 2.2. A comparison with the results reported in table

Table 2.2

Equation (2.19a): 1972–7

$$n_e - \beta_0 \frac{(g - \tilde{g})}{MES_e^{\beta_2}} + \beta_3 \frac{(1 + g)^{\beta_4}}{MES_e^{\beta_5}} \, \Pi_0^{\beta_6} \left(1 - \lambda_1 \frac{SU_e}{S_e} \, \Pi_0^{\lambda_2}\right) + u_1$$

Parameters	β_0	β_1	β_2	β_3	β_4	β_5	β_6	λ_1	λ_2
Estimates	0.257	1.015	−0.942	2.679	0.842	−1.075	1.353	1.509	1.262
	(0.470)	(0.413)	(0.294)	(0.571)	(0.413)	(0.080)	(0.327)	(0.526)	(0.594)

Number of observations, 264

Equation (2.20): 1977–82

$$\ln n_e = a_0 + a_1 \ln(1 + g) + a_2 \ln MES_e + a_3 \ln \Pi_0$$

$$+ a_4 \ln \left[1 - \left(a_5 \frac{SUM_e}{S_e} + a_6 \frac{SUB_e}{S_e}\right) \Pi_0^{a_7}\right] + \epsilon_1$$

Parameters	a_0	a_1	a_2	a_3	a_4	a_5	a_6	a_7
Estimates	−0.343	0.929	−0.893	0.672	0.748	0.703	−2.547	−0.613
	(0.802)	(0.242)	(0.102)	(0.326)	(0.248)	(0.165)	(1.675)	(0.206)

Number of observations, 250

2.1 seems to indicate that the conclusions of the paper are not sensitive to the time period chosen.

6 Summary

In this paper we have developed a simple model of firm entry decisions, fitted it to inter-industry data, and tested several important hypotheses.

Our results indicate that entry increases with the profit level of incumbents, holding fixed the expected losses that the entrant would suffer in the event of exit. These expected losses are greater the higher is the probability of an aggressive incumbent response and the larger are the sunk costs that must be committed by the entrant. The effects of sunk costs are significant (sunk costs deter entry and diminish the rate at which entry responds to positive incumbent profits), and incumbents are significantly more likely to react aggressively when they are both profitable and concentrated.

The estimated model provides some support to the hypothesis that market performance depends continuously on the degree of imperfection in its contestability. We find that sunk costs are a prime impediment to contestability. Sunk costs depend on the rate of depreciation and are affected by the availability of a rental market. These findings suggest a promising direction for public policy aimed at improving market performance. Such a policy might, for example, entail measures to reduce sunk costs by providing tax incentives for rentals, for re-use of old plant in new activities, and for rapid depreciation.

We have also attempted to provide a direct test of the hypothesis that advertising serves as a barrier to new competition. Our model isolates two separate effects of advertising on entry: the effect on the irrecoverable costs of entry, and the effect on the uncertainty underlying the environment faced by potential entrants. The empirical estimates show that, for the potential entrant, the need to advertise leads to an irrecoverable entry cost in the case of failure, and thus advertising creates a sunk cost barrier to entry. However, our estimates also establish the presence of a countervailing force due to advertising. We find that entrants perceive a greater likelihood of success in markets where advertising plays an important role. These two conflicting forces can balance either way, but over most of the sample the net effect of advertising is to facilitate entry. This evidence raises new questions about the appropriate interpretation of the observed positive correlation between advertising and profitability in cross section at the industry level.

Appendix

From the 1972 and 1977 *Census of Manufacturers* we obtained the number of firms in 1972 (1977) N_{72} (N_{77}), industry value added VA, industry payroll W, total industry sales S_0, tax depreciation charges for buildings DCB, tax depreciation charges for machines DCM, the expected sales of an entrant (simple average of the representative plants from the employment size distribution) $\bar{S}_e$, rental payments for buildings RB, rental payments for machines RM, growth in demand g (industry sales in 1972 divided by industry sales in 1967 minus 1.00), and the four-digit firm concentration ratio C_0.

From the 1971 *Annual Survey of Manufacturers* we obtained the fixed depreciable assets B and M in the form of buildings and machines respectively.

From the 1972 *Input–Output Tables for the US* and the 1974 *Annual Line of Business Report* we obtained industry advertising expenditures A_0.

We set the opportunity cost r of capital at 0.06. Estimates of the price elasticity of demand ϵ_p were generously provided by Richard Levin.

The price–cost margin was defined as

$$\Pi_0 = \frac{\text{VA} - W - (r + \text{DCB})B - (r + \text{DCM})M}{S_0}$$

Notes

1 For a deep analysis of the entry process see Spence (1977), Schmalensee (1978), Salop (1979), and von Weizsacker (1980). For empirical works see, among others, Orr (1974), Stonebraker (1976), Gort and Konakayama (1982), and Hause and Du Ritz (1984).

2 Clearly, this is a restrictive assumption. However, under imperfect information it is reasonable (rational) for the entrant to employ the current value of g in predicting future demand growth, even though the entrant's assessment may later be revised. Still, a more complete treatment would entail uncertain demand growth with the entrant assigning a probability $0 < \eta < 1$ that demand will expand by g, where η is a random variable with probability distribution $h(\eta)$. See Davies and Lyons (1982).

3 Lack of data prevents us from testing hypotheses about the entry-deterring effects of excess capacity. The role of excess capacity has been assessed in a recent paper by Masson and Shaanan (1986).

4 For an early in-depth treatment of exit barriers see Caves and Porter (1976). More recently, Baumol et al. (1982) present a formal analysis of sunk costs and their role as barriers to entry.

5 Since under rapid growth conditions, entry by outside firms will not necessarily reduce incumbent sales and depress their profits, such incumbents will

then have less of an incentive to engage in aggressive post-entry behavior. Thus $(1 - \alpha)/\alpha$ is likely to be function of g.

6 The "advertising = market power" view was developed by Chamberlin (1933) and pursued further by Bain (1956) and Comanor and Wilson (1974). For the "advertising = competition" view, see, among others, Telser (1964), Brozen (1974), and Nelson (1974).

7 It should be noted that the depreciation reported in the census is for tax purposes. The pertinent US tax code gives firms incentives to depreciate as much as the law permits. Thus tax depreciation is expected to exceed the true economic depreciation and this has been confirmed by Coen (1977), who provides estimates of the ratio of current cost depreciation to depreciation for tax purposes. We employed these estimates to construct alternative proxies for sunk costs based on the rate of true economic depreciation. We then formally discriminated between the two nonnested models (one employing true economic depreciation and the other depreciation for tax purposes). Our hypothesis testing rejects the true economic depreciation in favor of tax depreciation as the basis for constructing measures of sunk costs. This finding might potentially be related to the financial structure of the incumbent firms.

8 Since B and M are asset prices while RB and RM are rental streams, it would be more accurate to modify our proposed proxies as

$$ \text{SURB}_e = \left(1 - \frac{\text{RB}}{r_B B}\right) \text{SUB}_e $$

and

$$ \text{SURM}_e = \left(1 - \frac{\text{RM}}{r_M M}\right) \text{SUM}_e $$

where $r_B B$ and $r_M M$ are the maximum rental values of the industry's buildings and machines respectively. However, all this probably makes no difference in the estimation since it is just a normalization.

9 To economize on the number of parameters in our nonlinear estimation, we do not estimate z_1 and z_2 at this stage. Thus we simply set $\text{SU}_e = \text{SUB}_e + \text{SUM}_e$.

10 Using Hoel's comparison of forecasts method we tested hypotheses about the error structure. The t values for the Hoel test are 6.24 when the additive error structure is the null hypothesis and the multiplicative error structure is the alternative, and 1.58 when the multiplicative is the null and the additive is the alternative.

11 The pice elasticity term was found to be statistically insignificant, probably because of a poor proxy, and subsequently it was suppressed into the error term.

12 See Quandt (1970), Pesaran and Deaton (1978), and Chow (1980).

13 A standard F-test rejects the null hypothesis that incumbents expand at the same rate as industry demand grows at the 91.4 percent level.

14 See Goldfeld and Quandt (1972) for a description of the algorithms employed.
15 The fact that the estimates obtained are close to the theoretically predicted values might suggest that the omitted variables and simultaneity bias are not quantitatively important. However, it is possible that such bias is important and that it led us to commit a *type II error*.
16 These results differ sharply from those obtained by Orr (1974), who found no response to profitable signals. We should also note that many studies in this area have questioned the usefulness of the price–cost margin for purposes of economic analysis because of the generally accepted view that capital markets serve to equalize rates of return on investment, not on sales. Our results clearly demonstrate, however, that entry responds very strongly to profit margin signals. Thus, this measure of the profit rate is also a good indicator of the desirability of moving resources in or out of a given industry.
17 It should be noted that $\delta_1 = a_7 + 1$ where δ_1 is the coefficient of Π_0 in equation (2.17) specifying $(1 - \alpha)/\alpha$.
18 This result is obtained by setting $\partial n_e/\partial \Pi_0 = 0$ and solving for Π_0. Also, we drop SUB_e because its effect is statistically insignificant.
19 Some of these four-digit industries are the following: 2812, alkalies and chlorine; 2813, industrial gases; 2819, industrial inorganic chemicals; 2824, organic fibers; 2873, nitrogenous fertilizers.
20 Masson and Shaanan (1987), relying on Baron's (1973) intuition, argue that concentration could actually raise the incentive to enter in that, for a given minimum efficient plant scale and assuming a symmetric post-entry equilibrium, the larger the number of operating firms in an industry the more likely it is that entry will take place at a suboptimal scale and hence the lower will be the profitability of entry.

References

Bain, J.S. (1956) *Barriers to New Competition*. Cambridge, MA: Harvard University Press.

Baron, D.P. (1973) Limit pricing, potential entry, and barriers to entry. *American Economic Review* 62, 666–74.

Baumol, W.J., Panzar, J.C. and Willig, R.D. (1982) *Contestable Markets and the Theory of Industry Structure*. New York: Harcourt Brace Jovanovich.

Baumol, W.J. and Willig, R.D. (1981) Fixed costs, sunk costs, entry barriers, and sustainability of monopoly. *Quarterly Journal of Economics* 95, 405–31.

Brozen, Y. (1974) Is advertising a barrier to entry? In *Advertising and Society*, New York: New York University Press.

Caves, R.E. and Porter, M.E. (1976) Barriers to exit. In R.T. Masson and P.D. Qualls (eds.), *Essays in Industrial Organization in Honor of Joe S. Bain*, Cambridge, MA: Ballinger.

Chamberlin, E. (1933) *The Theory of Monopolistic Competition*. Cambridge, MA: Harvard University Press.

Chow, G.C. (1980) The selection of variates for use in prediction. In *Quantitative Economics and Development*, New York: Academic Press.

Coen, R.M. (1977) Alternative measures of depreciation, profits and rates of return in US manufacturing: 1947–74. US Treasury Department, Office of Tax Analysis, March, 1977.

Comanor, W.S. and Wilson, T.A. (1974) *Advertising and Market Power*. Cambridge, MA: Harvard University Press.

Davies, S.W. and Lyons, B.R. (1982) Seller concentration: the technological explanation and demand uncertainty. *Economic Journal* 92, 903–19.

Gallant, R.A. (1975) Nonlinear regression. *American Statistician* 29, 73–81.

Geroski, P.A. (1983) The empirical analysis of entry: a survey. Discussion Papers in Economics and Econometrics 8318, University of Southampton.

Goldfeld, S.M. and Quandt, R.E. (1972) *Nonlinear Methods in Econometrics*. Amsterdam: North-Holland.

Gort, M. and Konakayama, A. (1982) A model of diffusion in the production of an innovation. *American Economic Review* 72, 1111–20.

Hause, J.C. and Du Rietz, G. (1984) Entry, industry growth, and the microdynamics of industry supply. *Journal of Political Economy* 92, 733–57.

Masson, R. and Shaanan, J. (1986) Excess capacity and limit pricing: an empirical test. *Economica* 211, 365–78.

Masson, R. and Shaanan, J. (1987) Optimal oligopoly pricing and the threat of entry. *International Journal of Industrial Organization* 5, 323–39.

Nelson, P. (1974) Advertising as information. *Journal of Political Economy* 82, 729–54.

Orr, D. (1974) The determinants of entry: a study of the Canadian manufacturing industries. *Review of Economics and Statistics* 56, 58–65.

Pesaran, M.H. and Deaton, A.S. (1978) Testing non-nested hypotheses. *Econometrica* 46, 677–94.

Quandt, R.E. (1970) *The Demand for Travel: Theory and Measurement*. Lexington, MA: Heath Lexington Books.

Salop, S.C. (1979) Strategic entry deterrence. *American Economic Review* 69, 335–8.

Schmalensee, R. (1978) Entry deterrence in the RTE cereal industry. *Bell Journal of Economics* 9, 305–27.

Shubik, M. and Levitan, R. (1980) *Market Structure and Behavior*. Cambridge, MA: Harvard University Press.

Spence, M.A. (1977) Entry, capacity, investment and oligopolistic pricing. *Bell Journal of Economics* 8, 534–44.

Stonebraker, R. (1976) Corporate profits and the risk of entry. *Review of Economics and Statistics* 58, 33–9.

Telser, L.G. (1964) Advertising and competition. *Journal of Political Economy*, December, 537–62.

von Weizsacker, C.C. (1980) *Barriers to Entry: A Theoretical Treatment*. Berlin: Springer-Verlag.

Willig, R.D. (1982) Market structure and government intervention in access markets. Princeton University (unpublished).

3

Sunk Costs and Entry by Small and Large Plants

José Mata

1 Introduction

Since the seminal work of Bain (1956) the role of scale economies as a barrier to entry has been a highly controversial issue. Recently, the role of irrevocable commitments embodied in capital investment has been emphasized (Dixit, 1980), and durability has been identified as a source of such irrevocability (Eaton and Lipsey, 1980). Baumol and Willig (1981) first distinguished between fixed costs and sunk costs, and showed that while sunk costs create an entry barrier, fixed costs do not. Capital specificity is usually considered as a source of sunkness of costs, because once capital takes a specific form, it may be costly to transfer it to another use. Capital durability is also a source of sunkness of costs, because once a firm commits resources to a particular form, if it is not possible to resell capital, the firm must operate until the end of the capital's life to recover its value. Capital durability and capital specificity clearly interact to create an entry barrier.

However, there has been little empirical research on the role of sunk costs on entry deterrence. Only Kessides (1986; chapter 2 of this volume) has tested the influence of sunk costs on entry, finding a significant relationship between them. In his 1986 paper, however, he only accounted for the durability aspect of sunk costs. The purpose of the present paper is to make a test of the impact of sunk costs (both capital specificity and capital durability) on entry. For this, we use a general model of entry, in which statistical proxies to sunk costs are included. The model is tested using large-scale and small-scale entry as dependent

This research was partially supported by the Instituto Nacional de Investigação Cientifica. I am obliged to Paul Geroski, Stephen Martin and Nils-Henrik Mørch von der Fehr for helpful comments on an earlier version of this paper. Obviously, I am responsible for any remaining errors and omissions. I am also grateful to Jordi Jaumandreu and Gonzalo Mato for providing some of the data.

variables in order to ascertain whether these two types of entrants respond differently to entry barriers.

The remainder of the paper is organized as follows. The model is presented in the next section. Issues of measurement of sunk costs are dealt with in section 3. Empirical results are presented in section 4, and finally some concluding comments and suggestions for further research are made in section 5.

2 The Model

As in most empirical work on the subject, entry E is expected to vary directly with the expected profit rate π and negatively with every component of a vector of entry barriers BE:[1]

$$E = f_1(\pi, \text{BE}) \tag{3.1}$$

Expected profitability is an unobservable variable, and past profitability usually serves as a proxy. This is clearly an incomplete specification of *expected* profitability as it does not account for market evolution, and a growth measure (GR) is include to take this into account. Growth is assumed to attract entry because a market in rapid growth offers many profit opportunities for both incumbents and entrants. In addition, in a growing market entry does not necessarily occur at the expense of actual competitors, as it does in a stable market. Incumbents feel themselves less threatened by entry and are less likely to react aggressively. The response of entrants to profit stimulus is also conditional on market concentration C, as a proxy of the potential of collusion, because of either strategic deterrence or post-entry aggressive behavior, and on incumbent's diversification DO as a proxy of the incumbents' ability to sustain a post-entry fight. A substantial amount of entry simply replaces exiting firms, and occurs even if profits are at their long-run level. This flow of entry by replacement depends on the size of the market, and thus a measure of industry size (SIZE) is included in the model. The complete model is thus

$$E = f_2(\pi, \text{BE}, \text{GR}, C, \text{DO}, \text{SIZE}) \tag{3.2}$$

Whereas in early studies a quite restrictive definition of entry was used (*de novo* entry was the only kind of entry considered by Bain (1956), Mansfield (1962) and Orr (1974), it is now well recognized that entry barriers pose different problems to different types of entrants or modes of entry. Some recent studies employed alternative definitions of entry, and a few used the same data base to test for different effects of barriers to entry on different entrants.[2] However, despite the increasing interest of economists in small business, there has not yet been a study comparing entry by small and large entrants.

Entry barriers ought to affect entry in very different ways according to entrants' size. Large entrants are better positioned to overcome some types of barriers but, on the other hand, small entrants are more flexible and small-scale entry can be the way that entrants seek to avoid factors that deter large-scale entry (Scherer, 1980, p. 248; Shepherd, 1984). We shall now discuss the effect of each source of entry barriers in small- and large-scale entry. The entry barriers considered are economies of scale (MESM), product differentiation (PAT and ADV), capital requirements (KR) and two measures of sunk costs, which will be discussed in section 3.[3]

The capital requirements barriers, for example, act as a barrier to entry due to capital market imperfections. The usual hypothesis is that new firms encounter increased difficulties in raising funds, and this hypothesis has received generalized support from empirical work. A negative relationship should only hold for small-scale entrants, however. There are at least two reasons for this. The first is that, for large entrants, the percentage of plants that are *de novo* entrants is probably much smaller than that for small entrants, and therefore the previous argument does not apply. The second reason is purely statistical. If entry occurs in industries where economies of scale and thus capital require-ments are important, it is more likely to occur by large plants than in industries where economies of scale are not important. For large entrants, therefore, there is no reason why a negative relationship between capital requirements and number of entrants should exist.

In the absence of sunk costs the *scale economies* barrier can only be effective for entrants smaller than the minimum efficient scale, i.e. small entrants. However, with sunk costs it can constitute an obstacle for the entry of large plants. Given the size of the market, the larger is the scale at which entry must be attempted, the smaller is the number of firms in the market and the higher the reduction on output of each firm provoked by one more competitor will be. If sunk costs prevent easy displacement, there will be a strong incentive for incumbents to defend their position, and therefore economies of scale can imply an entry barrier to large entrants. However, the last argument made about capital requirements also applies here.

On the other hand, strategic entry deterrence and fear of aggressive behavior, proxied by *industrial concentration*, will only be important to large entrants. Retaliatory behavior is much more likely to occur if directed against large competitors. The payoff of an aggressive attitude against small entrants is very small compared with the sacrifice it may involve in terms of short-run profits, and is not a credible threat. Small entrants will not be deterred by fear of aggressive behavior, and concentration is not likely to be negatively related to small-scale entry unless it merely reflects a scale economies effect.

We would probably observe a similar effect in what concerns *sunk costs*. Sunk costs will presumably have a more significant effect on large-scale entry. For small-scale entry, investment is small and thus the loss would be small in case of failure, as the probability of finding a buyer for the equipment would be greater than in the case of large-scale entry. Therefore we should expect a negative effect of sunk costs on large-scale entry and no significant effect on small-scale entry.

Product differentation represents an increased obstacle to entry as the existence of differentiated products requires an additional effort from the potential competitor in order to build his own acceptance from buyers. This can be achieved through advertising or through product characteristics (R&D, product design). In both cases, this effort may involve substantial fixed costs, and may be of particular importance for small entrants. However, small entrants may be at an advantage *vis-à-vis* large entrants, as in differentiated markets it is easier to find niches which can be served with no need of large promotional campaigns and in which they can operate even with some cost disadvantages.[4]

Entry was measured as the gross increase in the number of new establishments in a industry. Gross entry is used because a net entry figure near zero may result either from zero entry and zero exit or from an equally large number of entries and exits. While the first case can reflect a situation in which entry is highly attractive, but entry barriers are also high, the second can stand for a situation in which, even if there are no barriers to entry, there is no room for more firms in the industry and profits are near the competitive level. Entry occurs together with exit and implies the substitution of a more efficient firm for a less efficient one. As we are investigating here the determinants and not the consequences of entry, a gross measure seems appropriate.[5]

3 The Measurement of Sunk Costs

Sunk costs are those costs which are irrevocably committed to a particular use, and therefore are not recoverable in case of exit. From the point of view of a potential entrant, the relevant costs for his decision to enter/not to enter the market are the costs he would not recover if and when he decides to leave the market. Clearly, these costs, which we shall denote SUNK, are dependent on the initial capital requirements (KR), the proportion of this investment that had depreciated at the time of exit (DEP), and the proportion of its net value that could be recovered by reselling the capital goods (RESEL). Assuming a linear depreciation, and denoting by ANDEP the annual rate of depreciation and by n the expected number of years that an entrant will be in the market in case of failure, we obtain

$$SUNK = KR(1 - n\,ANDEP)(1 - RESEL) \qquad (3.3)$$

A measure for KR has been extensively used in the literature and the annual rate of depreciation ANDEP can be computed from the expected life of capital assets or, if data are not available, replaced by the tax depreciation rate. The problem with (3.3) is then the choice of appropriate proxies for n and for RESEL.

We cannot observe n, and if we replaced it with the past average time of permanence of entrants that have been in the market for less than, say, the expected life of capital assets, we would obtain a result which would be the opposite of our original aim. What we want is an estimate for the time that an entrant can expect to be in the market if he fails to succeed in his entry attempt. However, the observed time of permanence is inversely related to the degree of sunkness; a small past average permanence time would not imply that an entrant should expect to face high sunk costs and suffer great losses in case of exit but, on the contrary, would result from the fact that it has been easy to resell capital goods with minor losses. As we cannot measure n, we shall try to capture its effect and account for the reasons that determine it. The expected time of permanence in the market, if entry fails, is probably influenced by two main factors: how aggressive the reactions of incumbent firms are, and the entrant's ability to fight after entry has taken place. The first of these aspects is taken into account by including measures of growth, concentration and diversification, and the second by performing separate regressions according to the scale of the entrant.

The estimation of RESEL requires the knowledge of two figures for capital goods sold on the second-hand market of each industry. We must know the actual value at which the transactions took place, and we should be able to evaluate the assets sold at the price they were bought net of depreciation and corrected for inflation. As the last figure is not very likely to be known, it is not easy to compute the real values of RESEL. We could replace RESEL with the ratio of capital assets sales to total capital stock, attempting to capture how easy it is (has been) to sell capital assets in the second-hand market. However, a measure such as this could be biased toward industry growth, for example. It could capture not only the ease of selling capital goods in the second-hand market but also the will of capital owners to sell it.

To overcome this problem, we should be able to have a measure is the ease of selling capital goods which is insensitive so differences in growth rates. This measure, I shall argue, could be the proportion of capital goods bought in the second-hand market by the firms in the sector relative to total capital acquisitions. The reasoning is the following. What we are trying to measure to the ease of selling capital goods as a proxy of capital specificity. If it has been easy to buy capital goods in the second-hand market, that is because the capital goods bought are not that specific, and if they are not specific it will also be easy to sell them if one wishes. This measure will not be biased toward growth like the previous one, at least in the small open economy, which happens to be the case in Portugal. Apart from constraints from the supply side of the capital goods market (which is ruled out as we are dealing with a small economy with a great openness to the world market), it is not obvious why growth should be a major determinant of the decision between buying new and buying used.

Different types of capital goods have different degrees of sunkness. Like Kessides (chapter 2 of this volume), I assume that machinery and other equipment are more firm specific than any other kind of capital goods, and for the purposes of measuring sunk costs, this is the only type of capital asset that I consider in this paper. In order to test for possible interactions between the different measures of sunk costs, all the measures should vary in the same way with SUNK and thus with entry. NEW is then defined as the sum of machines and other equipment bought new as a percentage of the total of machines and other equipment bought by the industry. For the same reason EQUIP, the average life of machines and other equipment, was used instead of ANDEP.[6]

4 Estimation and Results

Small-scale and large-scale entry are highly correlated when both are measured by the absolute number of entrants (correlation coefficient of 0.459). However, when entry rates are employed, correlation is almost null (-0.048).[7] This indicates that market size is probably a common determinant of both small- and large-scale entry, but also suggests that, after market size is taken into account, these two types of entry have different patterns and may be determined by different factors. To test more rigorously for this, two equations were estimated, one with small-scale entry and the other with large-scale entry as dependent variables.

The semi-logarithmic specification was employed for both equations. Khemani and Shapiro (1986) tested for different functional forms for entry equations, and reached the conclusion that the semi-logarithmic form was the most appropriate. A method also suggested by Khemani and Shapiro was used to deal with industries without any entry during the period: 1 was added to the number of entrants in each industry and logarithms were then taken in order to give the dependent variable. This is the easiest way to assure both that industries with one entry appear different from those with none, and that the value of the dependent variable for industries with zero entry is zero. This method was employed without further investigation.

Small-scale entry equation coefficients were estimated using the ordinary least squares (OLS) method, and White's (1980) procedure was employed to obtain heteroskedasticity-consistent estimates for the covariance matrix. Large-scale entry occurred only in 26 of the 73 industries that constitute our sample, and therefore OLS is not a suitable method. A tobit regression was run for large-scale entry, and results for both equations are provided in table 3.1.[8]

A concentration measure is not included in the reported results because of multicollinearity with market size. When included in the regressions concentration measures produced reversed SIZE signs, or substantially reduced its significance. In the latter case, the concentration coefficient was negative only for small-scale entry; the same occurred when SIZE was dropped from the list of regressors. These results do not support the view that strategic deterrence or aggressive behavior might have been an important determinant of entry, and as the fit was better than SIZE was included, concentration was excluded. For the remaining variables multicollinearity was not judged to be a major problem.

Results show that only the size of the market is a common determinant of entry by small and large establishments, which seems to suggest that entry for replacement, substituting more efficient for less efficient firms, is a rather important occurrence.

All the conventional entry barriers were found to be negative and significant in the small-scale entry equation, but not in the large-scale entry equation. Although it is generally believed that entry barriers are more effective in deterring large-scale entrants, these results are not unexpected. In industries where economies of scale are not important, risk aversion recommends that entry takes place on a small scale and only a small amount of large-scale entry will occur. On the contrary, if

Table 3.1 Regression results

VARIABLE	Small-scale entry	Large-scale entry
CONSTANT	2.755	1.845
	(1.515)	(0.557)
PROFIT	2.922	−0.813
	(2.093)	(−0.368)
SIZE	0.645	0.569
	(5.904)	(3.818)
GR	0.925	3.320
	(0.569)	(1.787)
MESM	−4.063	1.470
	(−3.611)	(1.476)
PAT	−0.186	0.107
	(−1.884)	(0.465)
ADV	−0.808	−0.206
	(−5.833)	(−0.305)
DO	−2.218	−1.130
	(−2.691)	(−0.812)
KR	−0.304	0.177
	(−2.425)	(1.331)
EQUIP	−0.397	−1.847
	(−0.903)	(−2.454)
NEW	−0.632	−3.182
	(−0.743)	(−1.925)
R^2/R^{-2}	0.70/0.66	0.54

t-ratios in parentheses. R^2 for the large-scale equation was computed according to Dhrymes (1986).

economies of scale are important, only a small number of establishments will enter but, if they enter, they will be large. This effect probably more than compensates any deterrent effect that scale economies or capital requirements may have had on large-scale entry. Results in what concerns product differentiation are also not unexpected: it seems that the scale effect is more important than the niche effect. With respect to diversification, however, the result, being somewhat surprising, is consistent with the observed lack of importance of concentration as a proxy for incumbents' aggressive behavior. Diversification, being a proxy for incumbents' ability to sustain a post-entry fight, is not likely to affect entry if incumbents are not likely to fight in case of entry. The observed negative relationship between small-scale entry and diversification probably merely reflects the fact that small entrants do not generally enter industries where there are more complex (diversified) incumbents.

On the contrary, sunk costs variables are only negative and significant for large-scale entry, which confirms expectations. Storey and Jones (1987) argued that small-firm formation is strongly related to the existence of a second-hand market, since entrepreneurs usually start their own businesses buying cheap second-hand equipment. They are probably right, in the sense that in markets for second-hand equipment buyers are mostly small firms. Nevertheless, the main effect that second-hand markets seem to have is to increase the possibility for large plants to sell the equipment they no longer need, thereby reducing the commitment to the market and the risk involved with entry.

The past profitability of industry only appears to be significant for small-scale entry. Since, in using PROFIT, an *a priori* 4 year lag is imposed and we have no previous information on the lag structure prevailing between profits and entry, average profit rates for other periods were used, allowing for lags of 3 years to 1 year and for no lags at all. In no case was past profitability revealed to be a determinant of entry by large plants. This could be due to the fact that, for large entrants, strategic considerations rather than overall industry profitability determine the decision of entering an industry. Or, as Highfield and Smiley (1987) and Geroski (chapter 3 of this volume) have argued, past profits are not a good proxy to expected profits for sophisticated entrants. Sophisticated entrants do not have naive expectations about future profits, and more elaborate methods should be employed in trying to forecast expected profits. Such careful modeling of expected profits was not attempted. However, results apparently indicate that entrants of different sizes differ in the way that they incorporate past profits into their entry decisions. If large entrants only respond to forecast profits, while small ones respond to past profitability, that would give some support to the view that large entrants act in a more sophisticated fashion.

The observed influence of pre-entry growth rates does not contradict this view. Growth can be viewed as an inverse measure of the incumbent's incentive to adopt a post-entry aggressive behavior, and can also be viewed as a signal of profit opportunities. As aggressive behavior was not found to be very important, the fact that only large entrants respond to industry growth reinforces our suggestion that market dynamics is only taken into account by these entrants.

From what has been said, it seems that small entrants are in a position of disadvantage relative to large entrants. Large entrants are able to overcome the majority of entry barriers to which small entrants are sensitive, and small entrants respond in a naive fashion to past profitability while large entrants do not. It has been hypothesized that small-scale entry could be the way to avoid the barriers to large-scale market entry. This does not seem to have happened in Portugal. The hypothesis that small-scale entry is a way of avoiding entry barriers assumes that small entrants are able deliberately to adopt small-scale entry as part of a strategic plan of market penetration, which involves a minimum size and organizational and managerial skills which I am not sure (I seriously doubt) that Portuguese small firms possess. The majority of Portuguese small firms are probably too small to achieve the minimum internal organization compatible with strategic choice, and probably in most cases small-scale entry is the only option left to entrants.

Nevertheless, despite these handicaps, or perhaps as a consequence as this lack of sophistication, sunk costs do not affect small entrants' decisions. This could be interpreted as being due to greater flexibility and greater ability to manage difficult situations or, and this is not a contradictory conclusion, to the fact that they pay less attention to risk.

5 Conclusions

In this paper we have presented an empirical test of the effect of sunk costs on entry by small and large plants. Empirical results suggest that entrants respond very differently to entry barriers, with small entrants being more sensitive to them. With regard to sunk costs, however, an opposite effect was found: sunk costs seem to be important only for large entrants.

This duality has also been observed with respect to the entry inducement factors . Pre-entry growth rates appear to be important only to large-scale entry decisions, while past profitability seems to attract only small entrants. Even if more sophisticated methods of forecasting profits should be attempted, in order to determine whether large entrants respond to them, the overall picture seems to suggest that large entrants are in a position of relative superiority *vis-à-vis* small entrants. Unlike small entrants, large entrants do not use naive projections of profits, incorporate market dynamics in their entry decisions, and are able to overcome the majority of entry barriers.

These results challenge the (already) conventional view of small business flexibility and their superior ability to succeed in environments where large firms fail. They suggest that, even if this view may hold for some countries, it does not seem to hold for the Portuguese case, and warn us against directly importing conclusions derived for more developed economies into less developed economies. The different roles that small business may play in different countries is certainly a question which deserves further investigation.

Appendix: Variables and sources

PROFIT   Residuals of a regression of PCM on RISK and KO. PCM was computed as the average price–cost margin and RISK as the standard deviation of PCM, both across the period 1979–82. KO was also defined as the average capital-to-output ratio across the period (see Duetsch, 1984; MacDonald, 1986).

SIZE   Logarithm of the number of workers of plants primarily classified in the industry in 1982.

GR   Annual rate of growth in industrial employment between 1979 and 1982.

MES   Half of the average number of workers in firms that, on average, operated 1.5 establishments in 1982 (see Lyons, 1980).

MESM   MES/SIZE.

KR   Logarithm of the amount of total capital required to operate a plant as large as MES.

ADV   Dummy variable: 1 when the industry is consumer oriented in Portugal and advertising intensive in Spain, and 0 otherwise.

PAT   Ratio of total expenditures in patents and trademarks to production (average for 1979–82).

DO   Ratio of the number of employees in establishments primarily classified outside the industry, belonging to firms primarily classified in the industry, to the total number of employees in firms primarily classified in the industry in 1982 (see MacDonald, 1984).

NEW   Machines and other equipment bought new as a percentage of the total of machines and other equipment bought by the industry (average for 1979–82). Figures are net of sales in the second-hand market.

EQUIP   Logarithm of the expected life of machines and other equipment.

The sample consists of 73 industries from the Portuguese manufacturing sector. Data on production, employment, wages, value added, gross investment, and patents and trademarks expenditures are published data from the National Institute of Statistics. The Institute is also the source for the classification of the industries according to the destiny of production (consumer/ producer). Data on capital stock are estimates, and were published by the Ministry of Industry for 79 industries, defined with a level of aggregation superior to the standard level at which industrial data are usually released. It was assumed that all the subsectors of each sector have the same capital-to-output ratio. Measures of concentration, diversification, and scale economies, as well as entry figures, are our own computations based on unpublished data from the Ministry of Employment. Data on the ratio of advertising to production in Spain are unpublished data from an official survey on the Spanish manufacturing sector used by Jaumandreu and Mato (1987), and were kindly provided by the authors.

Notes

1 See Geroski (1983) for a survey of empirical work on entry.
2 See MacDonald (1984, 1986), Shapiro and Khemani (1989), Acs and Audretsch (1987), and Schwalbach (1987) for different definitions of entry. Gorecki (1976), Shapiro (1983), Baldwin and Gorecki (1987), and Geroski (1990) compared foreign firm entry with national firm entry, Gorecki (1975) and von der Fehr (chapter 5 of this volume) distinguished and compared entry by new and already established firms, and Yip (1982) and Baldwin and Gorecki (1987) compared entry by acquisition and by plant construction.
3 A complete list of variables and their definitions can be found in the appendix.
4 Advertising intensity is commonly proxied by the ratio of advertising to sales. As there are no such data for Portugal, the variable used (ADV) was based on Spanish data. This was based upon the belief that Portuguese and Spanish markets are very similar, and that potentially differentiable industries are the same in both countries.
5 Entry figures were computed from four raw files (two files for 1982 and two for 1986). A file with all plants primarily classified in the manufacturing sector and another with all the firms owning plants primarily classified in the manufacturing sector were available for each year. The figures for entry were obtained by comparing the 1982 establishment file with the 1986 file. For each industry, a plant was classified as an entrant if it was present in 1986 but not in 1982. Very small plants (less than five employees) were then deleted, and the remaining entrant plants were classified according to their scale. Entrants were defined as small if they were employing from five to 50 persons, and large if they had more than 250 employees.
6 Similar measures were employed by Kessides (1988).
7 Entry rates were computed by dividing the number of small and large entrants by the *total* number of plants in the industry.
8 OLS estimates for the large-scale equation were also computed (not shown here). They were always smaller (in absolute value) than tobit estimates, except for the constant coefficient. In addition, GR is nonsignificant while MESM is significant. Another regression was run in which the dependent variable was the sum of large-scale and small-scale entry. Results were rather different from those of the small-scale equation, especially considering that we are dealing with the number of entrants and not with their market share.

Coefficient signs all remain as in the small-scale equation, but their absolute value decreases. Moreover, PROFIT, PAT, and KR are no longer significant.

References

Acs, Z.J. and Audretsch, D.B. (1989) Small-firm entry in U.S. manufacturing. *Economica*, 56 (222) 255–65.

Bain, J.S. (1956) *Barriers to New Competition*. Cambridge, MA: Harvard University Press.

Baldwin, J.R. and Gorecki, P.K. (1987) Plant creation versus plant acquisition: the entry process in Canadian manufacturing. *International Journal of Industrial Organization* 5 (1), 27–41.

Baumol, W.J. and Willig, R.D. (1981) Fixed costs, sunk costs, entry barriers, and sustainability of monopoly. *Quarterly Journal of Economics* 96 (3), 405–31.

Dixit, A. (1980) The role of investment in entry-deterrence. *Economic Journal* 90, 95–106.

Dhrymes, P.J. (1986) Limited dependent variables. In Z. Griliches and M.D. Intriligator (eds), *Handbook of Econometrics*, vol. 3, Amsterdam: North-Holland.

Duetsch, L.L. (1984) Entry and extent of multiplant operations. *Journal of Industrial Economics* 32 (4) 477–87.

Eaton, B.C. and Lipsey, R.G. (1980) Exit barriers are entry barriers: the durability of capital as a barrier to entry. *Bell Journal of Economics* 11, 721–9.

Geroski, P.A. (1983) The empirical analysis of entry: a survey. Discussion Paper in Economics and Econometrics 8318, University of Southampton.

Gorecki, P.K. (1975) The determinants of entry by new and diversifying enterprises in the U.K. manufacturing sector 1958–1963: some tentative results. *Appplied Economics* 7 (2), 139–47.

Gorecki, P.K. (1976) The determinants of entry by domestic and foreign enterprises in Canadian manufacturing industries: some comments and empirical evidence. *Review of Economics and Statistics* 58 (4), 485–8.

Highfield, R. and Smiley, R. (1987) New business starts and economic activity: an empirical investigation. *International Journal of Industrial Organization* 5 (1), 51–66.

Jaumandreu, J. and Mato G. (1987) Margins, concentration and advertising: a panel data analysis. Paper presented at the 14th EARIE Conference.

Kessides, I.N. (1986) Advertising sunk cost and barriers to entry. *Review of Economics and Statistics* 68 (1), 84–95.

Kessides, I.N. (1988) Market structure and sunk costs: an empirical test of the contestability hypothesis. Working Paper 88–50, University of Maryland.

Khemani, R.S. and Shapiro, D.M. (1986) The determinants of new plant entry in Canada. *Applied Economics* 18, 1243–57.

Lyons, B. (1980) A new measure of minimum efficient plant size in UK manufacturing industries. *Economica* 17, 19–34.

MacDonald, J.M. (1984) Diversification, market growth and concentration in the US manufacturing. *Southern Economic Journal* 50, 1098–111.

MacDonald, J.M. (1986) Entry and exit on the competitive fringe. *Southern Economic Journal* 52, 640–52.

Mansfield, E. (1962) Entry, Gibrat's law innovation and the growth of the firms. *American Economic Review* 52, 1023–51.

Orr, D. (1974) The determinants of entry: a study of the Canadian manufacturing industries. *Review of Economics and Statistics* 56 (1), 58–66.

Scherer, F.M. (1980) *Industrial Market Structure and Economic Performance*, 2nd edn. Boston, MA: Houghton Mifflin.

Schwalbach, J. (1987) Entry by diversified firms into German industries. *International Journal of Industrial Organization* 5, 442–54.

Shapiro, D. (1983) Entry, exit and the theory of the multinational corporation. In C. Kindleberger, and D. Audretsch (eds), *The Multinational Corporation in the 1980s*, Cambridge, MA: MIT Press.

Shapiro, D. and Khemani, R.S. (1987) The determinants of entry and exit reconsidered. *International Journal of Industrial Organization* 5 (1), 15–26.

Shepherd, W.S. (1984) Contestability versus competition. *American Economic Review* 74 (4), 572–87.

Storey, D.J. and Jones, A.M. (1987) New firm formation – a labour market approach to industrial entry. *Scottish Journal of Economic Policy* 34 (1), 37–51.

White, H. (1980) A heteroskedastic-consistent covariance matrix estimator and direct test for heteroskedasticity. *Econometrica* 48, 817–38.

Yip, G.S. (1982) *Barriers to Entry: A Corporate-strategy Perspective*. Lexington, MA: Lexington Books.

4

Domestic and Foreign Entry in the United Kingdom: 1983–1984

P.A. Geroski

1 Introduction

Economists interested in analysing market process are aware that what makes a market competitive is not only the number of firms that populate it, but also the types of firm that do so. For example, certain types of entrant may be more advantaged than others, and thus may enter more readily and present more of a competitive challenge to incumbents than other types. At a practical level, this type of observation often poses an interesting policy dilemma for policy-makers in small open economies: does the possibility of import competition obviate the need for policy-makers to be concerned with domestic market structure and, in particular, with entry into markets by domestic-based firms? The purpose of this paper is to cast some light on this question by estimating a simple model of entry applied to two types of competitor in UK markets, domestic and foreign-based entrants. The goal of the exercise is that of measuring the speed with which the two types of entrant respond to profitable market opportunities in the UK, and the height of the barriers to entry which they face.

Our exploration of the subject will proceed through a number of stages. To extract estimates of entry barriers from raw data on entry flows, we need to model entry and to do so in a way that enables us to calculate the level of profits which would be observed at a long-run

Portions of an earlier version of this report were prepared for, and with the support of the Office of Fair Trading (OFT). The comments and advice of several members of the OFT proved to be very helpful. I am also obliged to T. Vlassopoulos for assistance with the computing, and to D. Mueller, H. Yamawaki, B. Lyons, J. Schwalbach, and participants at the first (i.e. November 1988) meeting of the International Comparisons of Entry group for helpful comments on a first draft of this paper, and to J. Fairburn who collected the original data, did much of the early computing, and provided valuable feedback throughout. The usual disclaimer applies, however.

equilibrium in which no (net) entry occurred. The development of such a model of entry is the subject of section 2, and in section 3 the model is specified empirically (i.e. expressed in terms of observables) before being applied to the data. In most of our applied work we shall use a sample of data on entry into 95 three-digit UK Minimum List Heading (MLH) industries in 1983 and 1984, and our first empirical step – taken in section 4 – is to describe the basic features of these data. The second step is to apply the model to the data, and in section 5 we describe the results of this application. Finally, a brief summary of the results and an answer to our motivating question are presented in section 6.

2 A Model of Entry

Calculating the height of barriers to entry is an important part of assessing market processes because the existence of barriers is a necessary condition for any kind of anticompetitive device to have a sustained long-run impact on market performance. Barriers are not directly observable, however, and so must be inferred from observed data on market outcomes, an exercise that is not entirely straightforward. The problem is that long-run equilibrium positions (which is what we wish to observe) are counterfactual constructions which are not necessarily perfectly mirrored in actual market outcomes. If we truly believed that markets were always at or very near their long-run equilibrium positions, then high observed profits would clearly signal the existence of high long-run profits. However, if markets take any time at all to adjust to changes, then the data will be contaminated by disequilibrium factors, and we run the risk of confusing short-run disequilibrium outcomes with market performance in the long run. Observed current period profits are therefore likely to be an unreliable signal of profits in the long run, and so of barriers to entry.

There are two basic methods which have been used to try to overcome the problem of measuring the height of barriers to entry. The first, according to Bain (1956), involves carefully isolating and measuring the different types of barrier which are present in any given industry, and then summing their effects to arrive at an overall "condition of entry" for each industry. To measure each type of barrier, Bain constructed a hypothetical "most advantaged entrant," and speculated on the likely effects of entry in a particular sector by such a competitor. If this most advantageously placed entrant could not enter and make a profit in a market where incumbents were already profitably operating, then those "pre-entry" profits were deemed likely to persist even in the long run and entry was said to be "blockaded." Similar types of counterfactual construction would also identify situations where entry was "effectively impeded," "ineffectively impeded," and "easy." Although it has the potential to be very accurate, this type of explicit counterfactual construction is fairly time consuming and is much too expensive to consider seriously as a means of examining large numbers of industries. The second method, introduced by Orr (1974b), involves applying a particular model of entry to data on entry and industry profitability and then using the estimated parameters of the model to infer something about the size of profits that are likely to persist into the long run for each industry. At a long-run equilibrium, entry is zero by definition and this condition can be used, together with the estimated parameters of the econometric model, to infer the size of profits that incumbents will enjoy when all entry has ceased. This level of profitability – sometimes called the level of "limit profits" – is a natural measure of the height of entry barriers. As a method, this second approach suffers from all the inaccuracies which are introduced by the use of the kinds of variables that proxy barriers which are available for cross-section work. However, set against this is the fact that the method is relatively straightforward and inexpensive to use. Thus it seems suitable for the purposes of screening a wide range of industries, perhaps for use as a first step in identifying industries in which a more explicit and more detailed counterfactual analysis of entry conditions might pay dividends.

The basic empirical model that we shall use derives from Orr (1974a) and has a simple intuitive basis. If we think of entry as an error-correction mechanism which is attracted by and serves to bid away excess profits, it is natural to suppose that entry will occur whenever profits differ from their long-run levels. Given this maintained hypothesis, observations of actual entry rates and current (or expected post-entry) profits can be used to make inferences about the unobservable of interest – long-run profits. In particular, entry E_{jt} in industry j at time t, is hypothesized to occur whenever expected post-entry profits π_{jt}^e exceed the level of profits protected in the long run by entry barriers b_j; i.e.

$$E_{jt} = \gamma(\pi_{jt}^e - b_j) + \mu_{jt} \qquad (4.1)$$

where μ_{jt} is a random error and the levels of barriers b_j are assumed to be constant over time, and $E_{jt} = 0$ reflects net exit. The parameter γ measures the speed with which entrants respond to excess profits, and has the dimension of a flow per unit of time; b_j, however, is expressed in the same units as π_{jt}^e. The level of profits which can be sustained in perpetuity without attracting entry is clearly b_j, and these "limit profits" are a natural measure of the height of barriers to entry. Putting the matter in a different way, the flow of entry that would have occurred if there were no entry barriers is $\gamma \pi_{jt}^e$, and the difference between this and the actual flow E_{jt} is, on average, equal to γb_j, which clearly depends on the height of barriers to entry.

While equation (4.1) appears, on the face of it, to be a reasonable looking entry equation, it is worth considering its microeconomic foundations more explicitly.[1] The gain from so doing comes from being able to interpret γ, the parameter which describes the speed of response by entrants to excess profits, and expected post-entry profits π_{jt}^e, more precisely. Thus, suppose that firm i chooses output x_i and that total industry output is $x \equiv \Sigma x_i$. Let the good in question be homogeneous, demand be $p = p(x)$, and marginal costs be constant at a level of c_i per unit. Thus, current period profits net of fixed costs are

$$\Pi_i = x_i[p(x) - c_i] \tag{4.2}$$

Two constraints play an important role in affecting the choice of x_i by firm i in any period t. First, rivals are likely to respond to any attempt by i to expand (or, for that matter, to contract), and this response is likely to occur over time. Using conjectural variations, we suppose that firm i expects an initial aggregate response, $\partial x_t / \partial x_{it} \equiv \theta_0$, by all rivals and a subsequent response $\partial x_{t+1} / \partial x_{it} \equiv \theta_1$ to any output change that it makes in period t.[2] Since $\partial x / \partial x_i = 1 + \Sigma \partial x_j / \partial x_i$, $j \neq i$, then $\theta_0 = \theta_1 = 1$ describes a Courtnot reaction, and $\theta_0 = \theta_1 = 0$ describes a situation in which price is expected to remain constant when x_i changes. Thus the larger are θ_0 and θ_1, the less accommodating are rivals and so the larger is the price decline consequent on increasing x_i. Second, the choice of x_{it} in t may involve firm i in substantial short-run adjustment costs if $x_{it} \neq x_{it-1}$.[3] These adjustment costs $A_{it} = A(x_{it}, x_{it-1})$ are assumed (for simplicity) to be proportional to the increase in market share implied by the choice of x_{it} given x_{it-1}. That is, if $S_{it} \equiv x_{it}/x_t$, then marginal adjustment costs are assumed to be $\partial A_{it} / \partial x_{it} \equiv \partial_t (S_{it} - S_{it-1})$. Finally, we assume that $\partial_t / p_t \equiv \delta$, which is constant over time.

Given these assumptions, choices in t by firm i have future effects, and a sophisticated decision-maker will maximize the expected present discounted value of profits.

$$V_t = E_t \left(\sum_{\tau=0}^{\infty} \rho^{\tau} \{x_{t+\tau}[p(x_{t+\tau}) - c]\} - A_{t+\tau} \right) \tag{4.3}$$

where ρ is a discount factor, $E_t(\cdot)$ denotes the expectation at time t of the quantity in parentheses, and we have suppressed the subscript i to simplify notation. The sequence of x_{it} which maximizes (4.3) satisfies (see, for example, Sargent, 1979)

$$p_{t+\tau} - c + x_{it+\tau}p'(x_{t+\tau})\theta_0 - \delta_t(S_{it} - S_{it-1})$$

$$+ \rho E_t[x_{it+\tau+1}p'(x_{t+\tau+1})\theta_1 - \delta_{t+1}(S_{it+1} - S_{it})] = 0 \qquad (4.4)$$

Some fairly standard manipulation converts (4.4) into

$$m_{t+\tau} + S_{t+\tau}\left(\frac{\theta_0}{\eta}\right) - \delta(S_{t+\tau} - S_{t+\tau-1})$$

$$+ S^e_{t+\tau+1}\left(\frac{\lambda\theta_1}{\eta}\right) - \lambda\delta(S^e_{t+\tau+1} - S_{t+\tau}) = 0 \qquad (4.5)$$

where $E_t(S_{t+1}) \equiv S^e_{t+1}$, $\lambda \equiv \rho p_t/p_{t-1}$ and is assumed constant, and η is the elasticity of demand ($\eta < 0$). Collecting terms and suppressing τ, we obtain

$$\gamma_0 m_t + \gamma_1 S^e_{t+1} + \gamma_2 S_t + S_{t-1} = 0 \qquad (4.6)$$

where $m_t \equiv (p_t - c)/p_t$, i's price–cost margin, and $\gamma_0 = \delta^{-1}$, $\gamma_1 = [(\lambda\theta_1/\eta) - \rho\delta]\gamma_0$, and $\gamma_2 = [(\theta_0/\eta) - \delta + \lambda\delta]\gamma_0$. Under reasonable restrictions on the parameters, the solution to (4.6) is

$$S_t = \eta_1 S_{t-1} + \eta_1\gamma_0 \sum_{\tau=0}^{\infty} \left(\frac{1}{\eta_2}\right)^\tau m^e_{t+\tau} \qquad (4.7)$$

where η_1 and η_2 are such that $0 < \eta_1 < 1/\gamma_1 < \eta_2$. They are the roots of (4.6) and so are implicitly defined by the two equations $\eta_1 + \eta_2 = -\gamma_2/\gamma_1$ and $\eta_1\eta_2 = 1/\gamma_1$. It can be shown that increases in θ_0, θ_1, and δ all raise η_1 and lower η_2. Finally, defining

$$S^*_t \equiv \frac{\gamma_0\eta_1}{1 - \eta_1} \sum_{\tau=0}^{\infty} \left(\frac{1}{\eta_2}\right)^\tau m^e_{t+\tau} \qquad (4.8)$$

we can write (4.7) as

$$\Delta S_t = (1 - \eta_1)(S^*_t - S_{t-1}) \qquad (4.9)$$

Whether written as (4.6), (4.7), or (4.9), the model has a very natural and reasonable interpretation. Two observations may help to bring this out. First, if $\theta_1 = \delta = 0$, then the current choice of x_{it} has no effect on π_{it+1} and (4.5) simplifies to

$$m_t = \frac{-\theta_0}{\eta} S_t \qquad (4.10)$$

which is the standard Cowling–Waterson (1976) model of market structure and price–cost margins. Equation (4.5) then says that a firm choosing S_t, given $S_t > S_{t-1}$ and expecting that $S_{t+1} > S_t$, will earn less than $-\theta_0 S_t / \eta$; i.e. an expansion programme generates short-run costs of adjustment. Second, equation (4.9) is a natural way of relating the model to the standard dynamic models used in applied work. If $S_t^* = S^*$, then (4.9) describes a partial adjustment to a fixed target. In practice, we imagine that the target S^* will not be constant over time, and (4.8) makes plain not only that it does depend on the entire future stream of profits, but that it is also a target which depends on the expectations of these profits that are held at t. It is, therefore, likely to be a moving target, being updated continuously with the arrival of new information. The speed of adjustment is determined by η_1, which, in turn, depends on θ_0, θ_1, and δ. Adjustment is slower the larger are adjustment costs and the more severe are the adverse price consequences of rivals' reactions. In fact, these two sources of cost of adjustment are impossible to distinguish from each other in an equation like (4.4).

For an entrant in its year of entry, $S_{t-1} = 0$ and (4.9) simplifies to

$$E_t = (1 - \eta_1) S_t^* \qquad (4.11)$$

where E_t is its initial market penetration. Equation (4.11) says that entry will occur if the appropriately discounted present value of the stream of expected post-entry margins is positive, and that entrants will respond more quickly to a given S_t^* the more benign is the response of incumbents and the smaller are adjustment costs. However, (4.11) is incomplete as a model of entry, and, in particular, two problems exist with it as it stands. First, entrants may have to pay a fixed entry cost F to enter, and second, the level of costs c_i that entrant i incurs in producing output x_i is, in general, not observable. What is observable is the price–average cost margin of incumbents. Entry costs imply that marginal costs do not equal average costs, and absolute cost disadvantages imply that incumbents and entrants operate along different marginal cost schedules. With fixed costs, what are germane are price–average cost margins. Thus, if $(p - a_1)/p$ is the (observable) price–average cost margin of incumbents, then that of entrants is

$$\frac{p - a_1}{p} + \frac{a_1 - a_E}{p} \qquad (4.12)$$

where the difference in average unit costs between entrant and incumbent depends on both F and the difference in marginal costs between them. Writing $\pi \equiv (p - a_1)/p$, $b \equiv (a_E - a_1)/p$, and $\gamma \equiv (1 - \eta_1)$, and letting π^e denote the appropriately discounted expected present value of π, we can write (4.10) entirely in terms of "observables" as

$$E_{it} = \gamma(\pi_{it}^e - b_i) \tag{4.13}$$

for each entrant firm i in industry j. If γ is the same for all firms i in each j, then (4.13) can be averaged across entrants in j to yield a similar relation at industry level, namely that depicted in equation (4.1).

Equation (4.1) is our basic empirical model of entry. The model (4.2)–(4.12) provides a natural and intuitively appealing interpretation of γ, π^e, and b. The speed of response γ of entrants to excess profits depends upon the elasticity of demand, costs of adjustment, and the response of incumbents to entry. If there are no costs of adjustment and no future reactions by incumbents to current entry, then (4.10) reveals that entrants react to current profits and that their speed of reaction is equal to $|\eta/\theta_0|$, being higher the more elastic is demand and the smaller is the effect on total industry output (and thus on price) that entrants expect to induce. When there are future responses to entry and/or when costs of adjustment are high, then sophisticated entrants will respond to more than just current profits. In particular, they will consider the appropriately discounted stream of all future profits, trading off lower current returns caused by adjustment costs or aggressive responses by rivals for the (hopefully) higher returns that can be expected after transitory difficulties have been ironed out. In the long run, however, entry barriers may leave entrants permanently disadvantaged, facing higher unit costs than those faced by incumbents. These factors, collectively described by the parameter b, lower the expected present value of all current and future market operations and can be concisely described as the mark-up per unit of costs sustainable by incumbents forever in the face of entry.

3 Specifying an Empirical Entry Equation

To apply the empirical model (4.1) to data on entry requires two types of aggregation. First, (4.1) applies at industrty level (which is how our data are recorded), while the outcome of (4.2)–(4.12), namely (4.13), has been derived as a consequence of the decision of some firm i. As noted, provided that γ is broadly similar for all entrants – or, more precisely, for those relatively few entrants whose turnover dominates the total – then this type of aggregation does not create much of a problem, and both π_{jt}^e and b_j can be thought of as the average values of the corresponding magnitudes across all entrants i in each industry j.

Somewhat more serious is the temporal aggregation involved in using annual data. It seems hard to believe that most entrants have a horizon that lasts much beyond a year or two, and since possibly as many as 25 percent of those who enter in any given year do not even last a full year in the market, it may be that cash flows over a 6–8 month period are the most important concern of many entrants. Hence, it seems hardly worth considering a stream of future returns that extends much beyond t for entrants making their decisions in period $t - 1$. Thus, by expected future returns, we shall generally mean returns in the year of entry and possibly the subsequent year.

To turn (4.1) into a regression equation which can be used to measure γ and the height of entry barriers, we need to express it in terms of observables. The problem is that neither π_{jt}^e nor b_j are directly observable, the one being an expectational variable and the other pertaining to unobserved long-run outcomes. The usual procedure (see, for example, Orr, 1974a) has been to assume that entrants use lagged actual profits π_{jt-1} to proxy expected post-entry profits and to model "limit profits" b_j as being determined by a series of observable features of current market structure:

$$b_j = \beta_0 + \beta_1 X_j \tag{4.14}$$

where, for ease of exposition, we have assumed that only one observable measure of entry barriers X_j is used. These two assumptions transform (4.1) into the regression model

$$E_{jt} = \alpha_0 + \alpha_1 \pi_{jt-1} + \alpha_2 X_j + \mu_{jt} \tag{4.15}$$

where $\alpha_0 = \gamma\beta_0$, $\alpha_1 = \gamma$, and $\alpha_2 = \gamma\beta_1$. As all the parameters of interest in (4.1) and (4.14) are identified from (4.15), it follows that the level of profits in industry j that is sustainable against entry in the long run can be computed from the output of (4.15). Neglecting purely random transitory factors, $E_{jt} = 0$ in the long run, and using this condition to solve (4.15) for the level of limit profits π_j^* yields

$$\pi_j^* = \frac{\alpha_0 + \alpha_1 X_j}{\alpha_1} \tag{4.16}$$

If entrants expect no higher profits than π_j^*, then they will not be able to cover their entry costs and so will not enjoy a positive net return post-entry. Clearly, entry will not occur in this case, and incumbents will continue to enjoy π_j^* in the long run.

Numerous regressions with the basic structure of (4.15) based on a number of different samples drawn from different time periods and countries have been reported in the literature.[4] In general, the results suggest that π_j^* is significantly different from zero, implying the existence of barriers to entry in the wide majority of industries. Most scholars have been more concerned to explore the determinants of π_j^* than to calculate its height, and much energy has been invested in examining the data for evidence of significant barriers associated with product differentiation advantages, absolute cost advantages, and economies of scale. There seems to be quite a wide measure of agreement that advertising, capital requirements for entry, industry growth, R&D expenditure, and industry size all significantly affect entry rates in the expected manner. Further, advertising is undoubtedly one of the major factors associated with higher values of π_j^*, a result mirrored in the extensive literature examining the determinants of industry profitability (see Schmalensee (1987) for a recent survey). The effects of concentration on profits in the long run have also been the focus of some attention, since one of the hallmarks of contestability theory is that only entry barriers, and not market concentration, are likely to matter in determining market outcomes. The results reported on concentration have been fairly mixed, however, and no clear pattern is evident.

Although these results generally conform to our expectations, there are at least three conceptual problems with (4.15) that make us hesitant to accept them without reservation. First, the use of observed profits prior to entry, π_{jt-1}, to predict expected post-entry profits, π_{jt}^e, presumes that entrants have naive expectations. In assuming that outcomes will be the same post-entry as they were pre-entry, naive entrants neglect the effect that their entry will have on profits. Furthermore, in so doing they also open up the possibility that incumbents will be able to discourage them from entering by manipulating pre-entry profits strategically, say through limit pricing. It is hard to accept the proposition that entrants will necessarily be so naive, and it is far more reasonable to assume that they base their decisions to enter on expected post-entry profits rather than on observed pre-entry profits. Since the expectations that any but the most naive entrants are likely to hold are unlikely to be based directly on pre-entry observables, then we must mimic the kind of expectations formation process that entrants might use if we are to proxy π_{jt}^e properly.

The second problem with (4.15) was briefly noted above, and this is that it is often difficult to obtain good cross-section estimates of particular types of barriers to entry. For example, it is rather difficult to construct a variable which reflects the strategic control that incumbents may have over a scarce natural resource, or to measure nontariff barriers to trade. Further, the use of variables like advertising to measure product differentiation barriers is rather controversial and unsatisfactory. These observations suggest that it might be prudent to regard X_j as being measured with error and, more fundamentally, we might suspect that certain types of barrier are likely to be omitted from most regressions based on (4.15). If several important but unobserved barriers are omitted from (4.15), then inefficient estimates are likely to result. More worrying, if these omitted barriers are correlated with variables included in (4.15), then biased estimates are likely to result.

Third, and finally, (4.15) assumes that entrants respond at the same speed to profit opportunities in all industries; that is, that γ is a constant across all industries j. This type of assumption is usually made purely for convenience of estimation. It implicitly presumes that the pool of able entrants is similar industry by industry, that the time taken by entrants to mount a challenge is more or less independent of industry characteristics, and that the strategic response of incumbents to entry attempts also does not depend on industry characteristics. Neglecting this variation in γ across industries j may not be terribly serious *under* the factors which govern the size of γ industry by industry are correlated with the determinants of b_j or with π_{jt-1}, in which case neglecting to account for variations in γ will also lead to bias.

The basic model that we have constructed is shaped by the decisions that we have made with respect to each of these points. In most cases our decisions have led us on paths which differ somewhat from those typically followed in the literature, and, for this reason, it is worth dwelling on them.

π_{jt}^e is the level of profits expected by the entrant post-entry. As such, it is not observable prior to entry when the entrant makes its decision. However, an entrant who forms rational expectations will, make use of all the information available to it at the time that it does make its decision. This information comes in two forms: observed data reflecting past market outcomes, and a prior knowledge of how the market process operates. The two types of information complement each other because knowledge of market operations enables the entrant to establish a causal linking between the different observables in its information set. The most straightforward way to combine the two types of information is in a simple econometric model which enables the entrant to predict profits. Given observed data on profits π_{jt-1} and other variables Z_j, then we can model the interaction between entry and profitability by expressing each as a distributed lag function of the other plus exogenous variables. Solving the model by eliminating the entry variables yields an auto-regression in profits (plus other things):

$$\pi_{jt} = \lambda(L)\pi_{jt-1} + \phi Z_{jt} + \epsilon_{jt} \tag{4.17}$$

where $\lambda(L)$ is a polynomial in the lag operator L. The assumption of rational expectations implies that expectations are unbiased and will differ from realized values only randomly. Thus, if entrants' expectations are rational, then we can use the predictions from (4.17) in place of the unobservable latent variable π_{jt}^e.[5] Doing this insures that the information available to the entrant in $t-1$ will be used to make predictions of π_{jt}, and this in turn implies that ϵ_{jt} will be a regression error with classical properties. Thus, to model the signal that attracts entry to a market, we shall assume that entrants make their decisions rationally, using the predicted value of π_{jt} to proxy the latent variable π_{jt}^e.[6]

The second problem arises in measuring entry barriers. The work reported in the literature makes use of a number of easy-to-gather observables, but, as mentioned above, it is not proof against the possibility that certain important barriers may be omitted or measured with systematic error. The data set that we shall be working with in this study is particularly limited in this respect, and does not even include variables which are generally easy to gather (e.g. advertising). The key to our solution of this problem is the observation that the height of barriers to entry ought to be fixed in the short to medium run in most industries. Thus, although they may take a value specific in each industry, the height of barriers can be regarded as a constant over a reasonable time period. As a practical matter, then, we can measure the height of barriers to entry using

$$b_j = \beta_j + \beta_1 X_j \tag{4.18}$$

where the "fixed effects" β_j for the sample of industries $j = 1, \ldots, M$ are objects of estimation along with β_1, and X_j is an observable determinant of barriers. Substituting (4.18) into (4.1) as before generates an equation like (4.15), except now the constant α_0 takes a different value for each industry. The amended model becomes an equation with fixed effects, and, while not estimable using a single cross section, it can be estimated using panel data. The resulting $2M$ observations are sufficient to estimate the M values of α_0 plus the other unknown parameters in (4.15).

The third conceptual problem that needs to be addressed is the assumption that γ, the speed of response by entrants to market opportunities, is the same in all industries. This type of assumption implies that there are no differences across industries in the ability of entrants to

mount a challenge, and that the resistance put up by incumbents is
similar everywhere. Although we might genuinely wish to model the
determinants of variations in the response rates of entrants, our data are
too limited to do this job properly. Rather, what we wish to do is to allow
for the possibility that γ differs across industries. If we do not observe
it varying in response to a range of observable factors, then the assumption that γ is constant may not be too unreasonable. While it is difficult
to test this maintained hypothesis at all satisfactorily with limited data,
it is at least worth a try. To this end, we have collected a set of
observables W_i and have assumed that

$$\gamma_i = \gamma_0 + \gamma_0 W_i \qquad (4.19)$$

A test of the hypothesis that $\gamma_1 = 0$ is the appropriate test of the
maintained assumption that γ is constant across all j.

To sum up these various decisions, we propose estimating (4.15) using
a rational expectations estimator for π_{jt}^e. As the model includes fixed
effects to capture unobserved entry barriers, we shall work with two
combined cross sections of data for 1983 and 1984. The observable
variables that we shall use are fairly standard and do not require much
elaboration. They are industry size and industry growth. All the observables are assumed to be exogenous, and to insure that this assumption is,
in fact, consistent with the data, we shall use lagged values of all the
exogenous variables (e.g. 1983 industry size and growth in the 1984 entry
equation). Various minor data problems reduced the original cross
section of 104 industries to 95, giving a total of 190 observations over the
2 years included in our panel. After first estimating a linear version of
the model in which γ is constrained not to vary across industries, we shall
re-estimate it allowing γ to vary with industry concentration, size, and
growth. Tests will then be conducted to see whether this more general
version of the model can be simplified to a version in which γ does not
vary. Finally, the entry equation will be estimated separately for
domestic entrants (measuring entry as market penetration, net and
gross) and foreign entrants (measuring foreign entry by changes in
import penetration). These decisions leave us with a pair of entry
equations describing domestic and foreign entry E_{jt}^d and E_{jt}^f as linear
functions of expected post-entry profits π_{jt}^e industry size $SIZE_{jt}$, industry growth $GROW_{jt}$, and a set of industry-specific fixed effects f_j,
specific to each type of entrant:

$$E_{jt}^d = \gamma^d \pi_{jt}^e + \alpha_0^d SIZE_{jt-1} + \alpha_1^d GROW_{jt-1} + f_j^d + \mu_{jt}^d$$
$$E_{jt}^f = \gamma^f \pi_{jt}^e + \alpha_0^f SIZE_{jt-1} + \alpha_1^f GROW_{jt-1} + f_j^f + \mu_{jt}^f \qquad (4.20)$$

where μ_{jt}^d and μ_{jt}^f are assumed to be normally distributed white noise residuals.

4 Entry and Exit Flows in the United Kingdom: 1983–1984

To talk at all about "entry" requires careful definition of terms. Several types of decision must be made. First, is "entry" the entry of only newly formed firms, and is it to be measured as the sales realized only in their first year of arrival? The practical alternative to concentrating on new firm formation is to allow entry through merger by firms operating elsewhere, thus adding "new owners and management" to the conventional criteria of entry as "new plant by a new firm." Further, it is clear that entry by foreign firms through imports is entry, even if its impact as a competitive force may differ from that of domestic entry. Similarly, given the extremely high failure rate of new firms and the extremely slow penetration rates of new firms in markets, it is not obvious that the principal effects that one associates with "entry" necessarily occur in the main (or, indeed, at all) in the initial year of establishment. Finally, by "entry" do we mean the number of new firms or their market penetration, and, in measuring it, do we net out the displacement of firms caused by entry? That is, do we consider that it is the net or the gross entry rate which is the primary competitive force working to bid down profitability, and is the competitive force of this flow better measured by the numbers involved or by their collective market penetration?

There are, of course, no hard and fast answers to any of these questions, and in what follows we shall focus on entry measured as the net market share penetration of new domestic firms in their year of entry.[7] The focus on new firms in their year of entry is largely determined by the data at hand, and the concern with market share penetration arises from the suspicion that most recorded entry flows are merely the arrival of extremely small firms who seek to occupy (but not really expand in) particular specialized market niches. Only if the total sum of this type of activity is particularly large will leading firms be threatened, and market shares are a natural way to measure the size of this competitive challenge. Finally, the focus on net market shares arises from the empirical observation that entry and exit rates are extremely highly positively correlated, suggesting that much entry is merely displacement of one set of small firms by another.

Table 4.1 provides some descriptive statistics on this data. In terms of

Table 4.1 Entry and exit flows

	1983	1984
Number of entrants	210.5	216.9
Number of exiters	138.3	157.1
Market share of entrants	0.0683	0.0802
Market share of exiters	0.0629	0.0391
Market share of foreign entrants	0.0158	0.0143
Entry rate	0.214	0.151
Exit rate	0.129	0.111

Average figures across 95 MLH industries in the United Kingdom.

sheer numbers, the flow of entry into UK industries is quite impressive. The average number of new firms per industry recorded during the period 1983–4 was a little more than 200 per year (the maximum was roughly ten times that figure), and between one in five and one in seven firms observed in each industry in each year was newly created. These figures undoubtedly overstate the importance of entry for at least two reasons. First, entry almost certainly induces exit, and, even if it does not, the impact of a gross flow of entrants of any given size on market performance is much reduced when exit is high. Table 4.1 shows that, on average, between 140 and 160 firms exited from each industry per year (the maximum being more than ten times this figure in 1983, and more than 15 times in 1984), leaving a net flow of about 50 new firms per year. The rate of exit was about one firm in eight or nine, leaving a net entry rate (the net number of new firms as a percentage of the total population) of 8.5 percent in 1983 and 4 percent in 1984. Thus, of those firms newly observed in any given industry in any given year, between 1 in 12 and 1 in 25 represent a net addition to industry numbers.

The second reason why the gross number of new entrants exaggerates the importance of actual entry is that most entrants are, in fact, extremely small. The gross collective market share of new entrants was about 7 percent in both years, implying that the average entrant was between a third and half the size of the average incumbent. Further, while net entry rates averaged between 25 and 40 per cent of the size of gross entry rates, the net market penetration of domestic entrants averaged between 8 and 50 percent of gross market penetration (net penetration was negligible on average in 1983, and reached an average level of 4 percent in 1984). Although both entrants and exiters were of broadly similar size over the period 1983–4, exiting firms were larger on average relative to survivors in 1983 than in 1984, while entrants were larger on average relative to incumbents in 1984 than in 1983. Of course, total net entry includes entry by foreign firms, and the most interesting difference between domestic and foreign-based entrants is that foreign entry flows are more stable than domestic entry over time. Total (domestic and foreign) net entry market penetration was about 2 percent in 1983 and about 5.6 percent in 1984, figures far less impressive that the total number of new firms per industry or the gross entry rate per industry.

Table 4.1 suggests that there is some stability in the number of new firms which enter markets over time. Table 4.2, panel (a), confirms this impression, showing that, in addition, the gross market penetration of entrants was fairly stable across industries between 1983 and 1984. Exit and net penetration rates were far more variable over time. This observation suggests that correlations between different measures of entry will not be high or very stable over time, an impression confirmed in table 4.2, panels (b) and (c). Entry and exit rates across industries were highly positively correlated with each other in both 1983 and 1984, but virtually all measures of entry involving penetration were

Table 4.2 Correlations

(a) 1983, 1984

Entry rate	0.657
Exit rate	0.476
Share of entrants	0.510
Share of exiters	0.097
Share of foreign entry	0.194
Net entry share	0.159

(b) 1983

Entry	1	–	–	–	–
Exit rate	0.796	1	–	–	–
Share of entrants	0.293	0.353	1	–	–
Share of exiters	0.431	0.601	0.393	1	–
Share of foreign entry	− 0.082	− 0.174	− 0.015	− 0.094	− 1
Net entry share	0.165	0.169	0.945	0.041	0.017

(c) 1984

Entry	1	–	–	–	–
Exit rate	0.674	1	–	–	–
Share of entrants	0.151	0.096	1	–	–
Share of exiters	0.332	0.184	0.107	1	–
Share of foreign entry	− 0.075	− 0.107	− 0.158	− 0.1166	− 1
Net entry share	− 0.236	− 0.1245	0.382	− 0.877	0.031

Across 95 MLH industries in the United Kingdom.

weakly correlated. Correlations between gross entry penetration and exit weakened considerably between 1983 and 1984, as did correlations between gross and net penetration. That entry and exit were positively correlated implies that entry may often involve some displacement, but it seems clear that the extent of this displacement varies over time – being, for example, much less in 1984 than in 1983. Finally, it is worth noting that gross and net domestic entry penetration rates were largely uncorrelated with foreign net entry penetration. On the face of it, this observation suggests that the two types of flows may be complements rather than substitutes; that the response of domestic and foreign entrants to excess profits differs, and/or that the height of the barriers to entry that they face may differ across industries.[8] We shall return to this conjecture in section 5.

The vast majority of the entrants observed in our sample fell in the turnover size band £18,001–£2,000,000: 13 percent of entrants in 1983 and 17 percent of entrants in 1984 were either smaller in size than £18,000 or larger than £2,000,000. Disclosure rules made it impossible to be more precise than this for the whole sample, but it is possible to hazard some speculative inferences based on 17 unidentified industries in either 1983 or 1984 which were used for checking. These 17 industries generated 1,597 entrants in total, of which 236 (or about 15 percent) were of size less than £18,000, 1,245 (or about 78 percent) were of size £18,001–£500,000, 83 (or about 5 percent) were of size £500,001–£2,000,000, and finally 33 (or about 2 percent) were larger than £2,000,000. Thus it seems reasonable to suppose that most of the entrants who were outside the £18,000–£2,000,000 size band were, by and large, smaller than £18,000 (there were, no doubt, many more firms in this extremely small size class not recorded in the value-added tax (VAT) data). Given this, what is interesting about the data is that firms outside the £18,000–£2,000,000 size band accounted for about 88 percent of total gross sales by entrants in 1983 and just under 65 percent in 1984. Thus the collective market share penetration recorded by the 200 or so entrants who appear on average in each industry in each year may actually be largely the work of a handful of very large firms. Not surprisingly, entry penetration by firms outside the £18,000–£2,000,000 size band and total entry penetration was very highly correlated across industries (the correlation coefficient was above 0.96 in both years). Surprisingly, the percentage of exiters from outside the £18,000–£2,000,000 size band was a much higher percentage of the total number of exiters (40 percent in 1983 and 35 percent in 1984) than was the corresponding percentage of entrants. It is impossible to tell what percentage of these were larger than £2,000,000 and what percentage smaller than £18,000, but exits from this group do account for most of the shares of the market held by exiters in their year of exit.

The very high positive correlations between entry and exit and the relatively small size of net relative to gross entry suggests that most entry involves displacement. As table 4.1 indicates, only about 3 in 10 entrants represent a net addition to the stock of firms in each industry. We have no direct information on the life span of the 1983 and 1984 entry cohorts in our data, but information does exist for VAT firms in manufacturing as a whole for the period 1974–82.[9] Roughly 12.4 percent of entrants survived no longer than 6 months, 27.3 percent no longer than a year, 55 percent no longer than 2 years, and roughly 85 percent no longer than 4 years. Only 0.1 percent of the cohort of 1974 entrants were still operating in 1982. It would seem to follow from this that most of the entrants who appear in some year t are unlikely to survive more than 5 years, and that 7 out of 10 of them will probably be displacing entrants who had appeared in the 5 years preceding t. In terms of sheer numbers, it appears to be the case that 15–20 percent of the firms present in each industry in any year are part of a process of scrambling for position at the bottom of the industry size distribution which results in a considerable turnover of firms but only a small accretion in market share. The pool of firms involved in this turnover over a 5–10 year period is very large relative to the number of firms active in each year, enormous relative to the net number of new firms present in any year, and simply of an entirely different order of magnitude relative to those who survive throughout that 5–10 year period.

5 Some Empirical Results on Barriers to Entry

The raw data suggest that observed entry flows result from the actions taken by a very large number of very small firms, although, to be sure, gross market penetration figures may be dominated by the activities of one or two large entrants. Further, there appears to be an enormous amount of turnover in firms, with high entry rates correlated with (and almost certainly causing) high exit rates. The lack of permanence in the lives of most entrants, together with the fairly small scale of most entry attempts, seems, somehow, slightly alien to the spirit of the model developed in section 2. In particular, although high exit is quite consistent with the notion that barriers b_j are important, high entry rates can only be consistent with this if potential competitors systematically overvalue their chances in the market. While it is possible that the extent of this kind of miscalculation is related to the level of π_{jt}^e, it may also be unsystematic or just simply more focused on short-run factors than the construction of π_{jt}^e suggests ought to be appropriate. It follows, then, that we expect to observe the effects of an error of measurement in π_{jt}^e on the estimates of γ and b_j. While this type of error will almost certainly inflate the noise apparently observed in the data (and attributed to exogenous factors orthogonal to π_{jt}^e and b_j), it may, if correlated with π_{jt}^e, also lead to downward bias in the estimates of γ. Still, on the principle that a poor proxy is better than no proxy (e.g. McCallum, 1972; Wickens, 1972), we shall proceed using the model as finally formulated in (4.20).

The first step in estimating (4.20) involves generating the proxies for expected profits π_{jt}^e. Let us take this as given for the moment (we return to it below), and assume that π_{jt}^e is observable. To estimate the fixed effects in each equation requires using both the 1983 and 1984 cross sections pooled together, and the results of doing this are shown in table 4.3.

Inspection of the two equations in table 4.3 prompts several observations. First, domestic entry appears to respond much more rapidly than foreign entry to excess profits. The estimated value of γ^d is about four times the size of γ^f and, in fact, the latter is barely significantly different from zero. This implies that adjustment costs are far higher for foreign than for domestic firms, that the latter expect a milder response from incumbents than foreign entrants do, or that the demand for the products of domestic entrants is more elastic than that for foreign

Table 4.3 Regressions explaining entry

	Domestic entry E_{jt}^d	Foreign entry E_{jt}^f
π_{jt}^e	1.684	0.4479
	(2.192)	(1.06)
$SIZE_{jt-1}$	0.0741	0.0029
	(0.494)	(0.0542)
$GROW_{jt-1}$	−0.2599	−0.0505
	(1.83)	(1.21)
Log likelihood	178.492	460.955
$R^2/\bar{R}^2$	0.589/0.146	0.618/0.207
$F(97, 90)$	1.329	1.504

Both equations include a full set of industry fixed effects; absolute values of t statistics are given in parentheses below the estimated coefficients. π_{jt}^e is expected profits, measured as the predicted value of π_{jt} from equation (4.21), $SIZE_{jt-1}$ is the lagged log of total domestic production, $GROW_{jt-1}$ as the lagged rate of growth of domestic production, E_{jt}^d is the net market penetration of new entrants, and E_{jt}^f is the net change in import penetration.

entrants. The estimates in table 4.3 indicate that a rise of 10 percentage points in expected industry profits will increase entry penetration by about 2 percent, nearly 80 percent of which will be attributable to the activities of domestic entrants and will be more predictable than the 20 percent of total entry penetration attributable to foreign firms. One way or the other, it follows that domestic and foreign entry appear to be quite distinct types of competitive force. This impression is reinforced by considering a second interesting feature of the results shown in table 4.3. The R^2 for both equations are rather high, but, as the $\bar{R}^2$ show, that degree of explanation is bought at the cost of introducing numerous industry-specific parameters. The F statistics for the two equations are both low, and that in the domestic entry equation is barely significant at 5 percent levels. The upshot seems to be that both domestic and foreign entry flows are extremely noisy. They exhibit a systematic tendency to vary with excess profits, but the predictable component of this variation is difficult to discern in the raw data. Of the observables used to chart this variation, expected profits play a noticeable role, but variations in industry size and growth rates appear to have little effect on the height of barriers or, ultimately, on entry flows.

Three further points emerge from various respecifications of the model. First, net entry depends on both entry and exit, and it is possible that the determinants of entry will emerge more clearly if we consider gross entry flows. Replicating the domestic entry equation shown in table 4.3 but using gross entry penetration (not shown) produced the interesting result that the effect of expected profits on gross entry was much stronger and far more clearly observed than that on net entry, largely because exit and expected profits are relatively uncorrelated. Once again, the fixed effects proved to be collectively significant, but the industry size variable displayed a significant coefficient. Gross entry appears to be significantly higher in larger industries. This is likely to arise from one of two factors: large markets probably contain more specialized niches for small entrants to fit into, and in large markets it is easier for firms to reach minimum efficient scale without provoking responses from incumbents. Surprisingly, both gross and net domestic entry were lower, *ceteris paribus*, in faster-growing industries. Second, it is also the case that gross and net domestic entry on the one hand, and foreign entry on the other, respond far more strongly to expected future profits than to lagged profits. Introducing π_{jt-1} instead of π_{jt}^e into the equation shown in table 4.3 produced much smaller estimates of γ^f and γ^d, which were generally not significantly different from zero.[10] Third, the results in table 4.3 all pertain to estimated models in which γ was assumed to be constant. Equations were also estimated which allowed

γ to vary systematically with lagged industry concentration, industry growth, and industry size, but in all cases the null hypothesis that γ was constant could not be rejected. For what it is worth, the very weak systematic variation in γ that was observed suggested that γ might be slightly lower in more highly concentrated industries than in less concentrated ones. No obvious patterns with respect to industry growth or size were evident.

The next step is to use (4.16) and the estimated parameters of the model to solve for the level of profits sustainable in the long run against foreign and domestic entry. The estimates do not appear to vary much over the period 1983–4, and variations in industry size and growth rates appear to have little effect on them. Tests indicated that all the fixed effects could not be reduced to one sample-wide constant, suggesting that there were significant variations in the height of barriers across different industries. On average, the height of barriers facing domestic firms was 20.2 percent while that for foreign firms was 18.2 percent, a difference which is probably not significant given the uncertainty about precise parameter values shown on table 4.3. With two exceptions, all the estimates of the height of barriers facing domestic firms fell in the interval [0.0767, 0.4100], and were approximately normally distributed (the median height of the barriers was about 0.188). The height of barriers facing foreign firms fell in the interval [0, 0.500] and, again, was approximately normally distributed across industries (the median was 0.172). By any standards,[11] these are large numbers, indicating that incumbents can maintain prices about 15–20 percent above costs without attracting (net) entry. Table 4.4 shows the top ten industries ranked as having the highest barriers to domestic and foreign entry.

Finally, the estimates of the reduced-form estimates of (4.17) that were used to generate the proxy values of π_{jt}^e are

$$\pi_t = -0.422\pi_{t-1} - 0.261\pi_{t-2} - 0.0042\pi_{t-3} - 0.0712\text{SIZE}_{t-1}$$
$$\quad (4.132) \qquad (3.52) \qquad (0.056) \qquad (2.54)$$
$$\quad + 0.0643\text{GROW}_{t-1} - 0.042\text{EXP}_{t-1}$$
$$\quad (2.80) \qquad\qquad\qquad (0.472) \qquad\qquad\qquad\qquad (4.21)$$

where EXP is the export intensity, absolute values of t statistics are shown in parentheses under the estimated coefficients, $R^2/\bar{R}^2 = 0.968/0.931$, $F(100, 87) = 26.3373$, and the estimated equation contained a full set of industry-specific effects and a time dummy (suppressed here).[12] The estimated fixed effects in (4.21) are statistically very significant and cannot be simplified to a single constant. The implication is that industries have quite different long-run profit levels

Table 4.4 The height of barriers by industry

SIC		Name	Domestic entrant barriers	Foreign entrant barriers
Highest barriers to domestic entrants				
1	242	Cement, lime, and plaster	0.73	0.36
2	231	Stone, clay, and gravel	0.51	0.50
3	423	Starch	0.42	0.21
4	424	Spirit distilling	0.38	0.29
5	324	Machinery for food, etc.	0.36	0.39
6	241	Structural clay products	0.34	0.32
7	257	Pharmaceuticals	0.33	0.33
8	475	Printing and publishing	0.30	0.29
9	330	Office machinery	0.28	0.23
10	426	Wines, cider, etc.	0.25	0.25
Highest barriers to foreign-based entrants				
1	231	Stone, clay, and gravel	0.51	0.50
2	324	Machinery for food, etc.	0.36	0.39
3	495	Miscellaneous manufacturing	0.14	0.38
4	242	Cement, lime, and plaster	0.73	0.36
5	257	Pharmaceuticals	0.33	0.33
6	241	Structural clay products	0.34	0.32
7	245	Working of stone etc.	0.22	0.31
8	323	Textile machinery	0.19	0.31
9	412	Processing of meat	0.16	0.30
10	475	Printing and publishing	0.30	0.29

SIC, Standard Industrial Classification.

toward which they tend, and the coefficients on the three observable lagged exogenous variables suggest that these long-run levels are slightly higher in smaller fast-growing markets. The degree of explanation recorded in (4.21) is astonishingly high by the standards of inter-industry profitability equations. This arises partly from the inclusion of fixed effects, but also from the inclusion of the three terms π_{t-1}, π_{t-2}, and π_{t-3}. It is conventional to argue that cross-section work essentially involves a comparison of long-run equilibrium positions, and the strong dynamics recorded in the data make it plain that this view is somewhat untenable. Observed current profits in most markets are, by and large, a noisy signal of long-run profits. This said, it should also be noted that statistically significant coefficients mean only that effects are measured with a certain precision, not that they are large. The fact is that the dynamics captured by (4.21) translate into only fairly modest systematic movements in margins about their long-run levels. That is, the "between" variation in the data dominates the "within" variation:

84   *P.A. Geroski*

differences in margins between industries at any given time are much larger than differences in margins within the typical industry over time (see also Geroski and Toker, 1988).

More specifically, to assess the information conveyed by the model (4.17) and the estimates of its parameters shown in (4.21) about the character of market dynamics, we neglect Z_t in (4.17) and take the intercept to be industry specific. The resulting equation then describes a movement in profits from some starting point λ_0, to a long-run level of $\lambda_0/(1 - \lambda_3 - \lambda_4 - \lambda_5)$, where λ_3 is the coefficient on π_{t-1}, λ_4 is that on π_{t-2}, and λ_5 is that on π_{t-3}. It is useful to think of λ_0 as a situation of initial monopoly, and to think of the reduced-form profits equation as describing the erosion of that position. Using the estimates given in (4.21), we find that the percentage reduction of initial profits λ_0, in the long run that is due to entry turns out to be about 41 percent. If, for example, $\lambda_0 = 0.50$ and the initial monopoly profits π_0 are 0.50, then a simulation of (4.21) shows that competition reduces this to $\pi_1 = 0.289$ in period $t = 1$, to $\pi_2 = 0.2475$ in $t = 2$, to $\pi_3 = 0.318$, and so on, eventually reaching a level of 0.2955 by period $t = 8$.[13] The process oscillates around the long-run equilibrium level of 0.295, and could reasonably be said to require 3–8 years for convergence. It would seem to follow from this that total entry, potential and actual, has a fairly modest effect on profits, but one that is recorded rapidly.[14]

6 Summary and Conclusions

Our goal in this paper has been to assess the speed with which domestic and foreign-based entrants respond to profitable market opportunities and to measure the height of the barriers to entry that they face. Briefly, we have discovered that barriers are fairly high in most industries in the United Kingdom, and that they are of a roughly similar magnitude for domestic and foreign-based entrants. Domestic entrants appear to respond to high expected profits much more rapidly than foreign entrants, although it must be said that there is a lot of apparent noise in the behavior of both types of entrant. Finally, it appears that the dynamics of margins are rather modest, and that variations (systematic or not) in margins around their long-run levels for any given "typical" industry are dwarfed by variations in margins across industries.

The implications of these results are twofold. First, neither type of entrant appears to provide much in the way of a substantive challenge to incumbents in most markets. The effects of entry in both the short and long run, it would seem, are far easier to overstate than to understate.

Second, the fact that the heights of entry barriers facing each of the two types of entrant are broadly similar across industries means that neither is a substitute for the other (judged as competitive forces). When entry by one type of entrant is blocked, it is quite likely to be blocked for the other type of entrant as well. Our conclusion, therefore, is that (at least in the United Kingdom) the mere possibility of import competition does not obviate the need to be concerned with domestic market structure.

Appendix

Price–cost margins were computed as net output less the wage bill less net capital expenditures, all expressed as a percentage of gross output; all the data originated from the census. Concentration ratios were taken from the census and were adjusted by redefining the denominator as domestic production less exports plus imports, the latter two series being taken from the Business Monitor MQ10. The entry data were derived from VAT returns. These data are not strictly comparable with the UK entry data discussed in chapter 14, but a comparison of the two for 1983 suggests that they painted roughly the same qualitative picture in terms of the ranking of industries by numbers of entrants and exits, the relative size of net and gross entry penetration, and so on. Entry penetration was defined as the sales of all entrants divided by industry sales adjusted for trade flows. Both growth and industry size were defined in terms of domestic production alone.

Notes

1   What follows draws on Geroski and Murfin (1987). An alternative model is that of Kessides (1986) (see also chapter 2 of this volume), which uses a zero profit condition to derive the entry equation used in his empirical work and differs from the foregoing largely in being somewhat more static. The two formulations do not, however, appear to conflict on any fundamental points.

2   When goods are homogeneous, there is no need for any firm to isolate the response of any particular one of its rivals, and this makes it possible to characterize all individual firm responses using a single aggregate conjectural variation. For surveys of work on estimating conjectural variations, see Bresnahan (1987) and Geroski (1988b).

3   One source of these costs are the managerial constraints to growth discussed in Penrose (1959), although these are less likely to be of concern to entrants than to established incumbents attempting rapid expansion into new markets. For entrants, "getting the bugs out" of new processes of production and distribution are likely to be the main source of problem. Biggadike (1976) found enormous costs of adjustment for a sample of 40 entrants in the

United States, with short-run penalties to over-rapid expansion of the order of 35 percentage points in terms of rate of return.

4 For a brief survey of the results, see Geroski and Masson (1987), Geroski et al. (1988), and chapter 14 which summarizes the evidence presented in this volume. Gorecki (1975, 1976) makes comparisons between different types of entrant using an equation like (4.15).

5 For a discussion of how a reduced-form model like (4.17) emerges from a three-equation structural model of entry, market structure, and profits, see, for example, Mueller (1986), Geroski and Jacquemin (1988), and the papers in Mueller (1988).

6 This is standard practice in the literature involved with estimating rational expectations models (see Wallis, 1980; and Wickens, 1982). On the statistical properties of such two stage estimators see Pagan (1984, 1986).

7 The choice of net entry is largely dictated by the consideration that at the equilibrium of equation (4.1), $\pi_{jt}^e = bj$, we can observe positive gross entry if it is matched by exit. When $\pi_{jt}^e = bj$, however, net entry (i.e. the net expansion of industry supply) must cease. Set against this is the consideration that the choice-theoretic model that culminates in equation (4.13) is probably best interpreted as describing gross entry penetration; the decisions of exiters are possibly not well described by (4.2)–(4.12) and, in any case, individual agents probably do not choose net penetration targets.

8 For a comparison with UK data on entry for the 1970s, see Geroski (1988a) who reports results which suggest that neither of the two types of entrant–domestic or foreign-based – "crowd out" the other from profitable markets.

9 See various issues of *British Business*, particularly that of August 12, 1983.

10 This result is interesting in light of the very small estimates of γ reported in the literature (e.g Orr, 1974). Geroski (1989), Geroski and Murfin (1987), and Highfield and Smiley (1987) all report similar experiments on measuring expected profits, with similar effects observed on estimates of γ. The moral would seem to be that simple proxies of post-entry profits contain a systematic measurement error which leads to a substantial downward bias in estimates of γ, making entry appear slower in responding to excess profits than it truly is.

11 Including those of Bain (1956, p. 170) who argued that barriers were "high" if prices could be sustained 10 percent or more above costs, "substantial" if they could be sustained 7–10 percent above costs, and "moderate to low" if they could be sustained only 4–7 percent above costs.

12 Geroski (1989) found fairly similar results using somewhat different data for the 1970s. Barriers averaged about 17–18 percent in his sample, and were broadly similar for foreign and domestic firms. Foreign-based entry was much less responsive to variations in π_{jt}^e than domestic entry, and γ did not vary systematically with market growth, concentration, or advertising. Gross entry was also observed to be more sensitive to π_{jt}^e than net entry, again because exit was only weakly related to π_{jt}^e.

13 The general character of (4.21) proved to be extremely robust to a wide

variety of alterations in the set of observable exogenous variables (including the introduction of terms in import intensity and industry concentration).

14 Although (4.21) suggests that π_t and π_{t-1} are negatively correlated, this is only true conditional on the industry-specific fixed effects. That is, the negative correlation is, effectively, between $\pi_t - \bar{\pi}$ and $\pi_{t-1} - \bar{\pi}$ where $\bar{\pi}$ is the (industry-specific) average profits over time. The fixed effects (which effectively extract $\bar{\pi}$ from the data) are very highly correlated with π_t and π_{t-1}, meaning that the unconditional correlation between π_t and π_{t-1} is positive (and above 0.9).

References

Bain. J. (1956) *Barriers to New Competition*. Cambridge MA: Harvard University Press.

Biggadike, E. (1976) *Entry, Strategy and Performance*. Cambridge, MA: Harvard University Press.

Bresnahan, T. (1987) Empirical studies of industries with market power. In R. Schmalensee and R. Willig (eds), *Handbook of Industrial Economics*, Amsterdam: North-Holland.

Cowling, K. and Waterson, M. (1976) Price–cost margins and market structure. *Economica* 43, 275–86.

Geroski, P. (1988a) The interaction between domestic and foreign based entrants. In D. Audretsch, L. Sleuwaegan, and H. Yamawaki (eds), *The Convergence of Domestic and International Markets* Amsterdam: North-Holland.

Geroski, P. (1988b) In pursuit of monopoly: Recent quantitative work in industrial economics. *Journal of Applied Econometrics* 3, 107–23.

Geroski, P. (1989) The effect of entry on profit margins in the short and long run. *Annales d'Economie et de Statistique* 15–16, 333–53.

Geroski, P. and Jacquemin, A. (1988) The persisteance of profits: a European comparison. *Economic Journal* 98, 375–89.

Geroski, P. and Masson, R. (1987) Dynamic market models in industrial organization. *International Journal of Industrial Organization* 5, 1–14.

Geroski, P. and Murfin, A. (1987) Entry and industry evolution: the UK car market, 1958–83. Mimeo, London Business School.

Geroski, P. and Toker, S. (1988) Picking profitable markets. Mimeo, London Business School.

Geroski, P., Gilbert, R. and Jacquemin, A. (1988) *Entry and Strategic Competition*. London: Harwood.

Gorecki, P. (1975) The determinants of entry by new and diversifying enterprises in the UK manufacturing Sector, 1958–63. *Applied Economics* 7, 139–47.

Gorecki, P. (1976) The determinants of entry by domestic and foreign enterprises in Canadian manufacturing industries. *Review of Economics and Statistics* 58, 495–8.

Highfield, R. and Smiley, R. (1987) New business starts and economic activity. *International Journal of Industrial Organization* 5, 51–66.

Kessides, I. (1986) Advertising, sunk costs and barriers to entry. *Review of Economics and Statistics* 68, 84–95.

McCallum, B. (1972) Relative asymptotic bias from errors of omission and measurement. *Econometrica* 40, 757–8.

Mueller, D. (1986) *Profits in the Long Run*. Cambridge: Cambridge University Press.

Mueller, D. (ed.) (1988) *The Dynamics of Company Profits: An International Comparison*. Cambridge: Cambridge University Press.

Orr, D. (1974a) The determinants of entry: A study of the Canadian manufacturing industries. *Review of Economics and Statistics* 61, 58–66.

Orr, D. (1974b) An index of entry barriers and its application to the market structure performance relation. *Journal of Industrial Economics* 23, 39–49.

Pagan, A. (1984) Econometric issues in the analysis of regressions with generated regressors. *International Economic Review* 25, 221–47.

Pagan, A. (1986) Two stage and related estimators and their applications. *Review of Economic Studies* 54, 517–38.

Penrose, E. (1959) *The Theory of the Growth of the Firm*. Oxford: Basil Blackwell.

Sargent, T. (1979) *Macroeconomic Theory*. London: Academic Press.

Schmalensee, R. (1987) Interindustry studies of structure and performance. In R. Schmalensee and R. Willig (eds), *Handbook of Industrial Economics* Amsterdam: North-Holland.

Wallis, K. (1980) Econometric implications of the rational expectations hypothesis. *Econometrica* 48, 49–74.

Wickens, M. (1972) A note on the use of proxy variables. *Econometrica* 40, 750–61.

Wickens, M. (1982) The efficient estimation of econometric models with rational expectations. *Review of Economic Studies* 49, 55–67.

5

Domestic Entry in Norwegian Manufacturing Industries

Nils-Henrik Mørch von der Fehr

1 Introduction

In this chapter we aim to establish to what extent industry characteristics can explain inter-industry differences in entry patterns in Norwegian manufacturing industries. As such, it is more in the style of Schmalensee (1989) in that the orientation is exploratory and descriptive, rather than a stringent test of structural relationships. The study is in the main tradition of the structure–conduct–performance literature and the estimated model is of the one-equation reduced-form type. A number of variables that have been suggested as entry determinants by other studies are introduced, allowing the importance of the different variables for explaining entry in Norwegian industries to be estimated. In the last part, a "rough and ready" statistic for ranking industries according to overall entry conditions is suggested.

From an allocational point of view, an important question is to what extent barriers to entry exist in a given market. As argued by Geroski (chapter 4 of this volume), entry can be regarded as "screening criteria," reflecting the "competitiveness" of markets. Thus, low entry rates in the presence of above-normal incumbency profits may indicate high barriers to entry. In this study we attempt to measure how entry is influenced by profit possibilities as well as barriers to entry, thereby providing evidence on the performance of industries. This way of estimating the height of barriers to entry, that is, by using estimated parameters of a model

I am grateful to John R. Cable, Finn R. Forsund, Paul Geroski, Stephen Martin, and Dennis C. Mueller for helpful suggestions and comments on earlier work on this project. Financial support from the Norwegian Council for Applied Research in the Social Sciences (NORAS) is gratefully acknowledged. This paper is a somewhat shortened version of a working paper with the same title (von der Fehr, 1990). Readers interested in further details on theoretical and statistical considerations, as well as the results of the estimations, should consult this.

of entry, is in the tradition of Orr (1974). Since no attempt is made here to model exit the traditional no net entry (long-run) equilibrium 'limit profits' type of measure cannot be computed. However, an alternative way of normalizing profits is proposed thereby making it possible to rank industries according to overall entry conditions. Since only domestic entry is considered, extra caution is needed since foreign competition (imports) may facilitate good home market performance even if domestic entry is low.

An important feature of this study is the distinction made between different categories of (domestic) entrants. First, a distinction is made between *de novo* plants and plants which have previously been operated in other industries. Furthermore, establishments of firms with other (incumbent) plants in the same industry, establishments of firms with other plants in other industries, and single-establishment firms are treated as separate categories. Thus, six different entry equations are estimated, one for each type of entrant.

The results suggest that industry characteristics can take us some way towards explaining entry patterns in Norwegian manufacturing industries. In general the estimated coefficients are consistent with theory, and for the two single establishment categories, a fair amount of the variation in data is explained. The fit for the multi-establishment categories is poorer, which is perhaps not very surprising as one would expect firm characteristics to be more important in explaining why and how firms exploit economies of scale and scope. This study does not give much support for the conjecture that sunk costs are important entry barriers. Rather, the most important entry barriers seem to be the extent to which industries are concentrated and the amount of capital required for efficient production. Interestingly, there is a strong correlation between the height of entry barriers for different categories of entrants over industries. Furthermore, when a plant is considered for entry into a new industry, it does not seem to matter very much whether it is new built or has previously been operated in another industry.

The paper is organized as follows. In section 2 a general model of entry is presented. Some of the issues relevant to the measurement of entry are discussed in section 3. Problems of specifying the market properly are addressed in section 4. The specification of the barriers to entry employed in this study is presented in section 5, while the specification of the other dependent variables is presented in section 6. The estimation of the entry equation is discussed in section 7. The estimation results are presented in section 8, and, lastly, in section 9 industries are ranked according to the overall height of entry barriers

2 A General Model

Based on the discussion in Orr (1974), in chapter 4 of this volume, and most other studies in the field, a general entry estimation equation can be formulated as

$$E = E(\pi, \text{BTE}, X, \dot{X}, \mu, \sigma) \tag{5.1}$$

where E is entry, π is average industry profits, BTE denotes barriers to entry, X is market size, $\dot{X}$ is market growth, μ is industry turnover, and σ is industry risk. Entrants are supposed to be attracted by profit possibilities. In the model these are measured as average industry profits. However, for a given level of average industry profits, entry may vary between industries for several reasons. First, the height of barriers to entry may differ. Second, industries may differ with respect to size, growth, turnover rates, and risk. Profits, size, growth, and turnover rates are hypothetical entry inducements, whereas barriers to entry and risk supposedly reduce entry. (For more details on the underlying theoretical considerations of this model, see the above references as well as von der Fehr (1990), and the references cited therein.)

3 Measuring Entry

According to Khemani and Shapiro (1983), there are six outstanding issues relevant to the measurement of entry:

1 the method of calculation (net versus gross entry);
2 the unit of observation (plant versus firm entry);
3 the unit of calculation (number of entrants versus size of entrants);
4 the type of entrant (foreign versus domestic, existing versus *de novo*);
5 the use of entry rates versus absolute entry;
6 the transformation (if any) of the entry variable if absolute entry is chosen.

The first three of these questions will be addressed in this section, the fourth is discussed in the section on barriers to entry, while a discussion of the two last questions is undertaken in the section on estimation.

Whether the focus should be on plants or firms depends on the particular purpose of the study. If we are mainly interested in questions concerning market structure, such as the degree of concentration in the industry, the unit of observation should be the firm. If, on the other hand, the purpose is to analyze production technology such as measuring variations in production capacity, the unit of observation should be plant. In this study we focus on plants. However, since plants will be split into groups (see below) and separate equations are estimated for each group, four out of six of the equations are in fact firm entry equations.

We have chosen to investigate gross entry, i.e. the total number of plants entering an industry in a given year. Even if our main interest is in net entry, it is probably wise to estimate entry and exit using separate equations. This is because entry and exit may be determined by different forces and, furthermore, exit may be a determinant of entry and vice versa. In addition, there is the statistical identification problem that small net entry rates only signal that gross entry and exit are nearly equal, and not whether little or much entry is taking place.

Gross entry is the sum of plants entering *de novo* (i.e. new-built plants), inwardly diversifying or "moving" plants (i.e. plants previously employed in other industries), and re-opened mothballed plants (i.e. re-opening of plants which have been shut down for a certain period). As a starting point, these types of entrants should not be treated as equal. For example, whether to move a plant from one industry to another may be quite a different decision than whether to build a completely new plant. In this study, a distinction is made between moving plants and other entrants only, and separate equations are estimated for each category.

Entry can be measured in terms of both numbers of entrants and their size. However, Baldwin and Gorecki (1983) present evidence that the results are independent of the unit of calculation. To measure the impact of entry on market performance, market penetration by newcomers is important. For this reason, the size of the entrant should be taken into account. Furthermore, since market penetration rates of new plants are often slow, the effect of entry may not be significant long after the initial year of establishment. Based on such arguments, Geroski (chapter 4 of this volume) chose to measure entry as the net market share penetration of domestic firms in their first year of entry (concentration on the first year was determined by data availability). Since the focus here is not primarily on the effects of entry, but rather on the determinants of entry itself, it has been decided to measure entry by the number of entrants in a given year (see von der Fehr (1990) for alternative approaches).

4 Specification of the Market

The choice of market or industry is determined by (at least) two considerations. First, the level of classification should be chosen so as to approximate closely the economic concept of market. To maximize the homogeneity of products, a mixture of four-digit and five-digit industry classification levels is used here.[1] Second, the geographical dimension of the market should be specified properly. This choice has consequences for the measurement of market size and growth, as well as industry profits and R&D intensity and concentration.

Many studies implicitly use the size of the domestic industry as the market definition by employing the size and growth of the domestic industry as a measure of market size and growth. This is done by Orr (1974), Gorecki (1975), Khemani and Shapiro (1983), and Geroski (chapter 4 of this volume). In a closed economy (or a large economy with little foreign trade) the market does coincide with domestic industry. In a small open economy, however, the specification of the market is less obvious. One alternative is to use the home market, i.e. the size of the domestic industry, corrected for trade flows (plus imports, less exports). However, many domestic firms sell in both the home market and export markets, while foreign firms produce for their home market as well as for export to the country in question. Hence, the entry decisions of domestic firms are obviously affected by the possibilities for export. In other words, the relevant market is not the domestic market, and therefore the world market should be taken into account as well.

It seems reasonable to use average domestic industry profits as a proxy for profit possibilities. If shifts in consumer preferences, income, or technology affect products symmetrically, using data on a subgroup of the plants in a market should not cause problems. This is assumed here. A similar reasoning suggests that market R&D intensity may be well approximated by information based on domestic firms only. In addition, the amount of work required to produce data on the profits and R&D activity of foreign producers in the market prohibits alternative solutions.

On the other hand, it is not satisfactory to use the size of the domestic industry as a proxy for market size. Here we should at least include imports (and not exclude exports). We would also like to include some information on, for example, the size of the OECD or European Community (EC) market. Unfortunately, data limitations prevent taking foreign markets into account, and a "domestic market including export" definition of market is employed. Data limitation is also the reason that the concentration measure is based on domestic firms only.

5 Specification of Barriers to Entry

The choice and specification of entry barrier variables are of couse
mainly determined by data availability. The variables employed in this
study are sunk costs, minimum efficient scale, capital requirements,
industry concentration, and R&D intensity. A major drawback is the
lack of data on marketing and advertising expenditure.

Sunk cost is a major barrier to entry; in fact, according to the
contestability literature at is *the* barrier to entry. As discussed by, for
example, Baumol et al. (1981) and Mata (chapter 3 of this volume), the
sunkness of a capital good is determined by both its (firm and industry)
specificity and its durability. Capital goods which are highly industry (or
even firm) specific can only be transferred to other uses by inducing
heavy transfer costs. On the other hand, given the specificity of a capital
good, the shorter its potential productive life, the shorter time period the
firm has to operate the capital to recover its value. Thus we have to
construct variables which capture both dimensions of sunkness. Three
variables are used in this study. The first aims at measuring to what
extent well-functioning second-hand capital markets exist, and is given
by the ratio of total sales of capital from incumbent plants to total
industry capital acquisitions. This gives at least a rough indication as to
how large part of the market for capital used in a given industry consists
of used capital goods. The second variable measures the durability of
capital, and is given by the inverse of the depreciation rate. Since no
adequate measures of net investments or the volume of capital exist, the
depreciation rate is calculated as the gross investment rate less the
growth rate of employment, with the underlying hypothesis being
that capital and labor are used in fixed proportions. Because both of
these variables are – at best – only approximate measures of capital
specificity and durability respectively (see chapter 3), an additional
measure of capital sunkness is added. This is the ratio of machinery to
total real capital, i.e. machinery plus buildings. It seems reasonable to
assume that the degree of sunkness differs between types of capital. One
assumption is that machinery is more sunk than structure; the argument
being that machinery may be specific for different production processes,
whereas buildings may house different types of production. On the other
hand, machinery is probably less durable than buildings. Thus it is not
obvious which of machinery and structure is more sunk, and a negative
coefficient on the machinery capital intensity variable is taken as support
for the assumption that machinery is more sunk than buildings.

As argued by Orr (1974), there are two aspects of economies of scale:

first the fraction of industry output accounted for by a plant of minimum efficient size (MES), and second the degree to which average production costs are elevated at lower output levels. Orr includes only the first of these, measuring MES as the smallest plant size consistent with profitable operations in a year of normal economic activity. We shall employ this measure also, accounting for "normal" economic activity by measuring average profits over 3 years. This "supply effect" is supposed to indicate how much an entrant's output will depress industry price, thereby acting as a barrier to entry.

Capital requirements are measured as the capital requirements associated with MES. The hypothesis is that, with imperfect financial markets, average financial costs will increase with the amount needed to enter an industry. Furthermore, financial costs will presumably differ between agents according to their experience in this or other industries. If capital costs differ between entrants and incumbents, capital requirements acts as a barrier to entry. Thus, we would expect to see differences between types of entrants, with *de novo* firms facing higher barriers than firms already employed in this or other industries. (We shall return to this last point below.)

An industry concentration term is introduced to capture post-entry retaliatory behavior by established firms which is likely to be greater the more concentrated an industry is. Concentration facilitates collusion and parallel action; however, whether concentration will deter entry is a matter of some controversy. According to the contestability theory market concentration should not matter in determining market outcomes. The estimation results might therefore provide an additional indication of the strength of this theory. However, there are also arguments in favor of concentration as an entry-inducing variable. One argument is that, controlling for other entry determinants, high concentration may increase the probability of survival given that entry has occurred. Specifically, further entry at later stages may more easily be avoided. Since strategic actions supposedly are decided at the firm level, the number of firms rather than the number of plants should act as the basis of concentration measurement. Concentration can be measured in many ways. Khemani and Shapiro (1983) report best results with the Herfindahl index, as the four- and eight-firm concentration ratios were found to be highly collinear with other variables. Following their recommendation, we employ the Herfindahl index in this study.

R&D activity is measured as industry R&D expenditure as a percentage of gross (domestic) industry output. R&D can act as barrier to entry by raising (sunk) capital requirements. Furthermore, the use of patents can be directed to increase the cost of entry as well as improving the productivity of the inventor. On the other hand, in highly diversified industries as well as in industries with rapid technological development, entry may be facilitated by the opportunities for developing product niches. Furthermore, new innovations will often be exploited in plants spun off from the firm undertaking the R&D (see chapter 13) either because employees leave and start on their own, or because the parent firm opens up new plants. Thus, it is not obvious what sign of the R&D intensity term to expect.

If multi-plant economies of scale exist this would be reflected in lower barriers to entry for multi-establishment firms. Furthermore, the owners' experience in other industries (economies of scope) may matter. Therefore plants are categorized into three groups: (a) single-establishment firm plants; (b) plants of multi-establishment firms with other plants in the same industry (expanding firms); (c) plants of multi-establishment firms with no other plants in the same industry (diversifying firms). The hypothesis is, then, that barriers to entry may be different when entry occurs via expansion by firms already in the industry, via diversification by firms in other industries, and via entry of new firms (see Gorecki, 1975; Khemani and Shapiro, 1988). Inclusion of (dummy) variables in an overall equation amounts to the assumption that the independent variables affect the entry decision in the same way for all types of entrants. Alternatively, we can estimate separate equations for each type of entrant, and then test the extent to which they differ. This is done by Gorecki (1975) and Khemani and Shapiro (1988), and the conclusion is that the responses of diversifying and new entrants to several of the determinants of entry are systematically different. Taking this evidence into account, in this study separate equations are estimated for each type of entrant.

Several variables which may be important as barriers to entry have been omitted. Orr (1974) presents a long list including the slope of the long-run average cost curve generated by plants below MES, the impact of entry on factor prices, the degree of excess productive capacity, industry demand elasticities, marketing arrangements, and particular government regulations, programs or purchasing policies. Unfortunately, we have to add to this marketing and advertising expenditures, product specialization indices, and domestic versus foreign ownership. Furthermore, Khemani and Shapiro (1983) include a variable to account for the existence of regional industries caused by high transportation costs. Gilbert (1989) also discusses, among other things, network economies and consumer switching costs as entry barriers. These omissions should be accounted for when interpreting the results.

The exogeneity of the barriers to entry may be questioned. Some barriers may be erected by established firms as part of their strategic entry-deterring behavior. A first step to secure at least statistical exogeneity is to use pre-entry period data to measure barrier to entry variables. This is not entirely satisfactory, as the underlying assumption is naive expectations on behalf of (potential) entrants.

6 Specification of other Independent Variables

Profitability is measured as value added less the wage bill divided by real capital, i.e. as the return on assets. Real capital is measured as the fire insurance value of buildings and equipment. This profitability figure will understate the true profitability if true profits are larger than measured by our data, and overstate if true capital is larger. If the benefits of monopoly power are enjoyed as X-inefficiency or non-monetary rewards, profits will be understated. On the other hand, since types of (intangible) capital are omitted from measured assets, this will tend to overstate the average industry profitability. Both these effects will probably differ between industries, and it is impossible on *a priori* grounds to form any opinion on the net effect.

It is reasonable to assume that entry will be less the higher is the probability of earning below-normal rates of return, i.e. a risk premium will be required to undertake investments in risky industries. In this study three different indices are employed to account for such risk. First, the within-industry variability of profits is measured by the standard deviation of the profit rate over individual plants. Second, it is assumed that industries which are much exposed to foreign competition are more risky than sheltered industries. Thus, both an import share index and an export intensity index is included.

The industry turnover may also be employed as a measure of riskiness, for example measured as the number of exits as a percentage of the number of plants. On the other hand, in some industries rapid techno-logical progress may lead to high turnover rates, and entry may primarily be the replacement of exiters. Furthermore, as argued by Khemani and Shapiro (1983), there may be a considerable degree of symmetry between barriers to exit and barriers to entry, suggesting that the rate of exit may be positively related to the rate of entry. In addition, inclusion of an exit term in an entry equation may render the coefficients on the barrier to entry terms insignificant. This is, in fact, reported by Khemani and Shapiro. Nevertheless, a turnover rate is included in this study.

7 The Entry Estimation Equation

Various specifications of the entry equation could be tried out. As a starting point, however, the line of formulation and estimation of Khemani and Shapiro (1983, 1988) is followed. They advocate a semi-logarithmic form, and thus the estimation equation is

$$\log(\text{ENT}) = \beta_1 \log x_1 + \beta_2 x_2 + u \qquad (5.2)$$

where ENT is the number of entrants plus 1, x_1 is the market size and capital requirements, and x_2 are other independent variables. To overcome the problem of industries in which no entry occurs, the number of entrants is increased by 1. All terms are measured as deviations from the average over all industries in a given year.

Errors in variables caused by the omission of certain types of barriers to entry and measurement errors for those that are included should be taken into account in some way. Geroski (chapter 4) assumes that there are no measurement errors, and that omitted variables are constant over the time period considered, therefore introducing industry-specific fixed effects into the entry equation. These assumptions allow us to circumvent these misspecification problems. In the absence of any further information it seems that this solution, although somewhat unsatisfactory, may be the only alternative. In this study, however, as in most other studies in the field, no specific actions are undertaken to eliminate problems created by errors in variables; in particular, no fixed effects are introduced. Thus, one should be aware of this defect when reflecting over the results of the estimations, taking into account that coefficients may be biased.

8 Results

The entrants are divided into six groups: *de novo* firms, *de novo* plants of diversifying firms (the firms have other establishments, but none in this industry), *de novo* plants of expanding firms (the firms have other established plants in the same industry), moving firms (from other industries), moving plants of diversifying firms, and moving plants of expanding firms. The logarithms of these entry variables are regressed on the following average industry variables: the profit rate, the logarithm of market size (measured by sales), market growth rate (by sales), turnover (exit rate), MES, the logarithm of capital requirements (the real capital of the MES plant), concentration (measured by the Herfindahl index), sunk cost variables (the inverse of the depreciation rate, sales of real capital as a percentage of total capital acquisitions, and machinery as a percentage of total real capital), R&D intensity (R&D expenditure divided by sales), and risk variables (import's share of the home market, export's share of domestic production, and the standard deviation of the within-industry variation in profit rates). All terms are measured as the deviation from the average over all industries for a given year. In addition, all variables are lagged 1 year with the following exceptions. The R&D intensity variable is available only for 1985, and is thus constant over all years. The MES is based on figures for the 3 years preceding the date of the dependent variable, as is the capital requirements variable. For a more detailed description of the data, see the appendix. The estimation method used is ordinary least squares (OLS).

The results are shown in table 5.1, which gives the estimated coefficients of the independent variables with corresponding standard errors and the adjusted R^2 and F-values for each equation. Judged on the basis of the matrix of simple correlations, multi-correlation does not pose major problems. The estimated coefficients are robust with respect to estimation period (see von der Fehr, 1990).

Column 1 shows the results for the category "*de novo* firm." The fit is reasonably good, most coefficients are significant, and almost all signs are as expected. Profits earned by incumbents are significantly entry inducing. The results also confirm that large industries and industries with high turnover rates experience relatively more entry of *de novo* firms. All the risk variables have the expected negative sign. Both the profit variability and the export intensity coefficients are precisely estimated, whereas the import share term is insignificant. Some of the coefficients of the entry variables are also significant. Thus both the capital requirements and the concentration terms have negative coefficients with small standard errors. However, the sunk cost variables do not perform well and all are insignificant. The coefficient of the machinery intensity variable is negative, indicating that if an industry's capital stock is machinery intensive, less entry will occur. On the other hand, the coefficients of both the durability variable and the second-hand-market variable are of the wrong sign, albeit insignificant. This may, of course, reflect that these variables are not well designed to capture the sunkness of capital, rather than indicating that sunk costs are of little importance for the entry decision. However, all in all, these results do not give any support to the hypothesis that sunk costs are of major importance for the amount of entry into an industry by *de novo* firms. Mata (chapter 3 of this volume) found that sunk costs matter for large-scale entry, but not for small-scale entry. Since no attempt is made

Table 5.1 Regression results (ordinary least squares)

	(1) De novo firm	(2) De novo plant, diversifying firm	(3) De novo plant, expanding firm	(4) Moving firm	(5) Moving plant, diversifying firm	(6) Moving plant, expanding firm
Profits	3.752**	0.331	0.603	2.363**	0.263	−0.147
	(0.763)	(0.272)	(0.349)	(0.571)	(0.296)	(0.275)
Market size	0.404**	0.111**	0.109**	0.316**	0.084**	0.038*
(log sales)	(0.044)	(0.016)	(0.020)	(0.033)	(0.017)	(0.016)
Market growth	−0.000	−0.001	−0.002	−0.003	0.000	−0.002
(sales)	(0.004)	(0.001)	(0.003)	(0.003)	(0.002)	(0.001)
Turnover	3.197**	0.417	−0.466	2.205**	0.050	0.093
(exit rate)	(0.820)	(0.293)	(0.376)	(0.615)	(0.319)	(0.296)
MES	0.019**	0.002	0.002	0.012*	0.001	−0.002
	(0.007)	(0.002)	(0.003)	(0.005)	(0.003)	(0.002)
Capital requirements	−0.205**	−0.024**	−0.030**	−0.125**	−0.022**	−0.006
(log MES capital)	(0.023)	(0.008)	(0.011)	(0.017)	(0.009)	(0.008)
Concentration	−1.929**	−0.202*	−0.426**	−1.153**	−0.239**	−0.149
(Herfindahl index)	(0.239)	(0.086)	(0.110)	(0.179)	(0.093)	(0.086)
Sales of capital as a	−0.017	0.055	−0.032	0.075	0.024	0.007
percentage of	(0.130)	(0.046)	(0.059)	(0.097)	(0.050)	(0.047)
total acquisitions						
Capital durability	0.003	0.003*	0.001	0.004	0.002	0.001
(inverse of	(0.004)	(0.001)	(0.001)	(0.003)	(0.002)	(0.001)
depreciation rate)						
Machinery as	−0.315	−0.271*	−0.116	−0.510	−0.249	0.095
percentage of	(0.375)	(0.134)	(0.172)	(0.281)	(0.146)	(0.135)
total real capital						
R&D intensity	2.512	−2.059*	1.287	−0.032	−2.500**	−0.670
	(2.307)	(0.824)	(1.057)	(1.728)	(0.896)	(0.833)
Imports share of the	−0.007	−0.001	−0.002	−0.005	−0.002	−0.006*
domestic market	(0.007)	(0.002)	(0.003)	(0.005)	(0.003)	(0.003)
Export in	−0.599**	−0.117*	−0.206**	−0.382**	−0.073	−0.104*
percentage of	(0.133)	(0.047)	(0.061)	(0.100)	(0.052)	(0.047)
domestic						
prodution						
SD of within-	−9.145**	−0.218	−3.569**	−4.061**	−0.335	0.137
industry	(2.265)	(0.808)	(1.037)	(1.696)	(0.880)	(0.818)
distribution of						
profit rates						
R^2 adjusted	0.55	0.21	0.19	0.50	0.14	0.03
F value (471/14)	44.18	10.21	9.22	35.00	6.58	0.20

97 four- or five-digit ISIC industries; estimation period 1981–5. Standard error in parentheses.
  * Coefficient significantly different from zero at the 5 percent level
** Coefficient significantly different from zero at the 1 percent level

here to distinguish between the two, this may be one explanation for why the results show no strong effects. The coefficient of the only product differentiation variable in this study, the R&D variable, is positive, but not significantly different from zero. The coefficient of the MES variable is significantly positive, which seems a puzzle and hard to explain. One reason might be that, since the MES term is somewhat correlated with the market size and the capital requirement variables, much of the entry-reducing effect of the MES term is picked up by these variables. Anyway, in most industries the minimum efficient size measured by market share is very small, since in almost all industries highly profitable firms exist which are tiny relative to the size of the industry. Based on this we would not expect to find any strong negative supply effect of entry.

Column 4 shows the results for the category "firm moving from one industry to another." The results are very similar to those commented upon above, indicating that there is a strong symmetry in the entry processes of these two categories of entrants. The sunk cost variables are a little more precisely estimated, and here the second-hand-market variable is of the correct sign. The R&D term is negative in this equation, albeit definitely insignificant, whereas it was positive (and somewhat more precisely estimated) for the *de novo* firm category. Stretching the results a little, perhaps, it is nevertheless interesting to confront the differing results for the R&D variables of these two categories of entrants with the discussion in chapter 12, where Audretsch and Acs present evidence which suggests that entry may often be the result of spin-offs from existing firms, when for example key employees develop their own specialized knowledge and then leave their employer and start their own firm to exploit the market value of their innovations. If there is any truth in this story, one conjecture would be that the entry of *de novo* firms will be positively affected by the amount of R&D going on in the industry, whereas the entry decisions of existing firms will be less influenced by this feature. As shown, there is some support for this in the data. All in all, however, the symmetry between the results for the two categories is what stands out. Thus it seems that the entry of new undiversified firms into an industry, whether their productive resources have previously been employed in other sectors or not, is fairly well explained by industry characteristics and is determined by the same forces.

Columns 2 and 5 show the results for firms diversifying into an industry either by building new plants or by moving existing plants, while columns 3 and 6 show the results for firms expanding in an industry by building new plants or moving existing plants from other industries. For all these equations the amount of variance in the data explained by the independent variables is much less than for the categories discussed above. We should, perhaps, have expected this, since the decision to enter an industry by existing firms is believed to be determined by the desire to exploit economies of either scale or scope, and therefore is influenced more by firm characteristics than by industry characteristics. As for the single-establishment category, it seems that distinguishing between newly built plants and plants previously operated in other industries is of minor importance. In all four equations most coefficients are of the expected sign, but are insignificant. The following variables, however, seem to have explanatory power. The market-size term is positive and significant for all categories. Capital requirements and concentration both act as barriers to entry. The risk terms are of the expected negative sign in all equations (with the exception for the profit variability term in the "moving expanding" category), but only the export intensity coefficient is precisely estimated. Interestingly, the R&D variable plays a somewhat different role for diversifying and expanding entrants. For the two diversifying categories the coefficients are significantly negative, whereas they are insignificant (and negative) for the "moving expanding" category. However, the coefficient for the "*de novo* plant expanding firm" category is positive, although not very precisely estimated. The explanation may be that, to the extent that existing firms are able to keep innovations within the firm, they will often be exploited in newly built plants, whereas R&D acts as an entry barrier for firms with no experience in the industry. The only sunk cost term which behaves according to prior beliefs – the machinery intensity variable – seems to indicate that sunk costs are more of an entry barrier towards firms with no previous experience in the industry than they are toward incumbents. Thus the coefficient of the machinery capital share variable is significantly negative at the 10 percent level for the two diversifying categories, whereas it is insignificant in the two other equations. On the other hand, the risk characteristics in a given industry work more against expansion by incumbents than against firms which are diversifying into other industries. Thus, while the coefficients of the risk variables are (with one exception) insignificant in the diversifying equations, they are generally significant for the expansion categories. Thus it seems that firms are reluctant to expand in high risk industries, whereas firms in other industries are less influenced by the risk characteristics when considering diversification (perhaps to reduce the risk associated with their established investments).

   The hypothesis that the capital requirements term would behave differently according to entrants' experience in this or other industries receives no support. One would perhaps expect to see differences between types of entrants, with *de novo* firms facing higher financial barriers than firms already employed in this or other industries, but in fact the coefficients are negative in all equations and are strongly significant for all categories except for the "moving plant of existing firm" category. Furthermore, when we measure the influence of capital requirements on the overall entry conditions (see the next section), the impact of this term is very similar for the different categories. In fact, the regression results do not give any strong support for the conjecture that entry or mobility barriers vary much between types of entrants. It is true, as in the studies by Gorecki (1975) and Khemani and Shapiro (1988), that the estimated coefficients differ among types of entrants. As such, the size of entry barrier coefficients vary between equations, and are largest for the single-establishment categories. However, so are the profit rate coefficients. Thus, comparing industries, a given difference in incumbent profit rates will lead to relatively more entrants of the single-establishment type than of other types, but, on the other hand, so will a difference in one of the entry barrier variables. Therefore, to evaluate how different categories of entrants are affected by barriers to entry, we have to take into account both how they react to profit opportunities and how they are influenced by entry barrier characteristics. This is done in the next section, where an attempt is made to measure overall entry conditions.

9 A "Rough and Ready" Statistic for Overall Entry Conditions

The above results provide at least a rough guide for distinguishing between industries with high entry barriers and industries with no or only moderate barriers to entry. Some authors have based a measure of the overall height of entry barriers on a "no net entry" condition. The argument is that the profits sustainable in the long-run – this is defined as a situation of no positive or negative net entry – are an indication of how well incumbents are protected from the competition of entrants (see chapter 4 for a discussion). Having made no attempt to explain exit in this study, we propose another type of measure based on the gross entry equations.

The proposed index is a measure of the profits necessary to bring entry to a "normal" – that is, average – level, taking into account the entry barrier characteristics of the industry in question. Thus an industry index value is obtained by setting the entry equation equal to zero (remember that all variables are measured as deviations from the average over all industries in a given year), disregarding the market-size,

Table 5.2 Industries arranged according to decreasing height of entry barriers

Rank accorded to measured de novo firms	Sector	Sector name	(1) De novo firms	(2) De novo plant of diversifying firm	(3) De novo plant of expanding firm	(4) Moving firms	(5) Moving plant of diversifying firm
1	425	Manufacture of fertilizers and pesticides	64.3	131.6	77.0	67.0	165.8
2	525	Manufacture of primary aluminium	37.8	41.2	37.4	35.2	52.3
3	290	Manufacture of tobacco products	35.8	42.0	45.7	33.7	51.0
4	260	Manufacture of cocoa, chocolate, sugar confectionery	34.5	50.1	38.9	33.9	60.4
5	460	Petroleum refining	33.6	58.0	42.3	35.0	77.1
6	385	Manufacture of sulphate and sulphite pulp	32.6	69.3	35.9	35.4	71.6
7	235	Manufacture of vegetable oils	32.2	61.5	55.7	32.0	95.0
8	510	Manufacture of iron and steel	31.8	63.1	45.6	31.6	72.0
9	495	Manufacture of cement and lime	31.4	51.5	45.6	31.6	68.6
10	275	Manufacture of wine and spirits	27.1	22.8	38.3	23.8	30.1
43	550	Manufacture of metal furniture and fixtures	−3.5	−14.3	−6.5	−4.7	−10.7
44	435	Manufacture of paints, varnishes, lacquers	−3.6	3.0	−4.9	−4.9	7.0
45	545	Manufacture of hand tools and general hardware	−4.2	1.6	−5.5	−3.0	−2.6
46	660	Manufacture of aircraft	−4.4	−19.4	−4.7	−5.2	−21.0
47	565	Manufacture of metal netting, wire, etc.	−4.6	−7.3	−1.7	−5.0	−9.1

48	455	Manufacture of other chemical products	-4.6	2.5	-7.7	-3.4	-2.3
49	575	Manufacture of engines, turbines, agricultural machinery	-4.9	8.6	-8.7	-2.9	11.5
50	625	Manufacture of other electrical equipment	-4.9	-0.2	-9.7	-3.9	-1.0
51	250	Manufacture of grain mill products	-5.1	-12.4	-6.0	-5.6	-20.7
52	470	Manufacture and repair of rubber products	-5.2	-11.9	-5.9	-4.8	-11.8
53	205	Meat canning	-5.9	-14.8	-6.0	-6.9	-24.4
88	305	Manufacture of made-up textile goods, except clothing	-16.2	-28.5	-17.9	-16.9	-41.0
89	570	Manufacture of other metal products	-16.8	-32.9	-20.1	-16.8	-37.3
90	330	Manufacture of outer garments of textiles and plastics	-17.1	-31.5	-18.0	-17.3	-40.9
91	345	Maufacture of leather products, except clothing	-17.2	-62.9	-20.6	-22.5	-65.5
92	595	Repair of machinery	-17.9	-40.8	-22.8	-19.7	-47.6
93	635	Boat building	-17.9	-43.5	-21.5	-20.2	-54.4
94	370	Manufacturing building materials and other wood products	-18.0	-42.8	-21.4	-19.4	-50.9
95	355	Sawing and planing of wood	-19.6	-24.2	-20.4	-18.3	-36.0
96	265	Manufacture of food products n.e.c.	-22.8	-53.2	-24.8	-24.6	-57.8
97	395	Manufacture of fiber boards	-41.1	-37.0	-28.9	-37.0	-37.2

n.e.c., not elsewhere classified.

growth, turnover, and risk terms, and calculating the profit level as a residual when the actual values of the entry barrier variables are inserted. Of course, it is not possible to make precise statements regarding the extent to which an industry is ridden by entry barriers on the basis of this measure, and we would not want to make too much of the actual index values. However, the calculations make it possible to rank industries according to overall entry conditions, and thus the index provides a "rough and ready" statistic on which further investigations might be based.

Six candidates for overall entry condition indices are provided by this study, one for each of the categories of entrants.[2] It should, of course, not matter very much from an efficiency point of view whether entry appears via new or established firms or via the erection of new productive equipment or the movement of capital from one industry to another. Thus, in general, we shall be most interested in a maximin measure, i.e. in the language of Bain (1956), how difficult it is for the "most-favored entrant" to enter an industry. In addition, it is of interest to investigate whether entry barriers are symmetric for different types of entrants.

Table 5.2 shows the ten industries with the highest entry barriers, together with the ten industries with the lowest entry barriers, and ten industries with average entry conditions. The ranking is based on the entry equation for the category "de novo firms." However, as can be seen from the correlation coefficients in table 5.3 and the index values in table 5.2, statistics based on other categories generally coincide with this one. This should not be taken as an indication that if the entry barriers in a specific industry are high for one type of entrant, then they are necessarily high for other types of entrants as well. What is true is that if the entry conditions for one type of entrant are unfavorable in one industry relative to other industries, then so are the entry conditions for other categories of entrants. Nevertheless, it is interesting to see how similar the differences in entry conditions are between industries when entry conditions are measured with regard to different types of entrants. For example, if the extra profit that can be earned by incumbents in industry 290 without attracting entry from de novo firms and moving firms are x percentage points and y percentage points respectively, the corresponding figures are $x + 2.0$ and $y + 1.5$ in industry 525 (the industries are ranked as 2 and 3 in table 5.2). Thus, even if the entry conditions vary for different types of entrants in one industry, when two industries are compared the absolute difference in entry conditions for one type of entrant is often very nearly equal to the difference for another type.

Table 5.3 Correlation matrix of entry barrier indices based on different categories of entrants

	De novo firm	De novo plant, diversifying firm	De novo plant, expanding firm	Moving firm	Moving plant, diversifying firm	Moving plant, expanding firm
De novo firms	1.00					
De novo plant, diversifying firm	0.84	1.00				
De novo plant, expanding firm	0.98	0.78	1.00			
Moving firm	0.99	0.90	0.96	1.00		
Moving plant, diversifying firm	0.84	0.99	0.79	0.89	1.00	
Moving plant, expanding firm	0.73	0.75	0.77	0.74	0.79	1.00

Column 1 in table 5.2 corresponds to the "*de novo* firm" category. The general impression is that the height of entry barriers varies considerably between industries and thus that in some industries entry conditions are very unfavorable. The index values based on the "*de novo* firms" category range from 64.3 to − 41.1 percentage points, with 90 percent of the industries lying in the interval (− 18, 34). The results are similar for the other indices. If we break down the overall "*de novo* firm" category measure on different entry barriers, we find that the results are driven almost completely by the capital requirements and concentration terms. The sunk cost terms and the R&D terms contribute very little to the measure (as is the case with the MES term, even if it works in the "wrong" direction because of the positive coefficient in the estimated equation). Thus, these results suggest that sunk costs are of little importance as entry barriers. Those industries in which little entry of *de novo* firms is expected, even if incumbents earn above normal profits (taking into account risk, market size, and turnover characteristics), are very concentrated industries or industries in which minimum efficient scale demands large capital requirements. These two features do not have to be present at the same time to make an industry difficult to enter. For example, in the cement and lime industry it is not necessary to make huge capital investments to produce efficiently; however, the industry is extremely concentrated. Contrary to this, the concentration in the sulphite and sulphate pulp industry is at average; however, the economies of scale are very important.

For the other indices the picture is very much the same: unfavorable entry conditions are primarily due to high concentration or large capital requirements. The ony exception is that for the "diversifying" categories; sunk costs also matter to some extent. The machinery capital intensity is the most important sunk cost type of barrier, but the durability of capital also matters (with the wrong sign, however).

Appendix

This appendix gives some information on the construction of the data. For more details, see von der Fehr (1989).

Profits are measured as gross return on capital, i.e. total sales less materials, wages, and net taxes, divided by total real capital.

Market size is measured as sales of domestic plants (including exports) plus imports.

Market growth is measured as the percentage change in market size between 2 consecutive years.

Real capital is measured as the fire insurance value of buildings and equipment, machinery, and implements, not including motor vehicles, ships, and planes.

Turnover is measured by the gross exit rate, i.e. the number of plants active in year $t - 1$, but not in year t, divided by the number of plants in year $t - 1$.

Minimum efficient size is the market share of the smallest plant (measured by sales) in an industry with average profit rate above 20 percent over the 3 years preceding the date of the dependent variable.

Capital requirements are the real capital of the MES plant.

Concentration is measured by the Herfindahl index.

Sales of capital in percent of total acquisitions: for each plant sales of fixed durable assets in a given year are measured as total acquisitions of fixed durable assets, new and used, less gross capital formation. This is summed over plants in the industry and divided by the sum of total acquisitions.

Capital durability is measured by the inverse depreciation rate. The *depreciation rate* is measured as the gross investment rate less the growth rate of employment measured by the percentage change in the number of employees. In industries where the calculated value was less than 3 percentage points, the depreciation rate was set equal to 3 percent per year.

Machinery intensity is measured as the ratio of machinery capital to total real capital.

R&D intensity is measured as the ratio of total expenditure on R&D by firms classified to an industry to the total sales of these firms.

Imports share is measured as the ratio of imports to imports plus domestic production less exports.

Export intensity is measured as the ratio of exports to domestic production including exports.

Profit variability is measured by the *standard deviation of the within-industry variation of profits*, i.e. the standard deviation of the profit rates of all plants classified to an industry in a given year.

All data are taken from the census data of the Central Bureau of Statistics of Norway.

Notes

1 The need to mix four- and five-digit industries was because of the lack of data on imports and exports at the five-digit level.
2 The coefficient of the profit variable is of the wrong sign in the "moving plant expanding firm" equation, making it nonsensical to compute index values. However, it is still possible to rank industries according to overall entry conditions by using the estimated coefficients for the entry barrier variables.

References

Bain J.S. (1956) *Barriers to New Competition*. Cambridge, MA: Harvard University Press.

Baldwin, J. and Gorecki, P. (1983) Entry and exit to the Canadian manufacturing sector 1970–79. Discussion Paper 225, Economic Council of Canada, Ottawa.

Baumol, W., Panzar, J. and Willig, R. (1981) On the theory of perfectly contestable markets. In J. Stiglitz and F. Mathewson (eds), *New Developments in the Analysis of Market Structure*, Cambridge, MA: MIT Press.

von der Fehr, N.H.M. (1989) A micro establishment database for Norwegian manufacturing industries. Mimeo, SAF Center for Applied Research, Department of Economics, University of Oslo.

von der Fehr, N.H.M. (1990) Domestic entry in Norwegian manufacturing industries. Mimeo, Department of Economics, University of Oslo.

Gilbert, J. (1989) Mobility barriers and the value of incumbency. In R. Schmalensee and R.D.Willig (eds), *Handbook of Industrial Organization*, Amsterdam: North-Holland.

Gorecki, P.K. (1975) The determinants of entry by new and diversifying enterprises in the UK manufacturing sector 1958–1963: some tentative results. *Applied Economics* 7, 139–47.

Khemani, R.S. and Shapiro, D. (1983) Alternative specifications of entry models: some tests and empirical results. 10th EARIE Conference Paper, Bergen.

Khemani, R.S. and Shapiro, D. (1988) On entry and mobility barriers. *Antitrust Bulletin*, 33 (1), 115–34.

Orr, D. (1974) The determinants of entry: a study of the Canadian manufacturing industries. *Review of Economics and Statistics* 56, 58–66.

Schmalensee, R. (1989) Intra-industry profitability differences in US manufacturing 1953–83. *Journal of Industrial Economics*, 37 (4), 337–57.

6

Entry and Exit in Belgian Manufacturing

Leo Sleuwaegen and Wim Dehandschutter

1 Introduction

Entry by new firms and exit of established firms are key variables in the dynamic restructuring of an industry. According to neoclassical analysis, entry and exit ensure that industry supply will converge to a social optimal level leaving no excess profits in an industry. Within this theoretical framework, it is precisely excess profits that attract new entry, while insufficient profitability drives firms out of an industry. However, this supply adjustment process does not always happen as smoothly as theory suggests. A large literature has emerged on the many structural or corporate strategic factors that retard, impede, or completely block entry. Likewise, it has been found that many entry-impeding factors also act as barriers to exit from an industry. In particular, recent studies have emphasized the possible entry-deterring role of large investments with a sunk cost character, meaning that the opportunity cost of these investments becomes zero as soon as they are implemented (for an overview, see chapter 1).

Most empirical applications of entry and exit models were developed in national industry contexts which focus on domestic supply factors with little reference to international structural adjustment. However, it is clear that for a small open economy like Belgium, with imports and exports susbstantially higher than two-thirds of the Belgian gross domestic product (GDP), it is much harder to restrict the supply adjustment process to purely domestic factors.

Partial support from the Research Fund of the K.U. Leuven (OT/89/5) is gratefully acknowledged. The calculation of entry and exit rates was based on data provided by SERV/STV (Sociaal-Economische Raad van Vlaanderen/Stichting Technologie Vlaanderen). We are grateful to Harry P. Bowen, P. Geroski, P. Verdin, and H. Yamawaki for helpful comments. The usual disclaimer applies.

2 The Openness of the Belgian Economy and Entry and Exit

It is well known that Belgium, which is centrally located within Europe, is a very open economy, trading mainly with other countries in the European Community (EC). The degree of openness of the Belgian–Luxembourg economy, measured by the ratio of its imports to GDP, was 69.1 percent in 1987, compared with only 26.9 percent for the EC as a whole, and nearly 75 percent of Belgian exports are to other EC member states and 70 percent of its imports are from these countries.

Table 6.1, which displays the rate of import penetration in industries classified by R&D - intensity, shows that import penetration is particularly high in R&D intensive industries.

Table 6.2 shows average rates of entry and exit for Belgian manufacturing industries calculated over the period 1980–4. In this table the sample has been split up according to the rate of import penetration. Low import penetration means that less than 50 percent of total

Table 6.1 Rate of import penetration of manufactures (percent)

	High R&D			Medium R&D			Low R&D		
	1970	1975	1980	1970	1975	1980	1970	1975	1980
USA	4.8	7.7	14.3	7.0	8.9	11.2	4.8	5.7	6.1
Japan	6.6	6.4	7.9	5.5	5.0	6.9	3.5	4.4	5.4
FRG	21.6	28.4	42.5	22.8	27.4	33.4	16.8	21.6	27.4
France	23.1	23.3	28.8	23.7	26.0	31.6	11.8	14.7	17.7
UK	18.6	31.2	44.2	22.0	29.3	43.1	13.4	17.4	18.4
Italy	18.3	25.3	33.4	23.8	27.7	41.8	11.9	17.8	25.4
Canada	42.6	58.4	58.0	58.5	59.2	59.2	12.7	14.1	13.8
Australia	42.2	39.7	43.1	30.6	30.4	32.5	14.2	14.8	18.5
Netherlands	71.0	67.8	69.8	80.5	79.3	85.6	38.3	43.4	51.0
Sweden	44.9	46.1	54.6	44.4	48.1	53.5	23.1	27.2	28.3
Belgium	75.7	87.3	n.a.	88.0	86.3	n.a.	40.3	48.8	64.0
EC	25.1	32.1	41.7	28.1	33.3	42.4	16.0	20.5	25.4

Source: OECD, 1986, p. 74

Table 6.2 Import penetration and mean rates of entry and exit (average across industries and years, 1980–1984)

	Entry	Exit
Low import penetration	0.065 (0.045)	0.081 (0.030)
High import penetration	0.066 (0.038)	0.081 (0.028)

Standard deviation in parentheses.

domestic sales consists of imports, and high import penetration means that imports account for 50 percent or more of total domestic sales.

The entry rate ENTRY for industry i in year t is defined as the number of firms in operation in the industry in year t that were not in operation in year $t - 1$ (number NE of entrants in year t) divided by the total number NT of firms in operation in the industry in year $t - 1$:

$$\text{ENTRY}_i(t) = \frac{\text{NE}_i(t)}{\text{NT}_i(t - 1)}$$

The exit rate EXIT in year t is defined as the number of firms in operation in the industry in year t that are no longer in operation in year $t + 1$ (the number NX of exitors in year t) divided by the total number NT of firms in operation in the industry in year $t - 1$:

$$\text{EXIT}_i(t) = \frac{\text{NX}_i(t)}{\text{NT}_i(t - 1)}$$

Table 6.2 indicates that the degree of import penetration does not imply a significant difference in the average rates of entry and exit in Belgian manufacturing industries. This by no means suggests that international exposure is unimportant. Since there are few restrictions to establishment in Belgium, industries are highly contestable by foreign companies. Belgium is among the four countries with the highest foreign participation in industry. In 1985 the share of output in Belgian manufacturing controlled by foreign companies equaled 40 percent (Vanden Houte and Veugelers, 1989). Thus low import penetration may simply reflect a strong preference to locate in Belgium instead of exporting to the Belgian market. The results in table 6.2 are then consistent with the hypothesis that all industries are, directly or indirectly, subject to a strong discipline from international competition (on this point, see also Geroski's findings for the UK in chapter 4).

3 An Empirical Model of Entry and Exit in Belgian Manufacturing

In view of the high exposure of Belgian firms to international competition, it is unlikely that entry and exit can be explained by focusing only on purely domestic factors. In particular, we would expect Europe-wide factors to be among the key factors that explain the structure of Belgian industries. Because of their small size, several authors have argued, and empirically demonstrated, that in many industries Belgian firms tend to behave as price-followers in international markets (see, for instance, Kervyn de Lettenhove, 1979; Huveneers, 1981; Frantzen, 1985; Sleuwaegen and Yamawaki, 1988). Likewise, in high technology industries where Belgian firms tend to be dominated by a relatively small number of foreign firms, domestic firms tend to adopt a follower strategy with respect to several marketing and technological development instruments (De Bondt et al., 1988). This behavior is not without consequences for entry and exit behavior. If Belgian firms tend to be followers in international markets, we may also expect entry and exit to correspond to the behavior of a fringe with profit and growth possibilities largely determined externally by leading European competitors. This implies that potential entrants are basically attracted by profit opportunities in international markets. It also implies that, in conjunction with structural barriers to enter the industry, the number of entrants is restricted by the strategic behavior of the leading international companies in the European market. Within this scenario, the room for new entry will crucially depend on the relative cost competitiveness of Belgian firms with respect to these leaders. But even without the price-follower hypothesis, it is straightforward to argue that, because of the small size of Belgian industries, a number of firms will be very responsive to relative cost performance and international structural adjustments following changes in comparative advantages by countries.

These considerations suggest an empirical model of entry and exit which includes both domestic and international factors among the list of explanatory variables. Following Orr (1974), we adopt the following model:

$$\text{ENTRY}_t = \alpha_1^e \text{PROFIT}_{t-1} + \alpha_2^e \text{GROWTH} + \sum_{j=3}^{n} \alpha_j^e X_j$$

$$+ \alpha_{n+1}^e \text{EXIT}_{t-1} + \lambda_t^e + u$$

$$\text{EXIT}_t = \alpha_1^x \text{PROFIT}_{t-1} + \alpha_2^x \text{GROWTH} + \sum_{j=3}^{n} \alpha_j^x X_j$$

$$+ \alpha_{n+1}^x \text{ENTRY}_{t-1} + \lambda_t^x + u$$

where u is a stochastic disturbance term and X is a vector of the following industry characteristics:

FIXED   Net fixed assets as a percentage of total value of output in the industry.

EQ * SCALE   EQ stands for the capital outlays on machinery and equipment in the industry as a percentage of total sales. These outlays often involve investments with a sunk cost character which, in conjunction with the strategic behavior of incumbent companies and a high degree of uncertainty in the industry, may seriously discourage entry. In order to emphasize the possible entry-deterrence role, EQ is multiplied by SCALE, the minimum efficient scale of plant as a percentage of total industry output.

SCALE   Minimum efficient scale in the industry proxied by the average plant size in the upper class of plants ranked from large to small which accounted for 50 percent of industry output in 1985 (see Comanor and Wilson, 1967). SCALE is included as a separate variable in the regressions in order to account for the fact that entry or exit may only be possible at a large scale which may discourage entry or exit.

NUMBER OF FIRMS ($\times$ 10,000)   This variable reflects the size of the industry in terms of independent suppliers. It has been suggested that competition and resulting volatility is higher in large industries.

ADVD   Dummy variable which takes the value 1 for consumer goods that are heavily advertised and 0 otherwise. In order to identify such industries, the US counterpart industries with advertising expenditures greater than 3 percent of total sales were compared with fragmentary data on Belgian advertising by product group. This variable accounts for the possible entry-deterring effect of product differentiation.

R&D   R&D expenditure as a percentage of industry sales in Belgium in 1982. Like advertising, R&D expenditure often involves specific investments which become sunk as soon as they are implemented. However, high R&D expenditure also reflects important technological opportunities in an industry which may be an important driving force behind entry. When this expenditure is directed more toward development, entry often reflects the diffusion or adaptation of innovations to local market conditions by newly established firms.

REG   Dummy variable which takes the value 1 for energy industries which are strongly regulated and 0 otherwise.

The dependent variables ENTRY and EXIT are the rate of entry and the rate of exit, as defined previously.

Profit opportunities follow a naive extrapolation of the industry price–cost margin PCMBEL in year $t - 1$, measured as value added minus payroll, divided by the total value of sales. This definition of the price–cost margin is similar to that used by Dunne and Roberts (chapter 10 of this volume). The measure varies both over time and across industries with changes in profitability and expenditure on capital services. Capital cost is assumed to be linearly related to the ratio FIXED of net fixed assets in the industry to total sales. Industry growth prospects are proxied by GROWTHBEL, the industry growth rate in Belgium in the period 1980–5. It is calculated as the value of shipments in 1985 minus the value of shipments in 1980 divided by the value of shipments in 1980.

The variables defined above basically relate to Belgian conditions. In view of the international dimension of the operation of Belgian firms, it is perfectly arguable that Europe-wide price–cost margins and growth may constitute the real incentives to enter an industry. In order to take this possibility into account PCMGER, the price–cost margin of the industry in the FRG, Belgium's major trading partner, was nested as an independent variable in the regression model. Moreover, German firms often occupy a dominant position in European industries, which might explain the empirical finding that they typically tend to behave as price-leaders (see Kervyn de Lettenhove, 1979; Sleuwaegen and Yamawaki, 1988). Consequently, Belgian firms might consider the profitability of these companies as a relevant signal for viable entry into the industry. In all cases, entry is discouraged and exit becomes more likely if cost conditions, and as a consequence price–cost margins, in the Belgian industry show up as unfavorable in an international comparison. Likewise, given the Europe-wide dimension of the relevant market for many industries, a measure of Europe-wide growth is included in the model; this is GROWTHEC, the industry growth in the EC over the period 1980–5.

Finally, it has been argued that a great deal of entry consists of displacement of exiting firms and, in turn, that an important share of exit is induced by new entrants. As in other countries (see the other studies in this volume), turnover of firms in Belgian industries is indeed a more important phenomenon than either net entry or net exit. In order to take these displacement effects into account, the entry and exit equations include exit values lagged 1 year, EXITL, and entry values lagged 1 year, ENTRYL.

The estimation period covers the years 1980–4. Business conditions have changed substantially over this period. In order to take these effects into account, the model allows for a different intercept λ_t in each year, using dummy variables.

4 Empirical Results

The entry and exit equations were estimated using pooled cross-section and time series data for 109 three-digit NACE manufacturing industries over the period 1980-4 (see chapter 7 for a list of these industries; NACE, Nomenclature générale des activités économiques dans les Communautés européennes (General Industrial Classification of Economic Activities within the European Communities)). Since the left-hand variables are entry rates and exit rates we expected heteroskedasticity in the residuals. The results presented here were therefore derived using the method of weighted least squares. According to Glejser's (1969) test and in line with our *a priori* expectations, the "appropriate" weighting factor equaled the inverse square root of the number of firms in the industry.

The results are shown in table 6.3. Column 1 reports results for the equation explaining entry across industries. The results show a positive impact of the Belgian price–cost margin, growth and lagged exit. As previously discussed, the last two variables reflect room for new entry in an industry. The second entry equation extends the first equation by including international profit and growth prospect variables. When this is done, the coefficient of the Belgian price–cost margin is no longer significantly different from zero with the German price–cost margin encompassing the role of Belgian profitability. This result suggests that the incentive to enter in Belgian industry is strongly influenced by international profit opportunities, as proxied by those in the FRG, its major trading partner.

Similarly, the impact of Europe-wide growth prospects GROWTHEC shows up as an important explanatory variable, suggesting that room for additional capacity in the industry is largely determined on a Europe-wide scale. As expected, fixed assets exert a negative influence on entry, but it is not significantly different from zero. The point estimate suggests an implicit rate of return of about 4 percent on fixed assets (coefficient of FIXED divided by coefficient of PCMGER). However, this effect cannot be seen independently of the effect of EQ * SCALE, which shows up as a major entry-impeding factor. High machinery and equipment outlays, which often have a sunk cost character, seem to seriously discourage entry, especially the larger the efficient scale of operation in the industry. Similarly, in industries where product differentiation is important, as proxied by ADVD, entry in Belgian industries tends to be substantially lower. In contrast with the effect of advertising, R&D intensity in this linear specification does not

Table 6.3

Independent variable	(1) ENTRY	(2) ENTRY	(3) EXIT	(4) EXIT
PCMBEL	0.074** (0.031)	0.030 (0.034)	−0.036 (0.024)	−0.059** (0.026)
PCMGER		0.145*** (0.051)		0.084** (0.040)
GROWTHBEL	0.029*** (0.004)	0.026*** (0.004)	−0.013*** (0.003)	−0.014*** (0.003)
GORWTHEC		0.008*** (0.003)		0.002 0.002
FIXED	0.0002 (0.0067)	−0.006 (0.007)	−0.005 (0.005)	−0.009 (0.005)
SCALE∗EQ	−0.836** (0.357)	−0.783** (0.352)	0.323 (0.274)	0.330 (0.273)
NUMBER OF FIRMS	0.034*** (0.005)	0.029*** (0.006)	0.044*** (0.004)	0.042*** (0.004)
SCALE	0.125 (0.081)	0.123 (0.080)	−0.099 (0.062)	−0.096 (0.062)
ADVD	−0.028*** (0.006)	−0.027*** (0.006)	−0.009*** (0.004)	−0.009*** (0.004)
RDSAL	0.0007 (0.0008)	−0.0002 (0.0008)	0.0001 (0.0006)	−0.0003 (0.0006)
REG	−0.012 (0.032)	−0.014 (0.031)	0.015 (0.024)	0.014 (0.024)
EXITL	0.364*** (0.050)	0.336*** (0.050)		
ENTRYL			0.292*** (0.035)	0.276*** (0.036)
Time dummy 1980	0.026*** (0.006)	0.021*** (0.006)	0.072*** (0.005)	0.069*** (0.005)
Time dummy 1981	0.014* (0.007)	0.009 (0.007)	0.083*** (0.004)	0.080*** (0.004)
Time dummy 1982	0.018** (0.007)	0.015** (0.007)	0.078*** (0.004)	0.076*** (0.004)
Time dummy 1983	0.032*** (0.007)	0.030*** (0.007)	0.080*** (0.004)	0.079*** (0.004)
Time dummy 1984	0.037*** (0.007)	0.034*** (0.007)	0.072*** (0.005)	0.070*** (0.005)
R^2(adjusted)	0.615	0.623	0.741	0.741

Standard errors in parentheses.
* Significant at the 10 percent level.
** Significant at the 5 percent level.
*** Significant at the 1 percent level.
R^2 was computed without an intercept (see Theil, 1971, p. 164).

have a separate impact on entry. Also, the effect of regulation in energy industries is not fixed across these industries. As is found in most other studies, industries with a large number of firms are characterized by a higher entry rate. However, in contrast with many other studies, the results do not suggest a systematic separate effect of large scale on industry entry rates. Finally, the coefficients of the time dummies show that for the last two years, 1983 and 1984, the improvement in general business conditions resulted in relatively more entry than the years before.

Focusing on exit as the dependent variable in column 3 of table 6.3, we find that the exit rate is positively related to the number of firms and negatively related to industry growth. Past entry seems to induce exit of firms. The coefficient of lagged entry is, as is the case for lagged exit in the entry equation, susbstantially smaller than 1. This result suggests that displacement, under the 1 year adjustment structure, is only partial. However, the effects of lagged entry and lagged exit in the exit and entry equations respectively suggests a considerable turnover in the industries. When the model is extended to include Europe-wide factors (column 4) no separate effect is found for Europe-wide growth GROWTHEC. The inclusion of the German price–cost margin suggests that there is more exit when the difference between Belgian and German profitability increases. With few price differences between these countries, this result suggests that exit follows from unfavorable cost conditions in these industries in a wider international context. Among the other industry characteristics, the results indicate a smaller exit rate in highly differentiated consumer goods industries.

In summary, the results from the regression analysis suggest that while entry in Belgian industries is largely explained by favorable international profit and growth prospects, exit results from declining profitability and growth or, in other words, deteriorating international competitiveness of Belgian firms. Clearly, because of its small size and high openness to international trade, the structure of Belgian industries is very sensitive to international restructuring following changing comparative advantages among countries.

5 Conclusion

We have studied entry and exit in a cross-section time series sample of 109 Belgian industries over the period 1980–4. As has been found for other countries and reported in the other chapters in this volume, Belgian industries show a high turnover of firms. In testing an empirical model of entry and exit it is found that, in addition to domestic effects, entry by new firms in Belgian industries is largely explained by Europe-wide growth and profitability prospects. Product differentiation and the necessity to invest in equipment and machinery on a relatively large scale show up as significant entry-discouraging factors. Within a similar framework, exit across Belgian industries is explained by deteriorating domestic profit performance *vis-à-vis* its major trading partner (FRG) and declining growth of the industry in Belgium. These results are consistent with the hypothesis that entry and exit in Belgium closely follow international industry-restructuring processes. It is beyond any doubt that the sensitivity of entry and exit to international adjustment will increase with further European integration, coupled with the elimination of all remaining trade and production barriers.

References

Comanor, W.S. and Wilson, T. (1967) Advertising, market structure and performance. *Review of Economics and Statistics*, November.

De Bondt, R., Sleuwaegen, L. and Veugelers, R. (1988) Innovative strategic groups in multinational industries. *European Economic Review* 32 (4), 905–26.

Frantzen, D.J. (1985) Some empirical evidence on the behaviour of export and domestic prices in Belgian manufacturing industry. *Recherches Economiques de Louvain* 51 (1), 29–49.

Glejser, H. (1969) A new test for heteroskedasticity. *Journal of the American Statistical Association* 64, 316–23.

Huveneers, C. (1981) Price formation and the scope for oligopolistic conduct in a small open economy. *Recherches Economiques de Louvain* 47 (3), 209–42.

Kervyn de Lettenhove, A. (1979) Taux de change, inflation et compétitivité externe. *Recherches Economiques de Louvain* 45, 55–94.

OECD (1986) *Science and Technology Indicators*, 2, R&D, Invention and Competitiveness Paris: OECD.

Orr, D. (1974) Determinants of entry. *Review of Economics and Statistics* 56, 58–66.

Sleuwaegen, L. and Yamawaki, H. (1988) The formation of the European Common Market and changes in market structure and performance. *European Economic Review* 32, 1451–75.

Theil, H. (1971) *Principles of Econometrics*. New York: Wiley.

Vanden Houte, P. and Veugelers, R. (1989) Buitenlandse ondernemingen in België. *Tijdschrift voor Economie en Management* 34 (1), 9–33.

7

Entry, Exit, Concentration, and Market Contestability

Joachim Schwalbach

1 Introduction

The emergence of the theory of market contestability has stimulated research examining the role of actual and potential firm entry in disciplining incumbent firms. It departs from the conventional belief that a high level of concentration implies pricing above marginal costs, and instead suggests ". . . that a history of absence of entry in an industry and a high concentration index may be signs of virtue, not of vice" (Baumol, 1982, p. 14). Although Joe S. Bain similarly claimed more than 30 years ago that ". . . high concentration may be a relatively innocuous phenomenon if entry barriers can be reduced to a moderate level" (Bain, 1956, p. 218), virtually no empirical evidence is available as to whether such contestable markets exist.

In this paper we provide empirical insights into the relationship between entry, exit, concentration, and market contestability. First, the importance of entry and exit of firms in German manufacturing industries is analyzed. Second, the effects of entry and exit on the change of concentration are studied. Finally, a procedure to identify contestable markets is provided and tested.

2 Data Description

In a recent report the German Monopoly Commission published data on the cumulative number and size of entrants and firms exiting in selected

I would like to express my gratitude to David Audretsch, John R. Cable, Rainer Feuerstack, Paul A. Geroski, and the participants of both entry conferences in Berlin for helpful suggestions. I am also grateful to Andrea Barth, Stefan Csutor, and Sabine Hetebrüg for their help in collecting and processing the data.

Table 7.1 Entry and exit in German manufacturing industries, 1983–1985: descriptive
statistics

	Min	Max	Mean	Std	N
Number of entrants	0(17)	231	20.923	34.707	183
Entry rate	0	0.778	0.115	0.099	183
Entrants' market share	0	0.692	0.081	0.091	112
(employment sales)	0	0.256	0.049	0.040	113
Entrants' relative size	0.084	3.025	0.680	0.404	106
(employment sales)	0.017	3.403	0.699	0.514	106
Number of exiters	0(12)	187	24.716	35.695	183
Exit rate	0	0.500	0.138	0.072	183
Exiters' market share	0	0.320	0.092	0.060	112
(employment sales)	0	0.341	0.083	0.062	114
Exiters' relative size	0.046	5.023	0.653	0.504	126
(employment sales)	0.026	1.994	0.553	0.312	124

183 four-digit German manufacturing industries for the period 1983–5 in addition to the concentration statistics. The data allow rates, market shares, and relative sizes of entrants and exiters to be calculated. The data are summarized in table 7.1. It appears that there was no entry in only 17 out of 183 industries and no exit in only 12 industries. Table 7.1 also shows that the variances of entry and exit were relatively high. On average, about 21 firms entered an industry whereas about 25 firms exited. In the extreme, 231 firms entered the plastics industry and 187 firms left the wooden furniture industry between 1983 and 1985.

The entry rate was highest (0.778) in the electronic data processing industry whereas, on average, about 11 percent of all firms in manufacturing were newcomers. These firms captured, on average, 5 percent and 8 percent of market sales and employment respectively. The highest market shares were observed in the clothing industry (based on employment) and in the linen industry (based on sales). Table 7.1 also reveals that the relative size of the entrants (to incumbents) also varied greatly. In the linen industry, entrants were three times as large as the incumbents, but at the other extreme entrants in the mineral oil refining industry were only about 2 percent of the size of incumbents. Across all industries, entrants were, on average, about 70 percent of the size of incumbent firms.

The variance of exit rates was slightly smaller. In the plate glass industry, exactly half the firms exited, whereas on average about 14 percent of firms exited across all industries. The market share on sales of firms exiting reached a level of 34 percent in the concrete parts industry and, on average, about 8–9 percent across all industries. The relative size of firms exiting compared with incumbents based on employment was five times larger in the medical equipments industry and, based on sales, about twice as large in the glass bottles industry. Across all industries, the relative size of firms exiting was 55 percent and 65 percent of incumbents' average size based on sales and employment respectively.

Comparing entry and exit rates it appears that in most industries these occurred simultaneously. In industries like plate glass, concrete parts, and textiles for interior decoration, entry and exit rates were relatively high. Simple correlations between the various entry and exit measures vary between 0.342 and 0.550, which indicates that entry may have induced exit or was the result of exit, to name only two possible reactions. An additional stylized fact is that exiting firms were on average larger than entrants, but the size variation among entrants seemed to be higher than that among exiting firms.

3 The Effects of Entry and Exit on the Change of Concentration

In this section we examine the effects of entry and exit on the change of seller concentration. The conventional wisdom is that entry increases the number of competitors in a market and consequently contributes to deconcentration, whereas the opposite effects are expected from exit. The larger are the entrants' market shares, the higher will be the deconcentration effect. According to Hannah and Kay (1977, p. 57), ". . . entry will be most powerful in reducing concentration if the newcomer's size is equal to the effective average size of existing firms . . .," where concentration is represented by the numbers of equivalent measure.

For the empirical analysis we rely on the method introduced by Weiss (1965), who explained changes in concentration ratios in terms of entry, exit, mergers, internal growth, and displacement. Owing to data limitations, we condense Weiss's method and study only entry and exit separately, and combine the remaining factors. The functional relationship is specified as follows:

$$\Delta C_{it} \equiv E_{it} + X_{it} + R_{it} \qquad (7.1)$$

where

$$\Delta C_{it} \equiv CR_{it}^n - CR_{it-1}^n = \frac{S_{it}^n}{S_{it}} - \frac{S_{it-1}^n}{S_{it-1}}$$

J. Schwalbach

$$E_{it} \equiv \frac{S_{it}^n}{S_{it}} - \frac{S_{it}^n}{S_{it} - E_{it}^*}$$

$$X_{it} \equiv \frac{S_{it-1}^n}{S_{it-1} - X_{it-1}^*} - \frac{S_{it-1}^n}{S_{it-1}}$$

$$R_{it} \equiv \frac{S_{it}^n}{S_{it} - E_{it}^*} - \frac{S_{it-1}^n}{S_{it-1} - X_{it-1}^*}$$

and S_{it} is sales in the ith four-digit industry, S_{it}^n is the sales share of the n largest firms, E_{it}^* is the sales share of the entrants, X_{it}^* is the share of exiting firms, and t is the time period. In equation (7.1), the entry effect E_{it} measures the lost sales share by the n largest incumbent firms and the exit effect X_{it} reflects the opposite. The remaining effects R_{it} include all other effects such as mergers, internal expansion, and firms' displacement.

Table 7.2 summarizes the empirical results for industry groups, and table 7.A1 in the appendix shows the results for each four-digit industry

Table 7.2 Entry, exit, and change of concentration, 1982–1985: averages across industry groups

	Δ CR	Entry	Exit	Other effects	N
Manufacturing industry (total)					
CR_3	0.207	−1.408	2.126	−0.511	42
CR_6	0.285	−2.660	3.568	−0.624	67
CR_{10}	0.359	−2.889	4.532	−1.283	79
Production goods					
CR_3	0.076	−1.449	2.114	−0.559	25
CR_6	−0.043	−1.882	2.988	−1.148	40
CR_{10}	−0.450	−2.951	4.269	−1.768	50
Consumption goods					
CR_3	0.400	−1.304	2.144	0.440	17
CR_6	0.770	−3.811	4.428	0.154	27
CR_{10}	1.755	−2.783	4.985	−0.447	29
Growth industries					
CR_3	0.126	−1.404	2.138	−0.608	35
CR_6	0.189	−2.740	3.422	−0.492	56
CR_{10}	0.018	−2.904	4.032	−1.110	66
Stagnating industries					
CR_3	0.614	−1.431	2.066	−0.021	7
CR_6	0.773	−2.252	4.315	−1.291	11
CR_{10}	2.092	−2.816	7.068	−2.160	13

in the sample of 97 four-digit industries. Concentration ratios were considered for the largest three, six, and ten firms in the industry. Since the sales shares of the entrants and the exiters were measured for the period 1983–5, the concentration ratios were taken for the years 1982 and 1985.

If we first consider the results summarized in table 7.2, it appears that concentration increased only slightly for manufacturing as a whole. Entry reduced concentration between 1.4 and 2.9 percentage points, which implies that the market share by the n largest firms would have been that much higher if entry had not occurred. Exit, in contrast, contributes to an increase in the concentration ratios of between 2.1 and 4.5 percentage points. Interestingly, table 7.2 also shows that the effects of the remaining factors worked towards deconcentration but are considerably smaller than exit and entry effects.

Table 7.2 also presents the results for the industry groups consisting of production and consumption goods as well as growth and stagnating industries. In production goods industries, the effects of entry and the remaining factors overcompensated for the concentration effects caused by exit, so that the concentration ratios for the largest six and largest ten firms decreased. In the consumption industries, the exit effect was higher which resulted in an increase in the concentration ratios. The results for the growth and stagnating industries are similar and show that high exit led to higher concentration ratios, although to a lesser extent in the growth industries.

Industry-specific information about the effects of entry and exit on the change of concentration ratios is provided in table 7.A1 in the appendix. Table 7.A1 reveals that entry caused a deconcentrating effect of up to 6 percentage points in the majority of industries, indicating that entrants gained only a modest market share and were not able to challenge the competitive position of the market leaders significantly. The exit effects, however, were larger than the entry effects and all the remaining effects taken together in most industries, and therefore strengthened the market position of the dominant firms.

Table 7.A1 also reports some extreme results which are worthy of special attention. A large amount of entry was observed in the concrete products industry (2555), and it appeared to weaken the competitive position of market leaders significantly. In the period 1983–5, 24 new firms entered and 95 firms exited. At the end of 1985, 56 firms survived. Interestingly, this high turnover of firms did not have much effect on the market share of the largest ten firms, although a change in the ranking of these firms is expected to occur. The high level of exit was caused by the most serious crisis in the building industry since the Second World

War, which took place in 1981–2 and led to a reorganization of the industry resulting in the formation of new firms.

In the abrasive product industry (2580) no entry was observed but considerable exit took place, and this resulted in an increase in the concentration ratios of 7 and 18 percentage points in the shares of the largest three firms and largest ten firms respectively. Among these leading firms is the dominant firm Norton which (at that time) had a world market share of about 25 percent. The remaining firms in that industry are predominantly small and medium sized. In the radio and television receiving equipment industry, there was a small amount of entry but much more exit. This exit was due to plant closures by firms like Telefunken, Grundig, and Thomson–Brandt, but these had no effect on the concentration ratios. Another extreme case is the medical and ophthalmic equipment industry (3760), in which 65 firms entered and 68 firms exited, thereby leaving the total number of 651 firms virtually unchanged. Entry limited the expansion of incumbent firms and exit was too small to compensate. Finally, in the linen industry (6425) ten firms entered and 15 exited, and this led to the survival of 49 firms at the end of 1985. The entering firms had a significant impact on the incumbents' market share, but some incumbents seemed to have been relatively unaffected and actually gained market shares from the exiting firms.

4 Industry Characteristics affecting Entry, Exit, and Change of Concentration

The analysis in the last section showed that entry and exit had an effect on the change of concentration and therefore an impact on the structural development of incumbent firms. In the absence of entry the concentration ratios for the largest ten firms would have been higher by an average of about 3 percentage points, and in the absence of exit the ratios would have been about an average of 4.5 percentage points lower. All other factors had on average a deconcentration effect of about 1.3 percentage points.

We still require to determine which other industry variables are responsible for the variance of entry, exit, and the change of concentration across industries. One way of tackling this question is to commence with the familiar identity equation

$$\Delta C_{it} \equiv E_{it} + X_{it} + R_{it}$$

and regress each of these variables on selected industry variables such as scale economies, product differentiation, capital requirement, R&D outlay, industry growth, and market size. The first four variables may represent entry/exit costs which limit the mobility of firms. The estimated coefficients should reveal the effects that industry variables have on the change of concentration and which of these effects occur via E_{it}, X_{it}, and/or R_{it}.

The regression results show that among the selected industry variables only market size and capital requirement have a statistically significant effect on the change of concentration. The larger the market, the larger will be the deconcentration effect which occurs primarily via higher intra-industry mobility and to a lesser extent because fewer firms are exiting. Interestingly, according to the results entry is less likely in large markets and therefore does not contribute to deconcentration in these markets.

According to the results, markets in which the capital requirement is high exhibit a higher change toward more concentration whereas the driving forces are mergers and not entry or exit. Furthermore, the regression results indicate that scale economies limit entry and support exit significantly but they are unable to explain the change in concentration. Similarly, fast-growing markets attract new firms but their effect on the change of concentration is not statistically significant.

5 Identification of Contestable Markets

In this section we are also interested in the relationship between entry, exit, and concentration, but our analysis is oriented toward the identification of contestable markets and the detection of those which have a history of no entry and high concentration indices. According to Baumol (1982, p. 3), ". . . a contestable market is one into which entry is absolutely free, and exit is absolutely costless." Therefore the ability to estimate the costs of entry and exit is essential if contestable markets are to be identified.

We begin the analysis with the conventional assumption that observed nonzero economic profits in a market are a transitory disequilibrium phenomenon if entry and exit are free. Wherever positive profits exist, new firms will enter the market. If the incumbents experience negative profits, exit will be induced. The entry and exit process can be specified by the following simple model (see Orr, 1974):

$$E_{it+1} = \alpha(\pi_{it} - \pi_i^*) + \epsilon_{it} \tag{7.2}$$

where π_{it} is the observed economic profit of market i at time t and π_i^*

is the long-run profit level in market i. If $\pi_{it} - \pi_i^*$ is positive, entry by new firms can be expected, but exit may occur if negative profit differentials are observed. The parameter α measures the speed with which entrants and exiters respond to nonzero profit differences. The parameter ϵ_{it} reflects all other factors which effect the entry/exit process and are orthogonal to $\pi_{it} - \pi_i^*$.

The magnitude of long-run profits depends on the height of entry and exit barriers. If $\pi_i^* > 0$, barriers exist and consequently entry and exit is not costless. Therefore, π_i^* can be written as a function of entry and exit barriers as follows (see Geroski, 1988):

$$\pi_i^* = \beta_0 + \sum_{j=1}^{n} \beta_j B_{ij} \qquad (7.3)$$

In the long run, $E_{it} = 0$, and after substituting (7.3) into (7.2), we obtain a measure for the overall height B_i^* of barriers in market i, as follows:

$$B_i^* = \frac{\delta_0 + \sum_{j=1}^{n} \delta_j B_{ij}}{\alpha} \qquad (7.4)$$

where $\delta_0 = \alpha\beta_0$ and $\delta_j = \alpha\beta_j$.

We estimated equations (7.2)–(7.4) for 79 four-digit industries, where E_{it+1} is the gross entry rate, π_{it} is the price–cost margin derived from a reduced-form margins equation estimated for the period 1979–82, and B_{ij} are the exogenous entry barriers which are scale economies m_{it}, product differentiation a_{it}, capital requirement c_{it}, and R&D outlays r_{it}. Equation (7.2) was supplemented by other industry variables such as sales growth g_{it}, market size s_{it}, and industry dummies.

The preferred estimate of (7.2) was

$$E_{it} = 0.0933 + 0.226\pi_{it-1} - 0.932m_{it-1} + 0.0512a_{it-1}$$
$$\quad\quad (0.80) \quad\; (2.15) \quad\quad\; (-3.36) \quad\quad\quad (1.85)$$

$$- 0.0518r_{it-1} + 0.0001c_{it-1} + 0.0639g_{it-1} - 0.0107s_{it-1}$$
$$\quad (1.37) \quad\quad\quad (0.08) \quad\quad\quad (2.00) \quad\quad\quad (-1.64)$$

where $R^2 = 0.591$, $R^2(\text{adj}) = 0.375$, and $N = 79$, and we have suppressed estimates of the industry dummies. The estimates reveal that the speed of adjustment parameter $\alpha = 0.226$ is statistically significant at the 5 percent level. Therefore entry is encouraged by positive profit expectations, but the response of entrants to excess profits is relatively slow, i.e. for each additional 10 percent higher excess profit, the gross entry rate increases by 2.26 percent. The estimates presented above also show that entry barriers reduce the likelihood of entry by new firms. In contrast with the conventional wisdom, product differentiation and capital requirement barriers attract new firms, but it has to be remembered that only the parameter for product differentiation is statistically significant. On the other hand, scale economies and R&D activity function as entry barriers in a significant way. Other industry-specific variables like sales growth influence entry positively and significantly; large markets seem not to attract new firms.

Finally, estimates of (7.4) help to rank markets according to their height of entry barriers. Table 7.3 indicates the ten industries in which entry barriers are lowest among our sample and the corresponding values of B_i^*, the entry rate, and the concentration ratio. Among the ten industries are those which we are not surprised to find, like the various food industries. In nine of the ten industries, entry occurred during the period 1983–5, but in most industries the entry rate is below the average across the sample industries.

In table 7.3, the cigarette industry also shows low entry barriers, and no entry and high levels of concentration were observed. In addition, the asbestos industry exhibits low to moderate entry barriers, no entry, and high concentration ratios. Therefore these two industries reflect the formal specifications of a contestable market. However, it is difficult to determine whether zero economic profits prevailed in these markets. Case studies in the cigarette industry report that marginal cost pricing

Table 7.3 Industries in which entry barriers are low

SYPRO no.	Industries	B_i^*	Entry rate 1983–5	CR_6 1985
2525	Stone and nonmetallic mineral products	0.044	0.082	20.20
5110	Ceramic products	0.128	0.096	64.20
5691	Processing of paper and board n.e.c.	0.128	0.134	56.20
6911	Cigarettes	0.128	0.000	68.70 (CR_3)
2535	Cement, lime and plaster	0.141	0.167	59.80
6825	Fruit and vegetables	0.175	0.074	36.20
6821	Sugar	0.227	0.057	65.00
5620	Processing and printing of paper and board	0.310	0.079	36.70
6879	Soft drinks	0.380	0.057	35.40 (CR_{10})
6882	Other food products n.e.c.	0.419	0.141	36.40
2570	Asbestos products	0.716	0.000	77.2

SYPRO, Systematick der Wirtschaftszweige, rev. Fassung für die Statistik im Produzierenden Gewerbe (Systematic of industries, revised version for the statistic in the production industries); n.e.c., not elsewhere classified.
Descriptive statistics of B_i^*: mean, 0.84; standard deviation, 0.38; maximum, 2.684.

is not unlikely (see Brendel, 1984). In April 1981 the grocery chain ALDI introduced its own brand in its stores, which was priced about 14 percent lower than the current price in that brand segment. Other grocery firms followed, and those firms gained market shares of up to 10 percent in total. The incumbent firms reacted in spring 1983 by price adjustment toward the lower level.

In conclusion, the results show that entry is motivated by the existence of positive profits and demand growth expectation, while entry barriers limit entry effectively. In addition, we found that the cigarette and asbestos industries exhibited the characteristics of a contestable market.

6 Conclusions

The analysis reveals that entry and exit occurred in about 90 percent of German manufacturing industries between 1983 and 1985. The variance of entry and exit was high and, on average, every ninth firm entered and every seventh firm exited. Entrants and exiters were, on average, small, but exiting firms were larger than entrants.

The analysis also shows that entry and exit are more important in explaining the change in concentration than factors like mergers, internal expansion, and firm displacement. On average, however, the effects of entry and exit on changing concentration are rather limited. Industry factors like market size and capital requirement also had a significant effect on the change of concentration. In larger markets a deconcentration effect was observed owing to intra-industry mobility and not to higher entry or fewer exits. However, industries with higher capital requirements exhibited greater changes toward increased concentration, where the driving forces were mergers and not entry and/or exit.

Finally, the study shows that profits and growth expectations attract entrants, but entry barriers limit their mobility subsequent to entry. Interestingly, we detected industries which showed the characteristics of contestable markets. Among these are industries with low entry barriers but relatively high concentration ratios. It appears that future research should focus explicitly on the dynamics of these markets.

Appendix

Table 7.A1 Entry, exit, and change of concentration, 1982–1985

(1)	(2)	(3)	(4)	(5)	(6)	(7)	(8)	(9)
				Change of concentration				
						Effects		
SYPRO	Industry	CR	Concentration 1982	Total	Others	Entry	Exit	Concentration 1985
2200	Mineral oil refining	CR_3	50.60	–	–	–	0.55	–
		CR_6	81.10	-0.20	-0.86	-0.22	0.87	80.90
		CR_{10}	93.30	0.90	0.14	-0.25	1.01	94.20
2512	Natural stones	CR_3	–	–	–	-3.45	–	23.40
		CR_6	–	–	–	-4.57	–	31.00
		CR_{10}	38.80	0.10	2.74	-5.73	3.09	38.90
2516	Sand and gravel	CR_3	–	–	–	-1.54	–	17.40
		CR_6	–	–	–	-2.12	–	23.90
		CR_{10}	26.50	4.30	4.26	-2.73	2.77	30.80
2525	Stone and nonmetallic mineral products	CR_3	11.70	0.40	0.95	-1.32	0.77	12.10
		CR_6	19.60	0.60	1.51	-2.20	1.29	20.20
		CR_{10}	27.70	0.50	1.75	-3.07	1.82	28.20
2535	Cement, lime, and plaster	CR_3	51.90	–	–	–	2.67	–
		CR_6	61.90	-2.10	-0.78	-4.51	3.19	59.80
		CR_{10}	–	–	–	-5.20	–	69.00
2541	Bricks	CR_3	19.40	2.30	1.87	-1.71	2.14	21.70
		CR_6	27.70	3.00	2.36	-2.41	3.05	30.70
		CR_{10}	34.40	4.60	3.88	-3.07	3.79	39.00
2551	Lime, sand, stones	CR_3	9.90	14.10	14.20	-2.15	2.04	24.00
		CR_6	18.70	15.30	14.48	-3.04	3.86	34.00
		CR_{10}	28.90	15.50	13.51	-3.97	5.96	44.40
2555	Concrete blocks	CR_3	–	–	–	-18.29	–	29.00
		CR_6	–	–	–	-25.73	–	40.80
		CR_{10}	53.40	-2.50	2.31	-32.10	27.29	50.90

Table 7.A1 Continued

(1)	(2)	(3)	(4)	(5)	(6)	(7)	(8)	(9)
				Change of concentration				
				Effects				
SYPRO	Industry	CR	Concentration 1982	Total	Others	Entry	Exit	Concentration 1985
2559	Concrete products	CR_3	16.50	–	–	–	2.19	–
		CR_6	20.50	–	–	–	2.72	–
		CR_{10}	24.80	3.40	0.85	-0.74	3.29	28.20
2580	Abrasive products	CR_3	28.80	6.80	-0.37	0.00	7.17	35.60
		CR_6	–	–	–	0.00	–	57.10
		CR_{10}	71.50	-1.30	-19.10	0.00	17.80	70.20
2591	Ready-mixed concrete	CR_3	–	–	–	-1.35	–	8.50
		CR_6	–	–	–	-2.18	–	13.80
		CR_{10}	21.00	-1.70	-1.02	-3.06	2.37	19.30
2850	Nonferrous primary metal products	CR_3	33.10	-1.90	-4.74	-0.03	2.87	31.20
		CR_6	53.10	-5.60	-10.16	-0.04	4.60	47.50
		CR_{10}	63.50	-2.90	-8.35	-0.06	5.50	60.60
2910	Iron, steel blast furnaces	CR_3	28.60	–	–	–	2.08	–
		CR_6	41.40	-0.10	-1.56	-1.55	3.01	41.30
		CR_{10}	53.40	-0.70	-2.60	-1.98	3.88	52.70
2950	Nonferrous metal blast furnaces	CR_3	–	–	–	–	–	–
		CR_6	–	–	–	-0.80	–	33.00
		CR_{10}	42.10	-2.30	-2.55	-0.96	1.21	39.80
3015	Metal wires	CR_3	24.50	-1.20	-1.87	-2.51	3.18	23.30
		CR_6	37.10	-0.10	-0.94	-3.98	4.82	37.00
		CR_{10}	–	–	–	-5.08	–	47.20
3021	Steel pipe and tubes	CR_3	11.00	0.50	0.84	-1.77	1.42	11.50
		CR_6	17.50	0.20	0.65	-2.72	2.27	17.70
		CR_{10}	25.30	-0.90	-0.43	-3.74	3.28	24.40

Code	Industry	CR						
3025	Cold finishing of steel shapes	CR_3	8.90	-1.70	-1.76	-0.56	0.62	7.20
		CR_6	-	-	-	-0.87	-	11.10
		CR_{10}	17.40	-2.20	-2.22	-1.19	1.21	15.20
3030	Mechanics	CR_3	8.70	-	-	-	1.33	-
		CR_6	16.10	-4.60	-3.24	-3.81	2.45	11.50
		CR_{10}	23.80	-6.10	-3.86	-5.87	3.63	17.70
3111	Steel and light metal	CR_3	23.80	-15.00	-16.79	-1.04	2.83	8.80
		CR_6	28.60	-14.50	-16.24	-1.66	3.40	14.10
		CR_{10}	33.80	-15.40	-17.25	-2.17	4.02	18.40
3151	Metal cans and barrels	CR_3	32.70	0.50	-0.39	-2.71	3.60	33.20
		CR_6	45.00	1.40	0.23	-3.79	4.96	46.40
		CR_{10}	54.90	1.20	-0.27	-4.58	6.05	56.10
3210	Farm machinery	CR_3	35.30	-	-	-	1.81	-
		CR_6	46.50	18.20	16.96	-1.14	2.38	64.70
		CR_{10}	-	-	-	-1.25	-	70.90
3220	Metalworking machinery	CR_3	6.30	-	-	-	0.61	-
		CR_6	11.10	-0.50	-1.37	-0.20	1.07	10.60
		CR_{10}	16.60	-0.60	-1.89	-0.31	1.60	16.00
3230	Textile machinery	CR_3	20.10	2.30	2.32	-1.00	0.98	22.40
		CR_6	34.00	1.20	1.11	-1.57	1.66	35.20
		CR_{10}	45.70	1.40	1.27	-2.10	2.23	47.10
3240	Food machinery	CR_3	16.20	-	-	-	1.19	-
		CR_6	24.20	-1.30	-2.62	-0.45	1.78	22.90
		CR_{10}	30.30	-1.20	-2.85	-0.58	2.22	29.10
3256	Steel mills	CR_3	32.70	-4.10	-8.48	-1.09	5.47	28.60
		CR_6	41.80	-6.20	-11.84	-1.36	7.00	35.60
		CR_{10}	49.20	-6.10	-12.69	-1.65	8.24	43.10
3257	Construction materials	CR_3	19.20	-4.70	-5.18	-1.04	1.52	14.50
		CR_6	28.90	-5.90	-6.53	-1.65	2.29	23.00
		CR_{10}	39.90	-7.40	-8.22	-2.34	3.16	32.50
3260	Cogged and gear drives	CR_3	41.60	-	-	-	1.66	-
		CR_6	55.10	-0.80	-1.82	-1.17	2.19	54.30
		CR_{10}	61.30	-1.10	-2.24	-1.30	2.44	60.20

Table 7.A1 Continued

(1) SYPRO	(2) Industry	(3) CR	(4) Concentration 1982	(5) Total	(6) Others	(7) Entry	(8) Exit	(9) Concentration 1985
				Change of concentration				
					Effects			
3270	Machinery for other industries	CR_3	24.50	2.10	1.01	−0.45	1.54	26.60
		CR_6	35.50	2.80	1.22	−0.65	2.23	38.30
		CR_{10}	44.50	3.20	1.22	−0.81	2.79	47.70
3280	Machinery n.e.c.	CR_3	22.80	–	–	–	1.78	–
		CR_6	30.40	–	–	–	2.37	–
		CR_{10}	37.10	2.50	−0.09	−0.30	2.89	39.60
3314	Automobile parts	CR_3	18.90	−1.70	−2.27	−0.30	0.87	17.20
		CR_6	29.60	−1.50	−2.36	−0.49	1.36	28.10
		CR_{10}	39.50	−2.20	−3.36	−0.65	1.81	37.30
3316	Car bodies	CR_3	–	–	–	–	–	–
		CR_6	31.50	2.70	2.34	−4.68	5.04	34.20
		CR_{10}	40.70	2.60	2.01	−5.92	6.51	43.30
3390	Repair shops	CR_3	4.50	–	–	–	0.61	–
		CR_6	7.00	−0.50	−1.10	−0.36	0.95	6.50
		CR_{10}	9.40	−0.90	−1.71	−0.46	1.28	8.50
3620	Electrical equipment	CR_3	42.40	–	–	–	1.54	–
		CR_6	47.50	0.30	−0.75	−0.67	1.72	47.80
		CR_{10}	52.30	−0.40	−1.57	−0.73	1.90	51.90
3640	Electrical lamps	CR_3	–	–	–	–	–	–
		CR_6	–	–	–	–	–	–
		CR_{10}	48.90	4.60	3.89	−1.03	1.74	53.50
3650	Household electrical appliances	CR_3	47.10	–	–	–	2.29	–
		CR_6	60.90	−0.20	0.53	−3.69	2.96	60.70
		CR_{10}	71.50	0.40	1.30	−4.37	3.47	71.90

Code	Industry							
3660	Meters	CR_3	–	–	–	–	–	–
		CR_6	70.10	–	–	–	4.41	–
		CR_{10}	74.80	-4.90	-8.57	-1.03	4.70	69.90
3670	Television and radio	CR_3	55.30	–	–	–	16.71	–
		CR_6	69.10	0.20	-16.72	-3.96	20.87	69.30
		CR_{10}	76.10	2.50	-16.00	-4.49	22.99	78.60
3751	Precision mechanics	CR_3	20.30	-5.70	-6.09	-0.56	0.95	14.60
		CR_6	30.10	-5.00	-5.44	-0.96	1.40	25.10
		CR_{10}	39.50	-4.50	-5.00	-1.34	1.84	35.00
3760	Medical and orthopedic equipment	CR_3	19.90	8.00	13.07	-6.14	1.07	27.90
		CR_6	–	–	–	-7.80	–	35.40
		CR_{10}	–	–	–	-8.94	–	40.60
3821	Farm tools	CR_3	17.20	–	–	–	0.80	–
		CR_6	24.40	0.10	-0.27	-0.76	1.13	24.50
		CR_{10}	–	–	–	-1.04	–	33.50
3842	Steel-sheet goods	CR_3	6.10	0.90	0.70	-0.56	0.77	7.00
		CR_6	–	–	–	-0.94	–	11.70
		CR_{10}	–	–	–	-1.37	–	17.00
3844	Nonferrous sheet-metal goods	CR_3	–	–	–	-2.09	–	24.40
		CR_6	–	–	–	-3.18	–	37.10
		CR_{10}	45.30	-0.70	0.24	-3.83	2.89	44.60
3847	Metal furniture	CR_3	16.90	–	–	–	1.82	–
		CR_6	24.50	-2.60	-0.93	-4.31	2.64	21.90
		CR_{10}	33.10	-2.10	0.44	-6.11	3.57	31.00
3850	Locks	CR_3	14.10	–	–	–	1.77	–
		CR_6	24.20	6.00	5.95	-2.99	3.04	30.20
		CR_{10}	–	–	–	-4.08	–	41.20
3871	Cutting goods	CR_3	57.00	–	–	–	1.25	–
		CR_6	72.70	0.70	0.17	-0.99	1.59	68.30
		CR_{10}	–	–	–	-1.06	–	73.40
3882	Metals n.e.c.	CR_3	13.70	1.90	1.38	-0.71	1.24	15.60
		CR_6	24.40	2.10	1.11	-1.21	2.20	26.50
		CR_{10}	35.40	2.30	0.83	-1.72	3.19	37.70

Table 7.A1 Continued

(1)	(2)	(3)	(4)	(5)	(6)	(7)	(8)	(9)
				Change of concentration				
						Effects		
SYPRO	Industry	CR	Concentration 1982	Total	Others	Entry	Exit	Concentration 1985
3889	Metal haberdashery	CR$_3$	17.20	–	–	–	2.50	–
		CR$_6$	23.40	-0.90	-1.65	-2.66	3.41	22.50
		CR$_{10}$	29.50	-0.70	-1.59	-3.40	4.29	28.80
3931	Toys	CR$_3$	–	–	–	-0.87	–	32.50
		CR$_6$	–	–	–	-1.14	–	42.50
		CR$_{10}$	45.30	5.90	5.92	-1.37	1.34	51.20
3940	Sports goods	CR$_3$	–	–	–	-2.11	–	29.10
		CR$_6$	–	–	–	-3.20	–	44.20
		CR$_{10}$	51.40	7.30	-3.59	-4.25	15.14	58.70
3990	Photo and film laboratories	CR$_3$	25.60	–	–	–	1.45	–
		CR$_6$	–	–	–	-1.18	–	38.90
		CR$_{10}$	48.40	3.00	1.82	-1.56	2.74	51.40
4031	Basic chemicals	CR$_3$	49.40	–	–	–	1.13	–
		CR$_6$	67.30	-0.50	-1.63	-0.41	1.54	66.80
		CR$_{10}$	75.80	0.60	-0.67	-0.47	1.74	76.40
4034	Farm chemicals	CR$_3$	17.60	-1.80	-2.84	-0.18	1.22	15.80
		CR$_6$	23.20	-1.00	-2.36	-0.25	1.60	22.20
		CR$_{10}$	29.20	-0.80	-2.50	-0.32	2.02	28.40
4035	Pharmaceutical goods	CR$_3$	21.80	0.80	0.06	-0.68	1.42	22.60
		CR$_6$	32.20	0.90	-0.20	-1.00	2.10	33.10
		CR$_{10}$	42.20	0.20	-1.27	-1.28	2.75	42.40
4036	Soap and detergent	CR$_3$	49.90	–	–	–	1.45	–
		CR$_6$	61.50	0.70	0.77	-1.85	1.79	62.20
		CR$_{10}$	72.80	-0.60	-0.57	-2.15	2.11	72.20

Code	Industry							
4037	Photochemical goods	CR3	96.40	–	–	–	0.00	–
		CR6	98.40	-0.60	-0.22	-0.38	0.00	97.80
		CR10	99.50	-0.20	0.19	-0.39	0.00	99.30
4039	Chemicals goods n.e.c.	CR3	27.30	-0.60	0.93	-5.99	4.47	26.70
		CR6	–	–	–	-9.56	–	42.60
		CR10	53.30	0.70	4.10	-12.12	8.72	54.00
5080	EDP equipment	CR3	92.00	–	–	–	0.69	–
		CR6	–	–	–	–	–	–
		CR10	97.90	-3.90	-3.38	-1.25	0.73	94.00
5225	Glass containers	CR3	34.50	-3.50	-15.53	-0.75	12.78	31.00
		CR6	47.20	-0.70	-17.07	-1.12	17.49	46.50
		CR10	–	–	–	-1.47	–	60.70
5290	Glass manufacturing	CR3	46.00	-2.60	-3.08	-2.76	3.23	43.40
		CR6	–	–	–	-3.48	–	54.70
		CR10	–	–	–	-4.03	–	63.50
5311	Sawmills and planing mills	CR3	11.70	1.50	0.83	-1.19	1.86	13.20
		CR6	19.40	0.60	-0.68	-1.80	3.09	20.00
		CR10	26.90	0.30	-1.53	-2.45	4.28	27.20
5361	Prefabricated wood products	CR3	18.00	0.20	-0.62	-1.31	2.13	18.20
		CR6	28.30	0.40	-0.89	-2.07	3.35	28.70
		CR10	38.80	1.80	0.13	-2.92	4.60	40.60
5411	Wood construction goods	CR3	10.60	-2.80	-3.76	-1.17	2.13	7.80
		CR6	–	–	–	-2.03	–	13.60
		CR10	–	–	–	-2.99	–	20.00
5421	Wood furniture	CR3	6.20	1.10	0.75	-0.48	0.83	7.30
		CR6	10.40	1.80	1.21	-0.80	1.39	12.20
		CR10	14.90	1.70	0.80	-1.09	1.99	16.60
5424	Upholstered furniture	CR3	–	–	–	-1.50	–	17.70
		CR6	–	–	–	-2.39	–	28.20
		CR10	35.70	2.30	1.45	-3.21	4.07	38.00
5431	Wood packing goods	CR3	–	–	–	-2.60	–	19.80
		CR6	–	–	–	-3.91	–	29.80
		CR10	40.40	-1.00	-6.12	-5.17	10.29	39.40

Table 7.A1 Continued

(1)	(2)	(3)	(4)	(5)	(6)	(7)	(8)	(9)
				Change of concentration				
						Effects		
SYPRO	Industry	CR	Concentration 1982	Total	Others	Entry	Exit	Concentration 1985
5441	Wood products n.e.c.	CR_3	–	–	–	-2.83	–	17.70
		CR_6	–	–	–	-4.31	–	26.90
		CR_{10}	30.40	5.80	7.45	-5.80	4.14	36.20
5610	Paper and board products	CR_3	12.90	0.50	0.39	-0.74	0.85	13.40
		CR_6	19.40	1.00	0.86	-1.13	1.27	20.40
		CR_{10}	25.80	1.50	1.32	-1.51	1.69	27.30
5691	Processing of paper and board n.e.c.	CR_3	–	–	–	–	–	–
		CR_6	57.60	-1.40	-3.76	-2.01	4.37	56.20
		CR_{10}	–	–	–	-2.40	–	67.10
5700	Printing	CR_3	8.70	–	–	–	0.79	–
		CR_6	12.20	0.90	0.85	-1.06	1.11	13.10
		CR_{10}	15.80	0.80	0.70	-1.34	1.44	16.60
5800	Plastics	CR_3	6.90	0.20	-0.39	-0.06	0.66	7.10
		CR_6	11.00	-0.10	-1.05	-0.10	1.05	10.90
		CR_{10}	14.70	-0.30	-1.57	-0.13	1.40	14.40
5900	Rubber manufacturing	CR_3	37.10	-2.00	-0.72	-1.98	0.70	35.10
		CR_6	50.70	-3.70	-2.01	-2.65	0.96	47.00
		CR_{10}	62.70	-2.50	-0.30	-3.39	1.19	60.20
6100	Leather manufacturing	CR_3	23.50	–	–	–	1.79	–
		CR_6	36.90	2.10	-0.23	-0.49	2.81	39.00
		CR_{10}	50.30	4.10	0.94	-0.68	3.84	54.40
6211	Leather goods	CR_3	9.20	–	–	–	3.19	–
		CR_6	16.50	2.20	-1.02	-2.51	5.73	18.70
		CR_{10}	24.60	3.10	-1.72	-3.72	8.54	27.70

Code	Industry	Ratio	(1)	(2)	(3)	(4)	(5)	(6)
6332	Cotton weaving mills	CR₃	15.50	2.60	1.66	-0.68	1.63	18.10
		CR₆	25.20	3.70	2.15	-1.09	2.64	28.90
		CR₁₀	–	–	–	-1.47	–	38.90
6370	Knitting mills	CR₃	11.10	–	–	–	0.99	–
		CR₆	17.40	1.30	0.54	-0.79	1.55	18.70
		CR₁₀	23.80	2.30	1.28	-1.10	2.12	26.10
6413	Men's outerwear	CR₃	11.70	–	–	–	1.92	–
		CR₆	18.20	2.90	2.11	-1.14	2.99	14.60
		CR₁₀	–	3.80	2.52	-1.71	–	22.00
6414	Women's and children's outerwear	CR₃	9.60	–	–	–	1.11	–
		CR₆	14.00	2.20	0.86	-0.27	1.61	16.20
		CR₁₀	18.50	2.40	0.62	-0.35	2.13	20.90
6421	Underwear manufacturing	CR₃	20.40	2.30	0.72	-0.55	2.13	22.70
		CR₆	29.90	4.80	2.52	-0.84	3.12	34.70
		CR₁₀	–	–	–	-1.12	–	46.30
6425	Linen manufacturing	CR₃	40.40	–	–	–	17.26	–
		CR₆	50.80	8.70	39.18	-52.19	21.71	59.50
		CR₁₀	–	–	–	-61.48	–	70.10
6430	Sport and work cloth	CR₃	29.70	1.70	0.11	-1.20	4.82	11.70
		CR₆	–	1.20	1.55	-2.16	–	21.00
		CR₁₀	–	0.10	0.48	-3.23	–	31.40
6450	Headgear and cloth accessories	CR₃	14.40	1.20	1.83	-1.60	1.25	15.60
		CR₆	24.00	0.40	-0.68	-2.47	2.09	24.10
		CR₁₀	33.00	–	–	-3.51	2.87	34.20
6460	Fur goods	CR₃	35.30	–	–	–	2.78	–
		CR₆	49.20	-6.40	-12.99	-2.80	3.88	49.60
		CR₁₀	–	–	–	-3.25	–	57.50
6470	Bedclothes	CR₃	35.60	-11.20	-15.74	-0.98	8.24	17.20
		CR₆	–	-9.30	-14.53	-1.66	–	29.20
		CR₁₀	–	–	–	-2.32	–	40.90
6489	Other textiles	CR₃	36.80	–	–	–	7.64	–
		CR₆	47.40	–	–	-3.10	9.84	25.60
		CR₁₀	–	–	–	-4.62	–	38.10

Table 7.A1 Continued

(1)	(2)	(3)	(4)	(5)	(6)	(7)	(8)	(9)
				Change of concentration				
						Effects		
SYPRO	Industry	CR	Concentration 1982	Total	Others	Entry	Exit	Concentration 1985
6812	Farinaceous gods	CR$_3$	–	–	–	–	–	–
		CR$_6$	–	–	–	–	–	85.80
		CR$_{10}$	95.60	–0.90	–0.90	0.00	0.00	94.70
6818	Baking goods	CR$_3$	8.90	2.00	1.87	0.00	0.80	10.90
		CR$_6$	16.50	2.00	1.66	–0.67	1.48	18.50
		CR$_{10}$	–	–	–	–1.13	–	26.30
6825	Fruit and vegetables	CR$_3$	17.30	3.80	4.20	–2.34	1.94	21.10
		CR$_6$	30.10	6.10	6.73	–4.01	3.38	36.20
		CR$_{10}$	42.80	3.90	4.27	–5.18	4.81	46.70
6828	Confectionery goods	CR$_3$	33.20	–2.60	–2.71	–0.89	1.01	30.60
		CR$_6$	46.70	–3.00	–3.14	–1.28	1.42	43.70
		CR$_{10}$	57.60	–2.60	–2.74	–1.61	1.75	55.00
6831	Dairy goods	CR$_3$	11.60	–1.00	–1.31	–0.41	0.72	10.60
		CR$_6$	18.50	–0.80	–1.27	–0.68	1.15	17.70
		CR$_{10}$	25.50	–0.50	–1.12	–0.96	1.58	25.00
6852	Slaughter-houses	CR$_3$	40.50	–	–	–	4.71	–
		CR$_6$	53.70	–2.30	–3.69	–4.85	6.24	51.40
		CR$_{10}$	62.60	0.00	–1.37	–5.91	7.28	62.60
6853	Meat products	CR$_3$	14.30	–2.30	–2.43	–1.25	1.38	12.00
		CR$_6$	21.60	–1.50	–1.50	–2.09	2.09	20.10
		CR$_{10}$	28.60	–0.40	–0.23	–2.94	2.77	28.20

Code	Industry							
6854	Butcher shops	CR$_3$	–	–	–	–	–	–
		CR$_6$	16.20	–1.10	–1.52	–1.34	1.76	15.10
		CR$_{10}$	20.70	–0.20	–0.63	–1.82	2.25	20.50
6871	Beer breweries	CR$_3$	11.20	0.70	0.78	–0.84	0.76	11.90
		CR$_6$	26.60	–	–	–1.37	–	19.40
		CR$_{10}$	66.70	0.70	0.82	–1.93	1.81	27.30
6872	Malt breweries	CR$_3$	–	–	–	–	–	–
		CR$_6$	21.80	7.00	–17.31	0.00	24.31	55.20
		CR$_{10}$	34.00	–	–	0.00	–	73.70
6879	Mineral water	CR$_3$	–	–	–	–	–	–
		CR$_6$	–	–	–	–	2.09	–
		CR$_{10}$	–	1.40	0.05	–1.91	5.44	35.40
6882	Other food products n.e.c.	CR$_3$	19.30	4.30	7.71	–5.85	3.26	23.60
		CR$_6$	31.10	5.30	10.40	–9.02	2.43	36.40
		CR$_{10}$	43.20	5.50	12.12	–12.07	3.92	48.70
6889	Animal foodstuff	CR$_3$	24.70	–	–	–	4.51	–
		CR$_6$	40.70	2.90	–2.16	–2.37	7.43	43.60
		CR$_{10}$	51.80	2.30	–4.22	–2.94	9.46	54.10

n.e.c., not elsewhere classified.

142 *J. Schwalbach*

References

Bain, J.S. (1956) *Barriers to New Competition*. Cambridge, MA: Harvard University Press.

Baumol, W.J. (1982) Contestable markets: an uprising in the theory of industry structure. *American Economic Review* 72 (1) 1–15.

Brendel, H. (1984) Zigarettenindustrie. In P. Oberender (ed.), *Marktstruktur und Wettbewerb*, Munich: Vahlen, pp. 311–70.

Geroski, P.A. (1988) The effect of entry on profit margins in the short and long run. Working Paper Series 47, London Business School.

Hannah, L. and Kay, J.A. (1977) *Concentration in Modern Industry*. London: Macmillan.

Orr, D. (1974) The determinants of entry: a study of the Canadian manufacturing industries. *Review of Economics and Statistics* 56 (1), 58–66.

Weiss, L.W. (1965) An evaluation of mergers in six industries. *Review of Economics and Statistics* 67, 172–81.

8

Entry during Explosive Growth: Korea during Take-off

Kap-Young Jeong and Robert T. Masson

1 Introduction

When manufacturing industry in Korea is contrasted with that in other countries, there are many differences, several of which are revealed in chapter 14. Recent Korean manufacturing growth rates have often exceeded 20 percent per annum in real terms. The sample we examine had a real growth rate of 41 percent per annum over an entire business cycle, 55 percent per annum during the expansion, and 18 percent per annum during the contraction. This leads to different entry patterns from those in other more mature economies. In mature economies entry rates and disappearance/exit rates are approximately equal; "turnover" dominates. For our data, entry over 1977–81 was 51 percent of the number of firms in 1976, whereas disappearance was only 25 percent of this base. Although there is a consistently positive correlation between entry and disappearance in the mature economies, during the expansion there was a negative (significant) correlation in Korea: entry was taking place in some industries, and exit in others.

Results on profitability are also different. Gross return on assets, profits before deducting interest on debt or opportunity cost on equity, averaged 9.8 percent in the industries we considered, while "curb rate" interest was running over 20 percent. No doubt entry was aimed at longer-run profits. Our estimates indicate that net entry would be positive with gross profits of less than 3.5 percent on assets.

Some institutional characteristics are worth noting. Until after our data period, the government had virtually no antitrust policy. Rather,

We are indebted for suggestions from other participants, especially Paul Geroski. We should like to thank M. Roychoudhury for her help. We are particularly indebted to the National Bureau of Statistics, Economic Planning Board of Korea, for compiling the special data sets we used in this work.

it had more of a *protrust* policy. Mergers and agreements were not challenged, and at times were encouraged. Many markets were protected from import competition. Geography plays little role domestically; separate markets are separated by less than six hours by road. Conglomeration, as we know it, plays little role. (The various products manufactured under the name of Hyundai, for example, are manufactured by 33 legally independent firms.) Relative to most countries, there are well-defined firms in well-defined markets. But the invisible hand is not alone; industrial policy granted subsidies to target industries. This led us to introduce policy variables in our estimation.

Our initial work (Jeong, 1985; Jeong and Masson, 1990) defined the net numbers of new firms as "entry." In this project we developed other measures, but found weaker results with them. We are inclined to accept our initial measure as the "best" measure of increasing competition/entry for Korea, but not necessarily for economies where turnover dominates the statistics. This measure not only shows the greatest response to predicted profits, but realized profits following entry are suppressed the most using this measure.

In this paper we present the entry methodology first, followed by the data and the results. We then attempt to validate our measures by examining the effect of entry on profits. Finally we provide estimates of firm exit/disappearance.

2 Methodology and Data

We use a linear entry model[1] similar to the one presented in Masson and Shaanan (1982, 1987) or somewhat like that in Orr (1974).[2] Entry is a function of (a) profit rates, (b) entry barriers, (c) a government policy variable, (d) the concentration ratio, and (e) lagged growth:

$$E_t = \alpha_0 + \alpha_1 \frac{\Pi + rD}{A} + \alpha_2 \text{MES}^c + \alpha_3 \text{ASR} + \alpha_4 \text{CAP} + \alpha_5 \text{POL}$$

$$+ \alpha_6 \text{CR} + \alpha_7 \text{GRO}_{t-1} \tag{8.1}$$

A key element estimated in the studies in this volume is the profit rate at which there would be no entry. If exit were zero then this profit level defines a steady state. If net entry is zero in expected value, this defines a stochastic steady state. This also plays a central role in limit-pricing theory. Bain (1956) called this profit level the *entry forestalling level* Π^f. In some papers in this volume, it is also called "limit profits." Bain distinguished between limit profits and forestalling profits, as Π^f exists independent of whether firms limit price (or whether the limit price is equal to or greater than Π^f, cf. Masson and Shaanan (1982)). For Korea we find little support for limit pricing as the opportunity cost is too high, yet we can still estimate Π^f (cf. Jeong and Masson, 1990).

The meanings of Π^f across entry definitions with and without turn-over are not the same, and may not correspond to the concept defined in limit pricing,[3] but we do not analyze this here. Π^f can be solved by setting $E = 0$ in (8.1) and solving for Π:

$$\left(\frac{\Pi + rD}{A}\right)^f = -\left(\frac{\alpha_0}{\alpha_1}\right) - \left(\frac{\alpha_2}{\alpha_1}\right)\text{MES}^c - \left(\frac{\alpha_3}{\alpha_1}\right)\text{ASR} - \left(\frac{\alpha_4}{\alpha_1}\right)\text{CAP}$$

$$- \left(\frac{\alpha_5}{\alpha_1}\right)\text{POL} - \left(\frac{\alpha_6}{\alpha_1}\right)\text{CR} - \left(\frac{\alpha_7}{\alpha_1}\right)\text{GRO}_{t-1} \qquad (8.2)$$

2.1 Sample Selection

The data are for 62 manufacturing industries, 32 of which are consumer goods. We selected Korean Standard Industrial Classification (KSIC) industries that most closely reflect our idea of markets. We subjectively excluded industries which were defined too broadly, too narrowly, or too vaguely,[4] and four-digit industries if their five-digit subcomponents did not have similar concentration ratios. Our sample includes 48 four-digit and 14 five-digit KSIC industries. The mean concentration of our five-digit industries was 52 percent and the overall sample mean was 58 percent.

The time period t was defined in three ways. First we have a full business cycle (1977–81), next the expansion period (1976–8), and finally the contraction period (1979–81).[5]

2.2 The Independent Variables

Profits are gross profits on assets: net accounting profits Π plus interest on debt rD divided by assets A.[6] Thus the concept of "zero economic profits" is when $(\Pi + rD)/A = r$ (if the opportunity cost of equity is also r). For net entry equations using the price– cost margin and profits on equity see Jeong (1985). The measure we report was marginally better in explaining entry.

Following Geroski (chapter 4) we constructed $(\Pi + rD)/A$ to measure "predicted profits." This was done by regressing the entry period profits on pre-entry profits and all exogenous variables. For each time period we averaged the gross profit rates for that period and regressed them on the gross profit rates for the three preceding years plus all exogenous variables. These first-stage predicted profits are used in the entry equation.

Next we define three proxies for entry barriers, Minimum efficient scale (MES) is proxied by the Florence median: average plant size at the midpoint of industry output relative to the domestic market divided by the value of shipments VS minus exports X plus imports M. To capture the disadvantages of suboptimal operation we use the cost disadvantage ratio CDR (Caves et al., 1975). CDR is the ratio of the value added per worker in smaller plants to that for the remaining plants. MES is only a barrier if CDR is small, and so we use $MES^c \equiv MES(1 - CDR)$. The measure of MES was calculated based upon annual averages over the business cycle (1976 – 81).[7]

For product differentiation we use the traditional proxy–the advertising-to-sales ratio ASR. We assume that all advertising can be attributed to domestic sales and use $ASR \equiv Adv/(VS - X)$, where Adv is advertising. ASR was measured as the annual average over the relevant period (e.g. for the expansion period 1976–8 ASR is the annual average over 1976–8).[8] To measure an absolute capital cost barrier we use $CAP \equiv MES$ (industry assets).[9] Credit markets are less perfect in Korea, and so we might expect CAP to be important. Alternatively, since government policy was to stimulate some industries with subsidized loans (especially exporters and the heavy industry and chemicals sector), there is the possibility that government policy could be correlated with entry through CAP. We accordingly add a policy variable POL.

POL is a measure of subsidized government loans. In Korea, as in most less developed countries (LDCs) and newly industrialized countries (NICs), of which Korea is one, one outcome of poor capital markets is the formation of "business groups."[10] These are groups of firms that have a common internal capital market, yet are otherwise legally independent. In Korea these *Jaibul* groups are important sources of capital.[11] However, credit availability is a crucial constraint. The curb rate of interest in Korea was generally over 20 percent during the 1970s but the government subsidized some loans at under 10 percent. These subsidies are not across the board, but are preferential loans granted to target firms or industries, typically exporters and the heavy and chemical industries. POL measures these preferential loans. It is the ratio of preferential loans to firms in the industry to total industry capital.[12] Its expected sign could be positive or negative. These loans are typically (but not exclusively) granted to incumbents rather than as seed money for entrants. But potential entrants may view a high level of preferential loans in an industry as an opportunity to enter with the expectation of later receiving subsidized expansion capital.

The next regressor is the three-firm concentration ratio.[13] Inclusion of concentration is in part for comparability with other studies.[14] A *priori* there are many theories of how concentration may affect entry. These are reviewed by Masson and Shaanan (1987) who also show evidence that indicates that greater concentration increases entry in US data and decreases entry in Canadian data. There are many ways that concentration, conditional upon profits, might affect the incentive to enter. For example, there is fear of retaliation by incumbents. But barring extremely high concentration, predation seems unlikely to be a major threat.[15] Other plausible explanations depend upon potential entrants' assessments of the ease of collusion in the industry.

Suppose that a potential entrant thinks that collusion explains the profits in the industry, and that collusion is inherently fragile. It might fear entering unless concentration is high, expecting that if it enters at intermediate concentration levels the collusive profits may disappear as the agreement is destabilized. But it may feel that a highly concentrated industry would be able to maintain collusion, accepting the entrant into the agreement. As in the US data, entry would be more likely to occur if concentration were high than if it were at intermediate levels.

Unfortunately a very similar logic leads to the opposite conclusion for the entrant, and the opposite sign as an empirical prediction. Suppose that the potential entrant feels that collusion is difficult. If it observes intermediate levels of concentration it may conclude that profits are being generated despite competitive (in a Nash sense, noncooperative) behavior. Further, upon observing similar profit levels in a concentrated industry, it might conclude that these may come from collusion. If they come from collusion, and as hypothesized the entrant feels that collusion is hard to maintain, then it will feel that there is some chance that entry will destabilize the collusive agreement. This would mean that higher concentration, conditional upon observed profits, would lead to lower entry. Given both theory and past empirical studies, there is no *a priori* sign prediction for the concentration variable (therefore two-tailed t tests should be applied).

The final regressor is industry growth GRO_{t-1}. This is growth over the three preceding years. For the full cycle and the expansion period GRO_{t-1} is measured over 1973–5 and for the contraction of 1979–81 it is measured over 1976–8.[16]

2.3 Measures of Entry

Our initial entry measure was the net entry rate $\Delta N/N$, i.e. the net increase in the number of firms measured as a rate of change $100(N_\tau - N_{\tau-1})/N_{\tau-1}$. This is the type of measure used by Orr (1974) and Masson and Shaanan (1987) for Canadian data. For this project we were provided #New/N: the number of actual new entrants measured as a rate.[17] We also developed two proxies for net entry shares. The proxies are based upon our suggestion at the First Entry conference. They are $\Delta(H^{-1})/N$ and $\Delta(H^{-1})H$. That is, if H_τ is the Herfindahl index of concentration for time τ, our proxies are[18]

$$100 \, \frac{1/H_\tau - 1/H_{\tau-1}}{N_{\tau-1}} \quad \text{and} \quad 100 \, \frac{1/H_\tau - 1/H_{\tau-1}}{1/H_{\tau-1}}$$

The intuition follows from symmetric oligopoly for which $H \equiv \Sigma(1/N)^2 = 1/N$; hence $H_\tau^{-1} = N_\tau$ and $\Delta(H^{-1})/N = \Delta(H^{-1})H = \Delta N/N$. If symmetry is assumed, this is a measure of net entrant shares or the shares of entrants in τ net of the shares of exits displaced by entrants. We use two proxies because one of the independent variables is the three-firm concentration ratio CR. Although there is no strong *a priori* reason to assume that $\Delta(H^{-1})$ is spuriously correlated with CR, H may be spuriously correlated with CR. The proxy using $\Delta(H^{-1})H$ seems more appealing, yet it may also include a measurement error correlated with an independent variable. Accordingly we look at both proxies.

For asymmetric oligopoly the idea is similar, but not identical. This index has the possibility of measuring the size of net entry. if H is monotonically falling in net entry and if there are no changes in the relative size of incumbents. Clearly, we could construct examples in which large-scale entry actually increases the value of H. For example, if a single new entrant's output becomes virtually the entire market, then H will aprroach a value of 1. But a bound can be established which suggests that the Herfindahl index will almost always fall with entry. A sufficient condition that H is monotonically declining in larger entrant shares is that the size of the entrant does not exceed the mean firm size.[19]

The second restriction is that relative incumbent sizes also will not change. Clearly, this will generally not be true. Cable (undated) in fact proposed ΔH as one of 'two measures of market-share mobility and entry,' where the second measure was the decomposition of ΔH into the effects of entry, exit, and flux in surviving incumbents' shares. We do not control for the sub-ΔH effects in our proxies. To the extent that intra-industry mobility effects are similar to net entry effects, our proxies are some combined notion of a measure of increasing competition.

We were also able to obtain entrants' gross shares. These were compiled in two ways: impact shares and long-run shares. For the expansion period of 1975–8 we have the share of all entrants in these 3 years as of December 31, 1978. This is our measure of the impact share in the expansion period. Its long-run share is defined as the shares of these same entrants 3 years later on December 31, 1981. For the contraction period (1979–81) the impact share is measured on December 31, 1981 and the long-run share on December 31, 1984. For the full cycle (1976–81) the measures are made at year end 1981 and year end 1984.[20]

The entry impact shares seem more closely allied to the share definitions used in other investigations reported in this volume. The long-run shares are closer to the type of entry definition used by Masson and Shaanan (1982, 1984).

The correlations between entry measures are given in tables 8.1–8.3. A correlation coefficient of 0.211 is significant at the 90 percent level and a level of 0.250 is significant at the 95 percent level. Clearly, the measures are different.

The following patterns emerge. First #New/N is a better proxy for entrant shares than is $\Delta N/N$, possibly because the latter is not a measure of gross entry. The measures of net entry using the Herfindahl index are not strongly correlated with other measures, either gross or net.[21]

We keep all of these measures of "entry" for our empirical analysis. Although #New/N is possibly a better measure of "entry" than is net entry $\Delta N/N$, $\Delta N/N$ may be a better measure of structural change in a response to supranormal profits. (For example, an industry with an equilibrium structure may have a high turnover of firms and large #New/N without any increase in effective competition). Entrant shares have a similar interpretive problem. Although the measures based on the

Table 8.1 Correlation of entry measures (Pearson): entry 1977–1981, full cycle

	$\Delta N/N$	#New/N	$\Delta(H^{-1})/N$	$\Delta(H^{-1})/H$	*Share 1981*	*Share 1981*
#New/N	0.344	1.000				
$\Delta(H^{-1})/N$	0.111	0.036	1.000			
$\Delta(H^{-1})H$	0.188	0.220	0.482	1.000		
Share 1981	0.224	0.553	0.139	0.128	1.000	
Share 1984	0.128	0.448	−0.132	0.013	0.476	1.000
DIS	−0.598	0.466	−0.094	−0.008	0.270	0.222

$\rho \geqslant 0.211$ is 90 percent significant and $\rho \geqslant 0.250$ is 95 percent significant.

Table 8.2 Correlation of entry measures (Pearson): entry 1976–1978, economic expansion

	$\Delta N/N$	#New/N	$\Delta(H^{-1})/N$	$\Delta(H^{-1})/N$	Share 1978	Share 1981
#New/N	0.682	1.000				
$\Delta(H^{-1})/N$	−0.081	0.076	1.000			
$\Delta(H^{-1})H$	0.031	0.172	0.695	1.000		
Share 1978	0.472	0.586	0.118	0.238	1.000	
Share 1981	0.040	0.268	−0.134	0.093	0.560	1.000
DIS	−0.922	−0.409	0.236	0.130	−0.307	−0.129

$\rho \geqslant 0.211$ is 90 percent significant and $\rho \geqslant 0.250$ is 95 percent significant.

Table 8.3 Correlation of entry measures (Pearson): entry 1979–1981, economic contraction

	$\Delta N/N$	#New/N	$\Delta(H^{-1})/N$	$\Delta(H^{-1})/N$	Share 1981	Share 1984
#New/N	0.082	1.000				
$\Delta(H^{-1})/N$	0.104	−0.121	1.000			
$\Delta(H^{-1})H$	0.223	0.031	0.632	1.000		
Share 1981	0.077	0.365	0.026	0.146	1.000	
Share 1984	0.133	0.438	−0.021	−0.037	0.565	1.000
DIS	−0.895	0.350	−0.133	−0.196	0.086	0.090

$\rho \geqslant 0.211$ is 90 percent significant and $\rho \geqslant 0.250$ is 95 percent significant.

Herfindahl index are only rough proxies, they may capture the effects of entrant shares net of exits.

Finally, we come to the final line of each correlation matrix, DIS which measures firm disappearance.

2.4 Firm Disappearance

Disappearance is defined as a rate: $DIS \equiv (\#New/N) - (\Delta N/N)$. Disappearance means that a firm has disappeared from the sample as a result of exit or merger.[22] The implications of exit versus merger are hard to interpret. Successful operations may be purchased by rivals, possibly to acquire the successful firm's expertise and apply it to the products of both firms. If an undercapitalized firm has entered, it may have a negative present value, evaluated at the external rate of interest, but a positive value evaluated at some rival's internal opportunity cost of capital. If equity markets are not well developed and/or industry insiders are better equipped to evaluate the firm's productive capabilities, a productively successful firm may face financial stringency or even failure without being merged with a rival. Given the relatively inefficient capital markets in Korea, this would seem more likely than in the mature industrialized countries. In other cases merger is due to failure and the potential application of a successful incumbent's expertise to the failing firm's physical capital. Exit may also come from success or failure, although more commonly it is from failure. Exit is often accompanied by asset sales, where the assets remain in the industry. An entrant that discovers a superior process may find it more profitable to license that process to some large-scale producer on an exclusive basis (or to multiple incumbents) than to remain in the industry. Alternatively, in the case of failure, often some physical capital is more industry specific than firm specific and is sold to survivors. Although it is hard to distinguish the difference between success and failure from the method of disappearance, our intuition is that disappearance without merger is generally due to failure and disappearance with merger is more likely to be due to success.

Our intuition can be enhanced by an estimate of the degree to which DIS is due to merger. For 1982 and our 62 industries, mergers were 11.5 percent of DIS. The official merger rate for all manufacturing 2 years later was 15 percent. This suggests that exit dominates these statistics.

We also gain insight by knowing how much of DIS is composed of failed new entrants. From data on all manufacturing, this does not appear to be the case. Of all manufacturing entrants for 1977, 82.7 percent survived for at least 1 year. 70.2 percent for 2 years, 68.9 percent for 3 years and 62.4 percent for 4 years. The 4 year success rates for 1981 entrants were 90.2 percent, 88.4 percent, 87.4 percent and 84.6 percent respectively. Success rates were higher after 1981 (economic recovery) than for the years following 1977. Although 1978 was a peak cycle year, the success of 1977 entrants through 1978 was less than the 4 year success of 1981 entrants. The declining success of the 1977 entrants in 1979–81 may reflect the downturn.

In tables 8.1–8.3 we see that DIS is strongly negatively correlated with $\Delta N/N$, as it should be (DIS $\equiv$ (#New/N) $-$ ($\Delta N/N$)). Although the full-cycle pattern has DIS positively correlated with #New/N (e.g. there are high and low turnover rates), the correlation is negative for the expansion (e.g. during good times, industries that are doing well have few exits and more entrants).

3 The Determinants of Entry

The explanation of the entry measures is presented in tables 8.4–8.6. Table 8.4 presents the determinants of our six measures of entry for the

Table 8.4 Entry 1977–1981: full business cycle

	$\Delta N/N$	#New/N	$\Delta(H^{-1})/N$	$\Delta(H^{-1})H$	Share, Dec 31, 1981	Share Dec 31, 1984
Constant	-22.239	39.015***	-3.581	-197.864***	3.864***	12.317***
	(1.182)	(3.763)	(1.029)	(3.514)	(2.911)	(3.385)
$(\Pi + rD)/A$	1.778*	1.125*	0.034*	6.227*	0.021	0.666***
	(1.293)	(1.479)	(1.231)	(1.603)	(0.230)	(2.497)
MES^c	-0.909*	-0.220	0.107	-0.278	0.005	-0.157*
	(1.398)	(0.614)	(0.882)	(0.151)	(0.117)	(1.246)
ASR	-6.224**	-2.805*	-0.660	-36.666***	-0.290	0.391
	(1.732)	(1.415)	(0.985)	(3.601)	(1.207)	(0.561)
CAP	+0.909	-0.187*	-0.043	-0.557	-0.042***	0.005
	(0.393)	(1.633)	(1.125)	(0.955)	(3.024)	(0.120)
POL	-0.055	0.035	0.017	-0.877	-0.019	0.005
	(0.121)	(0.125)	(0.175)	(-0.596)	(0.546)	(0.146)
CR	0.543**	-0.015	0.062*	2.385***	-0.070	-0.101**
	(1.921)	(0.098)	(1.243)	(3.020)	(0.360)	(1.856)
GRO	0.226*	0.160**	-0.264	0.642**	0.011*	-0.013
	(1.513)	(1.950)	(0.794)	(1.981)	(1.454)	(0.465)
$\bar{R}^2$	0.202	0.272	0.124	0.341	0.303	0.297
Entry forestalling profits	3.23	-6.82	3.30	1.43	3.40 ⟨?⟩	-7.95
Mean profit rate	9.80					
Mean of entry measure	25.62	51.05	0.74	-15.57	7.22	12.74

t-ratios are in parentheses; ⟨?⟩ indicates an uncertain estimate of Π^f.

* Significant at the 10 per cent level.

** Significant at the 5 per cent level.

*** Significant at the 1 percent level.

entire business cycle, table 8.5 is for the expansion, and table 8.6 is for the contraction. For each measure and time period the mean of the dependent variable is the final line of the table. Two lines from the bottom we report the value of Π^f from each estimate (see equation (8.2)). Since Π^f is only relevant if entry responds positively to profits, the measures are suspect if this is not the case. Accordingly we put a question mark $\langle ? \rangle$ next to each value of Π^f that is based upon an equation which does not have predicted profits as a significant positive determinant of entry.[23] Below the estimates of Π^f we present the mean profit level for the sample period.

The most striking result is the lack of consistency in the results. There is no variable that has a consistent sign for all entry measures and each time period. There is one variable that is almost always consistent: higher expected profits almost always imply greater entry. Indeed, for the full cycle and for the expansion period, the influence of higher expected profits on entry is consistently positive, and is significant in all but two of 12 equations and significant at the 99 percent level for the measures of long-run entrant shares in both periods. For the contraction period the expected profit measure is not significant in five of the equations, and is negative in two of these five. It is possible that it is hard to estimate profits during a contraction by using pre-contraction data – that the measure of expected profits is poor for this period.[24] Alternatively, poor expected profits during the contraction may not be considered to be a good measure of longer-term profitability, and firms are able to project future profits by a superior mechanism. If we discount the contraction period as "atypical," our measure of expected profits seems to be a significant determinant of entry.

This is an important observation. First, it demonstrates that the measure of profits we employ is a measure of profitability that potential entrants feel demonstrates the potential for entrant profitability. Second, it follows that potential entrants do not feel that they are unable to duplicate pre-entry profits. That is, potential entrants neither see these profit measures as "accounting noise" (cf. Fisher and McGowan, 1983) nor as "superiority rents" which cannot be duplicated (cf. Demsetz, 1973). Third, if there are characteristics of an industry which cannot be observed by industry outsiders and if, in the absence of entry-deterring behavior, these are correlated with profits, then this suggests that signaling by the use of reduced realized profitability may be an effective strategic entry deterrent[25] (cf. Milgrom and Roberts, 1982; Matthew and Mirman, 1983).

Given that entry may be influenced by predicted profits, it is relevant to consider what profit rates would deter entry. Estimates of Π^f are

Table 8.5 Entry 1976–1978: economic expansion

	ΔN/N	#New/N	Δ(H⁻¹)/N	Δ(H⁻¹)H	Share, Dec 31, 1979	Share Dec 31, 1981
Constant	−7.511	20.037**	−1.164	−102.146***	2.966*	8.755*
	(0.220)	(2.165)	(1.183)	(3.226)	(1.575)	(1.404)
$(\Pi + rD)/A$	1.153*	1.014**	0.073*	4.001**	0.156**	1.319***
	(1.357)	(1.935)	(0.703)	(1.896)	(1.259)	(2.881)
MES^c	−0.590	−0.147	0.050	−1.111	0.051	−0.051
	(0.556)	(0.584)	(1.020)	(0.116)	(0.883)	(0.236)
ASR	−1.883	−2.214*	−0.453**	−16.885***	−0.353	0.133
	(0.328)	(1.564)	(1.684)	(3.306)	(1.134)	(0.112)
CAP	−0.078	−0.132**	−0.023*	−0.304	−0.042***	0.119**
	(0.231)	(1.688)	(1.503)	(0.986)	(2.341)	(1.733)
POL	−1.442**	0.051	−0.013	−0.583	0.043	−0.056
	(1.697)	(0.280)	(0.341)	(0.754)	(0.917)	(0.323)
CR	0.369	−0.018	0.044**	1.021***	−0.049**	−0.146*
	(0.819)	(0.173)	(2.092)	(2.480)	(1.864)	(1.561)
GRO	0.242*	0.150***	0.017**	0.028	0.042**	0.054**
	(1.313)	(2.648)	(1.505)	(0.104)	(2.571)	(2.088)
$\bar{R}^2$	0.155	0.349	0.216	0.296	0.371	0.307
Entry forestalling profits	2.12	−4.30	−0.19 ⟨?⟩	0.04	−3.20	−0.79
Mean profit rate	11.90					
Mean of entry measure	11.02	33.09	0.02	−7.78	4.01	15.81

t-ratios are in parentheses; ⟨?⟩ indicates an uncertain estimate of Π^f.
* Significant at the 10 per cent level.
** Significant at the 5 per cent level.
*** Significant at the 1 percent level.

Table 8.6 Entry 1979–1981: economic contraction

	$\Delta N/N$	#New/N	$\Delta(H^{-1})/N$	$\Delta(H^{-1})H$	Share, Dec 31, 1981	Share Dec 31, 1984
Constant	−19.593*	19.938***	−0.452	−21.844*	3.535**	14.692***
	(1.371)	(3.043)	(0.230)	(1.439)	(2.170)	(3.499)
$(\Pi + rD)/A$	1.986**	0.348	−0.015	0.287	−0.073	0.231
	(1.835)	(0.784)	(0.105)	(0.273)	(0.647)	(0.750)
MES^c	−0.298	−0.009	0.102*	0.343	−0.011	−0.228*
	(0.472)	(0.042)	(1.435)	(0.686)	(0.197)	(1.565)
ASR	−7.379***	−0.417	−0.240	−5.727**	−0.133	0.052
	(2.570)	(0.379)	(0.612)	(2.010)	(0.454)	(0.699)
CAP	−0.017	−0.096**	−0.022	−0.211*	−0.034**	−0.071*
	(0.097)	(1.489)	(1.004)	(1.338)	(2.001)	(1.542)
POL	−0.505*	0.174	0.026	−0.144	−0.001	0.013
	(1.383)	(1.067)	(0.046)	(−0.362)	(0.026)	(0.109)
CR	0.239	−0.015	0.005	0.387**	0.009	−0.071
	(1.098)	(0.162)	(0.166)	(1.813)	(0.401)	(1.133)
GRO	0.170*	0.051*	0.020*	0.144*	0.017**	−0.025
	(1.524)	(1.473)	(1.246)	(1.647)	(1.845)	(0.758)
$\bar{R}^2$	0.212	0.140	0.089	0.172	0.162	0.332
Entry forestalling profits	−8.20	−13.20 ⟨?⟩	0.69 ⟨na⟩	−6.43 ⟨?⟩	2.50 ⟨na⟩	−32.93 ⟨?⟩
Mean profit rate	5.80					
Mean of entry measure	15.80	26.94	0.86	2.08	9.41	10.70

t-ratios are in parentheses; ⟨?⟩ indicates an uncertain estimate of Π^f; ⟨na⟩ means not applicable, entry falling with profits.

* Significant at the 10 per cent level.

** Significant at the 5 per cent level.

*** Significant at the 1 percent level.

consistently less than the opportunity cost of capital. The profit measure is accounting profits plus cost of debt, so that if these do not exceed the opportunity cost of capital (weighted average of debt and equity) then economic profits are not being earned. The highest estimate of Π^f is 3.4 percent, which is lower than the lending rates for most government-subsidized loans. Suppose that we accept profits as a signal that may deter entry. Then even if we were to accept the highest estimate of Π^f as the true estimate, clearly the only way to deter *all* entry would be for incumbents to earn well below the opportunity cost of capital (which is not surprising given the explosive growth rates).

We next turn to the influence of entry barriers. First note that all signs (each barrier and each sample period) are, as expected for barriers, negative in the numbers measures of entry $\Delta N/N$ and $\#New/N$. In each case, the measure of the barrier for one of the equations is significantly negative. Turning to the Herfindahl-based measures $\Delta(H^{-1})/N$ and $\Delta(H^{-1})H$, we find that MES is sometimes positive and only ASR develops much negative significance. These results may reflect the fact that intra-industry mobility is more important than entry in this measure.[26] The means of the entry estimates suggest that this is true. The mean for the measure $(\Delta H^{-1})H$ is even negative for the full cycle and the expansion.[27] ASR may act as a mobility barrier, but if a new plant is not needed to re-position products within an industry, MES may not be an important mobility barrier. Finally, there are the two share measures, the "impact" share and the "mature" share. There is no sign consistency here. It appears that the influences on impact share and on mature share are different. For example, ASR is negative and insignificant in the impact share equations and positive and insignificant in the mature share equations; CAP for the expansion period is negative and significant in the impact share equation and positive and significant in the mature share equation. Factors that may deter entry or slow initial penetration may be overcome with time, or the measures and significance may not mean much.

The variable meant to capture government policy, the fraction of subsidized loans, did not explain much. It is generally insignificant and of indeterminate sign. The only mildly interesting result is in the $\Delta N/N$ equations. It is positive in the expansion and negative in the contraction. This could reflect a belief that loans would be forthcoming after entry during the expansion, and a belief that the government's primary focus during the contraction would be on protecting incumbents.[28] Equally plausible is that these loans reduced disappearance during the expansion period (this is supported at the 90 percent level in the section on disappearance) and that during the contraction the loans were insufficient to keep afloat firms that were only present because of subsidies (POL is positively, but insignificantly, related to disappearance during the contraction). The lack of a pattern on the other entry measures suggests that there is little evidence that POL actually influences entry rates.

The influence of concentration on entry is also mixed. CR is positive (and significant for the full cycle) in the numbers measure $\Delta N/N$, but negative for #New/N. CR was positive and highly significant for $\Delta(H^{-1})H$, but a measurement bias due to the correlation between CR and H might have been the cause. This can be discounted by looking at the results of the $\Delta(H^{-1})/N$ alternative. CR is still positive albeit somewhat less significant (and is insignificant for the contraction). In contrast, CR is generally negative for entry shares. It is negative and significant for both the impact and mature share in the expansion period and for the mature share for the full cycle.[29]

The implications of the fact that CR is positive and significant for $\Delta N/N$ and negative and insignificant ($t < 0.20$) for #New/N, implies that the influence of CR is not on entry of new firms but in the reduced disappearance of firms with high CR. This will be confirmed later in the examination of the DIS equations.

Finally we have the influence of past growth on entry. This performs as intuition would suggest for the numbers measures, but is lessened in the other measures.[30]

Results across entry measures are not robust, with the exception that profits appear to attract entry and that Π^f is low. That profits attract measured entry is perhaps some indication that our measures of entry are reasonable. The fact that there is entry with negative economic profits is not surprising in an economy that is growing explosively. Present values may be high, and accrue primarily to tomorrow's incumbents rather than tomorrow's entrants.

Other mixed results may reflect the fact that the proxies are poor, either generally or for Korea. For example, even if there are high barriers to entry in the Korean domestic markets, a firm might enter primarily for exports. There is also the possibility that our market definitions are too wide; entry may be occurring into well-defined submarkets that we did not define. To obtain some idea about the validity of our entry measures as measures of emerging competition, we look at the influence of entry on profits.

158   K.-Y. Jeong and R.T. Masson

4 A Validation Test: Does Entry Affect Profits?

In this section we examine the determinants of profits. If, for example, concentration CR has a strong influence on profits, we gain confidence in our market definitions. The results suggest that the markets are reasonably defined, as concentration is consistently significant in predicting profits.[31] They also suggest that $\Delta N/N$ is our best measure of increasing competition/entry.

We estimate profit equations as linear in the same factors affecting entry (dropping predicted profits). We also add ENTRY and two more variables. These are EXS (exports divided by domestic sales) and IMS (imports divided by domestic sales).

The results of the profit equation estimates are presented in tables 8.7, 8.8, and 8.9 for the full cycle, expansion, and contraction. Each equa-

Table 8.7 Profits 1977–1981: full business cycle

Definition of ENTRY	$\Delta N/N$	#New/N	$\Delta(H^{-1})/N$	$\Delta(H^{-1})H$	Share, Dec 31, 1981
Constant	−4.823***	5.465***	4.799***	4.700***	4.800***
	(5.681)	(5.800)	(5.478)	(5.012)	(5.114)
ENTRY	−0.011**	−0.011*	−0.034	−0.002	0.044
	(1.664)	(1.306)	(0.894)	(0.671)	(0.401)
CR	0.061***	0.056***	0.055***	0.057***	0.053***
	(4.280)	(4.078)	(3.975)	(3.797)	(3.874)
MES^c	−0.026	−0.019	−0.013	−0.016	−0.012
	(0.752)	(0.552)	(0.386)	(0.453)	(0.354)
ASR	0.690***	0.700***	0.733***	0.701***	0.764***
	(3.518)	(3.529)	(3.720)	(3.319)	(3.839)
CAP	−0.032***	−0.033**	−0.030***	−0.030***	−0.028***
	(3.011)	(3.037)	(2.826)	(2.826)	(2.822)
GRO	0.044***	0.044***	0.044***	0.044***	0.040***
	(2.912)	(2.833)	(2.829)	(2.796)	(2.449)
EXS	−0.006	−0.004	−0.007	−0.007	−0.007***
	(0.453)	(0.291)	(0.569)	(0.506)	(0.550)
IMS	−0.027**	−0.028***	−0.025**	−0.026**	−0.025**
	(0.324)	(2.391)	(2.112)	(2.206)	(2.092)
$\bar{R}^2$	0.605	0.598	0.591	0.588	0.586

t-ratios in parentheses.
*   Significant at the 10 per cent level.
**   Significant at the 5 per cent level.
*** Significant at the 1 percent level.

Table 8.8 Profits 1976–1978: economic expansion

Definition of ENTRY	$\Delta N/N$	#New/N	$\Delta(H^{-1})/N$	$\Delta(H^{-1})H$	Share, Dec 31, 1979
Constant	5.339***	5.433***	5.208***	5.378***	5.448***
	(6.999)	(6.882)	(6.686)	(6.830)	(6.559)
ENTRY	−0.004*	−0.008	−0.028	0.005	−0.048
	(1.432)	(0.850)	(0.318)	(0.638)	(0.656)
CR	0.038***	0.040***	0.040***	0.037***	0.038***
	(3.073)	(3.170)	(3.057)	(2.872)	(2.999)
MES^c	0.066**	0.066**	0.069**	0.066**	0.069**
	(2.086)	(2.106)	(2.191)	(2.101)	(2.207)
ASR	0.648***	0.631***	0.637***	0.673***	0.629***
	(3.576)	(3.448)	(3.417)	(3.614)	(3.408)
CAP	−0.027***	−0.029***	−0.027***	−0.026***	−0.029***
	(2.862)	(2.942)	(2.819)	(2.640)	(2.866)
GRO	0.039***	0.040***	0.037***	0.036***	0.039***
	(3.965)	(3.881)	(3.791)	(3.696)	(3.830)
EXS	0.004	0.004	0.002	0.002	0.003
	(0.333)	(0.314)	(0.171)	(0.125)	(0.226)
IMS	−0.022**	−0.022**	−0.020**	−0.021**	−0.021**
	(2.128)	(2.122)	(1.947)	(2.012)	(1.011)
$\bar{R}^2$	0.609	0.606	0.602	0.604	0.604

t-ratios in parentheses.
*   Significant at the 10 per cent level.
**   Significant at the 5 per cent level.
*** Significant at the 1 percent level.

tion is comparable with one in tables 8.4, 8.5, or 8.6 (e.g. the results for $\Delta N/N$ in table 8.4 are comparable with those for $\Delta N/N$ in table 8.7). No comparable equation is shown for "mature" share, as it is hard to see exactly how the share attained in the future should impact on current profits.[32] The entry measures listed across the top of each table are not the dependent variables, as in tables 8.4–8.6 but rather are the definition used for the independent variable ENTRY in that column's regression.

The results are consistent regarding most of the variables other than ENTRY. Concentration and growth are both positive and significant at the 99 percent level in each equation. (Note that the consistency within a table is not surprising; all variables except the independent variable ENTRY are invariant between regressions.) The consistency across time periods is interesting. Also of interest is that advertising is positive and significant and the capital variable is negative and significant in

K.-Y. Jeong and R.T. Masson

Table 8.9 Profits 1979–1981: economic contraction

Definition of ENTRY	ΔN/N	#New/N	$\Delta(H^{-1})/N$	$\Delta(H^{-1})H$	Share, Dec 31, 1979
Constant	3.847***	3.808***	3.718***	3.806***	3.749***
	(3.871)	(3.178)	(3.837)	(3.764)	(3.539)
ENTRY	−0.005	−0.001	−0.110	0.001	0.009
	(1.012)	(0.041)	(1.275)	(0.107)	(0.080)
CR	0.091***	0.093***	0.093***	0.092***	0.092***
	(4.916)	(5.021)	(5.167)	(4.877)	(5.034)
MES^c	−0.086*	−0.085*	−0.083*	−0.085*	−0.084*
	(1.597)	(1.570)	(1.560)	(1.577)	(1.536)
ASR	0.542**	0.519**	0.513**	0.527**	0.523**
	(1.999)	(1.905)	(1.950)	(1.940)	(1.954)
CAP	−0.031**	−0.032**	−0.033**	−0.032**	−0.032**
	(2.150)	(2.121)	(2.336)	(2.180)	(2.177)
GRO	0.031***	0.031***	0.033***	0.031***	0.031***
	(3.078)	(3.109)	(3.322)	(3.075)	(3.005)
EXS	−0.012	−0.010	−0.009	−0.011	−0.010
	(0.672)	(0.552)	(0.531)	(0.605)	(0.595)
IMS	−0.041***	−0.041***	−0.039***	−0.040***	−0.040***
	(2.736)	(2.643)	(2.675)	(2.704)	(2.680)
$\bar{R}^2$	0.521	0.519	0.533	0.519	0.519

t-ratios in parentheses.
*   Significant at the 10 per cent level.
**   Significant at the 5 per cent level.
*** Significant at the 1 percent level.

every specification. Imports are almost always negative and significant and MES seems to be positive in the expansion and negative in the contraction.

The strength of the concentration (growth and advertising) variables leads us to believe that we have at least reasonably defined our industries. Large capital expenses depress industry profits and do not act as would a barrier in a limit-pricing model.[33] But given that Π^f is very low in Korea, limit pricing may not be privately optimal (cf. Jeong and Masson, 1989).

Given the general appearance of validation of the data set, we turn to the entry measures. Do any of our measures appear to capture the concept of increasing competition? The answer seems to be yes, yet most of the entry measures present no evidence of indicating increased competition.

Our initial specification (cf. Jeong, 1985; Jeong and Masson, 1990) of $\Delta N/N$ seems to be a useful measure of increasing competition. Its influence is negative and highly significant for the full cycle, negative and somewhat significant for the expansion, and negative for the contraction as well. With the exception of #New/N, which is somewhat significant for the full cycle, there is no other measure that is significant in its influence on profits. An explanation for this seems, *ex post*, to be that net entry is best measured by this variable. Note that the share measure only captures gross entry, as does #New/N. The Herfindahl measures capture not only net entry, but also movements of incumbents' relative shares. The variable $\Delta N/N$ may be the "cleanest" measure of the net effect of entry and exit in our data, and hence the best measure of increasing competition/entry.

This is the "best" measure in our data set. However, this does not mean that it would be the best measure elsewhere. In the other studies in this volume the number of new entrants is about equal to the number of exits: turnover is high, and net entry is low. In our data, net entry is large: new entry is significantly greater than exit. In terms of the signal-to-noise ratio, $\Delta N/N$ may be a better measure of entry for an economy like Korea, than for a more mature economy. An "ideal" measure might instead be one that looks at entrant shares net of the prior period shares of the exits. Without such data, we remain agnostic, especially given the fact that the "correct" measure of entry depends upon the purposes of the measure. The correct measure of a human body may be height, breadth, weight, or some other measure, depending upon goals (boxers, jockeys, beautry queens). All our measures may be appropriate measures of entry, but $\Delta N/N$ may be the best measure of competitive effects, at least when net entry is large relative to turnover. We conclude after a brief description of the determinants of firm disappearance.

5 Firm Disappearance

Firm disappearance should primarily reflect exit/failure, as discussed above. Disappearance is defined as DIS $\equiv$ (#New/N) $-$ ($\Delta N/N$). We estimate DIS as we did the entry equations: the results are given in table 8.10.

Concentration CR is negative in each equation and significant for the full cycle and the expansion period. As noted above, this suggests that the influence of CR on net entry is operating through its effects on DIS and not through entry. As expected, growth GRO retains firms in the industry: GRO is negative for all periods and significant for expansion and contraction results. Advertising intensity ASR is positive and highly

Table 8.10 Estimation of disappearance DIS

	1977–81	*Expansion*	*Contraction*
Constant	56.265***	10.799	39.454***
	(3.693)	(0.555)	(2.898)
$(\Pi + rD)/A$	0.092	−0.326	−0.996
	(0.081)	(0.229)	(0.997)
MES^c	0.535	0.235	−0.384
	(0.996)	(0.350)	(0.814)
ASR	1.979	−4.310	6.303***
	(0.667)	(1.160)	(2.420)
CAP	−0.121	−0.233	−0.011
	(0.708)	(1.091)	(0.071)
POL	0.282	−0.811*	0.439
	(0.657)	(1.507)	(1.166)
CR	−0.519**	−0.465*	−0.215
	(2.233)	(1.595)	(1.053)
GRO	−0.020	−0.321**	−0.150*
	(0.166)	(2.080)	(1.392)
$\bar{R}^2$	0.157	0.173	0.197

t-ratios in parentheses.
* Significant at the 10 per cent level.
** Significant at the 5 per cent level.
*** Significant at the 1 percent level.

significant for contraction, yet negative and insignificant for expansion.[34] Interestingly, predicted profits are insignificant: they are negative for both the expansion and contraction periods, and positive for the full cycle.[35]

Care must be taken in drawing conclusions, especially with no *a priori* hypotheses. The negative effect of CR may indicate that high concentration industries maintain a profit umbrella – high prices retain less efficient firms – implying that the profit variable is not a perfect measure of viability.

6 Conclusions

The "correct" measure of entry is an illusive, if not meaningless, concept. What would be the correct measure of any multifaceted phenomenon. Each of our entry measures captures a different facet of entry. As the correlation matrix suggests, these measures may be interrelated, but are distinct. The measure that works best in terms of our prior expectations is $\Delta N/N$, our initial measure for testing our *a priori* hypotheses. As Bayesians we place our highest confidence on these results.

This does not mean this is the best measure elsewhere. Indeed, this "comparisons" volume seems to indicate that turnover is the primary phenomenon related to entry in more mature economies. If turnover had an expected value of zero, "entry," gross or net, would tend to be nonzero and yet meaningless in terms of the traditional "entry-deterrence" paradigms. Since turnover is less in our sample, i.e. entry dominates disappearance, our signal-to-noise ratio may be much improved. If this is the case, a crude measure of net entrant numbers may be a good measure of the effect of entry on competition. For more mature economies, some measure that weights the significance of the entrants' (shares) and takes into account the (previous time period) shares of those they replace/displace may be needed.

It is clear that the results for our explosively growing economy are different from others in this volume. The most significant of our results are (a) entry responds to profits (as in other studies) and (b) profits decline with entry (seldom studied elsewhere).

Notes

1 There was no problem of censoring. Owing in part to growth, there were virtually no "limit observations" (i.e. zero entry) for any entry measure, and so Tobit was not indicated.

2 No data on sunk cost measures were available and so we were unable to attempt a test of the type used in chapter 2. R&D data for examining innovation in entry (cf. chapter 12) were unavailable or questionable for most of the sample in the study period. Higher-power terms, such as growth squared as used in chapter 10, also added little to the model, with no significant changes in the other variables included.

3 In Bain's theory entry is seen as distinct from exit, yet according to Gaskins (1971) zero entry is part of a continuum between entry and exit. The fact that there is considerable turnover in the data does not mean that Bain's view is incorrect. Much of the turnover in numbers of firms in the automobile sector seems to be due to specialty cars such as racing cars, hand-built cars, or special purpose cars (e.g. dune buggies). Bain would not have considered these as entry or exit in the United States unless they were truly comparable with the "big three," as in the case of the penetration of Volkswagen and later Datsun, Toyota, and Hyundai. These entrants would not be counted in US Census data as entry unless (or until) a domestic plant were constructed.

4 For example, "not elsewhere classified" (n.e.c.) and "not specified by kind" (n.s.k.).

5 The full cycle does not start in the same year as the expansion period because of unavailability of data. Real gross national product (GNP) growth rates for the years 1975–82 were 6.8 percent, 13.4 percent, 11.7 percent, 11.0 percent, 7.0 percent, − 4.8 percent, 5.9 percent, and 9.0 percent.

6 The data on profits are taken from annual issues of the *Financial Statement Analysis* published by Bank of Korea, and the *Analysis of Financial Data* published by the Korea Development Bank.

7 The data for MES and CDR are estimated from annual issues of the *Report on Mining and Manufacturing Survey* published by the Economic Planning Board.

8 Most Korean exports were advertised by importers. Data were taken from annual issues of the *Financial Statement Analysis* and *Analysis of Financial Data*.

9 Asset data were taken from the *Financial Statement Analysis* and *Analysis of Financial Data*.

10 These provide internal capital markets to group members. "Trust" is a problem if creditworthiness is poorly known or contracts are not easily enforceable. This leads to internal credit markets based upon the information, trust, and sanction possibilities associated with families or other personal associations.

11 For example, as of 1988 Hyundai has 33 independent firms using its name and sharing capital resources. Separate firms are in automobiles, shipbuilding, electronics, and construction. They have a trading company, and securities and insurance companies which often serve as the group's financial intermediaries. Although many primary decisions are centralized (e.g. which members can invest from group funds), the firms are otherwise almost completely independent.

12 Data are from unpublished sources and were provided by Bank of Korea and the Korea Development Bank.

13 The Data are from the National Bureau of Statistics of the Korean Economic Planning Board and are published in Jeong (1985).

14 Clearly, Masson and Shaanan (1987) suggests some skepticism about the inclusion of concentration in an entry equation. Concentration may act as a proxy for economies of scale for the firm (MES is a plant measure). It could also act to reflect superiority of leading firms, as in Demsetz (1973). If superiority cannot be copied by insiders, it may well not be copied by outsiders. Either explanation would predict a negative relationship between concentration and entry without having any direct strategic interpretation (as explained below).

15 Recent theoretical models have also suggested that entrants may be "punished" even in markets with large numbers. This work (e.g. Harrington 1989), although intriguing and possibly supported by evidence (Madhavan et al., 1990), does not seem likely to reflect a dominant influence on entry.

16 In place of GRO we also tried the following disaggregated measures: growth of domestic sales, growth of imports, growth of exports. We also added the

square of GRO. No consistent patterns emerged, and the results were no stronger. Results are available from Jeong upon request.

17 For example, for the expansion period this is $100(\#\text{New}_{76} + \#\text{New}_{77} + \#\text{New}_{78})/N_{76}$, where N_{76} is the number at the beginning of 1976). (Note that if a 1976 entrant disappeared in 1977, it would still be part of the numerator.) These data were provided by the National Bureau of Statistics.

18 The data for this measure were obtained from the National Bureau of Statistics and the Korea Development Institute.

19 If $H \equiv \Sigma s_i^2$ and if the s_i distribution is characterized by some density function, then $H = \Sigma (n^{-1} + \epsilon)^2 = n^{-1} + n\sigma^2$. That is, the mean share is n^{-1}, and if we define each share by differences from means, the Herfindahl index is equal to mean share plus n times the variance in shares. If an entrant takes a share equal to e and relative incumbent shares are unaltered at s_i, then $H' = \Sigma[s_i^2(1 - e)^2 + e^2]$. Therefore $\partial H'/\partial e = -2H° + 2eH° + 2e$. This is negative if $e < H°/(1 + H°)$. Substituting the formula expressing shares at means, and assuming zero variance, this is the condition that $e < 1/(n + 1)$, that the entrant does not exceed mean firm size. Further, the right-hand side of the inequality is rising in σ, so that, as the distribution of firm sizes widens, the entrant size can exceed the mean incumbent size and H'. can still locally decrease with greater entry size. (Repeating the same logic for $H' - H°$, we find that a sufficient condition for H to fall with entry (conditioned on incumbent relative shares) is that the entrant not exceed the size of the largest incumbent.)

20 Data from the National Bureau of Statistics.

21 This is not because the proxies fail because of enormous entrant shares. Successful entrants attain long-run shares of 53 percent , 57 percent, or 50 percent of average firm size as measured for the full cycle, expansion, and contraction respectively. This makes them only about 4 percent, 5 percent, or 2 percent of the size of the top three firms for the same measuring periods.

22 As in the US data, there is the potential for spurious disappearance. A firm is measured as in an industry if it has a plant with its primary output in that industry. If this plant's primary output shifts, it will "disappear," even if it is still a major producer of its former primary product. This problem does not appear to be very large in the KSIC data. Firms are not generally very diversified (recall that the *Jaibul* are made up of independent firms).

23 Two estimates with negative signs are labeled ⟨na⟩. These estimates, taken literally, would imply that entry would increase with lower profit rates.

24 In a purely technical sense the first-stage instruments fit well, with an R^2 of 0.56 for contraction and 0.88 for expansion.

25 The fact that something is an effective entry deterrent does not imply that deterrence is optimal (cf. Bain, 1956; Dixit, 1980). Note also that if profitability is determined by an observable entry deterrent (e.g. excess capacity) that is not an included independent variable, then reducing profitability

(rather than increasing excesss capacity) may not be an effective entry deterrent.

26 The Herfindahl index can be thought of as a weighted average of shares, with the weights being shares. Hence if an entrant takes a share of X and a leading firm has a change of share of X, the effect of the leading firm's change on H will be weighted higher.

27 Note that the mean of $(\Delta H^{-1})H$ may be negative while that of $(\Delta H^{-1})/N$ is positive. Both measures are like weighted averages of ΔH^{-1}. $(\Delta H^{-1})H$ weights negative values of ΔH^{-1} relatively more strongly than does $(\Delta H^{-1})/N$.

28 In fact this was the policy during the contraction. One contraction period policy was to restrict entry into some industries; other policies were expanded financial support and organizing capacity reductions.

29 For Canada the sign of CR in $\Delta N/N$ was the opposite of the sign here, and for the United States the sign of CR on shares was the opposite of that shown here. This adds to our skepticism about the role of CR in entry, but may simply reflect the different economy.

30 Growth may attract entry at larger shares of the pre-entry market size, yet if growth spurs incumbent growth, realized entry shares may be lower.

31 If CR had been only weakly related to profits it could have meant poor market definition, poor data, or a poor hypothesis (e.g. the market power hypothesis is incorrect for Korea).

32 As part of the exercise we ran these equations, and the longer-term share was always insignificant.

33 Technically speaking, limit pricing only predicts similar influences of barriers on profits, and not necessarily positive influences. That is, with low barriers, firms may not limit price, but with higher barriers they may. In such cases we would expect that the signs on each barrier would be negative. In our results, the sign on CAP is negative and that on ASR is positive. This would not be predicted in a limit-pricing model. (Cf. Masson and Shaanan (1982) for discussion of signs or Gaskins (1971) for a limit-pricing model in which prices are monotonically decreasing in the level of barriers.)

34 These results may reflect the fact that the business fluctuations strongly affected export consumer goods.

35 Substituting actual profits in the DIS equation leads to negative and marginally significant (10 percent) effects in all three equations.

References

Bain, J.S. (1956) *Barriers to New Competition*. Cambridge, MA: Harvard University Press.

Cable, J.R. (undated) Two measures of market-share mobility and entry (unpublished).

Caves, R.E., Khalilzadeh-Shirazi, J. and Porter, M.E. (1975) Scale economies in statistical analyses of market power. *Review of Economics and Statistics* 57, 133–40.

Demsetz, H. (1973) Industry structure, market rivalry and public policy. *Journal of Law and Economics* 16, 1–9.

Dixit, A. (1980) The role of investment in entry deterrence. *Economic Journal* 90, 95–106.

Fisher, F.M. and McGowan J.J. (1983) On the misuse of accounting rates of return to infer monopoly profits. *American Economic Review* 73, 82–97.

Gaskins, D. (1971) Dynamic limit pricing: optimal pricing under threat of entry. *Journal of Economic Theory* 3, 306–22.

Harrington, J.E. (1989) Collusion and predation under (almost) free entry. *International Journal of Industrial Organization* 7, 381–402.

Jeong, K.-Y. (1985) Market structure and performance in an open developing economy. Ph.D. Dissertation, Cornell University.

Jeong, K.-Y. and Masson, R.T. (1990) Market structure, entry and performance in Korea. *Review of Economics and Statistics*, 72, 455–62.

Madhavan, A.N., Masson, R.T. and Lesser, W.H. (1990) Cooperation for monopolization: an empirical analysis of cartelization (unpublished).

Masson, R.T. and Shaanan, J. (1982) Stochastic-dynamic limit pricing: an empirical test. *Review of Economics and Statistics* 64, 413–22.

Masson, R.T. and Shaanan, J. (1984) Social costs of oligopoly and the value of competition. *Economic Journal* 94, 520–35.

Masson, R. and Shaanan, J. (1987) Optimal oligopoly pricing and the threat of entry: Canadian evidence. *International Journal of Industrial Organization* 5, 323–9.

Matthew, S.A. and Mirman, L.J. (1983) Equilibrium limit pricing: the effects of private information and stochastic demand. *Econometrica* 51, 981–96.

Milgrom, P. and Roberts, J. (1982) Limit pricing and entry under incomplete information: an equilibrium analysis. *Econometrica* 50, 443–59.

Orr, D. (1974) The determinants of entry: a study of Canadian manufacturing industries. *Review of Economics and Statistics* 56, 58–66.

9

The Effects of Business Conditions on Net Entry: Evidence from Japan

Hideki Yamawaki

1 Introduction

In this paper we explore the response of entry and exit of firms to demand fluctuations and cyclical business conditions. In particular, we show using panel data for Japanese manufacturing industries, that the extent of net entry fluctuates over business cycles and varies across industries.

Previous empirical work on entry has made significant contributions to identifying long-run tendencies of entry and its associations with various elements of market structure in cross sections of industries (e.g. Orr, 1974; Deutsch, 1975; Gorecki 1975, 1976; Iwasaki, 1976; Hilke, 1984; Kessides, 1986; MacDonald, 1986; Baldwin and Gorecki, 1987; Highfield and Smiley, 1987; Schwalbach, 1987; Shapiro and Khemani, 1987). More recent empirical studies have extended this traditional work to incorporate some dynamic aspects of entry through the use of longitudinal and panel data (e.g. Hause and Du Rietz, 1984; Masson and Shaanan, 1986; Highfield and Smiley, 1987; Lieberman, 1987a, b; Dunne et al., 1988a, b; Geroski, 1988, 1989a, b).

Despite these recent developments in empirical work on entry that stress the dynamics of entry and thus the distinction between short-run responses and long-run patterns surprisingly little is known about the response of entry to cyclical demand and business fluctuations. While entry is typically an investment behavior that involves long-run deci-

I am grateful to David B. Audretsch, Richard E. Caves, Paul A. Geroski, Stephen Martin, Hiroyuki Odagiri, and Joachim Schwalbach as well as to the participants at the Conference of Entry and Market Contestability in West Berlin, November 3–4, 1989, for their helpful comments. I thank Andrea Barth for computational assistance. Any remaining errors are, of course, my own.

sions, the timing of entry may be sensitive to cyclical disturbances. If entry decisions respond to short-run disturbances, it is important and worthwhile for public policy to evaluate the sensitivity of such short-run responses.

The only existing study that has examined the relationship between cyclical business conditions and the degree of entry is that of High-field and Smiley (1987). Using aggregate time series data, they found that lower rates of gross national product (GNP) growth, lower inflation rates, and greater growth in the unemployment rate preceded increases in the growth rate of new US incorporations. However, their aggregate macro data did not enable them to control for industry-specific factors.

In the empirical analysis in this paper we control for industry characteristics as well as aggregate demand fluctuations to explain the intertemporal variation of entry in a cross section of industries. Thus a panel data base covering 135 Japanese industries between 1979 and 1984 has been constructed to determine whether entry responds to cyclical business conditions and if its response systematically varies among industries with different industry characteristics.

The paper is organized as follows. In section 2 we describe the data set and show the distinctive net entry pattern in Japanese manufacturing. In section 3 we explain the statistical model and presents the results of the estimation. The pooled cross-section time series regression shows that both industry demand fluctuations and aggregate macro demand fluctuations have a procyclical impact on net entry. Other macro variables such as the price of investment goods and the rate of discount also show significant effects on net entry. The regression also suggests that the response of net entry to business fluctuations depends on industry characteristics and thus market structure. Finally, in section 4, a summary and conclusion are provided.

2 Patterns of Net Entry in Japanese Manufacturing

2.1 Descriptive Statistics

Data on entry in Japanese manufacturing industries were obtained from the *Census of Manufacturers: Report by Enterprises* (Ministry of International Trade and Industry). The degree of entry that is measured from this data source is the net change in the number of firms in an industry. While this measure of entry is limited because it does not distinguish between gross entry and exit, at present this is the only obtainable source concerning entry in Japanese manufacturing industries. The Japanese census publishes annually the number of firms in each of the 143 three-digit Standard Industrial Classification (SIC) industries. We selected 135 out of these 143 industries for which data are continuously available over the peroid 1979–84.[1] Thus, the data in the study cover 135 three-digit Japanese manufacturing industries for the period 1979–84.

Table 9.1 presents the descriptive statistics for the net entry data. Net entry is measured as the absolute change $N_t - N_{t-1}$ in the number of firms and the rate of change $(N_t - N_{t-1})/N_{t-1}$ in the number of firms for every consecutive year in the sample period. An interesting pattern that emerges from table 9.1 is that the means for both measures of net entry are not constant over the sample period. Rather, net entry in Japanese manufacturing industries fluctuates from year to year, with the largest amount of net entry occurring in 1980–1 and the smallest amount of net entry in 1981–2.

The second important pattern observed from table 9.1 is that the yearly fluctuation of net entry is likely to be associated with the cyclical movement of aggregate demand conditions. In particular, during the period 1981–2 for which the lowest net entry was observed within the sample period, the rate of real GNP growth was also the lowest in Japan since the 1974–5 recession. As the economy recovered from the recession in the ensuing years, net entry also increased in the periods 1982–3 and 1983–4. Thus a plausible conjecture for the time series pattern of net entry in Japanese manufacturing industries is that net entry responds to fluctuations in business conditions. This time series characteristic of net entry will be examined further using a statistical model.

Table 9.2 presents the cross-section pattern of net entry at the two-

Table 9.1 Descriptive statistics for net entry variables ($N = 135$)

Variable	Mean	Standard deviation	Minimum	Maximum
$N_{80} - N_{79}$	4.47	36.63	−85	248
$N_{81} - N_{80}$	20.90	64.36	−274	286
$N_{82} - N_{81}$	1.37	36.54	−198	164
$N_{83} - N_{82}$	9.55	53.34	−139	329
$N_{84} - N_{83}$	13.20	61.79	−113	463
$(N_{80} - N_{79})/N_{79}$	0.006	0.083	−0.226	0.500
$(N_{81} - N_{80})/N_{80}$	0.031	0.107	−0.333	0.800
$(N_{82} - N_{81})/N_{81}$	−0.007	0.090	−0.357	0.500
$(N_{83} - N_{82})/N_{82}$	0.007	0.068	−0.158	0.322
$(N_{84} - N_{83})/N_{83}$	0.010	0.082	−0.250	0.337

N is the number of firms in the three-digit industry and the subscript denotes the year.

Table 9.2 Net entry rate by two-digit Japanese industry, 1980–1984

Industry	$(N_{80} - N_{79})/N_{79}$	$(N_{81} - N_{80})/N_{80}$	$(N_{82} - N_{81})/N_{81}$	$(N_{83} - N_{82})/N_{82}$	$(N_{84} - N_{83})/N_{83}$
Food and kindred products	0.010	0.053	0.025	0.013	0.008
Textile mill products	-0.034	-0.007	-0.010	-0.015	-0.019
Apparel and other textile products	-0.002	0.046	0.028	-0.018	0.019
Lumber and wood products	-0.040	-0.094	-0.076	-0.060	-0.051
Furniture and fixtures	-0.029	-0.018	0.011	-0.038	-0.054
Pulp, paper, and allied products	-0.020	0.019	-0.013	0.029	0.018
Publishing and printing	0.009	0.057	0.023	0.016	0.011
Chemicals and allied products	0.020	0.006	0.022	0.011	0.012
Petroleum and coal products	-0.006	0.006	0.050	-0.042	-0.019
Rubber products	0.037	0.081	-0.006	0.050	0.007
Leather and leather products	-0.035	0.040	-0.056	-0.045	-0.015
Stone, clay, and glass products	-0.002	0.000	-0.009	-0.015	-0.027
Iron and steel	0.006	-0.024	-0.048	-0.006	0.008
Nonferrous metals	-0.026	0.016	-0.022	0.005	0.024
Fabricated metal products	0.006	0.037	-0.002	0.007	0.010
Machinery, except electrical	0.028	0.039	0.013	0.022	0.039
Electric and electronic equipment	0.060	0.124	0.027	0.099	0.106
Transportation equipment	0.037	0.052	-0.019	-0.002	0.043
Precision instruments	0.069	0.049	-0.069	0.023	0.004
Ordinance	0.000	0.000	0.000	0.200	0.333
Miscellaneous manufacturing industries	-0.007	0.053	0.006	0.054	0.048

N_t designates the number of firms in year t.

digit SIC level of Japanese manufacturing industry for each consecutive year within the sample period. The first observation that emerges from table 9.2 is the rate of net entry varies across industries for any observation year. For example, the rate of net entry tends to be positive and large for electric and electronic equipment and machinery, whereas it tends to be negative and small for textile and wood products. The second observation, which is more interesting and relevant to the analysis of this paper, is that the rate of net entry is not constant year by year in each industry, and its time series variation differs among industries. Thus the inter-temporal pattern of net entry seems to be influenced by industry-specific factors as well. Industries such as electric and electronic equipment, machinery, food and chemicals have positive net entry rates over the whole observation period, while industries such as textiles and wood products show consistent negative net entry rates over time. The net entry rates for other industries in table 9.2 alternate between positive and negative values over the observation years.

Therefore the findings from tables 9.1 and 9.2 indicate that the combined entry and exit behavior, or net entry, in Japanese manufacturing industries over the observation period fluctuates over time and also differs across industries. To examine this point further, table 9.3 lists the 15 Japanese industries with the largest extent of net entry in the sample for each of the five observation years. Net entry in the table is defined by the absolute change in the number of firms. Table 9.3 shows that the extent of net entry differs both across industries and over time. Some interesting examples will serve to indicate this pattern.

Communications equipment showed the largest net entry in the periods 1979–80 and 1980–1, but after these years net entry started to decline. This industry disappeared from the list of the top 15 net entry industries by 1983–4. Watches and clocks showed a more drastic pattern. This industry had 69 net entries in 1979–80 and was listed as the ninth largest in table 9.3. The industry's net entry declined after this year, reaching 1 in 1980–1, -58 in 1981–2, and -4 in 1982–3. Thus, by 1984, the watches and clocks industry had moved from the top 15 to the bottom 15 in the sample of industries.

In contrast, net entry in electronic components has constantly increased over time from 136 in 1979–80 to 463 in 1983–4, although it dropped to 35 in 1981–2. Other industries that stayed in the list over the sample period include electronic equipment and electrical industrial apparatus. Metalworking machinery, food products, and plastic products also show positive net entry throughout most of the sample period. While the extent of net entry in these industries indicates the long-run tendency for the flow of entrants to exceed the flow of exits, it has

Table 9.3 The industries with the largest amount of net entry (net entry in parentheses)

Rank	$N_{80} - N_{79}$	$N_{81} - N_{80}$	$N_{82} - N_{81}$	$N_{83} - N_{82}$	$N_{84} - N_{83}$
1	Communication equipment (248)	Communication equipment (286)	Electronic equipment (164)	Electronic components (329)	Electronic components (463)
2	Electronic components (136)	Electronic components (256)	Miscellaneous food products (150)	Plastic products (283)	Electronic equipment (263)
3	Motor vehicles (97)	Miscellaneous food products (223)	Electrical industrial appliances (108)	Electronic equipment (235)	Plastic products (222)
4	General machinery (96)	Plastic products (217)	Outer garments (97)	Electrical industrial appliances (167)	Electrical industrial appliances (210)
5	Electronic equipment (97)	Electronic equipment (210)	Miscellaneous machinery (90)	Miscellaneous machinery (110)	Motor vehicles (183)
6	Metal services (81)	Electrical industrial appliances (205)	Seafood products (73)	Miscellaneous food products (91)	Metal services (124)
7	Miscellaneous food products (76)	Outer garments (193)	Printing (50)	Office machinery (82)	Miscellaneous machinery (119)
8	Metalworking machinery (73)	Motor vehicles (151)	Plastic products (50)	Communication equipment (78)	Miscellaneous electrical machinery (90)
9	Watches and clocks (69)	Seafood products (142)	Electrical household appliances (39)	Metalworking machinery (72)	Metalworking machinery (90)

Table 9.3 Continued

Rank	$N_{80} - N_{79}$	$N_{81} - N_{80}$	$N_{82} - N_{81}$	$N_{83} - N_{82}$	$N_{84} - N_{83}$
10	Miscellaneous machinery (47)	Miscellaneous machinery (132)	Meat and dairy products (38)	Metal services (70)	General industrial machinery (85)
11	Electrical industrial appliances (47)	Printing (120)	Electronic components (35)	Electrical household appliances (67)	Electrical household appliances (75)
12	Printing (42)	Metalworking machinery (107)	Underwear (34)	Miscellaneous electrical equipment (65)	Outer garments (70)
13	Optical instruments (39)	Metal services (105)	Communication equipment (31)	Paper containers (47)	Paper containers (57)
14	Rubber belting (37)	Structural metal products (99)	Bakery products (30)	Printing (42)	Miscellaneous food products (46)
15	Miscellaneous iron and steel (31)	Cement (87)	Special industrial machinery (29)	Miscellaneous chemical products (38)	Electrical measuring instruments (46)

certainly fluctuated over time. These findings thus suggest that the inter-industry variation in net entry is not constant year by year, and the time-series variation in net entry varies among industries.

2.2 *Net Entry and Cyclical Disturbances*

To explore the effects of cyclical disturbances on the inter-industry variation of net entry, a simple cross-section model of net entry that uses an approach analogous to the model developed by Orr (1974) is estimated for each year between 1980 and 1984. The model is specified as

$$RN_i = a_0 + a_1 GR3_i + a_2 PCM_i + a_3 KS_i + a_4 AVPSZ_i$$
$$+ a_5 ADSL_i + e_i \qquad (9.1)$$

where e is the disturbance term and i denotes industry, $i = 1,\ldots,135$. The variables in equation (9.1) are defined as follows:

$$RN = \frac{N_t - N_{t-1}}{N_{t-1}}$$

is the annual rate of change in the number of firms N; PCM is value added minus total labor costs divided by the value of shipments and is equal to the industry price–cost margin;

$$GR3 = \frac{VSHIP_t - VSHIP_{t-3}}{VSHIP_{t-3}}$$

is the rate of growth of industry shipments VSHIP over the prior 3 year period; KS are gross fixed assets divided by the value of shipments; AVPSZ is the value added divided by the number of establishments (in logarithms); ADSL is the purchased advertising divided by the total output. All the variables except ADSL are constructed for each observation year. Because of the unavailability of data, ADSL is measured for 1980 and repeated for every year in the sample. The sources of these variables are reported in detail in the appendix.

In equation (9.1), industry growth GR3 and price–cost margin PCM are the factors that induce entry, and their cofficients are expected to be positive. In contrast, we might expect negative coefficients for capital intensity KS, average plant size AVPSZ, and advertising intensity ADSL when the variables are interpreted as surrogates for entry barriers. Barriers to entry would be higher for the industry with high capital intensity if the sunkness of investment costs increases with the industry's capital intensity. Average plant size and advertising intensity may

H. Yamawaki

represent entry barriers associated with economies of scale and product differentiation respectively.

The ordinary least squares (OLS) estimation result of equation (9.1) is presented for each observation year in table 9.4. The most important result that emerges from table 9.4 is that the estimated coefficients for the independent variables are quite unstable over the observation periods. In particular, the coefficients for PCM, KS, AVPSZ, and ADSL change their signs and are not constant year by year. The coefficient for KS takes a negative sign for 1980–1, 1981–2, and 1983–4, but has a positive sign for 1979–80 and 1982–3. Similarly, the coefficient for AVPSZ is negative for 1980–1, 1981–2, and 1982–3, whereas it is positive for the rest of the observation periods. The coefficient for ADSL is negative only for 1980–1 and 1981–2. Reflecting this instability, the overall fit of the regression also varies across different observation years between the highest adjusted R^2 (0.38) for 1980–1 and the lowest adjusted R^2 (0.01) for 1979–80. Thus the cross-section relationship between the rate of net entry and the market structural variables estimated in the Orr-type model is inter-temporarily unstable for Japanese manufacturing industries.

The second important finding from table 9.4 is that the effect of

Table 9.4 Cross-section regression of net entry rate RN, 1980–1984

Independent variable	Dependent variable = net entry rate RN				
	1979–80	1980–1	1981–2	1982–3	1983–4
GR3	0.042	0.247	0.064	0.171	0.139
	(1.213)	(8.484)	(1.720)	(6.685)	(3.992)
PCM	−0.036	0.059	0.184	−0.167	−0.023
	(0.306)	(0.494)	(1.434)	(2.072)	(0.202)
KS	0.069	−0.307	−0.141	0.216	−0.001
	(0.578)	(3.421)	(1.533)	(3.898)	(0.001)
AVPSZ	0.003	−0.010	−0.013	−0.022	0.009
	(0.235)	(0.581)	(0.750)	(2.143)	(0.686)
ADSL	0.972	−0.055	−1.250	1.424	1.155
	(1.693)	(0.094)	(2.001)	(3.662)	(2.100)
Constant	−0.030	0.022	0.013	0.021	−0.034
	(0.753)	(0.484)	(0.268)	(0.705)	(0.882)
$\bar{R}^2$	0.006	0.382	0.035	0.361	0.181
F	1.173	17.424	1.952	16.016	6.864

Absolute values of t statistics are in parenthesis. Significance levels for one-tailed $t(120)$ are 1 percent = 2.358 and 5 per cent = 1.658. All the equations are estimated by the OLS method.

industry growth on net entry is relatively robust over the observation periods. The coefficient for GR3 is consistently positive over the entire period 1980–4 and significant throughout most of the period, although its size varies across the years. Thus net entry in a Japanese manufacturing industry is strongly determined by its rate of growth.[2]

The strong performance of industry growth, along with the intertemporarily unstable performance of the market structure variables, indicates that the inter-industry pattern of net entry in Japanese manufacturing industry is influenced by demand and other cyclical disturbances. The analysis in the next section examines in detail the role of both aggregate and industry demand fluctuations in the industry's entry and exit processes.

3 Explaining Intertemporal Variation in Net Entry

The purpose of this section is to identify the link between net entry and business conditions that has been suggested in the descriptive analysis of the last section. The question of whether the extent of net entry is sensitive to aggregate and industry demand conditions is examined using a statistical model. This question is of empirical importance because, if entry into an industry responds to cyclical demand fluctuations, competitive pressure is injected into the industry with a cyclical pattern. Then the industry's economic performance may also be dependent on cyclical business conditions.[3] Thus an evaluation of the response of net entry to business conditions is important for public policy.

3.1 Statistical Framework

To address the sensitivity of net entry to cyclical business conditions, three different sources of disturbances are considered here: (a) industry demand fluctuations; (b) aggregate macrofluctuations in demand; (c) fluctuations in macroeconomic variables such as the price of investment goods and the rate of discount.

When a firm enters the market with greenfield plant, it is necessary to make substantial capital investments in production facilities and equipment in addition to investments in auxiliary facilities and intangible assets. The new entrant must build production capacity which can accommodate expected demand and organize distributional activities to promote sales. If the firm chooses to maximize the expected profits accruing from such entry and subsequent investment activities, its entry decision will depend on, among others, the expectation of market demand and the calculation of investment costs. As the theory of firm investment suggests, the firm may choose to enter the market and expand its capacity when the market is expanding and the cost of capital is relatively low.

Thus, to the extent that the factors determining the firm's investment decision also influence its entry decision we may expect that the extent of entry moves over time in a manner analogous to capital investment, and it becomes larger when business conditions are more favorable. Since fewer firms are likely to exit when demand is expanding, the extent of net entry is also expected to be larger in boom periods.

To test this hypothesis that the extent of net entry responds to fluctuations in demand and investment conditions and moves procyclically over time, the following cross-section and time series model of net entry is proposed:

$$RN_{it} = b_0 + b_1\ PCM_{it} + b_2\ GRl_{it} + b_3\ GNPGR_t$$
$$+ b_4\ PINV_t + b_5\ DISC_t + u_{it} \qquad (9.2)$$

where i is the industry, $i = 1, \ldots, 135$, t is the year, $t = 1980, \ldots, 1984$, and u is the disturbance term. RN is the rate of net entry, PCM is the industry price–cost margin, and both variables have been defined in the last section. The rest of the variables in equation (9.2) are defined as follows:

$$GRl = \frac{VSHIP_t - VSHIP_{t-1}}{VSHIP_{t-1}}$$

is the rate of growth of industry shipments VSHIP from the preceding year;

$$GNPGR = \frac{GNP_t - GNP_{t-1}}{GNP_{t-1}}$$

is the rate of growth of real gross national product (GNP) from the preceding year; PINV is the price index of investment goods; DISC is the rate of discount. GRl and GNPGR capture industry demand fluctuations and aggregate macrofluctuation respectively. PINV and DISC are the components of the cost of capital. It is assumed that the firm has rational expectations on these time-dependent variables.

3.2 Statistical Results

The regrsssion results of equation (9.2) are presented in table 9.5. Equations (1) and (2) in table 9.5 assume no industry fixed effects,

Table 9.5 Pooled time series and cross-section regression of net entry (the dependent variable is the net entry rate RN)

Independent variable	(1)	(2)	(3)	(4)	(5)
Constant	−0.007 (1.337)	4.099 (8.995)	–	–	4.009 (9.040)
PCM	0.008 (0.366)	0.039 (1.805)	0.070 (0.733)	0.162 (1.704)	0.024 (1.081)
GR1	0.244 (13.532)	0.327 (18.682)	0.144 (8.443)	0.221 (11.878)	0.320 (18.864)
GNPGR		0.004 (2.115)		0.005 (2.987)	0.005 (2.613)
PINV		−0.041 (8.823)		−0.040 (9.661)	−0.040 (8.842)
DISC		−0.011 (7.447)		−0.008 (6.104)	−0.001 (7.962)
KS					−0.065 (2.924)
ADSL					0.388 (3.210)
R^2	0.220	0.383	0.623	0.696	0.424

Absolute values of *t* statistics are in parenthesis. The number of observations is 675. All the equations are corrected for heteroskedasticity. Equations (9.3) and (9.4) include 134 industry intercept dummies to take into account the industry fixed effects.

while equations (3) and (4) allow for industry fixed effects by including industry intercept dummies. All the equations in table 9.5 are corrected for heteroskedasticity but not for autocorrelation. The estimation period is for 1980–4, and the number of industries is 135.

Equation (1) in table 9.5 shows that industry growth from the preceding year GR1 has a highly significant positive coefficient, whereas the price–cost margin PCM has an insignificant coefficient. Equation (2) in table 9.5 adds the three macrovariables, GNPGR, PINV, and DISC. The rate of GNP growth GNPGR has a positive coefficient, whereas both the price of investment goods PINV and the rate of discount DISC have negative coefficients as expected. Thus net entry in Japanese manufacturing industries responds to the measures of cyclical business fluctuations.

The importance of fluctuations in demand on net entry is evaluated from the estimated coefficients for GR1 and GNPGR. Evaluated at the sample means, the elasticities for GR1 and GNPGR are 1.79 and 1.56 respectively in equation (2) in table 9.5. Thus demand fluctuations at the industry level as well as at the aggregate macrolevel have strong procyclical effects on net entry.

To account for industry effects that are not captured by the variables included in the equation, the constant term is then allowed to vary across industries. The regressions with industry fixed effects are equations (3) and (4) in table 9.5, which include 134 industry intercept dummies.

A comparison of equations (1) and (3) or equations (2) and (4) reveals that the estimation result remains basically unchanged after controlling for industry fixed effects. In equation (4) the coefficient for GR1 is highly significant and has a positive sign, and the coefficient for GNPGR has a significant positive sign. The coefficients for PINV and DISC remain unchanged and have significant negative signs.

Evaluated at the sample means, the elasticities for GR1 and GNPGR are 1.21 and 2.02 respectively in equation (4) in table 9.5. While both elasticities indicate the procyclical effect of demand fluctuations on net entry, the elasticity for industry demand fluctuations becomes smaller after controlling for industry fixed effects. However, the elasticity for aggregate demand fluctuations in equation (4) becomes larger than that in equation (2).

Finally, equation (5) in table 9.5 controls for market structure by including capital intensity KS and advertising intensity ADSL. KS has a significant and negative coefficient, whereas ADSL has a significant and positive coefficient. However, the effects of other variables on net entry remain virtually unchanged from those obtained in the previous specifications. Thus this result reinforces the earlier conclusion that the extent of net entry responds to inter-temporal fluctuations in business conditions.

Having identified the effects of cyclical fluctuations on net entry, we then ask whether the response coefficients are constant across industries with different market structure characteristics. A sensitivity analysis was conducted by dividing the entire sample into subsamples according to the sample means of capital intensity and advertising intensity,[4] the extent of subcontracting,[5] and the product class. Table 9.6 shows the response elasticities of net entry with respect to GR1, GNPGR, and DISC, which are calculated at the means of each of these variables.[6]

One of the interesting hypotheses is whether industries with high capital intensity and advertising intensity show low response elasticities of net entry. If the sunk components of investment costs for tangible and intangible assets increase with capital intensity and advertising intensity, entry barriers should be high in industries with high capital

Table 9.6 The elasticities of net entry rate calculated at the means of each of the independent variables by subsamples

Sample	Net entry elasticity at the sample mean of		
	GR1	GNPGR	DISC
Capital intensity			
High	1.39	1.45	−5.16
Low	2.16	1.40	−8.15
Advertising intensity			
High	1.30	1.16	−2.96
Low	7.90	5.55	−39.59
Product class			
Consumer goods	2.81	3.15	−8.09
Producer goods	1.43	0.70	−6.53
Materials	1.73	0.71	−8.89
Subcontracting intensity			
High	1.56	1.82	−4.76
Low	2.23	0.29	−13.79
Full sample	1.79	1.57	−6.71

The elasticities are calculated at the means of each of the independent variables and are based on the coefficients estimated for each subsample with the specification of equation (2) in table 9.5.

intensity and advertising intensity. Then, a given incentive to enter should have a weaker impact on net entry in industries with high capital intensity and advertising intensity.

The estimated elasticities in table 9.6 seem to be consistent with this hypothesis. The elasticities with respect to GR1 and DISC are higher in industries with low capital intensity, although the elasticity with respect to GNPGR is virtually the same for the two samples. The difference in the elasticity among subsamples is more distinctive when the sample is divided according to advertising intensity. The elasticities of net entry with respect to GR1, GNPGR, and DISC are all higher in the low advertising sample. Thus net entry in industries with low capital intensity and advertising intensity responds more strongly than industries with high capital intensity and advertising intensity to a given change in the incentives to enter.[7]

However, whether the presence of entry barriers is solely responsible for the low response of net entry in the highly capital intensive industries cannot unequivocally be ascertained here. It is conceivable that entry into the highly capital-intensive industries is less sensitive to cyclical business fluctuations because investments in such industries are lumpy and hence require the gestation lag that is longer than in the less capital-intensive industries. The elasticities of net entry are, in fact, lower for industries that produce materials and capital goods (or producer goods)[8] than for the consumer good industries (table 9.6).

On the contrary, the effect of advertising on net entry observed in table 9.6 seems to be distinguished from the general entry pattern that is associated with each product class. As table 9.6 shows, the elasticities of net entry are higher in the consumer good industries than in the producer goods industries, whereas they are smaller in the high advertising industries which tend to converge with the consumer goods industries.

Another interesting question is whether entry and exit are more sensitive to cyclical business conditions in industries with high subcontracting intensity. The previous literature on Japan's industrial organization has suggested that large manufacturing corporations use small and medium subcontractors as a buffer to shift part of the risk of demand fluctuations.[9] The results in table 9.6 show that the estimated elasticities of net entry with respect to GR1 and DISC are smaller in industries with a high subcontracting intensity, whereas the elasticity with respect to GNPGR is larger in these industries. Thus the results do not seem to provide clear-cut evidence for the hypothesis.[10]

4 Conclusions

Using panel data for 135 three-digit Japanese manufacturing industries over the period 1979–84, we tested the hypothesis that net entry responds to cyclical fluctuations of business conditions. The pooled cross-section and time series regressions found that net entry is sensitive to industry demand fluctuations as well as to aggregate demand fluctuations, and responds to them procyclically. The statistical results of this paper also show that net entry is sensitive to the movement of the cost of capital and thus has a negative relationship with both the price of investment goods and the rate of discount.

Response of net entry to business fluctuations was also found to vary with market structure. The regression results showed that the response elasticities differ between industries with high and low capital intensity, and between industries with high and low advertising intensity, but they do not differ between industries with high and low subcontracting intensity.

High sensitivity of net entry to cyclical business conditions implies that competitive pressure will be injected into an industry with a cyclical pattern. This suggests further that business fluctuations could affect the industry's competitive performance through their effects on the firm's entry decisions. The statistical results of this paper imply that such competitive pressure might be injected into the industry with a procyclical pattern, and its magnitude varies with the height of entry barriers which are created by advertising in particular.

Thus evaluating the sensitivity of entry to busniess fluctuations and exploring its dynamics are important for public policy. Much future effort should be directed toward exploring the effects of business conditions on entry and market performance, and the importance of market structure as a determinant of the sensitivity of entry to cyclical disturbances.

Appendix: Data Sources

All the industry data in this study were compiled at the three-digit level of the Japanese Standard Industrial Classification (SIC) system. This level of classification is comparable with the three-digit US SIC. Although the total number of industries classified at the three-digit level is 143, eight industries were eliminated from the sample because of the missing information over the sample period 1979–84.

The rates of industry growth GR1 and GR3 and the price–cost margin PCM were constructed from the *Census of Manufacturers: Report by Industries* (Japan Ministry of International Trade and Industry (MITI)). The rate of net entry RN was constructed from the number of firms listed in *Census of Manufactures : Report by Enterprises* (MITI). GNPGR and DISC were taken from the *Economic Statistics Monthly* (Bank of Japan, Statistics Department). GNPGR is constructed from GNP at constant price, and DISC is central bank discount rates at the end of year. PINV was obtained from the *Price Indexes Annual: Wholesale Price Indexes* (Bank of Japan, Statistics Department).

Notes

1 The Japanese SIC system was changed in 1985, thus making it rather difficult to compare the statistics before and after 1985.

2 Previous cross-section work on entry has found that industry growth and the profitability were significant inducements for entry. For example, see Orr (1974), Deutsch (1975), Gorecki (1975), Iwasaki (1976), Kessides (1986), MacDonald (1986), Baldwin and Gorecki (1987), Highfield and Smiley (1987), Schwalbach (1987), and Shapiro and Khemani (1987). In particular, the strong effect of industry growth on entry has been observed by Hause and Du Rietz (1984) and Dunne and Roberts (chapter 10 of this volume).

3 Domowitz et al. (1986) have found that price–cost margins in US four-digit

industries are procyclical. Bils (1987), however, found that price–cost margins are countercyclical in the US two-digit industries. Using panel data for the United Kingdom, Geroski (1989a, b) finds a positive relation between entry and productivity growth that varies over time. Odagiri and Yamashita (1987) analyze the variation of price–cost margins in Japanese manufacturing over business cycles.

4 The sample mean over time and across industries is compared with the mean over time for each industry. Capital intensity and advertising intensity are defined in the preceding section.

5 The extent of subcontracting is defineed as the percentage of small and medium firms that are subcontractors. Small and medium firms are those with less than 300 workers. The numbers are adopted from Yokokura (1988, table 3). Those industries with higher than 65 percent in subcontracting intensity are defined as high subcontracting industries.

6 The regression equation has the specification of equation (2) in table 9.5.

7 This result on advertising intensity is not necessarily inconsistent with the result of equation (5) in table 9.5 where advertising intensity has a positive effect on the rate of net entry in the pooled regression. The rate of net entry becomes larger as advertising intensity increases, but the high advertising industries respond less to a given incentive to enter.

8 The producer good industries include industries that produce both materials and capital goods.

9 For example, see Caves and Uekusa (1976, pp. 112–15).

10 This conclusion is reinforced by the results on the elasticities in industries that produce materials. While subcontracting is high in the material or intermediate good industries, the estimated elasticities of net entry tend to be lower in these industries.

References

Baldwin, J.R. and Gorecki, P.K. (1987) Plant creation versus plant acquisition: the entry process in Canadian manufacturing. *International Journal of Industrial Organization* 5, 27–41.

Bils, M. (1987) The cyclical behavior of marginal cost and price. *American Economic Review* 77, 838–55.

Caves, R.E. and Uekusa, M. (1976) *Industrial Organization in Japan.* Washington, DC: Brookings Institution.

Deutsch, L.L. (1975) Structure, performance, and the net rate of entry into manufacturing industries. *Southern Economic Journal* 41, 450–6.

Domowitz, I., Hubberd, R.G. and Petersen, B.C. (1986) Business cycles and the relationship between concentration and price–cost margins. *Rand Journal of Economics* 17, 1–17.

Dunne, T., Roberts, M.J. and Samuelson, L. (1988a) Firm entry and post-entry performance in the US chemical industries. Mimeo, Pennsylvania State University.

Dunne, T., Roberts, M.J. and Samuelson, L. (1988b) Patterns of firm entry and exit in US manufacturing industries. *Rand Journal of Economics* 19, 495–515.

Dunne, T. and Roberts, M.J. (1989) Inter-industry variation in producer turnover in US manufacturing. Mimeo, Pennsylvania State University.

Geroski, P.A. (1988) Domestic and foreign entry in the UK: 1983–84, Mimeo, London Business School.

Geroski, P.A. (1989a) The interaction between domestic and foreign based entrants. In D.B. Audretsch, L. Sleuwaegen, and H. Yamawaki (eds) *The Convergence of International and Domestic Markets*, Amsterdam: North-Holland.

Geroski, P.A. (1989b) Entry, innovation, and productivity growth. Mimeo, London Business School.

Gorecki, P.K. (1975) The determinants of entry by new and diversifying enterprises in the UK manufacturing sector 1958–63: some tentative results. *Applied Economics* 7, 139–47.

Gorecki, P.K. (1976) The determinants of entry by domestic and foreign enterprises in Canadian manufacturing industries: some comments and empirical results. *Review of Economics and Statistics* 58, 485–8.

Hause, J.C. and Du Rietz, G. (1984) Entry, industry growth, and the micro-dynamics of industry supply. *Journal of Political Economy* 92, 733–57.

Highfield, R. and Smiley, R. (1987) New business starts and economic activity: an empirical investigation. *International Journal of Industrial Organization* 5, 51–66.

Hilke, J.C. (1984) Excess capacity and entry: some empirical evidence. *Journal of Industrial Economics* 33, 233–40.

Iwasaki, A. (1976) Shijokozoyoin to junsannyuritsu (Market structure and the net rate of entry). *Konan Keizaigaku Ronshu* 16, 86–99.

Kessides, I.N. (1986) Advertising, sunk costs, and barriers to entry. *Review of Economics and Statistics* 68, 84–95.

Lieberman, M.B. (1987a) Excess capacity as a barrier to entry: an empirical appraisal. *Journal of Industrial Economics* 35, 607–27.

Lieberman, M.B. (1987b) Post-entry investment and market structure in the chemical processing industries. *Rand Journal of Economics* 18, 533–49.

MacDonald, J.M. (1986) Entry and exit on the competitive fringe. *Southern Economic Journal* 52, 640–52.

Masson, R.T. and Shaanan, J. (1986) Excess capacity and limit pricing: an empirical test. *Economica* 53, 365–78.

Odagiri, H. and Yamashita, T. (1987) Price mark-ups, market structure, and business fluctuations in Japanese manufacturing industries. *Journal of Industrial Economics* 35, 317–31.

Orr, D. (1974) The determinants of entry: a study of the Canadian manufacturing Industries. *Review of Economics and Statistics* 56, 58–66.

Schwalbach, J. (1987) Entry by diversified firms into German industries. *International Journal of Industrial Organization* 5, 43–9.

Shapiro, D. and Khemani, R.S. (1987) The determinants of entry and exit reconsidered. *International Journal of Industrial Organization* 5, 15–26.

Yokokura, T. (1988) Small and medium enterprises. In R. Komiya, M. Okuno, and K. Suzumura (eds), *Industrial Policy of Japan*, San Diego, CA: Academic Press.

10

Variation in Producer Turnover Across US Manufacturing Industries

Timothy Dunne and Mark J. Roberts

1 Introduction

Recent efforts to measure entry and exit for a broad cross section of industries and countries have revealed a number of robust patterns.[1] Among these are substantial inter-industry variation in both entry and exit rates, a fairly high correlation between industry entry and exit rates at a point in time, and stability of an industry's relative entry and exit level over time. All these facts suggest, not surprisingly, that there are stable underlying inter-industry differences in demand conditions, technology, or firm behavior that give rise to these patterns of producer turnover.

In this paper we utilize a panel data set for the US manufacturing industries to summarize the inter-industry variation in producer turnover. We have two goals for this paper. The first is to identify some industry characteristics that are highly correlated with entry and exit and to assess their importance, relative to the set of unmeasured or unmeasurable industry characteristics, in explaining inter-industry differences in producer turnover. The second is to examine the magnitude and persistence of the inter-industry patterns of entry, exit, turnover, and net entry.

Throughout this paper we adopt the view that "inter-industry research in industrial organization should generally be viewed as a search for empirical regularities, not as a set of exercises in structural estimation" (Schmalensee, 1989, p. 1000) and focus on refining the set

We are grateful for helpful comments from participants at the Conference on International Comparisons of Entry, Berlin. This research was supported by National Science Foundation grants SES-84-01460 and SES-86-05844. We are also grateful to the Center for Economic Studies, US Census Bureau, for research assistance.

of empirical regularities on industry entry and exit. Of particular interest are the entry and exit relationships which are robust over time.

The empirical regularities identified in this paper suggest that inter-industry differences in the entry and exit process arise from differences in technology across industries. The technology determines a base rate of producer turnover that is very stable over time but varies substantially across industries. Added to this are yearly fluctuations in demand and longer-term changes in technology which result in a net change in the number of firms. Attempts to assess across-industry differences in the competitive effect of entry are most likely to be successful if they separate industries into those with high versus low rates of producer turnover.

The remainder of the paper is divided into four sections. In the next section, we briefly describe the data and general entry and exit patterns. In section 3 the partial correlations between entry, exit, and industry characteristics are examined. In section 4 we explore the implications of the high cross-sectional correlation between entry and exit for measures of net entry and turnover. The final section contains a summary and concluding remarks.

2 Summary Statistics of Entry and Exit in US Manufacturing Industries

The estimation of structural models of industry supply which incorporate firm entry and exit is an important goal in industrial organization. Before attempting structural estimation it is useful to understand how the basic patterns of entry and exit vary across time and industries. This exercise can help identify dimensions on which industries differ and suggest factors that must be controlled for in structural models. In addition, it can help the researcher decide whether the differences across industries in the underlying technology and demand conditions remain so large, and so difficult to control for, that structural models of entry and exit can only be implemented for individual industries or closely related groups of industries.

A detailed description of the data set we examine is given by Dunne et al. (1988). The data consist of the number and total size of all firms which enter and exit each of 386 four-digit Standard Industrial Classification (SIC) industries in the US manufacturing sector over four time periods. The time periods are 1963–7, 1967–72, 1972–7, and 1977–82.

Four entry and exit variables are measured for each industry in each of the time periods. The entry rate (share) is defined as the number (real output) of firms that are first observed in operation at the end of each time period relative to the total number (real output) of firms that were in operation in the beginning of the time period. The exit rate (share) expresses the number (output) of firms that are last observed in operation at the beginning of each time period as a proportion of the total number (output) of firms in operation at the beginning of the period. Notice that all four variables are defined relative to the number of firms or industry output at the beginning of each time period.[2] This will be useful later in the paper when we measure net entry and turnover rates.

Summary statistics for these entry and exit variables are reported by Dunne at al. (1988, 1989) and Cable and Schwalbach (chapter 14 of this volume). Several general conclusions can be drawn from them. First, there is substantial entry and exit in the US manufacturing industries. The mean entry rate across the 386 industries and four time periods is 0.386 while the average exit rate is 0.353. The entering and exiting firms are also responsible for a significant amount of industry production. The mean output share of the entrants is 0.190 and that of the exiter is 0.164.

Second, the degree of entry and particularly the degree of exit for each industry are fairly stable over time. In the case of entry rates the average of the simple correlations between adjoining time periods is 0.297 while the average correlation for the exit rate equals 0.698. The market shares of entering and exiting firms are more stable over time than the entry and exit rates. On average the simple correlation between the entry share in adjoining periods is 0.455 while the comparable correlation for the exit share is 0.780.

Third, entry and exit are positively correlated across industries in each time period. The simple correlation between the entry rate and exit rate in the same time period averages 0.270 over the four time periods. The same statistic for the entry and exit share is 0.515.[3] These correlations seem particularly large given that no controls have been made for the rate of growth of the industry during the time period. Changes in industry size would be expected to have opposite effects on an industry's entry and exit rate and thus reduce the simple correlation between the entry and exit measures.

3 Entry, Exit, and Industry Characteristics

In this section we examine the partial correlations between the entry and exit variables and some characteristics of the manufacturing industries. The empirical model that will be estimated in this section is

$$Y_{it} = \beta_0 + \beta_t + \sum_{k=1}^{K} \beta_k X_{kit} + U_{it}. \qquad (10.1)$$

Y_{it} is the observation on one of the four entry or exit statistics for industry i in period t. The variables $X_{1it} \ldots X_{kit}$ are a set of industry characteristics that vary over time. The first two variables in this set are the average annual rate of real output growth over the time period and its square. These are included as proxies for changes in industry demand. Four additional variables, all of which reflect characteristics of the industry's technology, are also included. These are the industry price–cost margin, the ratio of capital input to real industry output, the number of firms, and the average size of firms in the industry. A time-period-specific intercept is included to control for external conditions that affect all industries but which may change over time.

The industry price–cost margin is measured as the value of production minus expenditure on labor and materials expressed as a fraction of the value of production. The value of production is the sum of the value of shipments plus changes in inventories. This is the definition of the price–cost margin used by Domowitz et al. (1986). It will vary both over time and across industries with changes in profitability and expenditures on capital services. The capital-to-output ratio is measured as the industry's perpetual inventory capital stock divided by the level of real output. Both the price–cost margin and the capital-to-output ratio are measured as the average annual value for each of the four entry periods. The number of firms in the industry is measured in the initial year of each of the four entry periods. The average size of firms in the industry is measured as the average level of real output per firm in the initial year of each entry period. These last two variables control for inter-industry differences in the size distribution of producers.

The magnitude of time series variation in the entry and exit statistics differs substantially across industries, even after controlling for important industry characteristics. To control for this we assume that $\text{var}(U_{it}) = \sigma_i^2$. We estimate it as

$$\hat{\sigma}_i^2 = \frac{1}{T} \sum_{t=1}^{T} e_{it}^2$$

where the e_{it} are the ordinary least squares residuals from (10.1). The estimated industry-specific variances are then used to construct weighted least squares estimates of equation (10.1).

Table 10.1 reports the estimated coefficients from weighted least squares regressions of equation (10.1). The coefficients summarize the cross-sectional correlations in these variables. With only one exception

Table 10.1 Regression coefficients – no industry fixed effects (standard errors in parentheses)

Independent variable	Entry rate	Entry share	Exit rate	Exit share
Intercept	0.191*	0.136*	0.333*	0.203*
	(0.011)	(0.006)	(0.006)	(0.005)
Growth	0.614*	1.046*	−0.248*	−0.289*
	(0.061)	(0.039)	(0.034)	(0.035)
Growth^2	6.244*	6.814*	2.009*	1.748*
	(0.530)	(0.357)	(0.244)	(0.253)
Price–cost margin	0.150*	−0.268*	−0.053*	−0.237*
	(0.038)	(0.017)	(0.018)	(0.014)
Capital-to-output ratio	−0.045*	−0.032*	−0.032*	−0.033*
	(0.006)	(0.004)	(0.005)	(0.004)
Number of firms	0.014*	0.030*	0.015*	0.031*
	(0.002)	(0.002)	(0.001)	(0.002)
Average firm size	−0.080*	−0.077*	−0.106*	−0.065*
	(0.025)	(0.018)	(0.021)	(0.013)
Time dummy 1967–72	0.149*	0.101*	0.076*	0.045*
	(0.007)	(0.004)	(0.004)	(0.004)
Time dummy 1972–7	0.142*	0.058*	0.027*	−0.005
	(0.007)	(0.004)	(0.004)	(0.004)
Time dummy 1977–82	0.179*	0.094*	0.057*	0.026*
	(0.008)	(0.005)	(0.004)	(0.004)
$\bar{R}^2$	0.184	0.444	0.146	0.143

* Significantly different from zero at the $\alpha = 0.01$ level.

the signs of the coefficients are not sensitive to whether entry and exit are expressed in terms of the number of firms or amount of output. As a result the following discussion will focus on the correlations for the entry and exit output shares. First, industry growth has a positive and increasing effect on the entry share but a negative and diminishing effect on the exit share. Thus industry growth is correlated with increased entry and decreased exit.

The pattern for the next four variables is summarized by the fact that industry characteristics that are positively (negatively) correlated with entry are also positively (negatively) correlated with exit. When looking across industries, those with higher price–cost margins, higher capital intensity, smaller numbers of firms, and larger average firm size tend to have lower rates of both entry and exit. The only exception to this pattern is that the entry rate is positively correlated with the price–cost margin while the entry share and exit variables are negatively correlated. Finally, both the entry and exit regressions are characterized by significant time period effects. The positive coefficients indicate that the latter three time periods had higher levels of both entry and exit than the period 1963–7.

The conclusion to be drawn from these regressions is that, after controlling for industry growth and time period effects common to all industries, there are significant correlations between characteristics of the industry's technology and the degree of entry and exit. These correlations are all consistent with the view that industries with capital-intensive technologies and larger scales are characterized by less entry and exit. If, in the cross section, capital intensity is correlated with the magnitude of sunk costs, then the across-industry turnover patterns are consistent with arguments that sunk costs reduce both entry and exit. The negative correlation between the price–cost margin and both entry and exit shares could arise because industries with higher capital expenditures have high sunk costs and thus lower turnover or because industries with higher profits have been able to benefit from strategic or nonstrategic entry barriers.

While the industry characteristics examined in table 10.1 play a major role in most cross-sectional studies in industrial organization they are by no means an exhaustive list of the factors that researchers have found to be important in inter-industry studies of entry and exit. The multiple time periods available in the data set make it possible to control for these omitted industry-specific factors. The interesting questions which this raises are as follows: first, how important are these omitted factors, which could include variables like the level of entry costs or degree of entry costs which are sunk, relative to the more easily quantifiable factors; second, does controlling for these factors alter the signs of the correlations between entry or exit and the industry characteristics reported above.

To control for these omitted factors, industry-specific intercepts are included among the regressors. The second empirical model we examine is

$$Y_{it} = \beta_i + \beta_t + \sum_{k=1}^{K} \beta_k X_{kit} + U_{it}. \qquad (10.2)$$

In practice, because the number of industries is large, we estimate (10.2) after expressing each variable as a deviation from its industry mean:

$$(Y_{it} - \bar{Y}_i) = \beta_t \left(1 - \frac{1}{T}\right) + \sum_{k=1}^{K} \beta_k (X_{kit} - \bar{X}_{ki}) + (U_{it} - \bar{U}_i). \qquad (10.3)[4]$$

As in the previous model, we control for the likely pattern of heteroskedasticity in this data. We assume that $\mathrm{var}(U_{it} - \bar{U}_i) = \omega_i^2$ and estimate it as

$$\hat{\omega}_i^2 = \frac{1}{T} \sum_{t=1}^{T} v_{it}^2$$

where the v_{it} are the ordinary least squares residuals from (10.3). The estimated industry-specific variances are then used to construct weighted least squares estimates of (10.3).

The variables in equation (10.3) now reflect the time series fluctuations in each industry's values about their own industry-specific means. The regression coefficients now summarize whether higher than average values of the X variables are associated with higher than average or lower than average values for industry entry or exit.

The regression coefficients from the model with industry fixed effects are reported in table 10.2. The signs of the correlations between entry, exit, and the industry growth rate are not substantially altered when the

Table 10.2 Regression coefficients – with industry fixed effects (standard errors in parentheses)

Independent variable	Entry rate	Entry share	Exit rate	Exit share
Growth	0.483*	1.208*	−0.280*	−0.246*
	(0.047)	(0.031)	(0.023)	(0.021)
Growth^2	2.682*	6.392*	1.322*	1.222*
	(0.434)	(0.245)	(0.189)	(0.151)
Price–cost margin	0.313*	0.043*	0.114*	0.065*
	(0.080)	(0.046)	(0.038)	(0.026)
Capital-to-output ratio	−0.012*	−0.006	0.014*	0.010*
	(0.005)	(0.006)	(0.005)	(0.001)
Number of firms	−0.054*	0.008	0.008	0.008
	(0.015)	(0.006)	(0.005)	(0.005)
Average firm size	0.057	0.028	0.001	−0.009
	(0.044)	(0.020)	(0.018)	(0.008)
Time dummy 1967–72	0.124*	0.104*	0.068*	0.038*
	(0.005)	(0.003)	(0.002)	(0.002)
Time dummy 1972–77	0.103*	0.056*	0.020*	−0.005*
	(0.005)	(0.003)	(0.002)	(0.002)
Time dummy 1977–82	0.140*	0.099*	0.044*	0.015*
	(0.006)	(0.004)	(0.003)	(0.002)
$\bar{R}^2$	0.331	0.718	0.677	0.760
F-statistic: no industry fixed effects	8.541	19.570	27.292	33.874

* Significantly different from zero at the $\alpha = 0.01$ level.

fixed effects are included. Periods of higher than average growth for an industry are also periods of higher than average entry and lower than average exit.

The direction and interpretation of the remaining correlations are altered when the fixed effects are included. In particular, many of the correlations which rely on the within-industry time series fluctuations in the data have opposite signs to those of the inter-industry correlations. The price–cost margin is now positively correlated with all the entry and exit variables. Unlike the inter-industry variation, the time series variation in the margin is much more likely to reflect variation in profitability. The finding that periods with higher than average margins also have higher than average entry could reflect the effect of demand increases on prices, profits, and incentives to enter. The fact that these are also periods of higher than average exit could reflect displacement of existing producers by the entrants.

The capital-to-output ratio is negatively correlated with entry and positively correlated with exit when industry effects are included. This may arise, not from variations in the industry's measured capital input, but from variations in real output. Periods of low demand, and thus low output, have higher than average capital-to-output ratios with lower than average entry and higher than average exit.

The final two variables, the number of firms and their average size, generally have statistically insignificant coefficients. The exception is that the number of firms is negatively correlated with the entry rate which implies that time periods that begin with a larger than average number of firms in operation have a lower than average entry rate.

A final inference which can be drawn from a comparison of the results in tables 10.1 and 10.2 concerns the importance of the industry fixed effects. Even after including many of the industry variables that are typically found to be important in cross-section industry regressions the industry fixed effects are very important. One rough way of assessing their overall importance is to examine the change in the adjusted R^2 which occurs when they are included.[4] In the case of the two entry variables the industry fixed effects increase the adjusted R^2 by between 60 and 80 percent, from 0.184 to 0.331 for the entry rate and from 0.444 to 0.718 for the entry share. The effect is even more substantial for the exit variables where the percentage increase in the adjusted R^2 is of the order of 400 percent. Inclusion of the industry fixed effects raises the adjusted R^2 from 0.146 to 0.677 for the exit rate and from 0.143 to 0.0760 for the exit share.

The importance of the industry fixed effects is also illustrated by the test statistics for the hypothesis that all industries have the same intercept. The test statistics are reported at the bottom of each column in table 10.2. They are distributed as $F(385, 1150)$ and the critical value at the 0.01 significance level is 1.0. In all cases the hypothesis that the industries have equal intercepts is rejected. The values of the test statistic are particularly large for the exit variables.

Cross-section regression equations like (10.1) have been treated as structural equations and used to draw inferences about the effect of barriers to entry on the degree of entry. If the industry characteristics in equation (10.1), which include the price–cost margin, the capital-to-output ratio, and the average size of producers, are correlated with the disturbance, then ordinary least squares parameter estimates are inconsistent. Hausman and Taylor (1981) develop and apply specification tests which utilize panel data and allow the assumption of exogenous regressors to be tested.[5] We perform the specification test and the results indicate that we reject the exogeneity of the industry characteristics for all four of the entry and exit statistics. The test statistic for this test is distributed as a χ_9^2 random variable which has a critical value of 21.67 at the $\alpha = 0.01$ significance level. The values of the test statistic for the entry rate, entry share, exit rate, and exit share are 67.99, 37.37, 50.47, and 40.35 respectively. This rejection suggests that it is inappropriate to treat equation (10.1) as a structural entry or exit equation and estimate it with ordinary least squares using cross-section industry data.

4 Inter-Industry Differences in Turnover and Net Entry

Two results from the last section emphasize the fact that industries which have high entry also have high exit. First, the cross-section results reported in table 10.1 indicate that industry characteristics that are positively (negatively) correlated with entry are positively (negatively) correlated with exit. Second, the industry-specific intercepts are constructed using the results of the fixed effects model (equation (10.3)). The simple correlation between the intercepts for the entry rate and exit rate regressions in 0.603. The same correlation for the entry and exit shares is 0.866.

The high inter-industry correlation between entry and exit implies that industries can be characterized by whether they are relatively high entry *and* exit or relatively low entry *and* exit. This finding complements the view that the major source of barriers to entry into an industry is barriers to exit. Caves and Porter (1976), Eaton and Lipsey (1980), and Baumol et al. (1982, ch. 10) have all discussed how the presence of durable specific assets whose costs are sunk to incumbent producers can act as a barrier to entry. These sunk costs, which are not part of the opportunity cost of production for incumbents, provide the incumbents with a credible threat to remain in an industry in the face of entry. In addition they are costs which are relevant to firms contemplating entry. Industries in which sunk costs are substantial will thus tend to have lower rates of both entry and exit when compared with industries in which sunk costs are unimportant.[6]

The presence of sunk costs thus provides a justification for distinguishing industries on the basis of turnover rates. High turnover rates, but not necessarily high net entry rates, are consistent with few sunk costs. This focus on inter-industry differences in turnover contrasts with most of the existing cross-sectional empirical work which attempts to explain differences in net entry rates across industries. If industries differ significantly in the importance of sunk costs, as is likely given the substantial differences in production technology and the importance of advertising and R&D expenditures, then this should result in significant and persistent differences in industry turnover. Inter-industry differences in net entry and, to a lesser extent entry and exit, are much more likely to reflect factors that vary over time such as overall growth of the market.

In this section we examine the relative magnitude of across-industry and within-industry variation in producer turnover and summarize the persistence of the across-industry patterns over time. In addition to the entry and exit rates we also examine net entry, turnover, and a measure of producer volatility which attempts to summarize the rate of turnover in excess of that resulting from overall growth or contraction of the market. Two descriptive tools are used to examine these variables. The first decomposes the sample variance in each measure into an across-industry component and a within-industry component. The second summarizes the correlations over time for each varible.

The net entry rate for industry i in year t is defined as the difference between entry and exit rates: $NER_{it} = ER_{it} - XR_{it}$. The turnover rate is defined as the sum of the entry and exit rates: $TR_{it} = ER_{it} + XR_{it}$. The turnover rate is bounded from below by the absolute value of the net entry rate. If we view net entry as largely resulting from changes in the total size of the market, then turnover reflects both the response of the total number of producers to changes in market size and the replacement of existing producers by new producers. In particular this excess producer turnover – the amount of turnover in the identities of the firms producing in the market which is not due to changes in the size of the market – provides a useful measure of the extent of producer volatility.

We define the volatility rate for industry i in year t as the difference between the turnover rate and the absolute value of the net entry rate: $VR_{it} = TR_{it} - |NER_{it}|$. If the volatility rate is high, then there is significant producer turnover in excess of what might be reasonably ascribed to changes in demand. Low volatility implies little change in the identity of producers beyond that due to growth or contraction of the overall market.[7]

We measure NER_{it}, TR_{it}, and VR_{it} for each industry in each of the four time periods. Measures of net entry, turnover, and volatility using the output of entering and exiting firms rather than their numbers are defined similarly. The total sample variation across both industries and time for each of these six variables is

$$\sigma^2 = \frac{1}{NT} \sum_{i=1}^{N} \sum_{t=1}^{T} (Y_{it} - \bar{Y})^2.$$

Y_{it} represents one of the six variables, N is the total number of industries (386), and T is the total number of time periods (4). $\bar{Y}$ is the overall sample mean of the variable:

$$\bar{Y} = \frac{1}{NT} \sum_i \sum_t Y_{it}.$$

The total sample variation can be decomposed into the sum of within- and across-industry variation:

$$\sigma^2 = \frac{1}{N} \sum_i \sigma_i^2 + \bar{\sigma}^2 \qquad (10.4)$$

where

$$\sigma_i^2 \equiv \frac{1}{T} \sum_t (Y_{it} - \bar{Y}_i)^2$$

$$\bar{Y}_i \equiv \frac{1}{T} \sum_t Y_{it}$$

$$\bar{\sigma}^2 \equiv \frac{1}{N} \sum_i (\bar{Y}_i - \bar{Y})^2.$$

The first term in equation (10.4) is the average of the within-industry variances over all industries. The second term is the variance across industries in the industry mean values of the variable.

The variance decomposition is reported in table 10.3. The final column of the table reports the ratio of across-industry to total sample

Table 10.3 Variance decomposition

	Mean	Total sample variation σ^2	Average within-industry variation $(1/N)\sum\sigma_i^2$	Across-industry variation $\bar{\sigma}^2$	$\bar{\sigma}^2/\sigma^2$
Entry rate	0.386	0.081	0.046	0.035	0.432
Exit rate	0.353	0.015	0.005	0.010	0.667
Net entry rate	0.033	0.076	0.052	0.024	0.316
Turnover rate	0.739	0.117	0.050	0.067	0.573
Volatility rate	0.583	0.059	0.018	0.041	0.695
Entry share	0.190	0.044	0.021	0.023	0.523
Exit share	0.164	0.013	0.004	0.010	0.667
Net entry share	0.027	0.033	0.023	0.010	0.303
Turnover share	0.354	0.081	0.025	0.056	0.691
Volatility share	0.266	0.039	0.007	0.031	0.795

variation. In the case of the variables measured as rates, the volatility measure has the highest proportion of across-industry variation followed by the turnover, exit, entry, and net entry measures. In the case of the output shares the ranking is the volatility share followed by exit, turnover, entry, and net entry. In both cases the volatility measure has the highest proportion of its sample variation in the across-industry dimension while net entry has the least. In particular, across-industry variation accounts for 79.5 percent of the total variation in the volatility share but only 30.3 percent of the net entry share.[8]

This finding is consistent with the view that industries differ significantly in the ease of entry and exit, possibly because of differences related to the technology and importance of sunk costs. This gives rise to different base rates of producer turnover across industries. Added to this are changes in the overall size of the market, possibly due to fluctuations in demand, which contribute to changes in the number of producers. In this simplified view an industry's net entry rate reflects the time series fluctuations in the number of producers resulting from market growth. If the demand for an industry's output fluctuates over time, then we would not expect an industry's net entry rate to be stable over time. In contrast, if the volatility rate more accurately measures the ease of entry and exit in an industry and this depends upon the industry's technology, then there should be a substantial degree of persistence in an industry's volatility rate.

In order to examine the stability of the entry and exit variables over time we construct the simple correlations for each variable between

Table 10.4 Simple correlations between adjoining time periods

	1963–7 and 1967–72	1967–72 and 1972–7	1972–7 and 1977–82	Average
Entry rate	0.310	0.274	0.306	0.300
Exit rate	0.667	0.678	0.736	0.694
Net entry rate	0.074	0.124	0.132	0.110
Turnover rate	0.562	0.451	0.530	0.514
Volatility rate	0.643	0.705	0.748	0.699
Entry share	0.548	0.349	0.466	0.454
Exit share	0.776	0.778	0.786	0.780
Net entry share	0.335	0.003	0.105	0.148
Turnover share	0.699	0.630	0.728	0.686
Volatility share	0.824	0.822	0.838	0.828

adjoining periods. These are reported in table 10.4. The first three columns report the simple correlations between each of the three adjoining entry periods. For example, the simple correlation between industry entry rates from the period 1963–7 and the period 1967–72 is 0.310. The last column reports the average of the correlations over the different time periods. The pattern revealed in the last column of table 10.4 is simple. Regardless of whether it is measured as rates or output shares, the industry volatility measures are the most persistent over time. This is followed by exit, turnover, entry, and net entry. In particular, the average correlation between adjoining periods for the volatility share is 0.828, but it is only 0.148 for the net entry share.

The conclusion to be drawn from the patterns reported in tables 10.3 and 10.4 is that inter-industry differences in producer volatility are both more pronounced and more persistent over time than are differences in entry, exit, and, especially, net entry. Those industries with high rates of producer volatility would most likely be ones in which both entry and exit barriers are low. If we wish to identify industries in which entry is likely to have a substantial impact on the competitive, process, the high volatility industries are good candidates.

5 Conclusions

The purpose of this paper is to identify some of the empirical regularities between characteristics of an industry's technology and its rate of entry and exit. We find that inter-industry variation in both entry and exit are correlated with an industry's price–cost margin, capital-to-output ratio, number of firms, and average firm size. Industries with higher price–cost margins, higher capital-to-output ratios, fewer firms, and larger average firm sizes tend to have less entry *and* less exit. While these correlations are statistically significant and stable over time these characteristics collectively leave a substantial amount of inter-industry variation unexplained. The stability over time suggests that these correlations are largely determined by differences in technology across industries.

While these four industry characteristics capture important aspects of the inter-industry variation in market structure, they are by no means an exhaustive list of the relevant factors. In order to control for these omitted characteristics we also examine the correlations after including fixed industry effects in the empirical model. The inclusion of industry effects results in a substantial increase in the explained variation, particularly for the exit variables, and alters the signs of several of the correlations. In particular, price–cost margins are positively correlated with both entry and exit while the capital-to-output ratio is negatively correlated with entry and positively correlated with exit.

It is important to understand why the signs of these correlations change when fixed industry effects are included. One simple explanation is that the cross-section correlations are dominated by the relationship between the capital intensity of the industry's technology and the effect that this has on producer turnover. Industries in which capital intensity and large production scale are important tend to have less producer turnover. If differences in capital intensity across industries are positively correlated with the magnitude of sunk costs, then the empirical findings would be consistent with the view that sunk costs are the major source of entry barriers.

In contrast, the fixed effects correlations reflect the relationship between the within-industry time series fluctuations in industry characteristics, entry, and exit. Rather than being dominated by variation in the importance of capital, the within-industry variation more likely reflects fluctuations in demand and output. Periods of relatively high demand and output result in higher than average margins, lower than average capital-to-output ratios and higher than average producer turnover.

Together these findings suggests that, at a minimum, a much more detailed specification of industry characteristics will be needed before cross-sectional entry and exit measures can be used to uncover underlying strutural relationships. It will be necessary to control for the substantial differences in technology (and demand) across industries. Three factors suggest that this will be difficult. First, the industry characteristics we include are among the most important sources of variation across industries, yet, when included, fixed industry effects are responsible for much of the explanatory power of the model and alter the signs of the correlations. This suggests that the omitted factors are important. Second, the most likely variables to include in any expanded specification are the ones that are most difficult to measure: entry costs and the proportion of an entrant's investment which is sunk. Third, the specification tests indicate that the industry-specific effects, which proxy for these omitted industry characteristics, are correlated with the characteristics of the technology we have included. While this problem may diminish as the model specification becomes richer, it still emphasizes the importance of worrying about endogeneity issues when using cross-sectional industry data for structural estimation. The alternative direction for estimation of structural models is to rely on panel data at the industry level or time series data for individual industries. In either case the heterogeneity in industry technology and demand can be controlled for.

One interesting pattern revealed by the inter-industry comparison is the high correlation between entry and exit. This suggests that "barriers to exit" that arise from the sunk nature of incumbent firm's past investments may be an important source of "barriers to entry." It further suggests that turnover rather than net entry is a more useful measure of inter-industry variation in entry patterns. We propose a measure of producer volatility – the excess of the turnover rate above the net entry rate – which should reflect the degree of producer turnover in excess of the amount that could reasonably arise from changes in the market demand for the product. This variable, which largely captures inter-industry rather than within-industry variation, may be useful in identifying industries in which the entry and exit process is most likely to have an impact on industry competition.

Notes

1 See chapter 15 for a summary of this literature.
2 The definition of the entry share used here differs from that used by Dunne et al. (1988). There we use the entrants' total output at the end of the period relative to total industry output at the end of the period. The definition used here involves the use of entrant output and industry output in different years. In order to control for price-level changes over time we deflate the value of

entrant and industry shipments by the Bureau of Labour Statistics (BLS) industry price indexes for the relevant year.

3 The average correlation between the entry and exit shares in the same period is 0.776 using the definition of entry share in Dunne et al. (1988).

4 The adjusted R^2 is constructed using the sum of squared residuals and total sum of squares of the dependent variable which are not scaled by the estimated σ_i^2. This corresponds to equation 2.3.12 of Judge et al. (1985) with the usual degrees of freedom correction. This is done because we wish to measure the change in adjusted R^2 between the two models and the weighted least squares estimates of equations (10.1) and (10.2) use different estimates of the σ_i^2. We are also interested in measuring the relative importance of the industry fixed effects and industry characteristics in explaining the across-industry variation in the original data.

5 The specification test relies on a comparison of the parameter estimates of equation (10.2) under two alternative specifications. In the first specification the industry intercepts are treated as random variables. In the second the intercepts are treated as fixed constants. The specification test examines whether or not the random effects specification is correct. However, since the exogeneity assumption that underlies the random effects model, that the industry intercepts are uncorrelated with the other regressors, is the same assumption made when estimating equation (10.1), rejection of the random effects specification also implies rejection of the specification of equation (10.1).

6 The importance of sunk costs in a market is a difficult factor to quantify although considerable progress in this area has been made by Kessides (1986, 1989, 1990). Kessides (1986) uses the importance of advertising outlays. Kessides (1990) exploits differences in the mix of equipment and structures across industries. Kessides (1989) develops measures of the importance of rental markets, depreciation patterns, and the mix of new and used assets in an industry as proxies for the importance of sunk costs. He finds that these variables are important in explaining inter-industry variation in net entry rates or changes in industry concentration.

7 The volatility measure equals twice the smaller of the entry or exit rate. This is consistent with the goal of measuring the rate of producer turnover not due to changes in the size of the market. For example, if entry exceeds exit, giving positive net entry, the excess entry is attributed to changes in market size and only the amount of entry necessary to replace the exiting firms contributes to this base rate of producer volatility.

8 The across-industry variance is always larger when the variables are constructed using output rather than the number of firms. This may reflect the fact that measurement error is less likely to affect the output measures. Mismeasurement of entering and exiting firms will distort both variables, but if the errors are concentrated among the smallest entrants, as is likely, they will have a smaller effect on the output measures.

References

Baumol, W.J., Panzar, J.C. and Willig, R.D. (1982) *Contestable Markets and the Theory of Industry Structure*. New York: Harcourt Brace Jovanovich.

Caves, R.E. and Porter, M.E. (1976) Barriers to exit. In R.T. Masson and P.D. Qualls (eds), *Essays on Industrial Organization in Honor of Joe Bain*, Cambridge, MA: Ballinger.

Domowitz, I., Hubbard, R.G. and Peterson, B.C. (1986) Business cycles and the relationship between concentration and price–cost margins. *Rand Journal of Economics* 17(1), 1–17.

Dunne, T., Roberts, M.J. and Samuelson, L. (1988) Patterns of firm entry and exit in US manufacturing industries. *Rand Journal of Economics* 19(4), 495–515.

Dunne, T., Roberts, M.J. and Samuelson, L. (1989) Firm entry and post entry performance in the US chemical industries. *Journal of Law and Economics* 32, 233–71.

Eaton, B.C. and Lipsey, R.G. (1980) Exit barriers and entry barriers: the durability of capital as a barrier to entry. *Bell Journal of Economics* 11(2), 721–9.

Hausman, J.A. and Taylor, W.E. (1981) Panel data and unobservable individual effects. *Econometrica* 49(6), 1377–98.

Judge, G.E., Griffiths, W.E., Carter Hill, R., Lutkepohl, H. and Tsoung-Chae Lee (1985) *The Theory and Practice of Econometrics*, 2nd edn. New York: Wiley.

Kessides, I.N. (1986) Advertising, sunk costs, and barriers to entry. *Review of Economics and Statistics* 68(1), 84–96.

Kessides, I.N. (1988) Market structure and sunk costs: an empirical test of the contestability hypothesis. Working paper, Department of Economics, University of Maryland.

Kessides, I.N. (1990) Toward a testable model of entry: a study of the US manufacturing industries. *Economica* 57, 219–38.

Schmalensee, R. (1989) Inter-industry studies of structure and performance. In R. Schmalensee and R. Willig (eds), *Handbook of Industrial Organization*, Amsterdam: North-Holland.

11

Patterns of Entry, Exit, and Merger in Yugoslavia

Saul Estrin and Tea Petrin

1 Introduction

In this paper we examine the pattern of entry and exit of enterprises in the Yugoslav industrial sector with special reference to the period 1952–1973. Yugoslavia represents a convenient basis for a comparison of market dynamics between socialist and capitalist economies because most productive assets are not privately owned, and since 1952 Yugoslavia has used a market system to allocate many resources in the context of its own unique system of self-management market socialism (see Tyson, 1980; Estrin, 1983; Lydall, 1984). We focus upon both the conceptual and institutional issues and the actual rates of entry and exit over the period. This paper can also serve as a point of reference for the other papers in the volume. The rates of both entry and exit prove to be astonishingly small by the standards of Western economies; gross entry rates into the industrial sector rarely exceed 1 percent per annum and never exceed 2 percent per annum. Exit rates never reach 0.5 percent per annum. Moreover, entry does not appear to be motivated to any significant degree by economic factors. This leads us to examine the reasons for the paucity of entry and exit

Two broad themes emerge in the study. First, there is the peculiarity of the Yugoslav capital market. The Yugoslavs developed an ownership form, known as social ownership, to complement their unique enterprise self-management system. The idea is that, while workers in enterprises own the surpluses earned from it, capital is not itself marketable (see Prout, 1985). Capital markets are necessarily thin because the only available instrument is debt and the only financial institutions are banks (see Dmitrijevich and Masesich, 1973).

Thanks are due to Polly Vizard and Lina Takla for valuable research assistance. The authors would also like to thank Paul Geroski, Mark Schankerman, and Ales Vahcic for useful discussion and comment.

Second, in common with many Eastern European economies, in practice Yugoslavia has rarely limited the role of the state in investment decisions, whether the officials concerned be titled "planners" or are merely representatives of goverment agencies. This is particularly true in the industrial sector, upon which the data in this paper are concentrated. Hence, for much of the period, entry decisions have been much influenced by the state. In the following section we briefly outline the institutional background and the relevant elements of labor management theory. The information on entry by industry and branch is reported in section 3. In section 4 we go on to discuss the reasons and consequences of the lack of entry before concluding in section 5 with an evaluation of the social as against the private costs and benefits of entry.

2 Historical and Theoretical Background

In this section, we briefly outline the relevant aspects of Yugoslavia's recent history in order to understand the changing process of entry and exit, as well as summarizing the conceptual issues highlighted by the theory of labor-managed firms. The changing legal and institutional framework has profound implications for the process of entry and exit and for interpreting the data. The theory of labor-management is also relevant because it shows that entry and exit plays a disproportionately important role in ensuring allocative efficiency in such economies.

2.1 Institutional Background

On the basis of the dominant form of economic coordination, four phases can be distinguished in the development of the Yugoslav economic system to the present day: 1945–52, central planning; 1952–65, the so-called visible hand which is a compromise between a Soviet type development strategy and a self-managed market system; 1965–74, self-managed market socialism; 1974–88, contractual socialism. The implications of each period for enterprise entry and exit are as follows

1   The brief era of central planning has a significance for entry and exit far in excess of what might be expected from its duration or success. It was during this period that the fundamentals of the industrial landscape were laid out in terms of the foundation of firms, their size distribution, and the industrial strategy. It was in this period that the bias toward the large size of enterprises and toward manufacturing industry was

established and the role of private sector limited to its still insignificant role.

2   In the 1950s and early 1960s, investment decisions and international trade were for the most part planned centrally, especially in the early years of the period, though firms were given increasing autonomy to allocate any surpluses remaining after tax. At the same time, state ownership was transformed into social ownership by which workers were granted *usus fructus* over the assets in their firms. They could receive the income generated but they could not distribute them as income, nor sell them, nor keep them after they left the enterprise.

The changes introduced, however, did not create an environment conducive to enterprise. Debt was still the major source of investment financing (see Furboton and Pejovich, 1970), there was no equity financing for new ventures, and existing enterprises were not motivated to invest in new enterprises because the rights of ownership and to the surplus were automatically ceded to the new unit's self-management bodies once production had commenced. There was also no downward flexibility in the size of the labor force because of the high political priority to maintain employment in existing enterprises at any cost. Bankruptcy rarely occurred, with ailing enterprises being merged with healthy rivals. Survival of persistently loss-making enterprises was supported by soft budget constraints (Kornai, 1980) which created an important source of bias in capital markets in favor of incumbents at the expense of potential entrants. In addition, the legislation concerning joint ventures between domestic suppliers and foreign firms was so restrictive that in practice it eliminated any role for foreign producers in the entry process. The entry of private firms was also negligible owing to the legal restriction on the size of private firms (no more than eight workers) and an unfavorable tax environment.

3   The central allocation of investment was dismantled by reforms in 1965 which aimed to develop market self-managing socialism. However, this did not promote the entry of new firms. Banks received the balance of state assets and undertook to supply the bulk of investment finance, but little was available to potential new entrants. Banks were not independent financial institutions, but rather were directed in the interests of their founder-members – existing enterprises and local authorities – who made the decisions about how funds should be allocated and were responsible for the bank's debts. This arrangement was an important source of advantage to incumbents in the allocation of investment funds.

4   After 1974, market socialism was replaced by social planning – a system designed simultaneously to strengthen self-management in the workplace and national economic coordination, particularly with respect to investment. The enterprise was transformed (by laws introduced between 1971–6) into "Organizations of Associated Labor," which meant that each firm was formally broken down into establishments, which were then given their own legal identities as Basic Organizations of Associated Labor (BOALS). These arrangements stimulated integration and market concentration. Although the data on firm numbers show a tremendous increase post-1974, this is not because of entry but is the result of the change in definition: the information available between 1952 and the early 1970s concerns enterprises, while from then on it concerns BOALS.

At the same time, the market was partially replaced by social planning to strengthen coordination, with plans intended to represent a coordinating framework for operational planning by BOALS. Though the plans themselves were not directly operational, banks were required to give priority to investment projects that had been included in the 5 year plans, which created further advantages for incumbent firms *vis-à-vis* potential entrants.

In addition to the factors outlined above, there were three impediments to entry which acted in all four periods under the discussion:

1   the highly restrictive and complicated procedures for entry of new self-managed and private enterprises which effectively prevented individuals, or groups of individuals, from being founders of a social firm, except from 1965 to 1968 – new social firms had to be established by existing firms or sociopolitical communities;
2   a generally accepted view that large self-managed firms are more efficient and easier to control;
3   the suppression of entrepreneurial activity because of the belief that entrepreneurship is only compatible with capitalism.

2.2 The Theory of Self-Management and Entry

A considerable literature has emerged that analyzes the consequences of the fact that all firms in the Yugoslav social sector are self-managed (see for example Ward, 1958; Vanek, 1970; Estrin, 1983). Surprisingly, there has been no formal analysis of the entry process as yet, but the existing work indicates several points that such a theory should take into account.

First, it is normally argued that self-managed firms will maximize average earnings per head rather than profits. This is because, in such organizations, the labor force is the entrepreneurial group. In capitalist firms, maximization of profit per entrepreneur is the same as maximization of profit because the number of entrepreneurs does not influence supply decisions on the margin. Since output and profits vary with employment, maximizing profit per worker will clearly give a different answer to maximizing profits, and it is the former value that will be of interest to the worker-entrepreneurs.

The fact that earnings rather than profits are the motivating force of the system has several important implications for the entry and exit process. Consider the case of a self-managing labor force whose workers each receive an equal share of revenues net of non-labor costs. If we define what would be profits P under a capitalist system as revenue R minus labor costs (wages w times labor L) and capital costs (capital rental r times capital stock K, then average earnings y can be seen to be

$$y = \frac{R - rK}{L} = w + \frac{P}{L} \qquad (11.1)$$

a notional wage payment plus a share of profits. Hence, if we assume perfect competition, y^* is the level of earnings which would pertain when capitalist profits are zero and entry will occur when $y - y^* > 0$. More generally, y^* will depend on industry-specific entry barriers.

The argument is not necessarily symmetric for exit, however, depending on the supply price of labor. There may be circumstances in which worker-managers would choose to stay in the enterprise even if $y - y^* < 0$, for example, if the expected value of alternative earnings were below y^* because of unemployment. Hence labor entrepreneurs may be expected to keep enterprises open which under capitalism would be closed, if the organization continued to offer rents to the labor force.[1]

Vanek (1970) and Meade (1972) have stressed that entry and exit will play a relatively more important role in the allocative process than under capitalism. Essentially, this is because self-managed firms restrict output relative to their profit-maximizing counterparts when profits are positive (see Ward, 1958). Hence favorable demand or cost perturbations do not generate a sufficient industry supply response from existing firms and the system must rely disproportionately on entry. The same argument applies in reverse for welfare-reducing shocks.

The theory implies that private individuals will make up the pool of potential entrants. In practice, except for a brief period during the 1960s, entry by private individuals has been virtually nonexistent in Yugoslavia. This is in part because there are simply no incentives to invest one's own skill and savings in an organization which must revert to social ownership and self-management when employment exceeds eight workers. Moreover, banks discriminate against "private companies." According to Sacks (1973), in the 22 years between 1952 and 1974, only around 350 private firms were formed in Yugoslavia. They were all small, none grew, and not many survived for more than a few years.

The state – either federal or more recently republican and local – did play a significant role in the entry process, particularly in the visible hand period. But it is unclear whether their actions were motivated by market criteria or whether they were following their own agendas, oriented to employment and local status. We investigate this issue more formally below. The other potential founders of new enterprises in the Yugoslav system are existing firms seeking to diversify. At first sight there seems little motivation for them; the capital invested ends up socially owned and once a new enterprise is operational, it must be independently self-managed. However, it may be possible to generate higher returns by forming new companies, for example, by exploiting under-utilized assets or economies of scope.

3 Entry and Exit in the Yugoslav Industrial Sector, 1952–1974

In this section, we outline the pattern of entry and exit in the Yugoslav industrial sector since the inception of workers' self-management, in total and by industrial branch (approximately three-digit level). This is the first time that most of these data have been available in either English or Serbo-Croat.[2]

In table 11.1 we report separate data on firm numbers, gross entry, net entry, exit, and mergers for the industrial sector as a whole for the period when definitions are roughly constant, i.e. 1952–72. In fact, the data suggest that firms may have begun changing their structure on a significant scale in 1971, since in 1972 gross entry was small and the number of mergers considerable but "firm numbers" increased by more than over the previous 20 years put together.

The number of firms in the Yugoslav industrial sector is small, never exceeding 2,800 in total and fluctuating around an average of 2,500. Net entry rates were quite high, up to 10 percent per annum, but gross entry rates were typically extremely low, less than 1 percent per annum except

Table 11.1 Yugoslav industrial sector industry 1952–1973

Year	No. of firms	Gross entry	Net entry	Exit	No. of mergers	Gross entry rate (%)	Net entry rate (%)	Exit rate (%)
1952	2198	35	NA	NA	NA	1.6	NA	NA
1953	2330	14	132	NA	NA	0.6	5.6	NA
1954	2482	10	152	NA	NA	0.4	6.1	NA
1955	2530	14	48	NA	NA	0.6	1.9	NA
1956	2541	8	11	NA	NA	0.3	0.4	NA
1957	2525	9	−16	NA	NA	0.3	−0.6	NA
1958	2710	0	185	NA	NA	0.0	6.8	NA
1959	2474	0	−236	NA	NA	0.0	−9.5	NA
1960	2556	34	32	NA	87	1.3	3.2	NA
1961	2787	41	231	NA	96	1.5	8.2	NA
1962	2684	33	−103	NA	110	1.2	−3.8	NA
1963	2507	16	−177	NA	160	0.6	−7.1	NA
1964	2445	31	−62	NA	133	1.3	−2.5	NA
1965	2466	8	21	NA	98	0.3	0.9	NA
1966	2467	12	1	NA	68	0.5	0.0	NA
1967	2492	3	25	NA	46	0.1	1.0	NA
1968	2508	3	16	NA	28	0.1	0.6	NA
1969	2434	32	−74	NA	73	1.3	−3.0	NA
1970	2374	43	−60	2	144	1.8	−2.5	0.08
1971	2398	35	24	10	105	1.5	1.0	0.4
1972	2773	27	375	4	81	0.9	13.5	0.2
1973	3217	27	444	2	75	0.8	13.8	0.1

All firms belong to the social sector.

NA, not available.

Sources: Sacks, 1973; Petrin, 1981; Yugoslav National Year Books.

for 1952, when planners were still influential in forming new enterprises, and two short periods at the beginning and the end of the 1960s. There also appears to be no significant relationship between rates of gross and net entry: the periods of slow or zero gross entry are usually associated with fairly rapid increases in firm numbers, while those years in which gross entry exceeds 1 percent are frequently also years of negative net entry. The limited information available also suggests that exit rates were negligible over the period, never reaching even 0.5 percent of the firm population in a year. The movement in the number of firms therefore appears to have been driven primarily by mergers, with considerable declines in firm numbers during the merger booms of 1962–4 and 1969–71. The years of rapid net entry, for example, 1953–5, 1958, and 1961, are associated with organizational changes in which firms divided into their constituent parts along the lines later codified in the 1974 reforms.[3]

In table 11.2 we report firm numbers, and gross and net entry by industrial branches for 1956–68, the years when data are available. As in table 11.1, there is no obvious relationship between gross and net entry in any year, particularly since in most years there is no entry whatsoever in the majority of sectors. Only in the years of relatively rapid entry – 1960, 1962, and 1964 – do a majority of sectors enjoy positive gross entry.

The average rate of entry over the 13 year period was 16 percent, or slightly over 1 percent per year. However, this was biased upward by the 100 percent gross entry rate in the rubber sector. If this branch is excluded, the average entry rate falls to under 1 percent per annum. Entry rates were high in ferrous metallurgy, chemicals, paper, and metal products. They were less than 5 percent over the period in building materials, shipbuilding, and, of course, coal and coke. There is therefore no unambiguous evidence that entry rates were lower (or higher) in the planners' traditional preserve of heavy industry.

4 Explanations of the Pattern of Gross Entry

There is a large literature on entry in capitalist market economies, but no one has ever attempted to explain the entry process in a market socialist economy such as that of Yugoslavia. Our preliminary attempt to do so is contained in table 11.3.

Of course, Yugoslav entry rates are very low. The core reasons are the absence of potential entrants, capital market discrimination against them, and the lack of incentives for entry by the few agents legally

S. Estrin and T. Petrin

Table 11.2

Industrial branch	1956			1957			1958			1959			1960			1961		
	M	GE	ME	M	GE	ME	M	GE	ME	M	GE	ME	M	GE	ME	M	GE	ME
Electricity	118	4	NA	101	1	−17	95	0	−6	77	0	−18	153	2	76	146	0	−7
Coal and Coke	106	0		103	0	−3	99	0	−4	84	0	−15	82	0	−2	81	0	−1
Petroleum	9	1		9	0	0	9	0	0	9	0	0	9	0	0	9	0	0
Ferrous metallurgy	11	1	NA	12	0	1	14	0	2	13	0	1	14	0	−1	14	0	0
Nonferrous metallurgy	34	0		35	0	1	35	0	0	34	0	−1	36	1	2	37	1	1
Nonmetals	101	1		109	8	8	109	0	0	95	0	−14	97	0	2	87	0	−10
Metal products	258	1	NA	261	0	3	258	0	−3	276	0	18	279	3	3	313	9	34
Shiphuilding	22	0		22	0	0	22	0	0	19	0	−3	19	0	0	20	0	1
Electrical products	40	0		41	0	1	42	0	1	43	0	3	42	0	−3	51	0	−9
Chemicals	92	0	NA	95	0	3	101	0	6	98	0	−3	102	8	4	117	3	13
Building materials	377	0		364	0	−13	363	0	−1	354	0	−9	349	5	−5	356	2	7
Wood products	281	0		278	0	−3	263	0	−15	258	0	−3	263	3	5	290	3	27
Paper products	31	0	NA	30	0	−1	29	0	−1	21	0	−8	20	0	−1	32	0	12
Textiles	290	0		280	0	−10	277	0	−3	287	0	10	292	6	5	329	11	37
Leather goods	86	0		86	0	0	87	0	1	92	0	5	96	1	4	103	3	9
Rubber	6	0	NA	6	0	0	6	0	0	6	0	0	7	0	1	8	0	1
Food products	513	0		516	0	3	6	0	0	6	0	0	7	0	1	8	0	1
Printing	97	0		96	0	−1	509	0	−7	385	0	−124	364	3	−19	393	2	−1
Tobacco	68	0	NA	70	0	2	98	0	2	182	0	64	190	1	10	250	2	60
Miscellaneous	NA	NA					NA	NA	0	44	0	NA	47	0	3	45	0	−2

GE, gross entry; NE, net entry; NA, nor available.
Sources: Sacks, 1972; Yugoslav National Year Books

able and capable of so doing. The evidence suggests that the situation, which was not very good during the 1950s and early 1960s, has been continuously deteriorating since then, with the reforms of 1965 and 1974 placing ever more control over the entry process in the hands of incumbent firms. Our econometric work concentrates on the period when the state took some responsibility for entry, and seemed more willing to facilitate its occurrence.

Theory suggests that entry should follow average earnings. Hence to the extent that entry is decentralized, the possibility of enhancing earnings should be an important motivation. In the absence of profits as an indicator of efficiency, earnings are also the primary indicator to

1962			1963			1964			1965			1966			1967			1968		
M	GE	ME	M	GE	ME	M	GE	ME	M	GE	ME	M	GE	ME	M	GE	ME	M	GE	ME
146	1	0	128	0	−18	94	0	−34	94	3	−10	90	1	−4	79	0	−1	91	0	2
82	0	1	74	0	−8	71	0	−3	72	0	1	68	0	−4	66	0	−2	57	0	−9
9	0	0	9	0	0	6	0	−3	6	0	0	4	0	−2	3	0	1	3	0	0
13	0	−1	13	1	0	13	0	0	12	0	−1	14	0	2	13	1	−1	13	0	0
39	1	2	33	0	−6	32	0	−1	31	0	−1	33	0	2	33	0	0	31	0	−2
85	0	−1	75	2	−11	77	0	2	90	3	13	89	4	−1	91	1	2	89	0	−2
322	2	8	326	2	4	324	3	−2	345	1	21	347	3	2	357	1	10	358	0	1
20	0	0	21	0	1	21	1	0	20	0	−1	19	0	−1	18	0	−1	19	0	1
47	1	−4	51	0	4	53	2	2	57	0	4	73	0	16	75	0	2	78	0	3
109	2	−8	104	2	−3	143	5	37	151	0	8	145	1	−6	148	0	3	150	1	2
321	2	−35	278	0	−43	262	3	−16	294	0	−8	244	0	−10	244	0	0	243	0	−1
269	4	−21	250	2	−11	290	2	0	251	0	1	268	0	17	267	0	1	273	1	6
32	1	0	33	1	1	97	3	4	40	0	3	38	1	−2	38	0	0	38	0	0
330	10	1	324	3	−6	313	7	−11	320	0	7	328	1	8	339	0	11	341	0	2
101	1	−4	101	2	0	94	2	−7	92	1	−2	91	0	−1	92	0	1	94	0	2
11	3	3	11	1	0	12	2	1	12	0	0	16	0	4	16	0	0	16	0	0
334	3	−59	283	0	−51	249	0	−34	234	0	−15	201	0	−33	197	0	−3	200	1	2
249	0	−1	248	0	−1	274	1	26	281	0	7	305	1	24	320	0	15	333	0	13
74	1	−1	66	0	−8	60	0	−6	60	0	0	53	0	−7	43	0	−10	39	0	−4
58	1	13	51	0	−7	24	0	−27	25	0	1	23	0	−2	21	0	−2	19	0	−2

planners of capital shortage and should therefore also influence their allocation of funds to new entrants. Therefore the first question to be addressed is whether there is any evidence that the entry of new firms was related to previously observed levels and rates of change of average earnings in that industry.

A second important element of planners' motivation was probably employment. The creation of industrial employment was probably the most important single objective for the authorities in this relatively less developed and labor surplus economy. The idea was that planners would seek to invest in new capacity, including new firms, in sectors where employment growth was fastest. We test for this effect by including lagged rates of growth of sectoral employment in the gross entry equation.

S. Estrin and T. Petrin

Table 11.3 Explanations of entry into Yugoslav industry

	(1) Gross entry level	(2) Gross entry rate	(3) Gross entry rate (industries where entry is positive)	(4) Gross entry rate (industries where industry is positive/) log form
No. of firms$_t$	0.002 (0.003)	–		
Earnings$_{t-1}$	0.00002** (0.00001)	0.0000025 (0.0000015)	0.0000002 (0.0000004)	2.121** (1.174)
Δ earnings $_{t-1}$	−0.964 (1.70)	−0.45 (0.028)	−0.039 (0.059)	−0.376 (0.224)
Δ employment$_{t-1}$	−0.152 (0.77)	−0.016 (0.013)	−0.004 (0.013)	−0.091 (0.160)
Industry dummies	Yes*[a]	Yes*[c]	Yes*[e]	Yes*[g]
Time dummies	Yes*[b]	Yes*[d]	Yes*[d]	Yes*[h]
$\bar{R}^2$	0.4041	0.2607	0.8081	0.8215
No. of	247	247	78	78

Standard errors in parentheses.

[a] Industries 6, 7, 10, and 14 were all positive significant at the 95 percent level relative to industry 1.

[b] Years 1960, 1961, and 1962 were all positive and significant at the 95 percent level relative to 1957

[c] Industries 6, 10, and 16 were positive and significant at the 95 percent level relative to industry 1.

[d] Years 1962, 1963, and 1964 were all positive and significant at the 95 percent level relative to 1957.

[e] Industries 6, 10, and 16 were positive and significant at the 95 percent level relative to industry 1.

[f] Years 1964, 1965, 1966, and 1967 were negative and significant relative to 1960; years 1956–9 omitted.

[g] Industries 6, 13, and 16 positive and significant; industry 18 negative and significant at the 95 percent level relative to industry 1.

[h] Years 1965, 1966, 1967 and 1968 negative and significant at the 95 percent level relative to 1960; years 1956–9 omitted.

 * Statistically significant at the 95 percent level.

** Statistically significant at the 90 percent level.

Given that entry was largely a preserve of planners, either directly or indirectly via their influence over the banking system, one might predict that their traditional preferences for heavy rather than light industry would be visible in the sectoral entry pattern. We therefore experimented with a dummy for light industry, but opted for the full set of industry dummies in the reported regressions on the grounds of fit. Finally, the historical material suggests that we might expect differences in the entry pattern between periods, with the break occurring with the relaxation of central intervention in 1965. Year dummies provided a better explanation of gross entry than a single dummy for the visible hand period.

In table 11.3, we report four versions of our entry equation; in every case the dependent variable is based upon gross rather than net entry to avoid confusing the picture by reference to the entirely different processes of divestiture, merger, and exit. Columns 1 and 2 are estimated over the entire data set (247 observations), while columns 3 and 4 cover only the industries in which gross entry was positive (78 observations). The regressions in columns 1 and 2 differ only in that in 1 the number of entrants is the dependent variable, with the number of firms in the industry included on the right-hand side, while in 2 the equation explains the gross entry rate. We obtain a rather better explanation of entry levels than rates, though it is the latter which is of greater interest from an economic perspective.

Column 1 provides the only hint in the table that there could be any economic forces at all behind the Yugoslav entry process, with a weakly significant coefficient on lagged earnings (at the 90 percent level). The industry numbers in the footnotes to the table refer to those reported in table 11.2. Entry levels are particularly high, *ceteris paribus*, in the non metals, metals, chemical, and textile sectors, and in the pre-reform years of the early 1960s before capital markets were decentralized, and entry rates are high in the first and third of these four sectors plus rubber. In neither is a significant explanation provided by the rate of change of earnings or of employment. This suggests that the allocators of investment were not concerned to use the formation of new firms as a mechanism either to reduce scarcities indicated by high rents nor rapidly to create new jobs. Nor, as column 1 reveals, was gross entry related in any way to the number of firms currently operating in the industry. This may be because, given the limited variation in this variable, the effect is picked up in the industry dummies. In supplementary unreported regressions we also included average firm size and capital intensity as dependent variables to see whether planners were influenced by entry costs but these added nothing to the explanation in any formulation.

This picture of entry as a highly marginal process which is largely random once industry and time-specific factors are eliminated is confirmed by focusing on the determinants of gross entry rates in the sectors where entry did in fact occur, i.e. the regressions in columns 3 and 4 of table 11.3. The number of industries in the data set drops from 247 to 78, itself an indicator of the paucity of entry, though exaggerated because of the use of lagged independent variables. In column 3 we report a simple gross entry rate equation and in column 4 the same equation estimated in logarithms.[4] The fit improves markedly when all the zeros are eliminated from the right-hand side, but we are still unable to isolate significant effects from any of the economic variables above the 90 percent level. The equation in column 3 tells broadly the same story as those in columns 1 and 2, with entry relatively faster in the non metals, chemicals, and rubber sectors, and in the early 1960s. The logarithmic formulation offers the best fit, and, as in column 1, provides evidence at the 90 percent level that gross entry is driven by earnings levels, though by neither the change in earnings nor the change in employment. However, the industry- and time-specific factors show a similar pattern to that in the other columns, with the exception that two further industry dummies are significant – with a positive coefficient for paper products and a negative one for tobacco.

In conclusion, we therefore find that there is some systematic pattern to the entry process in Yugoslavia, but it derives almost entirely from the relatively more common permission granted to new entrants in particular sectors (primarily nonmetals, chemicals, and rubber), and to the fact that, presumably for political reasons, entry was greater in certain years (the early 1960s). While the sign on lagged average earnings is typically positive and sometimes weakly significant, taken as whole the regressions provide little evidence that economic factors encroach very far into motivating the minimal Yugoslav entry process.

4.1 Some Consequences of the Lack of Entry

In this section we try to pinpoint some of the characteristics of the economy which could be associated with an inadequate entry process. Before commencing, we note that the problems are intensified by other aspects of Yugoslav market socialism. Low entry rates would be of secondary importance if market signals were strong and undistorted, if incumbents reacted rapidly to market opportunities, and if the Yugoslav market structure were diverse and competitive. However, most observers stress the fragmented and distorted nature of market signals in Yugoslavia, even during the most decentralized period (1965–74) as well as the slow reaction of incumbents to market signals (see for example Schrenk et al., 1979; Prout, 1985).

The consequences of weak entry can be inferred to some extent by evidence on Yugoslav market structure in tables 11.4 and 11.5. In table 11.4 we present the size distribution of firms by employment in the Yugoslav social sector. In 1954, only 12 percent of firms employed fewer than 125 workers, and by 1973 this had declined to 4 percent. This compares with an average of 30 percent in OECD countries in the mid-1970s (see Petrin, 1981). By 1973, 57 per cent of Yugoslav industrial firms employed more than 1,000 workers compared with 35 percent in

Table 11.4 Size distribution for social sector in 1954, 1965, and 1973

		Size distribution (%)								
Year	>15	16–29	30–60	61–125	126–250	251–500	501–1000	1001–2000	>2000
1954	0	1	3	8	12	16	20	41	NA
1965	0	0	1	7	7	14	18	22	31
1973	0	0	1	3	7	14	18	24	33

NA, not available.
Sources: Petrin, 1981; Yugoslav National Yearbooks

Table 11.5 Four-firm (sales) concentration ratio in Yugoslav industrial branches

Industrial branch	Concentration ratio (%), 1959, and changes in concentration (%)			
	1959	1965/1959	1973/1965	1973/1959
Coal	58	144.8	100	144.8
Oil	100	96	93.7	90.0
Ferrous metals	86	101.2	96.6	97.7
Nonferrous	94	96.8	107.7	104.3
Nonmetallic	90	98.9	92.1	91.0
Metals	84	63.1	88.7	55.9
Shipbuilding	88	97.7	100	97.7
Electricals	76	110.5	86.5	96.1
Chemicals	78	94.9	97.3	92.3
Building materials	56	105.4	89.8	94.7
Wood	27	181.5	53.1	96.3
Paper	53	109.4	89.7	98.1
Textiles	37	108.1	77.5	83.8
Leather	44	154.6	77.9	120.5
Rubber	88	89.8	126.6	113.6
Food	42	111.9	93.6	104.8
Tobacco	51	103.9	113.2	117.6

Sources: Sacks, 1973; Petrin, 1981; Estrin, 1983

OECD countries. The highly skewed Yugoslav distribution pertains, even when the private sector is included. Given how few firms there were in total, the very high levels of concentration recorded in table 11.5 also come as no surprise.

The manner in which the size distribution shifts to the right over time in table 11.4 is consistent with the view that growth stemmed entirely from the expansion of incumbents or the entrance of relatively large firms. There was no continuous process of entry into the smaller-size classes characteristic of the other countries discussed in this volume. Moreover, in the period when entry rates were relatively fast, in the early 1960s, average concentration levels actually rose from their already high levels in ten sectors of the 17 reported in table 11.5. Indeed, despite a second flurry of new entry in the early 1970s, concentration ratios in 1973 were higher than those pertaining 14 years previously in almost one-third of sectors, and were only reduced by more than 10 percentage points in two sectors, textiles and metals. There appears to be some relationship between gross entry and changes in concentration levels over the period. Concentration ratios increased most in the coal and coke sector, where there was no entry, and declined most in sectors where gross entry was most rapid – metals, textiles, chemicals, and nonmetals – though causality cannot necessarily be inferred.

5 Conclusions

Geroski (Introduction to this volume) has argued that entry in contemporary Western market economies may have high costs and unclear benefits. In this paper we suggest that things look very different from the perspective of market socialism. We would speculate that in a semi-planned economy like that of Yugoslavia, where entry and exit rates are very low and barely influenced by economic factors, the fact that the costs of entry are negligible are more than offset by the loss of potential benefits in terms of resource allocation.

We hypothesize that there are several dimensions to this downside effect, in addition to the problems of market structure discussed above. On the demand side, we associate the lack of entry, and in particular the virtual absence of new small firms, with the severe lack of product diversity in Yugoslavia. This is more than a restatement of the imperfect market structure argument. As Sacks (1973) noted, there are very few producers for relatively few products. In 1968, of 759 industrial products, he finds that 16 percent were produced by a monopolist, 37 percent by three firms or less, and only 20 percent by more than 20 suppliers. To the extent that one associates product innovation with entry, the weakness of the entry process may be a further explanation for why Yugoslavia appears to have relatively few goods to buy and, even for those on offer, little diversity of style or content.

On the supply side, it is argued that the paucity of firms and lack of economically motivated entry leads to an insufficiency of subcontractors and shortages of numerous intermediate products and parts (see Petrin, 1981). This helps to explain why large firms in Yugoslavia continue to tend to autarchy in material inputs in a manner characteristic of Soviet-type economies, despite the fact that supply planning was abandoned in the 1950s. The inefficiencies resulting from this lack of specialization have been well documented elsewhere (e.g. Ellman, 1989).

These speculations suggest that, because of an institutional structure which greatly hinders the entry and exit process, Yugoslavia may be forgoing an important avenue for efficiency enhancement. This conclusion can be squared with that of Geroski if we consider the distinction between the private and social costs and benefits of entry. The above discussion suggests that the social benefits of entry may greatly exceed the private benefits, particularly when viewed from the extreme perspective of an economy virtually devoid of economically meaningful entry. The private costs of entry in a market economy seem very high because the accompanying exit rate is so high, and the benefits, at least according to some of papers in this volume, seem rather limited since entry appears not greatly to reduce persistent long-run profits. From the social point of view, however, the benefits may be higher because of the additional effects on product diversity, supply efficiency and innovation, especially when the market structure is severely imperfect and market forces are weak. At the same time, private costings of entry may overstate the social cost because the apparently excessive entry rate throws up information which is not otherwise available in the system, and which may be crucial to economic decision-making, especially in the absence of alternative information sources. In that sense, the paucity of entry may itself help to explain our inability to understand it from an economic point of view; by suppressing the entry process, the planners were cutting themselves off from a valuable source of information about efficient future development paths for the economy.

Notes

1   This point has particular significance in the Yugoslav context, where since 1952 profits have not even been defined as an accounting concept.
2   But see Petrin (1981) and Sacks (1972, 1973) for partial coverage. The questions have previously been considered by Petrin (1981).
3   Thus between 1953 and 1955 enterprises were decreasing in size by divestiture because it was felt that enterprises should not be larger than could be governed by a single Workers' Council. The latter two dates correspond to the introduction of "economic units" in larger enterprises, the precursors of the BOALs.
4   We do not control for the selection bias caused by focusing on this limited sample because the absence of significant results argues against the application of sophisticated methods. Nonetheless, the results in columns 3 and 4 should be treated as indicative.

References

Dmitrijevich, D. and Masesich, G. (1973) *Money and Finance in Contemporary Yugoslavia.* New York: Praeger.
Ellman, M. (1989) *Socialist Planning*, 3rd edn. Cambridge: Cambridge University Press.
Estrin, S. (1983) *Self-Management: Economic Theory and Yugoslav Practice*, Cambridge: Cambridge University Press.
Furboton, E.G. and Pejovich, S. (1970) Property rights and behaviour of the firm in a socialist state: the example of Yugoslavia. *Zeitschrift für Nationalökonomie* 30, 431–54.

Kornai, J. (1980) *Economics of Shortage*. Amsterdam: North-Holland.

Lydall, H. (1984) *Yugoslavia*. Oxford: Oxford University Press.

Meade, J.E. (1972) The theory of labour-managed firms and of profit-sharing. *Economic Journal* 82. 402–28.

Petrin, T. (1981) Analiza vzrokov koncentracije organizacijskih enot industrija in trgovini Jugoslavije v Letih 1954–78. RCEF, Ljubljana.

Prout, C. (1985) *Market Socialism in Yugoslavia*. Oxford: Oxford University Press.

Sacks, S. (1972) Changes in industrial structure in Yugoslavia. *Journal of Political Economy* 80, 561–74.

Sacks, S. (1973) *Entry of new competitors in Yugoslav market socialism*. Research Series 19, Institute of International Studies, University of California, Berkeley, CA.

Schrenk, M., Ardalan, C. and El Tatawy, N. (1979) *Yugoslavia: Self-Management Socialism and the Challenges of Development*. Baltimore, MD: Johns Hopkins University Press.

Tyson, L. (1980) *The Yugoslav economy and its performance in the 1970s*. Institute of International Studies, University of California, Berkeley, CA.

Vanek, J. (1970) *The General Theory of the Labor-Managed Market Economy*. Ithaca, NY: Cornell University Press.

Ward, B. (1958) The firm in Illyria: market syndicalism. *American Economic Review* 48, 266–89.

12

Innovation as a Means of Entry:
an Overview

David B. Audretsch and Zoltan J. Acs

1 Introduction

Much of the literature on entry is obsessed with identifying the impact that new firms will have on reducing prices and profits either by adding to market output or by fueling the embers of competition.[1] The role that entry plays in the process of technological change, as emphasized by Schumpeter (1911), Nelson (1984), Helmstädter (1986), and others, has generally been ignored in this literature. However, Geroski and Jacquemin (1985, p. 178) warn that "Entry is both a disciplinary and an innovatory force. As a discipline entry acts to bid away excess profits and drive industrial structure towards cost minimizing configurations. As a force for innovation, entry operates by throwing up new ideas embodied in the particular challenges of individual entrants to which incumbent firms must respond."

The purpose of this paper is to argue for the view that entry and innovative activity are complementary phenomena that are to a large extent driven by the evolution of the industry over the life cycle. Considering innovation and entry within a life-cycle context enables the resolution of several apparent contradictions. For example, Mueller and Tilton (1969, p. 578) argued that R&D could constitute a barrier to entry, because "The chief component of these barriers generally is the extent of economies of scale in the R&D process. The second major factor contributing to R&D entry barriers is the accumulation of patents and know-how on the part of incumbent firms." The notion that R&D impedes entry has at least some empirical suport. Orr (1974) found that Canadian net entry was adversely affected by R&D intensity, and Baldwin and Gorecki (1987) found that entry via plant creation is

We wish to thank Paul Geroski, Steven Klepper, and F.M. Scherer for their helpful suggestions on parts of this paper. All errors and omissions remain our responsibility.

negatively related to R&D.[2] At the same time, a casual reading of the popular literature reveals that, especially in so-called high technology industries, there has been a wave of entry and new firm start-ups (Scherer, 1991).

The resolution of this contradiction lies in examining the various roles that R&D, innovation, innovation-producing knowledge, and entry play as an industry evolves over the life cycle. Thus, in secion 2 we introduce a model relating innovation and entry to the industry life cycle. The implications of this model are examined in section 3 within the context of several empirical cross-section studies. In section 4 lessons from several case studies are considered. Finally, conclusions are provided in section 5. We conclude not only that innovation and entry are complementary phenomena reflecting the stage of the industry life cycle, but also that they play a key role in understanding the dynamic evolution of markets.

2 Innovation and Entry over the Industry Life Cycle

The notion that market structure is largely influenced by technology has a long tradition in industrial organization. As early as 1948, Blair (1948) argued that the firm-size distribution was a direct result of the prevailing technology. In particular, he hypothesized that, owing to specific innovations and fundamental shifts in technology within certain industries, the trend toward increasing firm size would be replaced by an opposite trend toward smaller firms. More recently, Dasgupta and Stiglitz (1980) and Dasgupta (1986) have proposed a "new industrial organization" whereby certain characteristics of technology are decisive determinants of market structure.

However, specification of the exact manner in which technology affects market structure, and the size-distribution of firms in particular, has generally remained vague at best. One of the more specific models relating technology to market structure was introduced by Winter (1984). The driving force of the dynamic market evolution inherent in his model is what Winter terms the "technological regime." According to Winter (1984, p. 297), "An entrepreneurial regime is one that is favorable to innovative entry and unfavorable to innovative activity by established firms; a routinized regime is one in which the conditions are the other way around."

Although never rigorously tested, there is at least some empirical evidence consistent with the notion of separate technological regimes which are alternatively conducive to innovative activity by incumbent and new firms. Acs and Audretsch (1987, 1988) found that innovative activity of small firms is promoted by a rather different economic environment than that for large firms. While small firms do not necessarily imply new firms, Evans (1987) found a definite positive correlation between firm size and age. Thus, to the extent that large firms can be associated with incumbent enterprises and small firms tend to be new companies, or at least relatively new entrants, the finding of distinct environments promoting large and small innovative activity is consistent with the existence of separate technological regimes.

Gort and Klepper (1982) suggested that there are two distinct sources of information about new product technology – from firms already in the market and from firms outside the set, or on the fringe, of the major incumbent producers. The first information source is the product of experience and contains both transferable and nontransferable components. Gort and Klepper emphasize that the accumulated stock of nontransferable information is the product of learning by doing, which, by definition, firms outside the industry cannot possess. The greater is the role which the accumulated stock of nontransferable information plays, the greater will be the extent to which innovative activity emanates from the major incumbents.

In Gort and Klepper's (1982) model, entry behavior is derived directly from these technological regimes. Under the routinized regime, innovation as a vehicle for entry is less of a viable alternative for firms either outside or on the fringe of the market. However, entry by outside firms is induced when innovation-producing information from outside the industry is relatively more important. Arrow (1962), Williamson (1975), and Mueller (1976) have all pointed out that when such information created outside of the industry cannot be easily transferred to those firms existing within the industry, perhaps because of organizational factors, the holder of such knowledge has no choice other than to enter the industry in order to exploit the market value of his/her knowledge.[3]

While Winter (1984) and Gort and Klepper (1982) take the technological regime to be exogenous in their models, an implication from Mueller and Tilton (1969) is that it is likely to be directly related to the stage of the product in the industry life cycle. The most complete version of the product life cycle ascribes four distinct phases that characterize the evolution of a typical industry (Vernon, 1966; Wells, 1966).[4] Theses four phases – introduction, growth, maturity, and decline – are typically defined by relating the change in the volume of sales to time. In the introduction phase, when the product is new, not only are sales increasing but the rate of increase in sales is also increasing, i.e. the second derivative of sales with respect to time is positive. In the growth phase, sales volume is still increasing, but the rate of increase is no longer increasing as well. The first derivative of sales volume with respect to time is still positive, while the second derivative is negative. Once the industry has evolved to the mature stage, the level of sales is no longer increasing and has stabilized, implying that the first derivative is zero. Finally, in the last phase sales volume is declining, implying that the first derivative is negative.

Several important market structure and firm characteristics have been observed to vary along with the evolution of the life cycle. The most significant of these is the observation that the product is the most technologically advanced, relative to the stock of knowledge, during the early phases, but through a process of technological atrophy has become relatively standardized by the time that it has evolved into the mature and declining phases. In the introduction and growth stages, no singular product design and concept dominates the industry. Firms must experiment with the design in short production runs, making significant modifications after observing consumer response. Products tend to be distinguished by real technological differentiation and competition is more technology oriented than price oriented.

It has also been observed that, as the industry evolves toward the mature and declining stages, the product design becomes more standardized and uniform, and the premium attached to technological superiority recedes. Product differentiation may in fact intensify, but this tends to be through image differentiation rather than through technology differentiation. There is at least some evidence suggesting that market structure characteristics, and in particular technological conditions, vary along with the evolution of the life cycle. After classifying 382 four-digit Standard Industrial Classification (SIC) industries according to their stage on the life cycle, Audretsch (1987) found that those industries in the earlier life-cycle stages tended to be more innovative, less capital intensive, use a higher component of skilled labor, and devote a smaller percentage of sales toward advertising than did industries characterized as being in either the mature or the declining phase.

A major conclusion of Mueller and Tilton (1969) is that the amount of R&D required to enter an industry is relatively low during the earliest life-cycle stage and then subsequently rises until the product has been fully standardized. At the same time, however, the uncertainty associated with the R&D is greatest during the earliest phase, before the product is standardized, and then subsequently diminishes as the industry evolves towards maturity. Thus the cost of innovation as a means of entry is relatively low during the early life-cycle stages but subsequently rises as the industry evolves towards maturity.

226 *D.B. Audretsch and Z.J. Acs*

An implication of Mueller and Tilton (1969) is that under the routinized regime the source of innovation-producing knowledge tends to emanate from R&D laboratories of firms within the industries. This is *not* likely to be the case under the entrepreneurial regime. However, this is not to suggest that innovation-producing knowledge is unrelated to R&D under the entrepreneurial regime; rather, the knowledge is more likely to emanate from R&D laboratories outside the industry entered by the new firm. In fact, it is the desire to appropriate the rents accruing from the generation of such innovations by R&D outside the industry that leads to entry into a new industry.

During the early stages of the life cycle, the ratio of firm innovative output to R&D input should be relatively high, but subsequently declines along with the evolution of the industry over the life cycle. How can this be reconciled with the relatively well-known correlation between R&D and innovative output? Such correlations have typically been made at the *industry* level, where, for example, Acs and Audretsch (1988) found a simple correlation coefficient of 0.746 between industry R&D expenditure and the total number of innovations for 247 four-digit industries. Similarly, they identified a correlation of 0.440 between the number of patented inventions and R&D expenditures at the industry level. However, the relationship between R&D and innovative output is considerably weaker at the *firm* level. Based on 732 R&D firms, the correlation between innovative output and R&D expenditures – at the firm level – falls to 0.399. Thus, while knowledge may be the decisive input in producing innovations, that knowledge does not necessarily have to emanate from the innovating firm's own R&D laboratory–especially under the entrepreneurial regime.

Considering innovation as a means for entry suggests a considerably different economic role for entry than is implicitly assumed in the standard model applied in the individual country studies throughout this volume. In this standard model, entry is assumed to be induced by the presence of economic rents (controlling for entry costs). The product, method of production, inputs used, etc. are assumed to remain fixed. In this view, entry is essentially an equilibrating function, in that the new firms provide the necessary additional output required to restore equilibrium in the market so that economic profits approach their long-run equilibrium level.

However, a more evolutionary view of markets suggests a considerably different economic function for entrants – agents of change. That is, by producing different products or employing different production techniques than the incumbent firm, entrants serve as the mechanisms by which markets change over time. And, as we have argued above, the extent to which entrants serve as agents of change in a market is closely related to the stage of the product life cycle.

3 The Cross-Section Evidence

There exists a substantial body of empirical evidence which implies either directly or indirectly that innovation and entry are complementary phenomena related by the evolution of the industry life cycle. In one of the most important studies, Gort and Klepper (1982) constructed a data base consisting of observations on the number of firms, output, and price for 46 new products. While some of the new products were introduced in the nineteenth century, others did not appear on the market until after the Second World War. After tracing the pattern of firm entry, technological change, output and prices until 1972, Gort and Klepper found that the nature of innovative activity tends to change over the product life cycle. In particular, they found that the life-cycle stage affects the character, importance, and sources of innovations. More importantly, they conclude that, "There appears to be an association between rises and declines in the rate of innovation and the rate of entry into new markets. We interpret the causal relation as being positive, and flowing primarily from innovations to entry rates during the period of positive net entry" (Gort and Klepper, 1982, p. 651).

More recently, Klepper and Graddy (1989) have extended Gort and Klepper's original data set through 1981. Classifying the 46 products according to the change in the number of firms in the industry, Klepper and Graddy identified three discernible stages. The first stage is characterized by an increase in the number of firms. There is a decline (which they term "shakeout") in the number of firms in the second stage. Finally, in the third stage the number of firms stabilizes. Klepper and Graddy find that during the growth and shakeout stages, output tends to grow (at a decreasing percentage rate) and the price level tends to fall (also at a decreasing percentage rate). Once the stabilization stage has been attained, the percentage fall in price and rise in output level off and remain constant over time.

Thus, in both these studies a substantial amount of entry is found to occur along with the introduction of a new product, typically characterized by a wave of innovative activity. As the industry matures, however, the nature of innovative activity tends to change and net entry becomes replaced by net exit until stabilization is attained.

These results are consistent with the findings of Acs and Audretsch (1989a,b). Acs and Audretsch (1989a) employ a cross-section regression model using 247 four-digit SIC industries and find that net entry (the change in the number of firms between 1978 and 1980) is negatively related to the total ratio of R&D to sales for the industry (using 1977 Federal Trade Commission Line of Business Survey data), but positively related to the small-firm innovative rate (measured as the number of innovations by firms with fewer than 500 enployees divided by small-firm employment). These results suggest that entry is relatively greater in those industries in which small firms are particularly innovative. That is, while an R&D-intensive environment may inhibit the start-up of new firms, technological conditions conducive to small-firm innovation are a catalyst for entry.

Of course, the net entry measure used suffers from two well-known deficiencies. First, the change in the number of firms does not account for enterprises which exited from the industry over the relevant period. That is, given an amount of gross entry, the measure of net entry will increase as the number of exits from the industry decreases. Thus it is quite conceivable that an industry could have a negative amount of net entry if many firms actually entered the industry (i.e. if gross entry was positive) but even more firms exited from the industry. Because the pattern of industry exits varies across industries, the extent to which net entry deviates from actual gross entry will also vary from industry to industry. Second, the traditional entry measure is weighted by the number of firms, or in several cases plants, but not by either the sales or employment of the entrants.[5] Although most entry is by small firms, the entry of a single large firm can more than offset (in terms of sales) the entry of hundreds of small firms. Thus, inter-industry comparisons based on numbers of firms obscure differences because of the varying sizes of entering firms.

To avoid these two measurement deficiencies, Acs and Audretsch (1989b) use a measure of gross-employment-weighted entry, or industry births, provided for in the USELM file of the US Small Business Data Base.[6] They find that birth rates (births adjusted for industry employment) are negatively related to total innovative activity but positively related to small-firm innovative activity. These relationships hold not just for small firms, but also for large-firm births. Again, it appears that an environment enabling small firms to innovate invites entry of firms of all sizes. However, holding the extent of small-firm innovative activity constant, the greater the amount of innovative activity in an industry, the more entry (as measured by births) will be inhibited.

The results of these two studies by Acs and Audretsch are consistent with the notion that not just the amount of innovative activity but rather the nature of that innovative activity will determine the concomitant entry behavior. To the extent to which small-firm innovative activity can be viewed as reflecting the entrepreneurial regime and large-firm innovative activity as the routinized regime, there is at least some support of Gort and Klepper's hypothesis that innovation is an important means for entry under the entrepreneurial regime but not under the routinized regime.

Geroski (1989b) finds that total productivity growth in 79 three-digit manufacturing industries between 1976 and 1979 in the United Kingdom is positively related to entry (the market share of all new firms appearing in each annual census) and the number of innovations (using the SPRU innovation data base from Sussex), and negatively related to foreign entry (the change in import share). He includes lags of 1 and 2 years as well as contemporaneous observations. Geroski (1989b, p. 1) argues that these results support the view that ". . . competition promotes efficiency, that a vigorous competitive process throws up alternatives in the form of new firms and new ideas, and that selection amongst them induces movements to, and movements of, the production frontier." He views his three explanatory variables as representing θ in the usual production function:

$$Y = aK^{b_1}L^{b_2}\theta$$

where Y represents output, L represents labor, K represents capital, and "Our goal is to associate variations in θ with the degree of competition in markets" (Geroski, 1989b, p. 2).

However, in view of the discussion in the previous section, it may be more fruitful to consider θ not as the degree of competition in markets, but rather as knowledge generating innovative activity. When an industry is in the early stages of the life cycle, it is more likely to be characterized by the entrepreneurial regime. As previously explained, the knowledge generating innovative activity tends to come from outside the industry, and is transferred into the industry through the entry of a new firm. Thus, while considerable resources, such as R&D, may have been expended in generating the knowledge, it is from outside the industry and therefore not measured as an input in producing industry output. Thus large increments in this type of knowledge – transmitted through the entry of new firms – lead to the measurement of large increases in total factor productivity. In the early stages of the life cycle, therefore, three economic phenomena tend to occur simultaneously – a high amount of innovative activity, entry, and high productivity growth.

However, as the industry evolves towards maturity, the industry is more likely to be characterized by the routinized regime. In this case the expenditure of resources from within the industry (generally by the major incumbents) provides the major source of innovation-generating knowledge. Under the routinized regime, fewer resources expended outside of the industry contribute to producing innovations within the industry, and subsequently there is less entry. Thus, in the later stages of the life cycle a simultaneously decrease in innovative activity, entry, and productivity growth is observed.

Viewed in this life-cycle context, Geroski's findings of a negative relationship between import share and productivity are not surprising. Vernon (1966), Wells (1966), and Gruber et al. (1967) emphasized that as the increment to knowledge required in the production process approaches zero, less developed countries are able to copy the production technique with a cost advantage for inputs, and developed countries can expect to shift from being net exporters to being net importers. Similarly, the result that entry lagged 2 years is negatively related to subsequent productivity growth is also consistent with a life-cycle interpretation. As Mansfield (1962), Evans (1987), Hall (1987), and others have found, the survival rate of small firms tends to be significantly less than that of their larger counterparts. While substantial entry may accompany a wave of innovations in the early stage of the life cycle, many of the new firms will stagnate and ultimately fail. Thus, several years subsequent to entering (perhaps even as soon as 2 years later, as Geroski's results imply), the presence of stagnating firms and those on the path to exiting from the industry exerts a negative influence on productivity. In general, Geroski's (1989b) results may as much reflect the tendency for innovative activity and entry to be complementary characteristics which evolve together over the life cycle of industries (along with productivity growth), as they represent the competitive discipline of innovation and entry on productivity growth.

From these cross-section empirical studies several stylized facts have emerged: (a) entry and innovative activity are positively correlated; (b) entry is inhibited in industries where R&D plays an important role but promoted in markets where small-firm innovative activity is high. These stylized facts are consistent with the life-cycle view of innovation as a means for entry presented in the previous section.

4 Case Study Evidence

The evidence from cross-section regression models discussed in the previous section is generally consistent with observations made about the relationship between innovation and entry over the industry life cycle in a rich literature focusing on individual case studies. The semiconductor industry provides one of the best examples of innovation-generating knowledge emanating from firms outside the industry (Winter's (1984) entrepreneurial regime) during the industry's formative years but then shifting to knowledge from experience within the industry as the industry evolved.

The semiconductor industry began with a series of basic technological breakthroughs by a team of scientists led by William Shockley and Gordon Teal at Bell Laboratories in the early 1950s (Derzoutos et al., 1989). Teal departed from Bell Laboratories in 1951 to join the fledgling Texas Instruments, and Shockley left 3 years later to start his own firm. In 1957 eight of Shockley's former employees attracted enough venture capital to form Fairchild Semiconductor (Braun and Macdonald, 1982). According to Florida and Kenney (1988), the formation of Fairchild and the subsequent wave of entrepreneurial spin-offs fueled by venture capital proved to be the catalyst underlying the formation of the Silicon Valley innovation complex. As key employees developed their own specialized knowledge, they frequently departed from their employer and started their own firm to exploit the market value of their innovation(s).

Of the 23 semiconductor producers in Silicon Valley in 1971, 21 were started by former employees of Fairchild. By the middle of the 1970s Fairchild had produced 41 high-technology entrepreneurial spin-offs. Table 12.1 lists the entrants into the semiconductor industry during this phase of the industry's development (1966–76). Particularly noteworthy is the high concentration of entrants emanating from Fairchild and found in the Silicon Valley area. Most of these new start-ups were based on new technology and most were founded by management and technical personnel from existing firms (Office of Technology Assessment, 1984). It is clear that during this stage of the industry's evolution,

Table 12.1 Entry into the US semiconductor industry

Year	Company	City	Previous employment of founders[a]
1966	American Microsystems	Cupertino	Philco-Ford (4)
1966	National Semiconductors	Santa Clara	Fairchild (3)
1967	Electronic Arrays	Mountain View	Philco Ford (4) Bunker-Ramo (2)
1968	Intersil	Sunnyvale	Union Carbide (3)
1968	Advantek	Santa Clara	Applied Technology (4)
1968	Integrated Systems Technology		Philco-Ford (3)

Table 12.1 Continued

Year	Company	City	Previous employment of founders[a]
1968	Intel	Santa Clara	Philco-Ford (2)
1968	Nortec Electronics Corporation	Santa Clara	Fairchild (3)
1968	Computer Microtechnology	Santa Clara	Fairchild (3)
1968	Qualidyne	Sunnyvale	Intersil (1), Fairchild (2), Lehrer (1)
1968	Advanced Memory Systems	Sunnyvale	Fairchild (1), IBM (2), Motorola (1), Collins (1)
1969	Communications Transistor	San Carlos	National Semiconductor (3)
1969	Precision Monolithic	Santa Clara	Fairchild (3)
1969	Monolithic Memories	Santa Clara	IBM (1)
1969	Advanced LSI Systems	Santa Clara	Nortec (1)
1969	Mostek	Carrollton (TX)	Texas Instruments
1969	Signetics Memory Systems	Sunnyvale	Signetics (2), IBM (2), HP (1)
1969	Advanced Micro Devices	Sunnyvale	Fairchild (8)
1969	Spectronics	Richardson (TX)	Texas Instruments
1969	Four Phase	Cupertino	Fairchild (6), General Instruments (2) Mellonics (1), other (1)
1970	Litronix	Cupertino	Monsanto (1)
1970	Integrated Electronics	Mountain View	Fairchild (2)
1970	Varadyne	Mountain View	Fairchild (2)
1971	Caltex	–	Texas Instruments (2) Nortec (4)
1971	Exar	Sunnyvale	Signetics (3)
1971	Micropower	Santa Clara	Intersil (2)
1971	Standard Microsystems	Hauppague (NY)	Four Phase (1), Electro-Nuclear Labs (1), Nitron (1)
1971	Antex	–	–
1971	LSI Systems	–	–
1972	Nitron	Cupertino	–
1972	Frontier	Newport Beach	Caltex (1)
1972	Interdesign	Sunnyvale	Signetics (1)
1974	Synertek	Santa Clara	CMI (3), AMI (4), Fairchild (1)
1974	Zilog	Cupertino	Intel (2)
1975	Maruman	Sunnyvale	National Semiconductor (2)
1976	Supertex	Sunnyvale	Fairchild (1)

[a] The number of founders emanating from the designated company is listed in parentheses.
All cities are located in California, unless noted otherwise.
Source: US Senate (1978, p. 91)

there was little product standardization and considerable competition in design played a major role.

By the mid-1970s, a new stage in the industry's development had been reached – the development of large-scale integration. With the introduction of the microprocessor by Intel in 1971, electronic systems began to be replaced by components. This led to the integration of semi-conductor firms into the electronics market. Between 1975 and 1983 at least 14 independent semiconductor firms, including Fairchild and Signetics, were acquired by companies outside the United States (Borrus et al., 1983). Since then, technological competition has come almost exclusively from firms already existing in the industry.

Towards the end of the 1970s the semiconductor industry experienced a marked metamorphosis. Market share began to depend less upon radical product innovations and more upon the development of manu-facturing techniques essential in the mass production of the more elaborate chips using very large scale integration (VLSI). As predicted by Mueller and Tilton's (1969) thesis, large R&D laboratories became more important along with substantial capital investments. Derzoutos et al. (1989) emphasize that with the maturation of the semiconductor industry, the smaller venture-capital-financed American merchant firms face an increasingly severe competitive disadvantage *vis-à-vis* the larger well-financed firms, which are generally in Japan.

Beginning with the VLSI Project for 1976–9, involving a budget of $32.3 million for R&D from the government, four major government-funded R&D programs were undertaken in Japan. These included the Supercomputer Project ($104.5 million, 1981–9), the Optoelectronics Project ($81.8 million, 1979–86), and the New Function Elements Project ($113.6 million, 1981–90) (Audretsch, 1989).

These projects began to pay off when Fujitsu became the first semi-conductor firm to sell the 64K random access memory (RAM) in 1979. By 1980 Hitachi, Toshiba, and Mitsubishi were also producing 64K RAMs (Semiconductor Association of America, 1983). In the earlier generations of RAM semiconductors, there had been 14 US and eight Japanese producers for the 1K generation, 15 US and six Japanese producers for the 4K, and 12 US and six Japanese producers for the 16K (US International Trade Commission, 1983).

Derzoutos et al. (1989) attribute the decline of the American semi-conductor industry to an industry structure that is adept at production during the earlier stages of the life cycle but not in the more advanced stages. In contrast, they argue that the Japanese firms have developed the requisite size, financial resources, and R&D facilities which enable them to become the global leaders in the semiconductor industry.

Another striking example of the complementarity between innovation and entry over the life cycle is the video display terminal (VDT) industry. During the first half of the 1980s the VDT industry was characterized by high annual growth rates (20–25 percent), rapid technological change in the form of new products, new product features and expanded product capabilities, low entry barriers but high survival barriers, and product life cycles averaging less than 3 years (Link and Zmud, 1984).

The three major submarkets in the VDT industry comprise (a) glass teletypes, which have little internal processing capabilities and are known as "dumb" VDTs, (b) VDTs with internal circuitry enabling programmed processing such as line editing and data manipulation, which are referred to as "small" VDTs, and (c) VDTs capable of sophisticated information processing as a result of complex internal circuitry, storage, and software , which are known as "intelligent" VDTs (Link, 1981).

The first generation of dumb VDTs was introduced in the early 1970s. Since the technology and production process has been standardized for some time, dumb VDTs can be classified as being in the mature phase of the life cycle. Because their technological capabilities were still evolving but becoming increasingly narrower and more homogeneous, smart VDTs could best be characterized as being at the latter end of the growth stage in the mid-1980s.

The intelligent VDT market is clearly in an earlier life-cycle stage than the other two major submarkets. By the mid-1980s there still existed a wide variance in technological capabilities as well as prices (between $2,500 and $8,000). Link and Zmud (1984) emphasize that competition is mainly in terms of new technical features, such as improved software and color graphics.

By comparing patterns of R&D, new product innovations, and entry and exit among these three submarkets in the VDT industry, Link and Zmud (1984) find that the stage of the life cycle plays a crucial role. For example, in the dumb and smart VDT submarkets, R&D projects are oriented toward incremental market-induced product innovations. Major technical breakthroughs are not frequent, and entry is relatively unimportant. In contrast, in the intelligent VDT submarket, R&D is of a more risky nature, but the potential return from R&D – if successful – is greater. Smaller firms account for a greater share of the product innovations. While innovative output is found to be positively related to R&D input, ". . . the marginal returns of increasing size are significantly less than proportional" (Link and Zmud, 1984, p. 113).

Like the semiconductor industry, the biotechnology was formed by a cluster of entrepreneurial start-ups exploiting innovation-generating knowledge (generally produced elsewhere). Biotechnology is particularly dependent upon science, and relies on techniques such as recombinant DNA and hybridomas.[7] The actual scientific breakthroughs triggering the formation of the biotechnology industry were made during the first half of the 1970s. However, there was little recognition at this time that these scientific breakthroughs could have commercial applications. Robert Swanson, who had been a manager at Kleiner Perkins, joined with Herbert Boyer, who was a molecular biologist at the University of California, to form the first biotechnology company, Genetech, in 1976. Swanson served in the role of venture capitalist by bringing an initial $100,000 from Kleiner Perkins to finance the new venture (Kenney, 1986a).

As in the semiconductor industry during its formative years, a proliferation of small-entrepreneurial high technology start-ups quickly ensued Genetech's initial success. Kenney (1986b) emphasizes that most of these entrants were motivated by an attempt to exploit the potential market value of major innovations.

Virtually all the firms in the industry are small (fewer than 1,000 employees) and are specialized in a particular technology niche (Dibner, 1986). Table 12.2 shows the number of new formations in the biotechnology field over the last 25 years. The number of new firm formations peaked in 1981, before declining slightly in 1982–3. In particular, new firm formation in immunology and genetic engineering fell substantially after 1981.

Although there have been numerous attempts by large established firms in the chemical and pharmaceutical industries to enter the biotechnology industry, they have generally been unsuccessful. Florida and Kenney (1988) attribute this to the inability of the large drug and chemical companies to attract and hold high quality scientists. As a result, these large companies have resorted to forming "strategic partnerships" with small firms. In fact, these large firms have often been a source of venture capital for new start-ups. For example, Lubrizol, through its venture capital subsidiary, first invested in Genetech in 1979. It subsequently increased its investment to $15 million, accounting for 20 percent of the equity share in Genetech. Similarly, the Innoven Corporation, which is a joint venture concern funded by Monsanto and Emerson Electric, provided $20 million of venture capital for Biogen Inc. As part of the agreement, Biogen will provide Monsanto with access to its research findings (International Trade Administration, 1984). An appendix listing 57 agreements between small biotechnology firms and

Table 12.2 New firm formations in biotechnology, 1965–1985

	Pre-1965	65	66	67	68	69	70	71	72	73	74	75	76	77	78	79	80	81	82	83	84	85
Animal biotechnology[a]	3	0	0	0	0	0	0	0	2	0	2	1	1	0	1	3	3	1	1	7	2	1
Cell cultures	7	0	0	0	2	2	0	1	1	1	1	4	2	0	1	4	2	5	2	5	1	0
Catalysts	0	0	0	0	0	0	0	0	0	0	1	0	0	1	0	1	2	0	1	2	1	0
Bioelectronics	1	0	0	0	0	0	0	0	0	0	0	0	0	0	0	0	0	0	0	0	0	0
Biotechnology equipment	9	1	1	2	1	1	2	4	0	5	0	1	7	1	3	3	3	3	6	0	1	1
Enzymes	1	0	0	0	1	0	0	0	0	0	2	0	1	2	1	1	2	5	2	7	4	0
Genetic engineering	4	0	0	0	0	0	0	0	4	1	0	0	6	1	4	3	3	16	13	3	1	0
Immunology	3	0	0	0	0	0	1	0	2	1	0	0	1	1	1	3	2	10	1	9	1	5
Biomass/biochemicals	6	0	0	0	1	2	0	0	0	0	0	1	1	0	5	0	2	5	4	5	0	0
Biomaterials	0	0	0	0	0	0	0	1	0	0	1	0	0	0	0	0	0	4	1	3	0	0
Proteins	0	0	0	0	0	1	0	0	2	0	0	0	3	0	0	0	1	1	1	0	0	0
Plant biotechnology	1	0	0	1	0	0	0	0	1	1	0	0	0	1	0	1	2	4	1	0	0	0
Bioprocessing	1	0	0	0	0	0	0	0	1	0	0	0	2	0	1	2	0	2	2	1	0	0
Biological testing	0	0	0	0	0	0	0	0	0	0	1	0	0	0	0	0	0	0	0	0	0	0
Other biotechnology	1	0	0	0	0	0	0	0	0	0	0	0	0	0	0	0	0	0	0	0	0	0

[a] Includes new firms in biotechnology fields not listed.

Source: National Science Foundation, 1987, p. 311

large corporations in the United States is available from the authors upon request.

Kaplinsky (1983) examined the development and evolution of the computer-aided design (CAD) industry and identified four distinct phases which affected the nature of both innovation and entry. The first phase, which consisted of the initial technological breakthroughs (the light pen and screen) by large firms in the military, aerospace and aeronautical, and computer industries lasted from the early 1950s to 1968. The second phase, which occurred between 1969 and 1974, consisted of a wave of entry by new small firms which were spin-offs from other industries. Kaplinsky found these new entrepreneurial start-ups to consist of two distinct groups. The first group comprised people formerly in the software and electronics industry from firms such as IBM. The second group comprised people from the aerospace and transportation equipment industries who had specific experience in CAD software.

The third phase began in 1974 and lasted until 1980, when there was a shakeout of CAD producers. Not only did the rate of innovative activity within the industry slow, but most innovations emanated from firms already existing within the industry, such as General Electric. Subsequently, the average size of firms increased as did the market shares of the leading firms. In fact, Kaplinsky (1983) characterizes this phase as "the trend to concentration."

The final phase, maturity, began in 1980. Kaplinsky (1983) has identified the re-emergence of new small entrepreneurial firms. These firms have been oriented toward specific niches left unfilled by the larger corporations.

Kaplinsky (1983) found that R&D intensity in the industry was minimal prior to 1969, when it increased drastically for several years, before falling to about 12 percent of sales in 1975. Subsequently, R&D intensity in the industry has been declining.

While the above case studies all clearly illustrate the formation of new industries based on the entry of new firms exploiting, or hoping to exploit, product innovations emanating from a relatively low R&D effort, it should be emphasized that there is also an abundance of examples documenting entry and innovation under quite different circumstances and scenarios.

For example, Geroski and Jacquemin (1985) refer to the potato crisp industry in the United Kingdom, in which an incumbent (Smiths) responded to product innovation by an entrant with its own counter-innovation. Golden Wonder based its entry in the market on continuous frying coolers, and emphasizing marketing for home consumption rather than for pub consumption. Confronted by an innovative entrant, Smiths responded by introducing a host of new product varieties (Bevan, 1974).

Similarly, Brock (1975) examined 21 major innovations in the computer industry and attributed only six to IBM. Brock (1975) found that the three important generations of computers prior to the mid-1970s emanated from the challenge posed by entrants. When confronted by entry, IBM typically would copy the innovation(s) quickly and then develop them more effectively than the entrant. Thus, in these cases, the innovations were contributed in part by the entrants and in part by the incumbent responding to the threat of entry.

5 Conclusions

One of the more startling results that has consistently emerged in empirical studies of entry is that new firms are apparently not substantially deterred from entering capital-intensive industries. Acs and Audretsch (1989a, b) find that even small firms are not significantly deterred from entering industries which are relatively capital intensive. This raises several questions. How is it that small firms are able to enter an industry at suboptimal scale? And how are they able to survive subsequent to entry?

The answers to these questions are implied to some extent by the view posited in this paper that entry and innovation are complementary phenomena reflecting the stage of the industry life cycle. When knowledge from outside the industry is a more important input into the generation of innovations, as represented by the entrepreneurial regime, entry is more likely to occur. Of course, those firms which are unable to learn and adopt successfully will subsequently fail. Consistent with this is the finding that small-firm turbulence, a concept derived from Beesley and Hamilton (1984), is actually greater in capital-intensive industries (Acs and Audretsch, 1990, ch. 7).[8] Small firms that successfully innovate will become viable, but many of the remaining firms will recede and ultimately fail. That is, small-firm turbulence is particularly high in capital-intensive industries, where firms must quickly learn or else face extinction.

In contrast, when the knowledge obtained from actual experience in the industry is a crucial input in producing innovative activity, as characterized by the routinized regime, fewer firms will attempt to enter the industry and subsequently fewer will fail, leading to relatively low rates of turbulence.

As reflected by a rich case study literature, it is turbulence in markets – the process by which firms enter, survive and grow, and ultimately exit – that is inherently imbedded in the underlying technology in an industry. Rather than focusing on static relationships between innovation and entry, new directions for understanding market dynamics would be well advised to consider how market structure and technological change evolve over the life cycle of industries.

Notes

1 For examples of this literature see von Weizsäcker (1979), Schmalensee (1981), Baumol et al. (1982), Demsetz (1982), and Shglitz (1987).
2 It should be noted that Baldwin and Gorecki (1987) used an interactive variable consisting of R&D expenditures multiplied by the number of firms in the industry.
3 For further explanations see Mueller and Tilton (1969) and Tilton (1971).
4 One of the earliest discussions of the industry life cycle is given by Dean (1950), who emphasized pricing strategies. Cox (1967) subsequently emphasized marketing strategies, and Hayes and Wheelwright (1979a, b) and Porter (1980) emphasized the nature of technological change.
5 Exceptions include Schwalbach (1987), who measured diversified entry between 1977 and 1982 as the share of production in 1982 by firms which have their base industry in another market, and Geroski (1989a).
6 It should be noted that the US Small Business Administration Data Base is derived from the Dun and Bradstreet DUNS file. Further explanations are given by Phillips and Kirschhoff (1989).
7 A hybridoma is defined as "The cell product of the fusion of two different types of cells whilch possesses new combinations of properties inherited from both distinct parent cells. For example, in the preparation of *monoclonal antibodies*, one parent is a cell (lymphocyte) which produces a specific antibody. The other parent is a tumor cell from a myeloma, a cell which can propogate indefinitely ('immortal') in cell culture. Once these two parent cells are combined/fused, a hybridoma (hybrid melanoma) is formed that after cloning and selection, can propagate indefinitely in cell culture and can produce large amounts of monoclonal antibody. This antibody recognizes only one specific antigen" (International Trade Administration, 1984, p. 216).
8 The turbulence rate is defined as (births + expansion + contraction + deaths)/employment. For further explanations see Acs and Audretsch (1990).

References

Acs, Z.J. and Audretsch, D.B. (1987) Innovation, market structure and firm size. *Review of Economics and Statistics* 69, 567–75.

Acs, Z.J. and Audretsch, D.B. (1988) Innovation in large and small firms: an empirical analysis. *American Economic Review* 78, 678–90.

Acs, Z.J. and Audretsch, D.B. (1989a) Small-firm entry in US manufacturing. *Economica* 56, 255–65.

Acs, Z.J. and Audretsch, D.B. (1989b) Births and firm size. *Southern Economic Journal* 56, 467–475.

Acs, Z.J. and Audretsch, D.B. (1990) *Innovation and Small Firms*. Cambridge, MA: MIT Press.

Arrow, K.J. (1962) Economic welfare and the allocation of resources for invention. In R.R. Nelson (ed.), *The Rate and Direction of Inventive Activity*, Princeton, NJ: Princeton University Press, pp. 609–26.

Audretsch, D.B. (1987) An empirical test of the industry life cycle. *Weltwirtschaftliches Archiv* 123, 297–308.

Audretsch, D.B.(1989) *The Market and the State*. New York: New York University Press.

Baldwin, J.R. and Gorecki, P.K. (1987) Plant creation versus plant acquisition: the entry process in Canadian manufacturing. *International Journal of Industrial Organization* 5, 27–42.

Baumol, W., Panzar, J.C. and Willig, R.D. (1982) *Contestable Markets and the Theory of Industry Structure*. New York: Harcourt Brace Jovanovich.

Beesley, M.E. and Hamilton, R.T. (1984) small firms' seedbed role and the concept of turbulence. *Journal of Industrial Economics* 33, 217–32.

Bevan, A. (1974) The UK potato crisp industry, 1960–72: A study of new entry competition. *Journal of Industrial Economics* 22, 281–97.

Blair, J.M. (1948) Technology and size. *American Economic Review* 38, 121–52.

Borrus, M., Millstein, J.E. and Zysman, J. (1983) Trade and development in the semiconductor industry: Japanese challenge and American response. In L. Tyson and J. Zysman (eds), *American Industry in International Competition*, Ithaca, NY: Cornell University Press, pp. 142–248.

Braun, E. and Macdonald, S. (1982) *Revolution in Miniature: The History and Impact of Semiconductor Electronics*. New York: Cambridge University Press.

Brock, G.W. (1975) *The US Computer Industry*. Cambridge, MA: Ballinger.

Cox, W.E., Jr (1967) Product life cycles as marketing models. *Journal of Business* 40, 375–384.

Dasgupta, P. (1986) The theory of technological competition. In J.E. Stiglitz and G.F. Mathewson (eds), *New Developments in the Analysis of Market Structure*, Cambridge, MA: MIT Press.

Dasgupta, P. and Stiglitz, J. (1980) Industrial structure and the nature of innovative activity. *Economic Journal* 90, 266–93.

Dean, J. (1950) Pricing policies for new products. *Harvard Business Review* 28, 45–53.

Demsetz, H. (1982) Barriers to entry. *American Economic Review* 72, 47–57.

Derzoutos, M.L., Lester, R.K. and Solow, R.M. (1989) *Made in America: Regaining the Productive Edge*. Cambridge, MA: MIT Press.

Dibner, M.D. (1986) Biotechnology in the United States: A report to the NSF Science Indicators Unit. North Carolina Biotechnology Center, Research Triangle Park, NC.

Evans, D.S. (1987) The relationship between firm growth, size, and age: estimates for 100 manufacturing industries. *Journal of Industrial Economics* 35, 567–81.

Florida, R.L. and Kenney, M. (1988) Venture capital-financed innovation and technological change in the US *Research Policy* 17, 119–37.

Geroski, P.A. (1989a) The interaction between domestic and foreign based entrants. In D.B. Audretsch, L. Sleuwaegen, and H. Yamawaki (eds), *The Convergence of International and Domestic Markets*, Amsterdam: North-Holland, pp. 59–83.

Geroski, P.A. (1989b) Entry, innovation and productivity growth. *Review of Economics and Statistics* 71, 572–8.

Geroski, P.A. and Jacquemin, A. (1985) Industrial change, barriers to mobility, and European industrial policy. *Economic Policy* 1, 169–204.

Gort, M. and Klepper, S. (1982) Time paths in the diffusion of product innovations. *Economic Journal* 92, 630–53.

Gruber, W., Mehta, D. and Vernon, R. (1967) The R&D factor in international investment of United States industries. *Journal of Political Economy* 75, 20–37.

Hall, B.H. (1987) The relationship between firm size and firm growth in the US manufacturing sector. *Journal of Industrial Economics* 35, 583–605.

Hayes, R.H. and Wheelwright, S.C. (1979a) Link manufacturing process and product life cycles. *Harvard Business Review* 78, 133–40.

Hayes, R.H. and Wheelwright, S.C. (1979b) The dynamics of process-product life cycles. *Harvard Business Review* 78, 127–36.

Helmstädter, E. (1986) Dynamischer Wettbewerb, Wachstum und Beschäftigung. In G. Bombach, B. Gahlen, and A.E. Ott (eds), *Technologischer Wandel* – Analyse und Fakten, Tübingen: Schriftenreihe des Wirtschaftswissenschaftlichen Seminars Ottobeuren.

International Trade Administration, US Department of Congress (1984) *Biotechnology*. Washington, DC: US Government Printing Office.

Kaplinsky, R. (1983) Firm size and technical change in a dynamic context. *Journal of Industrial Economics* 33, 39–60.

Kenney, M. (1986a) Schumpeterian innovation and entrepreneurs in capitalism: the case of the US biotechnological industry. *Research Policy* 15, 21–31.

Kenny, M. (1986b) *Biotechnology: The University–Industry Complex*. New Haven, CT: Yale University Press.

Klepper, S. and Graddy, E. (1989) The evolution of new industries and the determinants of market structure. Unpublished manuscript.

Link, A.N. (1981) *Research and Development Activity in US Manufacturing*. New York: Praeger.

Link, A.N. and Zmud, R.W. (1984) R&D Patterns in the video display terminal industry, *Journal of Product Innovation Management* 2, 106–115.

Mansfield, E. (1962) Entry, Gibrat's law, innovation, and the growth of firms. *American Economic Review* 52, 1023–51.

Mueller, D.C. (1976) Information, mobility, and profit. *Kyklos* 29, 419–48.

Mueller, D.C. and Tilton, J. (1969) Research and development costs as a barrier to entry. *Canadian Journal of Economics* 56, 570–9.

National Science Foundation (1987) *Science and Engineering Indicators – 1987.* Washington, DC: US Government Printing Office.

Nelson, R.R. (1984) Incentives for entrepreneurship and supporting institutions. *Weltwirtschaftliches Archiv* 120, 646–61.

Office of Technology Assessment, US Congress (1984) Technology, innovation, and regional economic development. OTA-STI-238, Office of Technology Assessment, Washington, DC.

Orr, D.(1974) The determinants of entry: a study of the Canadian manufacturing industries. *Review of Economics and Statistics* 56, 58–66.

Phillips, B.D. and Kirchhoff, B.A. (1989) Formation, growth and survival: small firm dynamics in the US economy. *Small Business Economics* 1, 65–74.

Porter, M.E. (1980) *Competitive Strategy.* New York: Free Press.

Scherer, F.M. (1991) Changing perspectives on the firm size problem. In Z. Acs and D.B. Audretsch (eds), *Innovation and Technological Change: An International Comparison*, Ann Abor, MI: University of Michigan Press, 24–38.

Schmalensee, R. (1981) Economies of scale and barriers to entry. *Journal of Political Economy* 89, 1228–38.

Schumpeter, J.A. (1911) *Theorie der wirtschaftlichen Entwicklung: Eine Untersuchung über Unternehmergewinn, Kapital, Kredit und den Konjunkturzyklus*, 5th edn, 1952. Berlin: Duncker & Humblot.

Schwalbach, J. (1987) Entry by diversified firms into German industries. *International Journal of Industrial Organization* 5, 43–50.

Semiconductor Industry Association (1983) *The Effect of Government Targeting on World Semiconductor Competition: A Case History of Japanese Industrial Strategy and its Costs for America.* Washington, DC: Semiconductor Industry Association.

Stiglitz, J.E. (1987) Technological change, sunk costs, and competition. *Brookings Papers on Economic Activity* (3), 883–937.

Tilton, J. (1971) *International Diffusion of Technology: The Case of Semiconductors.* Washington, DC: Brookings Institution.

US International Trade Commission (1983) Foreign industrial targeting and its effects on US industries, Phase I: Japan. USITC Publication 1437, Washington, DC.

US Senate, Committee on Commerce, Science, and Transportation (1978) *Industrial Technology.* Washington, DC: US Government Printing Office.

Vernon, R. (1966) International investment and international trade in the product life cycle. *Quarterly Journal of Economics* 80, 190–207.

von Weizsäcker, C.C. (1979) *Barriers to Entry: A Theoretical Treatment.* Berlin: Springer-Verlag.

Wells, L.T. (1966) *The Product Life Cycle and International Trade*. Cambridge: Cambridge University Press.

Williamson, O.E. (1975) *Markets and Hierarchies*. New York: Macmillan.

Winter, S.G. (1984) Schumpeterian competition in alternative technological regimes. *Journal of Economic Behavior and Organization* 5, 287–320.

13

Entry, Exit, and Productivity Growth

John R. Baldwin and Paul K. Gorecki

1 Introduction

Entry and exit have long been claimed to play an important role in the evolution and adaptation of an industry to change. In other papers we have described and documented this portion of the turnover process in Canada's manufacturing sector (Baldwin and Gorecki, 1987, 1989, 1990a, b, 1991b). Its magnitude is impressive. Although entry and exit are relatively unimportant in the short run, being dwarfed by the rise and fall of incumbents or continuing firms, this is not so in the long run. The importance of entry cumulates inexorably as new cohorts arrive and growth in the old cohorts offsets exits. Indeed, over the decade of the 1970s the change in market share due to entry and exit was as important as that due to the expansion and contraction of incumbents. In this paper we take the analysis a step further by quantifying the contribution that entry and exit make to productivity growth in Canada's manufacturing sector.

2 The Market Share of Entrants and Exits

Entry and exit can take place either through acquisition and divestiture of existing plants or through the opening and closing of plants. In this paper, we focus on the latter. Plant openings and closures are divided into those associated with firm entry and exit and those made by continuing firms. Because the plant characteristics of each differed so much it would be a mistake to treat plant openings or closures as a homogeneous group.

We should like to thank the Economic Council of Canada and Statistics Canada for financial support and R. Turvey, J. Evans, P. Geroski, and T. Hazledine, as well as participants at the First and Second International Comparisons Conference held in November 1988 and November 1989, for their comments. The usual disclaimer applies.

Since earlier work showed that the cumulative magnitude of entry and exit over a decade was large in absolute terms and relative to change in continuing firms, while this was not the case in the short-run, the longer period is adopted here for measuring the impact of entry and exit on productivity. Plant and firm status in 1970 are compared with those in 1979. An entrant is defined as a plant or firm that existed in a particular four-digit industry in 1979 but not in 1970, an exit is a plant or firm that existed in a particular four-digit industry in 1970 but not in 1979, and a continuing firm or plant existed in the same four-digit industry in both 1970 and 1979. The characteristics of entrants are measured for 1979, the characteristics of exits are measured for 1970, and the characteristics of continuing firms or plants are measured for both years. Thus, what is being measured is the cumulative effect of successive entry cohorts in 1971, 1972, . . . , 1979 that survive to 1979. On the exit side, it is the cumulative exit from the 1970 population of firms over the next 10 years that is being measured.[1]

The mean of various characteristics of the entrant, exit, and continuing firm/plant categories was estimated across 167 four-digit Canadian manufacturing industries. New and exiting plant each accounted for about 20 percent of industry shipments. The plant turnover process is dominated by firm entry (16.9 percent) and exit (15.0 percent) rather than incumbent firm plant opening and closure (4.5 percent and 5.0 percent respectively). Exiting firms have similar characteristics to firm entrants not only in terms of market share but also in terms of size. Plants of exiting firms and of entering firms are 52.5 percent and 60.7 percent of the average plant size. A similar finding holds for incumbents that open and close plants, where the corresponding percentages are 111.2 percent and 119.7 percent respectively. This is consistent with the view that there are groups of firms with different characteristics in an industry.

3 Productivity and Firm Turnover

The contribution of firm and plant turnover to productivity change depends not only on the market shares of these categories but also on their relative productivity. The measure of productivity used here is value added per worker, which is defined as total value of production less the cost of materials, fuel, and electricity divided by the number of wage and salary earners.[2]

Productivity comparisons of entrants and exiters require a benchmark for comparison. One such standard is the productivity of continuing plants, which account for the vast majority of industry output.[3] This benchmark has the advantage that it varies industry by industry, continues throughout the decade, and potentially reflects all other factors that were changing productivity in an industry.

Relative productivity for each industry is estimated as the median productivity level for the particular entry or exit class of plants divided by the median productivity level of the continuing plant group.[4] The mean of this ratio is then estimated across all 167 industries. The result, presented in columns 1 and 2 of table 13.1, shows that the closed plants of exiting firms were less productive than continuing plants, while new

Table 13.1 Relative productivity of various firm and plant entry and exit categories compared with continuing plants for 167 four-digit manufacturing industries, Canada, 1970–1979

Category	Ratio of productivity of the firm/plant category to that of continuing plants[a]			
	Mean[b] (standard error of mean) (%) (1)	Significance of rank test for first differences[c] (2)	Regression coefficient[d] (3)	Level at which stastically different from zero (4)
1970				
Firm exits by plant closure	0.79 (0.02)	<0.001	0.90	0.0001
Continuing firm plant closure	0.96 (0.04)	0.003	1.00	NS[e]
1979				
Firm entry by plant opening	1.04 (0.03)	NS[e]	1.16	0.0001
Continuing firm plant opening	1.15 (0.05)	0.006	1.31	0.0001

[a] Productivity is measured for plant exits as of 1970 and for entrants as of 1979 relative to continuing plants that did not change ownership over the decade.

[b] The mean is calculated across 167 industries; it is the average for each industry of the ratio of the median estimate of the productivity of each category divided by the median estimate of the productivity of the continuing category.

[c] The probability of a greater absolute value of the signed rank statistic for the mean difference in the medians of productivity in each entry class less that of the continuing class.

[d] A regression of plant productivity on plant size with industry and firm/plant category dummy variables was estimated. The omitted firm/plant category was continuing plants that did not change ownership over the decade. A pooled regression for plant productivity for 1970 and 1979 was estimated. The table reports the coefficient on the firm/plant category dummy variable.

[e] NS, not significant at the 5 percent level.

Source: Baldwin and Gorecki (1990b) based on Special Tabulations, Business and Labor Market Analysis Group, Statistics Canada

plant of entrants were more productive. Continuing firms closed plant that was slightly less productive and opened plant that was much more productive than the benchmark. These numbers suggest that productivity gains would have been associated with entry and exit – if the former replace the latter in each category.

A simple comparison of the mean productivity differences at the four-digit level may conceal the true significance of exiters and entrants, especially if they are concentrated in only a portion of all four-digit industries. Moreover, it does not standardize for other factors such as capital-to-labor ratios that may differ by plant size. Exiting plants of exiting firms are smaller than average and small plants are generally less productive. This may be all that the exit productivity ratios are capturing.

To investigate this possibility, a regression of productivity was estimated using the entire plant sample with industry and entry/exit dummy variables as well as plant size as explanatory variables.[5] The results, reported in columns 3 and 4 of table 13.1, indicate that, once plant size is taken into account, the productivity associated with firm exit and continuing firm plant opening were, as before, both significantly different from the continuing sector – lower in one case, and higher in the other. The productivity of exiting plants of continuing firms are, however, now not significantly different than the continuing sector, while new plants of firm entrants have become significantly more productive.

It is noteworthy that the productivity disadvantage of plant closures by exiting firms remains even after the size effect has been removed. Such plants do not close just because their smallness causes a productivity disadvantage. These plant exits are, on the whole, smaller than the population average, but they suffer even more of a productivity disadvantage than might be expected given their size. Exit is therefore not just a random phenomenon brought about by variation in demand that might affect smaller plants more intensively. The evidence suggests that a natural selection process is at work.

4 The Contribution of Entry and Exit to Productivity Change

Productivity growth is the difference between the weighted average of value added per worker of various plant categories in 1970 and 1979:

$$\text{TOT} = (\text{SHE}_9 \cdot \text{APE}_9 + \text{SHC}_9 \cdot \text{APC}_9) - (\text{SHE}_0 \cdot \text{APE}_0 + \text{SHC}_0 \cdot \text{APC}_0) \tag{13.1}$$

where APE and APC represent output per worker in the entering/exiting and the continuing sectors respectively, SHE and SHC are the labor shares for each category, and the subscripts 9 and 0 refer to the years 1979 and 1970 respectively. APE_9 thus refers to the productivity of entrants in 1979, and APE_0 to the productivity of exits in 1970.

Change in productivity can be arbitrarily broken down into terms that involve entry and exit. One such method is to take a standard orthogonal transformation of the change. Unfortunately the different methods involve different underlying assumptions about the replacement process at work. Therefore it is best to proceed from a specific assumption to the final estimating formula. Here two such assumptions are employed and the results are tabulated.

The first assumption is that entrants replace exits. Using this approach yields[6]

$$TOT = SHE_9(APE_9 - APE_0) + SHC_9(APC_9 - APC_0)$$
$$+ (SHC_9 - SHC_0)(APC_0 - APE_0) \qquad (13.2)$$

The first term captures the change that is due to the productivity difference between entrants and exits. The second term represents the growth in productivity due to progress in continuing plants. Both the first and second terms capture that component of total change due to entry or continuing plant progress, assuming that shares are held constant. The last term captures the effect of share changes.

An alternative assumption is implicit in the work of Hazledine (1985), which examined productivity growth slowdown in Canadian manufacturing in the 1970s. The implicit assumption contained therein was that entry and exit were independent and that entrants displaced continuing firms. There is some evidence to suggest that entry does occur without exit; thus some entrants can be considered to replace existing firms. Using this assumption yields

$$TOT = (APC_9 - APC_0) + SHE_9(APE_9 - APC_9)$$
$$+ SHE_0(APC_0 - APE_0) \qquad (13.3)$$

In this formulation, the second and third terms can be interpreted as capturing the effect of entry and exit respectively, though in a very different sense than does equation (13.2).

Equations (13.2) and (13.3) were estimated for each of the 167 four-digit manufacturing industries. The results were robust to the use of different samples. In the case of equation (13.2) and for all industries with positive real productivity growth between 1970 and 1979, on average, firm entrants and exits accounted for 24.0 percent of the productivity growth, and new and closed plants of continuing firms accounted for 5.1 percent. For equation (13.3) entry had a negative impact of -5.1 percent, and exit a positive impact of 14.2 percent. Hazledine (1985) also found that entry had a negative impact and was puzzled by this result. His suggestion was "that there are adjustment costs which prevent new plants from immediately achieving scale-efficient operating levels," with the result that "in the short-to-medium term time horizon . . ., new plants do not contribute to productivity growth" (Hazledine, 1985, p. 322).

Choosing between the two approaches when the continuing sector is treated as a homogeneous group is difficult. The counterfactuals discussed above involve discrete choices between entrants replacing exits or entrants supplanting continuing plants but not both. Reality probably lies somewhere in between. But when continuing plants are treated as one group, the difficulty in treating entrants as replacing continuing plants which are, on average, about as productive as entrants is all too obvious.

A natural breakdown of the continuing sector is into those increasing and those decreasing market share. The magnitude of continuing plant market share change is substantial. Between 1970 and 1979 about as much market share was being transferred from plants that lost market share (contracting) to those gaining share (expanding) as was transferred by the entry and exit process (Baldwin and Gorecki, 1990b, figure 1). This movement in relative position was associated with substantial changes in relative productivity. In 1970 the mean ratio of the productivity of expanding to contracting plants across 167 four-digit manufacturing industries was 0.98 (standard error of mean, 0.02), which was not significantly different from unity; in 1979, the ratio had increased to 1.34 (standard error, 0.09), which was significantly different from unity. Success and failure as measured by changing relative position was closely related to changing relative productivity.

The ratio of the productivity of entrants to contracting and expanding plants for 1979 is presented in table 13.2. Plant openings, whether by new or continuing firms, were more productive than contracting plants, while new plants of continuing firms were as productive as expanding plants. On the basis of these relative productivity ratios, it is reasonable to consider entrants as replacing not only exits but also those continuing plants than lost market share. Continuing plants that gained market share should have done so at the expense of both declining continuing plants and exits.

The nature of the tradeoff between the various firm/plant categories was investigated using regression analysis. There are three groups that

J.R. Baldwin and P.K. Gorecki

Table 13.2 Relative productivity of plant entrants compared with continuing plants that gained and lost market share for 167 four-digit manufacturing industries, Canada, 1970–1979

Category	Mean[a] (%)	Standard error of mean	Median (%)	Significance of rank test for first differences[b]
I Relative to continuing plants gaining share				
Firm entry by plant opening	0.97	0.03	0.91	<0.0001
Continuing firm plant opening	1.08	0.04	0.99	0.532
II Relative to continuing plants losing share				
Firm entry by plant opening	1.24	0.07	1.10	<0.0001
Continuing firm plant opening	1.32	0.06	1.20	<0.0001

[a] The mean and median were calculated across the ratio of the median estimates of the productivity for each category relative to the median estimate of productivity for the given continuing category for each of the 167 industries. All ratios refer to 1979.
[b] The rank sign significance level for differences in the means of the median levels of productivity.
Source: Baldwin and Gorecki (1990b) based on Special Tabulations, Business and Labor Market Analysis Group, Statistics Canada

lose market share – contractions (SHCRT), firm exit via plant closure (SHE_0^1), and continuing firm plant closure (SHE_0^2) – and three that gained market share – expansions (SHEXP), firm entry via plant opening (SHE_9^1), and continuing firm plant opening (SHE_9^2). SHCRT is the absolute difference in market share of plants that contracted between 1970 and 1979; SHEXP is the absolute difference in market share for those plants that expanded between 1970 and 1979. By definition, the 1970 market share of the losers is equal to the 1979 market share of the gainers.

Table 13.3 reports the coefficients estimated by regressing[7] each of the categories that lost market share on the share of those that gained market share. For example, the first row of the table consists of the coefficients from the equation

$$SHE_0^1 = a_0\,SHE_9^1 + a_1\,SHEXP + a_2\,SHE_9^2 \qquad (13.4)$$

The remaining two rows are the same except that the dependent variables are SHCRT and SHE_0^2 respectively. The coefficients show the

Table 13.3 The relationship between share gain and loss of various firm and plant categories across 167 four-digit manufacturing industries, Canada, 1970–1979

| | Regression coefficients[a] | | | |
| | Share gain[b] | | | |
Share loss[b] regressor	Firm entry by plant opening SHE_9^1	Continuing plant expansion SHEXP	Continuing firm plant opening SHE_9^2	R^2
Firm exit by plant closure SHE_0^1	0.673 (0.037) (0.0001)	0.832 (0.053) (0.001)	−0.067 (0.116) (0.5641)	0.88
Continuing plant contraction SHCRT	0.295 (0.035) (0.0001)	−0.026 (0.049) (0.6001)	0.718 (0.108) (0.0001)	0.58
Continuing firm plant closure SHE_0^2	0.030 (0.024) (0.2180)	0.193 (0.035) (0.0001)	0.340 (0.077) (0.0001)	0.44

[a] The values in parentheses are the standard error of the estimator and the probability that a higher *t* value could have been obtained under the null hypothesis of a zero effect.
[b] The market share was measured in employment. The categories are defined in the text.
Source: Baldwin and Gorecki (1990b) based on Special Tabulations, Business and Labor Market Analysis Group, Statistics Canada

effect of a 1 percent increase in a particular firm/plant category that gains market share on the various categories that lose market share. For example, a 1 percentage point change in the share of new plants of new firms SHE_9^1 leads to a 0.67 percentage point change in the share of exiting plants of exiting firms SHE_0^1, but only a 0.30 percentage point change in the market share of contracting plants SHCRT. The coefficients suggest that there is more to the replacement process than entrants displacing exits and incumbents replacing incumbents (i.e. the diagonal coefficients). The displacement pattern is broadly that suggested by the relative productivities presented in tables 13.1 and 13.2.

These estimates can be used to quantify the contribution of each gaining firm/plant category to productivity. Each of the gainers can be allowed to replace each of the losers in the fashion given by the estimated coefficients in table 13.3. The first step is to estimate the change due to each category in the industry value of productivity between 1970 and 1979. For example, the effect of firm entry by plant opening would be[8]

$$SHE_9^1[0.673(APE_9^1 - APE_0^1) + 0.832(APE_9^1 - APCRT_0)$$
$$- 0.067 \ (APE_9^1 - APE_0^2)]$$

where AP is average productivity. The sum of the terms inside the square brackets denotes the productivity change due to a 1 percentage point increase in the market share of firm entrants by plant opening. Each of the terms reflects the impact on productivity of displacement with respect to a particular category that lost market share. When multiplied by the market share of firm entrants by plant opening, the dollar contribution of that firm/plant category to industry productivity is derived. The second step is to express this as a proportion of the productivity change for the industry. The result is the proportion of industry productivity change accounted for by entrants via plant opening. A similar exercise can be conducted for the other firm/plant categories that gain market share.

The change in productivity for each of the plant entry categories for each of the 167 four-digit manufacturing industries was estimated in the manner discussed in the previous paragraph. The results were robust to different samples. The table presents results for those industries where real growth in productivity was positive in the 1970s.

Each component was expressed as a percentage of total productivity growth[9] and the means and the standard error of these ratios are reported in table 13.4, panel I. The new plants of entering firms contributed 20 percent of the total growth in productivity, on average;

Table 13.4 Plant turnover and the proportion of productivity growth accounted for by each entry and exit source across those four-digit Canadian manufacturing industries experiencing positive real productivity growth, 1970–1979

Source of productivity growth[a]	Mean (%) (standard error of mean)
I Share growth due to plant opening	
(a) By new firms	19.5
	(2.8)
(b) By continuing firms	7.0
	(1.7)
II Share loss due to plant closure	
(a) By exiting firms	31.8
	(2.9)
(b) By continuing firms	8.1
	(1.4)

[a] For derivation see text.

Source: Baldwin and Gorecki (1990b) based on Special Tabulations, Business and Labor Market Analysis Group, Statistics Canada

continuing firm plant births accounted for 7 percent. This is very similar to that reported above using the formulation in equation (13.2).

The contribution that turnover made can be examined in reverse. Instead of asking what effect the growth in a particular entry category had, the effect of an exit category can be estimated in a completely analogous fashion – except that the effects are summed across all entry classes. The results are also presented in table 13.4, panel II. The displacement of plants closed by exiting firms account for 32 percent, and the closure of continuing firm plants account for 8 percent of total productivity growth.

5 Conclusion

This paper and associated work demonstrate the necessity of careful measurement if the importance of entry and exit is to be fully appreciated. In the short run, the change associated with entry and exit is dominated by expansion and contraction in the continuing sector. Therefore short-run estimates of entry and exit suggest that the process has little importance. Because most studies in the past have had to rely on such estimates, the impression has been left that entry and exit are insignificant. In the absence of much entry, conclusions to the contrary have had to rely on the threat of entry rather than evidence of actual entry. The development of panel data for the Canadian manufacturing sector (Baldwin and Gorecki, 1991a) has meant that such indirect methods need not provide the sole method of evaluating the effect of entry. These panel data show that over time the importance of entry and exit accumulates inexorably and can no longer be dismissed as either absolutely or relatively unimportant.

In this paper we extend this analysis by looking directly at the contribution of entry and exit to productivity growth. It does not rely on correlation or regression analysis to examine the relationship between entry intensity and productivity. Rather, it looks directly at the relative productivity of entrants and exits and calculates the contribution that both make to productivity growth. It extends the previous analysis from simply delineating the magnitude of entry and exit to measuring one dimension of its importance. Previous work on Canadian data (Hazledine, 1985) had left the impression that the effect of entry was unimportant, indeed that it was negative. In this paper we find this not to be the case. Entry and exit make a healthy contribution to total productivity growth.

In doing this, we also show that industries are not homogeneous – a point that Marshall stressed but that has been often ignored (Reid, 1987). Entrants arrive in industries at sizes well below the average. While they grow, they are still well below the average by the end of 10 years even though they have moved their average level of labor productivity up to the average by this time. More importantly, the pattern of substitution that is discovered has new firms supplanting exiting firms, and new plant of continuing firms supplanting closed plant in the same sector. While there is some interaction between the two groups, there is clearly a distinction that means that it is useful to think of differences of inter- and intra-group rivalry (Caves and Porter, 1977). This is also important for those who model entry. Most work that is based on the early research by Orr (1974) has some more or less complicated version of a limit entry model behind it in which entrants and leading firms are held to interact. The results of this paper suggest that entrants have little effect on incumbents and instead basically replace other small firms that exit. Shepherd (1984) was correct when he observed that large existing firms do not generally have to worry about entry. They have to worry about which of the large number of entrants will move out of the fringe and challenge them.

Notes

1 The creation of the longitudinal panel data set that was used to track firms and their plants through time is described by Baldwin and Gorecki (1989c).
2 Value added in 1979 was deflated to 1970 using an output price deflator for the calculations in table 13.4 (David, 1961, 1966). The results reported herein were also calculated using shipments per worker deflated by an output price index. The results of the alternate methods were qualitatively similar.
3 The comparisons for this section are for continuing plants that did not change ownership over the decade 1970–9. All other comparisons refer to all continuing plants.
4 The median was used because the occasional outliers in the micro data strongly biased the arithmetic average in a few cases.
5 Dummy variables for a much larger set of firm/plant categories were used. Only the results for entry and exit categories are reported here.
6 This is equivalent to assuming that, in the absence of entry, exiting plants would not have disappeared. It can be written in the same form as equation (13.1) except that the values of entrants' shares and/or average productivity are replaced with comparable values drawn from the exiters. In this case, the increase in productivity that would have occurred in the absence of entry can be written as

$$\left(\text{SHC}_9 \cdot \text{APC}_9 + \text{SHE}_9 \cdot \text{APE}_0\right) - \left(\text{SHC}_0 \cdot \text{APC}_0 + \text{SHE}_0 \cdot \text{APE}_0\right)$$
$$(13.1^L)$$

Equation (13.1^L) is just equation (13.1) except that the productivity of entrants in 1979 is replaced with that of exiters for 1970. The difference between total growth (equation (13.1)) and growth without entry (equation $(13.1^L)'$) is the effect of entry. It is given by the first term in equation (13.2) for the assumption embedded in equation (13.1′). (Note that equation (13.2) could also have been written with 1970 share weights.)

7 Ordinary least squares was used. The restrictions across equations did not have to be imposed since they were met in the original set of equations. Seemingly unrelated least squares was also employed but made no difference.

8 In the results reported in table 13.4 a slightly modified version of table 13.3 was used. Since the two negative coefficients were highly insignificant and very low in value they were set equal to zero and the remaining coefficients in the column were adjusted downward so that they summed to unity.

9 The proportions were calculated relative to total estimated productivity growth and not of actual productivity growth. Using the actual growth as denominator did not affect the relative size of the various components.

References

Baldwin, J. R. and Gorecki, P.K. (1987) Plant creation versus plant acquisition: the entry process in Canadian manufacturing. *International Journal of Industrial Organization* 5, 27–41.

Baldwin, J.R. and Gorecki, P.K. (1991b) Firm entry and exit in the Canadian manufacturing sector. *Canadian Journal of Economics*, forthcoming.

Baldwin, J.R. and Gorecki, P.K. (1989b) Measures of market dynamics: concentration and mobility statistics for the Canadian manufacturing sector. *Annales d'Économie et Statistique*, forthcoming.

Baldwin, J.R. and Gorecki, P.K. (1991a) Measuring firm entry and exit with panel data, in A.C. Singh and P. Whitridge (eds.) *Analysis of Data in Time.* Ottawa: Statistics Canada.

Baldwin, J.R. and Gorecki, P.K. (1990b) The contribution of the competitive process to productivity growth: The role of firm and plant turnover. Research Paper #23f. Analytical Studies Branch, Statistics Canada.

Baldwin, J.R. and Gorecki, P.K. (1990a) Intra-industry mobility in the Canadian manufacturing sector. Research Paper #23b, Analytical Studies Branch, Statistics Canada.

Caves, R.E. and Porter, M. (1977) From entry barriers to mobility barriers: conjectural decisions contrived deterrence to new competition. *Quarterly Journal of Economics* 91, 241–61.

David, P. (1961) The deflation of value-added. *Review of Economics and Statistics* 44, 148–55.

David, P. (1966) Measuring real net output: a proposed index. *Review of Economics and Statistics* 48, 419–25.

Hazledine, T. (1985) The anatomy of productivity growth slowdown and recovery in Canadian manufacturing. *International Journal of Industrial Organization* 3, 307–26.

Orr, D. (1974) The determinants of entry: a study of the Canadian manufacturing industries. *Review of Economics and Statistics* 56, 58–66.

Reid, G. (1987) *Theories of Industiral Organization.* Oxford: Basil Blackwell.

Shepherd, W.G. (1984) Contestability versus competition. *American Economic Review* 74, 572–87.

14

International Comparisons of Entry and Exit

John Cable and Joachim Schwalbach

1 Introduction

In previous chapters of this book the entry and exit process and its determinants for a number of individual countries have been investigated, paying appropriate regard to the circumstances and factors specific to each. In this chapter and the next attempts are made to draw out such general results and overall conclusions as can be discerned in the rich detail of the individual country reports. International comparison is useful in any context because of the additional insights which results from other countries can sometimes bring to the interpretation of individual cases. In the case of market entry there are, in addition, important questions at the supranational level as to how far the entry process operates, or fails to do so, in a "culture-free" fashion. Here, as we shall see, our studies bring to light substantial inter-country variations which remain to be explained in future work.

In this chapter we first summarize the evidence on entry and exit rates which our studies have unearthed. We find gross entry and exit proceeding at broadly similar rates in most countries, and net entry very low and often negative at the overall level. However, more detailed analysis at industry level reveals evidence of systematic inter-industry movement, as well as the replacement of exiting firms by entrants in the same industry. There also appear to be some international regularities in the observed patterns of high and low entry industries.

We then focus on those countries where the researchers have estimated the Orr (1974a, b) model, or something very close to it, and attempt a comparison of the results they have obtained. The country studies covered in this way are the United Kingdom, the FRG, Norway, Portugal, Belgium, and Korea. All countries find some evidence of profit opportunities acting as a statistically significant determinant of entry, but with a number of qualifications and with a marked heterogeneity of

258 J. Cable and J. Schwalbach

findings with respect to the role and importance of individual barriers to entry.

Empirical results for three other countries – the United States, Yugoslavia, and Japan – are treated separately and in a slightly different way. In part this is because the theoretical and/or empirical models employed in these studies are somewhat more removed from the Orr framework, but in the case of Yugoslavia and Japan it is also because of rather important "special" features of the institutional and cultural context which are specific to these countries.

2 Entry and Exit in Eight Countries

International comparisons of entry and exit are complicated by a number of noncomparabilities in the data. Thus, market share and relative size data are by employment for Belgium and Portugal, but by sales for other countries; figures relate to establishments in Belgium, Canada, and Portugal, but to firms elsewhere; there are differences in time period and aggregation level (see, for example, appendix table 14.A1). In addition, some countries give entry data cumulated over varying numbers of years, though these can be annualized on fairly innocuous assumptions.[1] In view of these complicating factors, the following commentary should be treated with an appropriate degree of caution.

Table 14.1 summarizes the entry and exit data from appendix tables 14.A1 and 14.A2. In terms of the number of entrants, the (unweighted) average gross entry rate (ER) in manufacturing across all eight countries is slightly under 6.5 percent, with all countries except Portugal falling within the fairly narrow band of 3.3–8.2 percent. Given the time period to which the data relate (1982–6), the outlying Portuguese figure (12.3 percent) may have been inflated by a surge of entry prior to entry into the European Community (EC) in 1986. In the one case where data for service industries are available (Belgium), we observe an entry rate more than double that for the country's manufacturing sector, but we have no way of knowing whether this is typical of other countries. In terms of market share (EMS), entry is much smaller – on average only 2.8 percent in manufacturing industries across the eight countries, and within the very narrow range 1.1–3.2 percent except for Portugal (5.8 percent) and the Belgian service sector (4.4 percent). This of course reflects the fact that entrants' relative size (ERS) is on average less than one-fifth (18.1 percent or 19.7 percent including Belgian services) that of incumbent firms, though with a notable exception in the case of the

Table 14.1 Entry, exit, and net entry in eight countries (annual averages)

	Time period	Cross entry			Gross exit			Net entry[a]		Sample
		ER	EMS	ERS	XR	XMS	XRS	NER	NEMS	
Belgium[b]										
(a) Manufacturing	1980–4	0.058	0.016[c]	0.285[c]	0.063	0.019[c]	0.213[c]	−0.005	−0.003	130 three-digit manufacturing industries
(b) Services	1980–4	0.130	0.044[c]	0.328[c]	0.122	0.041[c]	0.322[c]	0.008	0.003	79 three-digit service industries
Canada[b,d]	1971–9	0.040	0.030	0.096	0.048	0.034	0.078	−0.008	−0.004	167 four-digit industries
FRG[d]	1983–5	0.038	0.028	0.221	0.046	0.028	0.188	−0.008	0.000	183 four-digit industries
Korea[d]	1976–81	0.033	0.022	0.121	0.057	–	–	−0.024	–	48 four-digit + 14 five-digit industries
Norway	1980–5	0.082	0.011	0.126	0.087	0.010	0.113	−0.005	0.001	80 four-digit industries
Portugal[b,d]	1983–6	0.123	0.058[c]	0.080[c]	0.095	0.055[c]	0.118[c]	0.028	0.003	234 five-digit industries
UK	1974–9	0.065	0.029	0.449	0.051	0.033	0.612	0.014	−0.004	114 three-digit industries
USA[d]	1963–82	0.077	0.032	0.067	0.070	0.033	0.069	0.007	−0.001	387 four-digit industries

[a] Net entry here is derived from the gross entry and exit statistics: NER = ER − XR; NEMS = EMS − XMS.
[b] Establishment level data (figures for other countries are for firms).
[c] By employment (figures for other countries are by sales).
[d] Annualized cumulative figures (see note 1).

United Kingdom where entrants are shown to be 45 percent of the size of incumbents.

The gross exit statistics follow a very similar pattern. The average entry rate across manufacturing sectors is 6.5 percent in terms of numbers (XR) and 2.7 percent in terms of market shares (XMS), while exiting firms are on average 19.9 percent the size of incumbents (XRS). Moreover, the exceptional and outlying cases occur for the most part in the same places as for entry. Because the entry and exit statistics correspond so closely in this way, net entry (NER) is very small and frequently negative.[2] In terms of numbers NER is less than 1.5 percent in absolute terms, except for Korea (2.4 percent) and Portugal (2.8 percent), and in terms of market share (NEMS) net entry/exit is never more than 0.5 percent and on average less than 0.25 percent of market share. More detailed direct net entry data are set out in appendix table 14.A3.

Even with zero net entry overall, there could still be an economically significant entry/exit process at work if the relevant gross flows represented the systematic movement of firms from industries with low profit opportunities to industries with high opportunities, as opposed to the mere replacement of firms within the same industries. However, at times in previous chapters attention has been drawn to evidence of the latter. Table 14.2 provides more systematic evidence on this issue, in the form of correlation coefficients between entry and exit across the industry samples for each country. If the entry/exit process were solely composed

Table 14.2 Correlations between entry and exit[a]

	Number of firms	Market share	Relative size
Belgium[b]	0.660	0.161	0.890
Canada	0.039	0.682	0.393
FRG	0.342	0.572	0.525
Korea			
1976–8	−0.409	–	–
1979–81	0.350	–	–
Norway	0.488	0.219	0.180
Portugal	0.030	0.170	0.010
UK	0.318	0.513	0.872
USA	0.270	0.520	0.600

[a] Correlations of entry and exit in individual industries for the time periods shown in table 14.1. Columns show the correlation between ER and XR, EMS and XMS, and ERS and XRS respectively.
[b] Manufacturing only.

of the first kind of inter-industry flows (so that no individual industry would simultaneously exhibit both entry and exit), we would expect negative correlations, whereas if all that is happening is that entrants are replacing exiters in the same industry, a positive correlation approaching unity will be seen. On the evidence of table 14.2 it would appear that the second "replacement" effect tends to dominate in practice. All coefficients are positive save one, the exception being Korea in the period 1976–8. Significantly, perhaps, this period was a downswing phase in the Korean business cycle, when "push" would strongly reinforce "pull" factors and systematic moves from less profitable to more profitable industries might be expected to predominate; consistent with this, we observe that a positive correlation is re-established in the following upswing phase in 1978–81. However, though positive correlations are the norm in table 14.2, their values vary considerably (both across countries and across entry measures for given countries) and on average by no means approach unity. We therefore conclude that, while the intra-industry turnover effect appears to predominate, there is also some evidence of more systematic inter-industry movement at work. We also conclude from the relative size correlations that there is a distinct tendency for exiters to be replaced by firms of similar size, especially in Belgium and the United Kingdom and, to a lesser extent, in the United States and the FRG.

Further evidence of the coincidence of entry and exit in particular industries can be seen *inter alia* in the detailed appendix tables 14.A4– 14.A6. We also note the repeated appearance of certain industries, e.g. electronics, in the "highest entry" lists for several countries in table 14.A4 and some, though not overwhelming, similarity of entry and exit pattern across countries at the two-digit level in tables 14.A5 and 14.A6.

3 Comparative Results from the Entry Determinants Models

3.1 Recapitulation of the Orr Model

As previous chapters have variously explained, entry in the Orr model is assumed to respond to profit opportunities:

$$E_{jt} = \gamma \left(\Pi_{jt}^{e} - \Pi_{j}^{*} \right) + u_{jt}$$

where E_{jt} is entry into industry j at time t, Π_{jt}^{e} is the entrant's expected post-entry profit, and Π_{j}^{*} denotes the profit which would be earned by incumbents in the long-run limit after all entry has ceased. "Limit profit" in this sense (not to be confused with the entry-forestalling profit-level associated with limit-pricing behavior, since entry is permitted in the present model[3]) depends on entry barriers:

$$\Pi_j^* = \beta_0 + \sum_{m=1}^{M} \beta_m \, X_{mj}$$

where X is a vector of entry barrier determinants of Π_j^*. Substituting, we obtain

$$E_{jt} = \alpha_0 + \alpha_1 \, \Pi_{jt}^e + \sum_{m=1}^{M} \alpha_m \, X_{mj} + u_{jt}$$

with $\alpha_0 = -\gamma\beta_0$, $\alpha_1 = \gamma$, and $\alpha_m = -\gamma\beta_m$. In long-run equilibrium $E_{jt} = u_{jt}$ and $\Pi_{jt}^e = \Pi_j^*$. Hence

$$\widehat{\Pi_j^*} = \widehat{\beta_0} \sum_{m=1}^{M} \widehat{\beta_m} \, X_{mj} = \frac{-(\widehat{\alpha_0} + \sum_{m=1}^{M} \widehat{\alpha_m} \, X_{mj})}{\widehat{\alpha_1}}$$

Thus the parameters of the model can be used to generate an estimate of the level of limit profits in any industry j or, in effect, of the height of entry barriers in that industry as well as evidence on both the responsiveness of entry to profit opportunities (reflected in the estimate of the γ coefficient) and the importance of individual elements in the entry barrier vector X (captured in the estimates of the β_m parameters).

3.2   Specifying the Empirical Model

Table 14.3 summarizes the ways in which the country research teams have operationalized the model in specifying the variables Π_{jt}^e and E_{jt} and the vector X.[4]

Most employ a naive expectations model, proxying Π_{jt}^e with lagged actual profits (in the case of Portugal using up to fourth-order lags), though the UK and Korean analyses feature rational expectations involving a prior autoregression in profits and other observables. E_{jt} is most commonly specified as an entrant count, though market share measures are used exclusively in the case of the United Kingdom amd as an alternative in the case of Korea. Amongst the entrant count measures, gross entry or gross entry rates are used in four studies, and net entry in two. A drawback of gross entry measures is that they are of course bounded at zero, whereas the model can predict negative entry, and this could cause problems in estimation. Turning to the specification of X, the distinction in practice between entry barriers *per se* and variables included to normalize for other extraneous influences is inevitably less than complete. As regards the selection of entry barrier variables themselves, the inclusion of some (such as the traditional market-structural characteristics like concentration and capital requirements) might be regarded as contentious in the present state of the theoretical literature on entry. However, with the theoretical debate as yet unsettled, there is a strong case for inclining toward the most general empirical specifications that data considerations will allow, if for no other reason than that the ensuing results all add grist to the theorists' mill. Seen in this light the X_j specifications in table 14.3 are in many cases impressive, and the attempts to include measures of sunk costs alongside more traditional entry barrier variables in the cases of Norway and Portugal are particularly noteworthy. As can be seen, the time periods covered by the various studies are broadly similar and the samples are of comparable size, but the level of aggregation varies from three- to five-digit level, and this must be borne in mind when comparing the results. The special features of the studies, briefly indicated in the final column of table 14.3, highlight some of the ways in which the individual research teams have elaborated their analyses around the central core; though some are referred to in passing below, further details should in general be sought from the relevant country chapters.

3.3 Empirical Findings from Orr-type Models

Precise comparisons of the parameter estimates from the different country studies are vitiated by the previously mentioned differences in the level of aggregation and, in particular, in the specification of the dependent variable. When interpreting table 14.4, which attempts to indicate the most "representative" result in each case, it should also be borne in mind that the individual country estimates are in some cases nonrobust and sensitive to changes in specification and time period. Also, as can be seen, explanatory power varies considerably, with the models explaining from as little as 10 percent of the variation in the dependent variable (adjusted for degrees of freedom) to nearly 80 percent. Nevertheless it is noteworthy that, in their own terms, all studies currently under review find *some* evidence of entry responding to profit opportunities. Thus, at some point, statistically significant γ coefficients are reported in all cases, and this constitutes important evidence contrary to the view of Demsetz (1973) and others on the interpretation of observed profit differentials as "superiority rents"; this, it appears, is not how entrants themselves, on average, see them. However, the result does not hold in the United Kingdom for foreign as opposed to domestic entrants, nor in Portugal for large as opposed to small entrants, while, in the special case of Belgium, the response is to "Europe-wide" profit

Table 14.3 Specification of the Orr model

	Π^e_{jt}	E_{jt}	X_j	Sample	Special features
UK	RE	(i) Net market share penetration of new domestic firms in year of entry (ii) Net change in import penetration	Size (−1) Growth (−1)	95 MLH industries in 1983 and 1984 (panel)	Separate regressions for domestic and foreign entrants Analysis of entry record
FRG	Π_{jt-1}	Gross entry rate (entrants/all firms)	Scale economies Product differentiation Capital requirements R&D Size Growth	79 four-digit industries 1983–5	Effect of entry (and exit) on concentration (Weiss) (183 industries) Entry/exit record Identification of "contestable markets"
Norway	Π_{jt-1}	Gross absolute entry (log)	Sunk cost (−1) MES (−1, 2, 3) Log capital requirements (−1, 2, 3) Concentrations (−1) R&D (1985 only) Growth (−1) Log size (−1) Exit rate Risk (var Π)	141 five-digit industries 1981–5 (panel)	Separate regressions for six types of entrant

Country	Dependent variable	Independent variables	Sample	Notes
Portugal	Π_{it-4} (also −0, −1, −2, −3) Gross absolute entry (log)	Scale economies Sunk costs {equipment, new} Capital requirements Advertising intensity Diversification Patents + trademarks Size Growth[a]	73 industries 1982–6	Separate (OLS) regressions for small-scale and (Tobit) for large-scale entry Focus on sunk costs
Belgium	Π_{it-1} (PCM) (i) Net entry rate (ii) Gross entry rate (iii) Gross exit rate	Fixed assets Growth (Belgium) Growth (EC) Profits (FRG) Product differentiation (US/advertising) R&D MES	109 three-digit industries 1980–4	Focus on small open economy: "follower behavior" hypothesis
Korea	RE (i) Net entry rate (ii) New entry rate (iii) Entry shares	MES Advertising intensity Capital requirements Loan subsidy Concentration (CR_3) Growth (−1)	62 four- or five-digit industries, 1977–81	Entry-forestalling profits calculated Determinants of profits Firm disappearances

[a] Concentration dropped because collinear with size.
Numbers in parentheses denote lags.
RE, rational expectations; MES, minimum efficient size; PCM, price-cost margins.

opportunities rather than specifically Belgian conditions. Moreover, as a number of the authors point out, the results tend to suggest that the entry response is relatively slow to operate and limited in its extent; in the United Kingdom, for example, a 10 percentage point rise in expected profit prompts entry penetration of only 2 percent, 80 percent of which is domestic (and more predictable than the 20 percent due to foreign firms). Thus, though there is evidence of a *statistically* significant entry response as the theory would predict, the *economic* significance of entry is questionable; there is little to suggest that entry operates as a swift and severe constraint on the behavior of incumbent firms.

Other evidence from the studies is consistent with this conclusion. When the parameters of the models are taken together, the implied long-run "limit profits" after entry has ceased are generally substantial, on average permitting prices up to 15–20 percent above costs in the UK case, for example. Moreover, where the researchers report details of the entry and exit record, as in the cases of the United Kingdom, the FRG, and Belgium, we observe further confirmation of the general finding that, while gross entry may be large, so is gross exit, and correlations suggest much turnover at the fringes of industries with only small net market share effects.

To the extent that this adds up to a general lack of evidence of entry acting as an economically significant discipline on incumbents, all the more interest attaches to the question of what is preventing it from doing so, i.e. in the context of the Orr model, to the results relating to individual variables in the X vector. As can be seen from table 14.4, the results are more than somewhat mixed. Reading across the columns for individual countries we see that capital requirements and sunk costs attract the negative signs that are expected for such entry barrier variables whenever they are included, and are generally significant at or about the conventional significance levels. However, all other variables that are included more than once exhibit a pattern of mixed signs and significance levels. In the cases of product differentiation/advertising and patents/R&D the inconsistencies might arguably be explained in terms of these acting as the means through which entry is effected rather than as entry barriers in some circumstances. But this argument would not apply elsewhere, e.g. to the scale economies, concentration, size and growth variables, and to this extent it must be admitted that the results as a whole leave the ultimate mysteries of entry barriers far from solved.

Table 14.4 Empirical estimates of entry determinants in six countries[a]

Variable	UK	FRG	Norway	Portugal	Belgium	Korea
Expected profits	+**[b]	+**	+***	+**[c]	−, NS[d]	+*
Industry size	+, NS	−*	+**	+**		
Industry growth	−*[b]	+***	+, NS	+**	+*	+*
Scale economies		−**	+**	−**	+**	−*
Product differentiation/advertising		+*		−**[c]	−(*)	−**
Capital requirements			−**	−**[c]	−***	−, NS
Concentration			−**			+**
Sunk cost			−*(*)			
Equipment				−*(*)[e]		
New				−**[e]		
Exit rate			+**			
Risk			+, NS			
Patents/R&D				−**[c]	+**	
Diversification				−**[c]		
Π (FRG)					+**[d]	
Growth (EC)					+*	
$\bar{R}^2$	0.146–0.207	0.375	0.77	0.78–0.59	0.10	0.20

* Significant at the 1 percent level.
** Significant at the 5 percent level.
*** Significant at the 10 percent level.
NS, not significant.
[a] The table shows the "representative" result for each country (see text).
[b] Not significant for foreign entrants.
[c] Not significant for large entrants.
[d] Entry responsive to "Europe-wide opportunities", proxied by German profits (see text).
[e] Not significant for small entrants.

3.4 *Other Empirical Findings*

Although emanating from an entirely different theoretical framework, the estimating equation for the United States in chapter 2 is not wholly dissimilar to those already considered and, in general, the results tell broadly the same story as that outlined above. Thus entry is again found to respond to perceived profit opportunities while sunk costs (proxied by the intensity of investment in machinery rather than buildings) deter, and incumbents are found to be significantly more likely to react aggressively to entry when they are both profitable and concentrated. As the author stresses, the role of advertising is ambiguous: on the one hand the need to advertise generates an unrecoverable (sunk) cost in the event of failure but, on the other hand, entrants may perceive a greater likelihood of success in markets where advertising plays an important role. While the balance can clearly go either way (which, as we have already seen, table 14.4 also confirms), it turns out in the US analysis that over most of the sample advertising facilitates entry.

The two remaining country studies of entry determinants, for Japan and Yugoslavia, differ from the rest in finding at best very weak or no responsiveness of entry to excess profits (or in the case of self-managed Yugoslav firms, excess earnings). A possible explanation in the case of Japan may lie in the suggestion by Odagiri (1981, 1982) and others that, for cultural and other reasons, the pursuit of growth is a much more plausible objective for Japanese than is the pursuit of profit, and this gains credibility from the additional main finding reported in chapter 9 that entry responds procyclically to both industry and aggregate growth (subject to negative influences from the price of investment goods and the discount rate). If this interpretation is correct, it would be appropriate to regard entry in the Japanese case as essentially the same kind of equilibrating force as in the cases previously discussed; however, with growth replacing profit as the "signal" or "trigger" for the equilibration process, all welfare implications and the like dependent on profit-maximizing assumptions would of course not apply. In some other respects the Japanese results are in any event familar, in particular, the subsample regressions showing a higher elasticity of response of entry in industries with low capital intensities (suggesting the presence of a capital requirements/sunkness barrier) and, adding to the existing confusion of results in this area, in industries with *low* advertising intensities.

In the case of Yugoslavia it is hard to judge whether there *is* a response of entry to earnings differentials which we are unable to pick up statistically from the data because entry is, in the author's words, "astonishingly low" in comparison with the other countries, or whether the virtual absence of both responsiveness to earnings *and entry itself* is due to the absence of potential entrant groups, and/or capital market discrimination against them, and the inability of entrants to appropriate any benefits from entry in the longer term, as discussed in the chapter. Either way, the fact that all that can be discerned is some industrial pattern to entry, perhaps reflecting the preferences of planners, and virtually no response of entry to economic factors, is surely a matter of concern, especially as theory shows that entry is even more important under self-management than under capitalism.

4 Conclusions and Implications for Further Work

Except for the rather special case of Yugoslavia, our studies have all revealed nontrivial levels of industrial entry and exit, and they have also shown that entry does respond to profit opportunities as hypothesized and as any well-functioning market system crucially demands. However, the typical rate and pattern of entry, and the typical magnitude and speed of its responsiveness to profit opportunities which our estimates imply, suggest a process capable of visiting substantially less than swift and certain retribution on incumbent firms straying from the strict path of competitive behavior.

Though our studies constitute the largest coordinated and internationally comparative program of research on entry of which we are aware, they by no means exhaust the scope of useful empirical work on entry. The variable explanatory power of our models indicates that in most cases there is much about the entry process for which the variables we have included do not account, and the inter-country variations in the effects of certain variables raise further questions about possible omitted influences which could be interacting with them and intruding on present results. A number of potentially fruitful lines of future enquiry suggest themselves.

First, future work might profitably attempt to incorporate more microlevel information, in particular on the characteristics of entrants, and investigate any systematic differences that are revealed between entrants and incumbents. In our work we have modeled profit opportunities in terms of the industry average Π_{jt}^e. But where entrants are different from incumbents, or at any rate view themselves as being different (e.g. because of some product or process novelty which they possess, or some perceived superior marketing or organizational skill), what should attract entry is the *firm-specific* profit expectation Π_{jt}^e, where $i = 1, 2, \ldots, h$ are entrants. One way to allow for this in industry analyses would be to introduce variables capturing any average tendency for entrants to differ from incumbents. The potential fruitfulness of this kind of approach is, perhaps, illustrated by the Portuguese study, where a broad distinction is made between large and small entrants, and significant differences are observed both in entry behavior and in the degree of deterrence presented by different kinds of entry barriers (table 14.4).

Second, individual industry studies would have much to commend them as an alternative way of utilizing microlevel data, permitting detailed attention to the characteristics of individual incumbent and entrant firms. Interpreted against the backdrop of cross-section results from our own studies, the results from such industry case studies could help remove remaining uncertainty about the entry process. In the light of the not inconsiderable commonalities across countries revealed in our own work, for example, in the identities of high and low intensive entry industries, retention of an internationally comparative dimension in any such industry case study approach would seem attractive. Indeed, future researchers might easily do worse than select a small group of industries for intensive analysis from our own high and low entry lists.

Third, whether in the context of industry studies or otherwise, the effects on entry of country-specific institutional features merit further enquiry. Amongst the countries in our studies, prime candidates here would include the bank-based systems of industrial finance in the FRG and Japan *vis-à-vis* the market based systems of the United Kingdom and the United States, and the impact of industrial groups in Japan and Korea.

Finally, and more fundamentally, the most promising avenue for further research could well lie in treating entry as a special case of the more general phenomenon of market share mobility or turnover (Caves and Porter, 1977). In the absence of collusion amongst incumbent firms, the effective sanction of firms' behavior is potential loss of market share, whether this be to existing or new competitors. To be sure, there is no generally accepted theory of dynamic market share behavior on which to draw; after more than a decade of theoretical advance in industrial organization the sad conclusion is that, depending on whether we assume that prices or quantities are choice variables, on whether we deal in discrete or continuous time, and on whether market "moves" are sequential or simultaneous, and so forth, as far as theory is concerned, almost anything can happen (Schmalensee, 1988). In this situation, careful empirical observation and systemizing of observed behaviour, the development of appropriate measures and analytic constructs, and the identification of such empirical regularities as are there to be found, could not only advance our knowledge of entry and the more general process of market turnover, but also contribute towards a "solid base of facts" (Schmalensee, 1988) with which to discipline future theoretical advance.

Appendix

Table 14.A1 Entry in various countries

Year	Belgium[a]						Canada[b]			FRG[c]		
	ER		EMS by employment		ERS by employment		ER	EMS by sales	ERS by sales	ER	EMS by sales	ERS by sales
	(1)	(2)	(1)	(2)	(1)	(2)						
1963												
1964												
1965												
1966												
1967												
1968												
1969												
1970												
1971												
1972												
1973												
1974												
1975							0.363	0.268	0.867			
1976												
1977												
1978												
1979												
1980	0.055	0.125	0.014	0.043	0.246	0.320						
1981	0.054	0.128	0.015	0.041	0.305	0.321						
1982	0.057	0.127	0.018	0.043	0.295	0.329						
1983	0.061	0.127	0.017	0.046	0.315	0.350						
1984	0.067	0.142	0.018	0.048	0.265	0.320				0.115	0.084	0.663
1985												
1986												

[a] Annual averages, 130 three-digit NACE industries. 2, annual averages, 79 three-digit NACE service industries.
[b] Cumulative entry 1971–79, 167 four-digit manufacturing industries; 1979 base year for denominator.
[c] Cumulative entry 1983–85, 183 four-digit manufacturing industries; 1982 base year for denominator.

Table 14.A1 Continued

	Korea[d]			Norway[e]			Portugal[f]			UK[g]			USA[h]	
ER	EMS by sales	ERS by sales	ER	EMS by sales	ERS by sales	ER	EMS by employ-ment	ERS by employ-ment	ER	EMS by sales	ERS by sales	ER	EMS by sales	ERS by sales
												0.307	0.136	0.369
												0.427	0.185	0.359
									0.145	0.064	0.455			
									0.077	0.026	0.304	0.401	0.142	0.280
									0.069	0.028	0.384			
0.110	0.040	0.339							0.043	0.022	0.478			
									0.034	0.018	0.451			
									0.020	0.016	0.622			
0.090	0.094	0.384	0.075	0.023	0.292							0.408	0.169	0.324
			0.075	0.007	0.083									
			0.067	0.008	0.105									
			0.082	0.010	0.115									
			0.091	0.009	0.092	0.490	0.230	0.320						
			0.103	0.008	0.069									

[d] Annual averages 1976–78 and 1979–81, 48 four-digit and 14 five-digit manufacturing industries.
[e] Annual averages, 80 four-digit manufacturing industries.
[f] Cumulative entry 1983–86, 234 five-digit manufacturing industries; 1982 base year for denominator.
[g] Annual averages, 114 three-digit manufacturing industries.
[h] Cumulative entry 1963–67, 1968–72, 1973–77, and 1978–82, 387 four-digit manufacturing industries.

Table 14.A2 Exit in various countries

Year	Belgium[a] XR (1)	XR (2)	XMS (1)	XMS (2)	XRS (1)	XRS (2)	Canada[b] XR	XMS	XRS	FRG[c] XR	XMS	XRS
1963												
1964												
1965												
1966												
1967												
1968												
1969												
1970												
1971												
1972												
1973												
1974												
1975							0.429	0.309	0.699			
1976												
1977												
1978												
1979												
1980	0.055	0.122	0.011	0.037	0.186	0.312						
1981	0.076	0.114	0.016	0.054	0.267	0.376						
1982	0.077	0.125	0.030	0.036	0.184	0.292						
1983	0.083	0.121	0.018	0.036	0.221	0.297						
1984	0.078	0.127	0.018	0.043	0.206	0.334				0.138	0.083	0.563
1985												
1986												

[a] See table 14.A1.
[b] 1970 base year for denominator.
[c-h] see table 14.A1.

Table 14.A3 Net entry in various countries

Year	Belgium[a] Mean	Std	Min	Max	Canada[b] Mean	Std	Min	Max	FRG[c] Mean	Std	Min	Max	Japan[i] Mean	Std	Min	Max
1963																
1964																
1965																
1966																
1967																
1968																
1969																
1970																
1971																
1972																
1973																
1974																
1975					-0.066	0.231	-0.667	0.875								
1976																
1977																
1978																
1979																
1980	-0.001	0.042	-0.125	0.158									0.006	0.083	-0.226	0.500
1981	-0.023	0.072	-0.500	0.300									0.031	0.107	-0.333	0.800
1982	-0.020	0.060	-0.167	0.235									-0.007	0.090	-0.357	0.500
1983	-0.022	0.075	-0.333	0.259									0.007	0.068	-0.158	0.322
1984	-0.011	0.052	-0.174	0.182					-0.023	0.101	-0.273	0.555	0.010	0.082	-0.250	0.337
1985																
1986																

[a] Manufacturing industries only.

Table 14.A2 Continued

Korea[d]	Norway[e]			Portugal[f]			UK[g]			USA[h]		
XR	XR	XMS	XRS	XR	XMS	XRS	XR	XMS	XRS	XR	XMS	XRS
										0.308	0.144	0.367
										0.390	0.191	0.367
							0.084	0.051	0.548			
							0.062	0.035	0.531	0.338	0.146	0.310
							0.045	0.026	0.511			
0.231							0.046	0.032	0.673			
							0.040	0.030	0.709			
0.111	0.061	0.008	0.129				0.029	0.022	0.701	0.372	0.173	0.344
	0.102	0.007	0.065									
	0.100	0.010	0.096									
	0.081	0.011	0.121									
	0.084	0.012	0.128	0.380	0.220	0.470						
	0.095	0.014	0.138									

Table 14.A3 Continued

Korea[d]				Norway[e]				Portugal[f]				UK[g]				USA[h]			
Mean	Std	Min	Max	Mean	Std	Min	Max	Mean	Std	Min	Max	Mean	Std	Min	Max	Mean	Std	Min	Max
																-0.001	0.220	-0.617	1.250
																0.037	0.348	-0.595	2.125
												0.060	0.066	-0.179	0.296				
												0.015	0.052	-0.106	0.214	0.062	0.293	-0.385	1.396
												0.025	0.037	-0.087	0.196				
0.117	0.269	-0.636	1.431									-0.003	0.034	-0.118	0.102				
0.071	0.187	-0.500	0.570									-0.006	0.030	-0.104	0.088				
0.186	0.295	-0.444	1.500									-0.008	0.029	-0.136	0.072				
0.090	0.288	-0.308	2.000													0.036	0.218	-0.621	1.141
0.067	0.271	-0.567	1.250	0.004	0.049	-0.167	0.105												
-0.025	0.333	-0.667	1.370	-0.023	0.058	-0.195	0.143												
0.084	0.169	-0.333	0.610	-0.032	0.071	-0.286	0.200												
				-0.009	0.092	-0.444	0.333												
				-0.004	0.081	-0.400	0.333	0.090	0.320	-0.520	2.020								
				0.001	0.066	-0.250	0.188												

Table 14.A4 Highest entry and exit rates by industries

	Belgium		Canada		FRG		Korea	
Ranking	NACE	Industries[a]	SIC	Industries	SYPRO	Industries	SIC	Industries
Entry								
1	364	Aerospace equipment	2593	Particle board	5080	Electronic data processing	3901	Jewellery and related products
2	348	Electrical equipment	3243	Commercial traders	6481	Textiles for interior decoration	3320	Wooden furniture
3	330	Office and data processing machinery	1852	Felt mills	5211	Plate glass	33113	Plywood
4	417	Manufacture of spaghetti, macaroni, etc.	1094	Wineries	5160	Industrial ceramics	3220	Apparely (except footwear)
5	474	Publishing	2640	Office furniture	2555	Prefabricated concrete parts	3833	Electrical appliances
6	372	Medical and surgical equipment	3180	Office and store machinery	5461	Cork cane and wicker	3240	Footwear
7	500	Building and civil engineering work	2543	Prefabricated buildings	3660	Meters, telephone counter	3812	Metal furniture and fixtures
8	419	Bread and flour confectionery	1831	Fibre and flament yarn	6841	Edible oils	35139	Synthetic resins and fibers
9	452	Production of hand-made footwear	3150	Miscellaneous machinery and equipment manufacturing	3670	Radio, television and recording	3720	Non-ferrous metal
10	365	Manufacture of transport equipment, n.e.c.	2920	Steel pipe and tube mills	3690	Assembly of electrotechnical products	3560	Plastic products
Exit								
1	364	Aerospace equipment	3290	Miscellaneous vehicles	5211	Plate glass		
2	500	Building and civil engineering work	3242	Non-commercial trailer manufacturing	2555	Pretabricated concrete parts		
3	501	Construction of buildings' etc.	3570	Abraslves	6481	Textiles for interior decoration		
4	504	Building completion work	1093	Breweries	6816	Potato products		
5	503	Installation	1810	Cotton, yarn and cloth mills	2553	Building materials		

Table 14.A4 Continued

Norway		Portugal		UK		USA	
	Industries	CAE	Industries	SIC	Industries	SIC	Industries
3849	Other transport equipment	38511	Optical material	339	Other machinery	3573	Electronic computing equipment
3845	Aircraft	38392	Batteries	367	Radio, radar and electronics	3751	Motorcycles, bicycles, parts
3909	Miscellaneous	39095	Bone, horn and ivory products	411	Man-made tibres	2452	Prefabricated wood buildings
3610	Ceramics	36923	Non-hydraulic lime	366	Electronic computers	2754	Commercial printing
3902	Musical instruments	35921	Essential oils	276	Synthetic and plastic products	2648	Stationery products
3121	Food products n.e.c.	35403	Lubricant oils	212	Bread and flour confectionery	3448	Prefabricated metal buildings
3319	Wood products n.e.c.	35300	Oil refineries	311	Iron and steel	3652	Phonograph records
3829	Machinery n.e.c.	38241	Food machinery	462	Wires and cables	2795	Lithographic platemaking
3831	Electric motors and electrical parts	38292/3	Elevators	419	Carpets	2448	Wood palets and skids
3852	Photographic and optical goods	33202	Ready-made clothes	494	Toys, games and others	2519	Household furniture n.e.c.
3902	Musical instruments	31218	Eggs	339	Other machinery	2519	Household furniture n.e.c.
3849	Other transport equipment	36999	Other nonmetal products	412	Spinning and doubling	3822	Environmental controls
3610	Ceramics	33202	Wicker furniture	413	Weaving of cotton, linen, etc.	2492	Special products sawnills
3512	Fertilizers and pesticides	38414	Maritime engines	366	Electronic computers	2385	Waterproof outergarments
3232	Fur dressing and dyeing	35402	Briqueties	444	Overalls, shorts, underwear, etc.	3574	Calculating and accounting machinery

Table 14.A4 Continued

		Belgium		Canada		FRG		Korea
Ranking	NACE	Industries[a]	SIC	Industries	SYPRO	Industries	SIC	Industries
6	494	Toys and sports goods	2599	Miscellaneous wood industries, n.e.c.	6425	Household, bed and table linen		
7	495	Miscellaneous manufacturing industries	1840	Cordage and twine	6821	Sugar		
8	454	Bespoke tailoring, dress making	3511	Clay products	2542	Coarse stone		
9	319	Other metal workshops n.e.c.	3915	Dental laboratories	2551	Limestone		
10	492	Musical instruments	1094	Wineries	6875	Spirits		

n.e.c., not elsewhere classified.
[a] Manufacturing only.

Table 14.A5 The distribution of entry across industries

	Two-digit US SIC sectors	Belgium[a]			Canada[b]			FRG[c]		
		ER	EMS	ERS	ER	EMS	ERS	ER	EMS	ERS
20	Food processing	0.051	0.021	0.748	0.308	0.214	0.676	0.069	0.050	0.943
21	Tobacco	0.025	0.017	0.660	0.606	–	–	0.051	–	–
22	Textiles	0.041	0.018	0.420	0.338	0.265	0.791	0.058	0.045	0.729
23	Apparel	0.058	0.026	0.444	0.265	0.270	0.903	0.189	0.118	0.791
24	Lumber	0.045	0.019	0.497	0.435	0.362	1.082	0.119	0.075	0.494
25	Furniture	0.056	0.021	0.506	0.364	0.304	0.753	0.143	0.119	0.713
26	Paper	0.033	0.014	0.359	0.371	0.236	0.684	0.085	0.049	0.395
27	Printing	0.078	0.019	0.246	0.274	0.295	1.180	0.179	0.075	0.291
28	Chemicals	0.041	0.015	0.327	0.359	0.238	0.689	0.122	0.060	0.494
29	Petroleum and coal	0.007	0.001	0.165	0.437	–	–	0.133	0.003	0.014
30	Rubber and plastics	0.057	0.016	0.270	0.514	0.264	0.414	0.185	0.075	0.327
31	Leather	0.027	0.009	0.310	0.273	0.250	0.983	0.074	0.072	0.769
32	Stone, clay, glass	0.049	0.016	0.308	0.317	0.294	0.804	0.091	0.085	0.824
33	Primary metals	0.031	0.004	0.107	0.396	0.139	0.442	0.116	0.054	0.491
34	Fabricated metal	0.059	0.021	0.358	0.417	0.357	0.802	0.112	0.102	0.725
35	Nonelectrical machinery	0.039	0.009	0.281	0.634	0.320	0.481	0.111	0.068	0.535
36	Electric machinery	0.076	0.013	0.174	0.443	0.245	0.379	0.174	0.068	0.262
37	Transportation equipment	0.093	0.034	0.175	0.359	0.238	0.689	0.123	0.076	0.348
38	Instruments	0.092	0.061	1.601				0.105	0.076	0.669
39	Miscellaneous	0.086	0.032	0.436	0.274	0.303	2.394	0.100	0.048	0.436

[a] 1980–4, means across years (manufacturing only).
[b] 1971–9.
[c] 1983–5.

Table 14.A4 Continued

Norway		Portugal		UK		USA	
	Industries	CAE	Industries	SIC	Industries	SIC	Industries
3909	Miscellaneous	38519	Instruments n.e.c.	213	Biscuits	2794	Electrotyping and stereotyping
3214	Carpets and rugs	33204	Mattresses	232	Soft drinks	2369	Children's outerwear n.e.c.
3221	Outer farments of textiles and plastics	36094	Bijouteries	218	Fruit and vegetable products	2335	Women's and misses' dresses
3229	Wearing apparel n.e.c.	31312	New brandies	272	Pharmaceuticals	2363	Children's coats and suits
3121	Food products n.e.c.	36921	Cement	441	Weatherproof underwear	2339	Women's outerwear n.e.c.

Table 14.A5 Continued

Korea[d]			Norway[e]			Portugal[f]			UK[g]			USA[h]		
ER	EMS	ERS	ER	EMS	ERS	ER	EMS	ERS	ER	EMS	ERS	ER	EMS	ERS
0.072	0.025	0.370	0.052	0.006	0.117	0.470	0.280	0.440	0.054	0.021	0.274	0.239	0.148	0.313
–	–	–	0.000	0.000	0.000	0.000	0.000	–				0.205	0.026	0.107
0.107	0.028	0.240	0.076	0.007	0.085	0.420	0.180	0.300	0.084	0.029	0.364	0.372	0.244	0.374
0.153	0.049	0.290	0.107	0.016	0.145	0.630	0.470	0.510	0.074	0.047	0.687	0.403	0.370	0.512
0.116	0.042	0.490	0.075	0.011	0.139	0.440	0.270	0.470	0.068	0.060	0.999	0.497	0.419	0.424
0.154	0.068	0.400	0.065	0.009	0.087	0.530	0.330	0.440				0.471	0.367	0.383
0.100	0.047	0.420	0.037	0.003	0.076	0.390	0.150	0.280	0.069	0.030	0.657	0.314	0.159	0.304
0.052	0.020	0.100	0.091	0.014	0.147	0.360	0.190	0.410				0.490	0.329	0.407
0.101	0.035	0.320	0.071	0.001	0.082	0.460	0.140	0.200	0.074	0.024	0.335	0.325	0.132	0.217
0.065	0.022	0.320	0.060	0.000	0.003	0.660	0.200	0.130	0.035	0.001	0.015	0.337	0.230	0.354
0.090	0.018	0.160	0.072	0.013	0.191	0.500	0.330	0.510	–	–	–	0.431	0.189	0.224
0.047	0.042	0.200	0.054	0.006	0.140	0.480	0.210	0.280	0.057	0.051	1.076	0.294	0.252	0.476
0.092	0.052	0.610	0.067	0.010	0.142	0.430	0.180	0.290	0.063	0.028	0.472	0.344	0.183	0.330
0.117	0.037	0.290	0.031	0.001	0.015	0.500	0.140	0.160	0.089	0.014	0.209	0.319	0.182	0.329
0.126	0.063	0.440	0.099	0.026	0.260	0.520	0.220	0.260	0.049	0.035	0.733	0.429	0.310	0.376
0.098	0.049	0.470	0.119	0.041	0.379	0.530	0.200	0.230	0.084	0.103	0.505	0.465	0.253	0.299
0.117	0.037	0.290	0.111	0.009	0.070	0.530	0.270	0.330	0.096	0.022	0.193	0.461	0.213	0.216
0.073	0.038	0.380	0.082	0.009	0.100	0.370	0.130	0.250	0.052	0.019	0.250	0.465	0.276	0.257
0.097	0.020	0.160	0.095	0.035	0.469	1.230	0.230	−0.060	0.078	0.043	0.649	0.603	0.368	0.224
0.139	0.053	0.370	0.135	0.020	0.127	0.390	0.230	0.460	0.075	0.036	0.544	0.402	0.271	0.351

[d] 1976–81, means across periods.
[e] 1980–5, means across years.
[f] 1983–6.
[g] 1974–9, means across years.
[h] 1963–82, means across periods.

Table 14.A6 The distribution of exit across industries

Two-digit US SIC sectors	Belgium[a]			Canada[b]			FRG[c]		
	XR	XMS	XRS	XR	XMS	XRS	XR	XMS	XRS
20 Food processing	0.071	0.019	0.429	0.404	0.256	0.520	0.128	0.074	0.567
21 Tobacco	0.039	0.024	0.530	0.439	–	–	0.119	–	–
22 Textiles	0.072	0.016	0.232	0.456	0.363	0.967	0.955	0.057	0.401
23 Apparel	0.087	0.032	0.350	0.447	0.361	0.701	0.236	0.112	0.441
24 Lumber	0.071	0.017	0.297	0.428	0.374	0.981	0.156	0.107	0.650
25 Furniture	0.091	0.033	0.443	0.471	0.412	0.807	0.208	0.102	0.575
26 Paper	0.052	0.009	0.182	0.280	0.269	1.005	0.120	0.052	0.385
27 Printing	0.095	0.021	0.198	0.418	0.265	0.531	0.173	0.066	0.341
28 Chemicals	0.047	0.008	0.138	0.365	0.239	0.583	0.083	0.039	0.494
29 Petroleum and coal	0.003	0.0001	0.048	0.459	–	–	0.167	0.010	0.053
30 Rubber and plastics	0.054	0.015	0.339	0.419	0.183	0.369	0.144	0.040	0.219
31 Leather	0.075	0.023	0.279	0.411	0.357	1.016	0.180	0.124	0.635
32 Stone, clay, glass	0.094	0.017	0.224	0.473	0.315	0.538	0.155	0.101	0.690
33 Primary metals	0.060	0.002	0.039	0.340	0.175	0.443	0.116	0.020	0.677
34 Fabricated metal	0.080	0.027	0.304	0.437	0.402	0.969	0.103	0.068	0.610
35 Nonelectrical machinery	0.048	0.005	0.112	0.425	0.269	0.576	0.121	0.060	0.503
36 Electric machinery	0.085	0.008	0.072	0.495	0.295	0.468	0.129	0.062	0.417
37 Transportation equipment	0.085	0.026	0.676	0.478	0.316	0.557	0.168	0.110	0.506
38 Instruments	0.044	0.012	0.261	0.440	0.327	0.811	0.119	0.031	0.260
39 Miscellaneous	0.094	0.026	0.279				0.112	0.064	0.453

[a] 1980–4, means across years (manufacturing only).
[b] 1971–9.
[c] 1983–5.

Notes

1 The averages shown in table 14.1 are derived from the data in tables 14.A1 and 14.A2 as follows. Where the original data are on an annual basis, table 14.1 shows a simple unweighted average of the annual figures: $\Sigma\ (E_t/N_t)/T$, where E_t is the number of entrants at time t, N_t is the number of firms in the industry, and T is the number of years for which data are available. Cumulative data from tables 14.A1 and 14.A2 were annualized simply by dividing by T. The two sets of figures approximate each other to the extent that the number of firms N remains constant since, obviously, $\Sigma(E_t/N_t)/T = \Sigma\ E_t)/NT$ if N does not vary.

2 Note that the net entry figures in table 14.1 were obtained by subtraction. See table 14.A3 for alternative direct net entry statistics.

3. See chapter 8 for estimates of "limit profits" in the alternative sense.

4. See also individual chapters for discussion of specification issues concerning fixed effects and possible nonconstancy of the parameter γ.

Table 14.A6 Continued

Norway[d]			Portugal[e]			UK[f]			USA[g]		
XR	XMS	XRS	XR	XMS	XRS	XR	XMS	XRS	XR	XMS	XRS
0.070	0.010	0.137	0.370	0.280	0.640	0.046	0.023	0.311	0.313	0.123	0.303
0.067	0.010	0.015	0.000	0.000	–				0.223	0.032	0.110
0.098	0.020	0.183	0.360	0.190	0.410	0.064	0.037	0.489	0.372	0.179	0.355
0.143	0.036	0.225	0.400	0.260	0.520	0.067	0.056	0.855	0.453	0.292	0.517
0.092	0.019	0.199	0.400	0.250	0.500	0.048	0.067	1.478	0.442	0.265	0.452
0.087	0.021	0.229	0.410	0.340	0.730				0.431	0.241	0.418
0.061	0.004	0.057	0.250	0.100	0.360	0.053	0.033	0.584	0.299	0.122	0.324
0.074	0.014	0.171	0.260	0.160	0.520				0.429	0.243	0.439
0.082	0.001	0.016	0.320	0.180	0.460	0.054	0.024	0.372	0.285	0.081	0.213
0.027	0.000	0.002	0.370	0.140	0.270	0.034	0.008	0.066	0.297	0.144	0.372
0.075	0.012	0.150	0.310	0.190	0.500	–	–	–	0.302	0.133	0.315
0.109	0.037	0.307	0.370	0.240	0.550	0.059	0.052	1.127	0.390	0.240	0.487
0.071	0.009	0.121	0.400	0.260	0.530	0.050	0.027	0.508	0.307	0.138	0.357
0.050	0.003	0.040	0.320	0.080	0.180	0.052	0.020	0.348	0.277	0.120	0.341
0.094	0.019	0.184	0.390	0.260	0.540	0.042	0.039	0.803	0.355	0.182	0.406
0.097	0.016	0.156	0.380	0.250	0.550	0.062	0.099	0.657	0.373	0.161	0.328
0.091	0.011	0.118	0.340	0.190	0.440	0.057	0.027	0.356	0.351	0.119	0.240
0.095	0.021	0.119	0.350	0.150	0.320	0.037	0.029	0.222	0.327	0.117	0.233
0.086	0.014	0.138	0.410	0.160	0.270	0.049	0.037	0.782	0.468	0.182	0.254
0.134	0.026	0.186	0.410	0.310	0.630	0.052	0.039	0.609	0.410	0.222	0.430

[d] 1980–5, means across periods.
[e] 1983–6.
[f] 1974–9, means across years.
[g] 1963–82, means across periods.

References

Caves, R.E. and Porter, M.E.(1977) From entry barriers to mobility barriers: conjectural decision and contrived deterrence to new competition. *Quarterly Journal of Economics* 91, 241–61

Demsetz, H.(1973) Industry structure, market rivalry and public policy. *Journal of Law and Economics* 16, 1–9.

Odagiri, H.(1981) *The Theory of Growth in a Corporate Economy: Management Preference, Research and Development, and Economic Growth*. New York: Cambridge University Press.

Odagiri, H.(1982) Anti-neoclassical management motivation in a neoclassical economy: a model of economic growth and Japan's experience. *Kyklos* 35(2), 223–43.

Orr, D.(1974a) The determinants of entry: a study of the Canadian manufacturing industries. *Review of Economics and Statistics* 61, 58–66.

Orr,D.(1974b) An index of entry barriers and its application to the market structure performance relationship. *Journal of Industrial Economics* 23, 39–49.

Schmalensee, R.(1988) Industrial economics: an overview. *Economic Journal* 98, 643–81

15

Some Data-Driven Reflections on the Entry Process

P.A. Geroski

1 Introduction

No matter how strong one's preconceptions are, it is impossible to work with empirical data for any length of time without discovering something new and unexpected. Although this often takes the form of not discovering the statistical regularities that one expected (or hoped) to find, it can also frequently involve uncovering properties of the data that are both more interesting and more puzzling than those one set out to explore. Indeed, empirical projects can often end up as voyages of discovery that lead one to abandon initial hypotheses in pursuit of quite different models designed to account for quite different phenomena. One way or the other, at the end of the day one often finds that one has been more data led than one would like to admit (at least to the profession's methodological purists), but none the worse for the experience.

The recent flurry of empirical work on entry has proved to be no exception to this rule. Right from the start, scholars have had some trouble in reconciling the stories told about entry in standard textbooks with the substance of what they found in their data. Very few have emerged from their work feeling that they have answered half as many questions as they have raised, much less that they have answered most of the interesting ones. The subject of entry still commands much interest, but the reasons why it does so have begun to subtly shift. In view of this, it seems worth pausing for a moment to collect together a number of the interesting things about entry processes that have been uncovered and to speculate on what they might mean.

I am obliged to the IIM in Berlin for their hospitality and support, to all the participants at both of the Entry Conferences held in Berlin for contributing to a useful general discussion during which many of these issues were raised, and to Paul Gorecki for comments on the first draft. The usual disclaimer applies.

Acting very much in this spirit, our goal in this paper is to provoke people to pause, to collect, and most of all to speculate. We propose to work toward this goal by building a slightly ramshackle edifice of more or less well-founded conjecture on the base of four interrelated empirical observations that have cropped up over and over again in empirical work on entry (see the data surveyed by Schwalbach in chapter 7). The discussion in sections 2–5 takes up each empirical observation in turn, and the object of the exercise is to explore some of the implications of each for theory, for public policy, and for subsequent empirical work.

2 Success and Failure

The first and, in many ways, the most striking property of the data is that many firms attempt entry each year, but that few survive for more than a year or two. The average entrant is, it seems, basically a tourist and not an immigrant, enjoying a life that is often nasty, brutish, and, above all, short.

While it is fairly certain that this is what the life of a standard entrant is like, what is much less clear is why this should be so. There are perhaps three types of explanation worth considering. The first is that the survival experience that we observe arises because entrants are presented with profitable opportunities that have strictly finite lives. There are many reasons why the window of opportunity open to entrants might shut quickly, including the possibility that incumbents may be slow to react but are lethal when they eventually do so. One way or the other, however, the finite nature of the opportunities that are presented to entrants are probably best exploited through something more than faintly reminiscent of hit-and-run entry, and that, the argument goes, is what we observe. In view, low survival rates are as much a given feature of the environment as not, and the problem for entrants is to face up to this reality by choosing an appropriate life-cycle strategy.

By contrast, a second explanation of observed survival rates is that entry may be both a learning and a selection process. Since it is usually all but impossible to know beforehand exactly what the consequences of doing something new will be, it is unlikely that entrants will ever know their post-entry operating costs for sure, prior to entry. The immediate post-entry period is, then, likely to be a period of learning in which those entrants who reveal themselves to be efficient will be selected as survivors. For entrants who introduce some sort of innovation, entry is – at least initially – a type of market research conducted at the most direct and most practical level possible. In this view, then, low survival rates reflect the unavoidable need to use practical experience to separate genuinely talented entrants from the dross.

Third and finally; low survival rates may reflect either systematic errors made by entrants in forecasting post-entry returns, or a positively risk-taking attitude taken towards the post-entry assessments that are made. Entrants, like all decision-makers operating under conditions of incomplete information, may invest too few resources in acquiring information, and, like many decision-makers operating under uncertainty, they may systematically underweight unfavorable outcomes. What is at issue in this third view is not that a market test is required to establish an entrant's worth, but, rather, that although it is, in principle, possible to acquire full information prior to entry, few entrants manage to do so in practice. One way or the other, "mistakes" are made, and as long as each entrant has some unique characteristic that may account for its success or failure, the large number of entry "trials" that occur over time in any given market may not generate enough information to reduce the rate at which "mistakes" occur. What this third view asserts, then, is that the high turnover of firms that we observe is the consequence of "mistakes" made and then quickly rectified.

It would, of course, be interesting to try to discriminate between these three views, but, unfortunately, there is very little hard information in the raw data on observed survival rates which gives one a sound basis upon which to do so. At best, one might be able to distinguish the first explanation from the second and third. Finite windows of opportunity impose a mortality rate on entrants that is exogenous to the entry process, the type of entrant involved, and the post-entry experience of the entrant. Learning or discovering mistakes, however, depends on actual experience and the abilities of entrants, and therefore ought to induce systematic variations in survival across entrant types and markets. Thus support for the propositions that entry is a learning experience or that failure is the result of a "mistaken" evaluation of the market might be found in the frequently made observation that *de novo* entrants have rather higher failure rates than entrants who are diversifying into the market from elsewhere. If finite windows of opportunity were the main determinant of entrant mortality, then one might expect to observe little variation in life spans across types of entrant. Conversely, learning is likely to be facilitated by the deep pockets of a parent firm who may, in addition, provide some assistance in evaluating market opportunities.

Consistent with this but more persuasive is the evidence that emerges from an examination of the actual post-entry experience of entrants. Biggadike (1976) studied a sample of 40 entrants in the United States during the late 1960s and early 1970s. All of them had parent firms in the Fortune 200 who had had plenty of experience with entry. Nevertheless, most of these entrants experienced severe losses through their first 4 years of operation. Mean and medium returns on investment were -78 percent and -40 percent respectively in the first 2 years of operation, and only 10 percent reported positive net income during those years. The poor financial performance of these firms seemed to be largely due to high marketing and R&D expenditures (41 percent and 51 percent of revenue respectively), and the gradual improvement in their financial performance over time mainly resulted from reductions in these ratios (to 25 percent and 23 percent respectively in the second 2 years of operation). This reduction seems to have been due to a more rapid growth in sales revenues (87 percent on average) than in advertising (51 percent) or R&D (33 percent) expenditures. In fact, some analysis of the data by Biggadike suggested that these entrants might need as much as 8 years to achieve positive returns, and 10–12 years to establish levels of returns comparable with those enjoyed by incumbents.

Whether entry is determined by short-lived windows of opportunity or, as seems rather more likely, is essentially a trial under fire, the basic data on entry and survival suggest a revision in conventional conceptualizations of both the nature and sources of entry barriers. The raw data suggest that entry is, apparently, rather easy and, by implication, that entry barriers are rather low. However, what is much more difficult is post-entry market penetration and, indeed, survival. That getting in is easy but that staying (much less expanding) in is difficult, suggests that the obstacles that entrants face are more in the nature of mobility barriers than entry barriers (e.g. Caves and Porter, 1977). Entrants and small established firms are, it appears, part of a rapidly churning flow of firms in and at the fringes of the market; a churn whose speed increases the higher the mobility barriers and the lower the entry barriers.

More subtly, one's view about the nature of the obstacles that entrants face depends upon exactly why one thinks that the observed turnover of firms occurs. The three views discussed above boil down to two different conceptions of the decision process used by entrants. The view of entry as a hit-and-run process sees observed entry as a rational response to finitely lived opportunities, while the other two views focus on the notion that entry may be a learning experience, a type of "trial." If entry really is hit and run, then obstacles to entry must be essentially transitory factors that are continually being created and demolished during the course of normal market operations. If one follows Bain (1956) in insisting that barriers are permanent structural features of markets, then the hit-and-run view of entry suggests that their malign effects are regularly (but temporarily) undermined by favorable demand- or supply-side shocks. Either way, the implication is that there is no stable long-run equilibrium market structure involving a fixed population of perhaps unevenly sized "insiders" protected from "outsiders" by certain permanent features of the environment. Equilibrium in this world is characterized by some exogenously determined flow of shocks which keeps the supply-side structure market in a permanent state of flux.

By contrast, the view of entry as a trial suggests that barriers are a kind of "cost of adjustment," a challenge which must eventually be hurdled to insure long-run viability. Barriers, in this view, are not so much obstacles to action as they are demands for action. They form a list of necessary prerequisites (as it were) that any competitor must have to its credit if it is to succeed. One might think of them as a set of skills that must be mastered, or scarce special assets that are a crucial fixed input into the process of generating net revenue. The problem for entrants is not that these skills or assets cannot be acquired or created *de novo*, but that it is costly to do so quickly. In order to expand from zero output to some level sustainable in the long run, an entrant must incur these costs, but once it has reached that output level, no further expenditures are necessary (save, perhaps, maintenance expenditure).

If entry is a type of learning experience, then it must, at base, be viewed as an investment decision. The data suggest that the interesting problems do not center around the question of whether entry will occur, but, rather, around the question of how much time and money has to be sunk by entrants to overcome the obstacles that they face, and how much creative imagination or plain good luck will be needed along the way. Adopting the view of entry as an investment and market expansion program subject to possibly severe costs of adjustment eventually brings one to the conjecture that conditions of finance are likely to play a major role in affecting the outcome of any given entry attempt. To the extent that success is just a question of getting up some steam and approaching obstacles from the right angle, then the problem of successfully overcoming barriers to entry is mostly a matter of diligent effort and time. If it can last long enough to learn the tricks of the trade, virtually any entrant can, in this view, become a perfectly viable competitor. Different entrants may, of course, require more or less time to make the grade, but time and the accumulation of experience is the key. That is, success may be as much a question of buying time as it is of surmounting any particular obstacle. The implication is, of course, that selection may be determined as much by capital market forces as by product market forces; the competition that entrants face is not so much that provided by incumbents in a given product market as that provided by all agents in the economy seeking funds in the capital market. At base, understanding why entrants fail may require no more understanding than why bankers pull the plug on them when they do.

3 The Measurement of Entry

The second interesting feature of the data that we wish to comment on is that different measures of entry (net and gross entry measures, entry measures based on sales or number of firms) are not very highly related to each other. This, in turn, seems to be the result of two more basic properties of the data. The first we have seen before. The high mortality rate of entrants discussed in section 2 manifests itself in several ways, and one of these is that entry and exit rates across industries are highly positively correlated. The second interesting property of the data is that entrants are typically quite small.

To assess what all this means, it is worth stepping back from the data and briefly exploring at least three of the choices that are made (implicitly or explicitly) when measuring entry. The first and perhaps simplest choice is between using a gross or a net (of exit) measure of entry. The fact that entry and exit are positively correlated suggests that there is liable to be a meaningful and not entirely random difference between gross and net measures. Not only may net entry be substantially less variable than gross entry, but its variation across industries and over time may differ in subtle ways from that of gross entry. As always, what matters is the uses to which the information will be put, and, in this case, on whether the displacement of small incumbents by small entrants matters or not. The classical conception of entry, for example, is of an increase in industry supply, and a net entry measure seems to be the appropriate measure to reflect it. Conceptions of competition which turn on the number of firms, by contrast, may find a truer reflection in a gross entry measure that indicates the increase in the size of the pool of players from which market winners (and losers) will be selected. The difference between net and gross measures, then, turns on whether the effect of entry on market performance depends on the number of survivors of the entry process, or on the total number of participants.

The second type of choice that is made is between measuring entry as a rate of new firm formation, or in terms of the sales penetration of

entrants. The important difference here arises from the fact that entrants
are typically much smaller than incumbents, and thus command a much
smaller market share on average than incumbents do. This type of choice
is likely to be important whenever it matters whether the entrant merely
maintains a presence in the market, or whether a substantive transfer of
sales takes place between entrant and incumbent. One imagines that, for
most purposes, what matters from the point of view of effective competition is that an actual transfer of sales takes place. Measures of market
penetration (and, in particular, net market share penetration) are
therefore likely to be particularly useful in measuring the strength of the
competitve force associated with entry. However, insofar as an entrant
in position is a potential acquirer of sales, then the distinction between
the rate of entry and the market penetration of entrants might be
thought of as roughly corresponding to the distinction between actual
and potential competition. The rate of entry, in this view, might be
thought of as an increase in the pool of potential players, and thus as a
proxy for the competitive threat posed by entry. The difference between
entry rate and entry penetration measures, then, turns on whether one's
conception of competition stresses the number of participants in the
process, or the scale of the actions that they take.

Of course, not all entrants are small, and even if one believes that
what matters most is how many firms there are in the market, one may
still have in mind measuring the number of "effective competitors" in the
identified market by firms larger than some minimum size. The idea
here is that only substantial entrants attract the attention of incumbents
and make an impact on the market. Most markets have many niches in
which competition is localized, and what may matter from the point
of view of market competition is the number of broad-line volume
producers in the market, and not the numerous smaller fry that inhabit
the fringes. One way to make this type of distinction is to count only
new firms that reach a given minimum size as entrants; another is to
measure entry as a change in some numbers equivalent measure to
concentration.

Finally, the third type of choice that is made when measuring entry
is between measuring sales penetration by the initial impact entrants
make on the market or by some medium-term impact, say 5 years post-
entry. In practice, most measures of entry record the sales of entrants
during their first year of operation (or during that part of their first year
that falls within the census year). Many of these new firms do not,
however, survive for many years, and those that do occasionally grow
at spectacular rates. It is not clear why typical measures of entry should
stress only the initial impact of entrants, and it is not hard to think

of alternatives that give a more accurate assessment of the long-run (or permanent) impact of entrants on their chosen market. If it is thought to be important to focus on the activities of survivors of the entry process, then it matters whether or not one includes possibly transitory activities.

There is, of course, nothing more boring than an abstract discussion of measurement issues, and there is nothing perceptive about the assertion that the right choice of measure depends on the purpose of the exercise. The issues are important, however, and it is therefore worth making the point by developing a specific illustration. Consider the effect of entry by a number of small firms into a nearly monopolized market in which the incumbent elects to act as a classic dominant firm *vis-à-vis* entrants and fringe firms (e.g. Worcester (1959), Gaskins (1971), and others). This means that the incumbent will maximize profits defined on residual demand (i.e. total market demand less the sales of entrant and fringe firms), and its degree of market power is reflected in the slope of the residual demand curve. The force of the competition that it faces depends on the difference between total and residual demand, and the increase in competition induced by entry is clearly the sales of entrants less those of exiting firms, i.e. roughly net entry penetration. A measure based on gross entry penetration would, by contrast, exaggerate the erosion in the dominant firm's market position because new entrants take sales not only from the dominant firm but also from exiting firms and contracting fringe firms. If, in the limit, entrants did no more than displace fringe firms, then the dominant firm would suffer no erosion of market power regardless of gross entry penetration.

Notice that there is no significance whatsoever to be attached to the number of entrants in this model (all that matters is the collective sales of the group), and so no entry rate measure would be appropriate. Indeed, it is rather hard to justify the use of any measure of entry at all since entry and fringe firms are effectively interchangeable as far as the working of the model is concerned. It follows that there is no particular significance to be attached to the sales made by entrants in their first year of operation, or, indeed, to anything other than the cumulative flow of net entry recorded since the formation of the dominant firm's monopoly. This slightly startling conclusion follows from the implicit assumption in the model that entrants and fringe firms free-ride *forever* on attempts made by the dominant firm to restrict prices. They thus cause a *permanent* erosion in the dominant firm's market power. All entrants are alike in this respect, and there is no point in differentiating these by cohort, or, indeed, of signaling the arrival of any new cohort. If, by contrast, entrants begin to cooperate with the dominant firm over time as they become better established in the market, then the impact of a given cohort of entrants will vary systematically over time. Entrants and fringe firms would not be interchangeable, and it would be necessary to keep track of which cohort any particular entrant (or fringe firm) belonged to. Clearly, using a measure of entry based on initial market impact would record different effects from a measure based on, say, penetration over 5 years.

The bottom line seems to be that entry is a multi-dimensional phenomenon, and the real question may be less that of ascertaining whether "entry" has an effect on market performance than that of discovering what kinds of effects are associated with the various dimensions of entry that one observes using the range of conventional measures available. If there are noticeably different effects associated with different dimensions of the entry flow, then it is possible that important policy choices ought to be made, that one ought to move beyond an earnest desire to encourage "entry" toward more focused policies that help to design a flow of entry with the "right" characteristics. After all, if what matters is the total pool of players in a market (rather than survivors), then one will want to maximize the gross entry rate. If, however, what matters is flattening the residual demand curve of a dominant firm, then one ought to be concerned with entry penetration. In practical terms, this means that one might choose to think carefully about the relative desirability of policies that encourage new firm formation and those more concerned with providing continuing assistance to new start-up firms.

4 Types of Entrant

The third interesting feature of the data on entry is that there are a range of different types of entrant, and some are more successful at penetrating markets or surviving in them than others. While this observation suggests that barriers to entry are entrant specific to some extent, it also carries the further implication that different types of entrant are likely to have rather different effects on market performance.

The interesting question that is raised by these results is whether there is any sense in which one type of entrant tends to crowd other types out of the market, and therefore whether there is any systematic pattern to the arrival and departure of different types of entrant. Suppose that a market is dominated by a large incumbent who, for some reason, myopically restricts supply and keeps prices artificially high. If there are no major barriers to entry, this restriction in supply will, in due course, induce a flow of entry sufficiently large to undermine the restriction in supply. Individual entrants will respond with a speed that depends on their specific characteristics, and each will make a contribution toward expanding industry supply that also depends on its specific characteristics. Imagine some particularly advantaged entrant that is both quick to react and has a substantial impact on the market. Since the restriction in supply is finite and does not increase over time, the more entrants there are of this type, the less there will be of any other type. Advantaged entrants will simply crowd out rival entrant types, and one will only ever observe that type of entrant in the market.

A second pattern that one might observe in the data is one of successive waves of activity by entrant type. Suppose that, although they have a substantial impact on the market when they do arrive, advantaged entrants are slow to take advantage of market opportunities. Crowding out will then occur as before, but only over time. Rival entrants may be quicker to enter the market, and one will therefore observe actual entry by rival types. However, the superior competitive ability of advantaged firms is likely to mean that, when they eventually arrive, advantaged entrants will to some extent displace rival entrants. One will observe something like waves of entry by entrant types, followed by waves of exit as less advantaged cohorts are squeezed out of the market to make room for more advantaged cohorts of entrants.

Studying the interaction between entrants is interesting for a number of reasons, not least because it may matter which type of entrant populates markets. At the simplest level, one might prefer to see most of the restriction in supply made good by domestic entrants rather than by imports. One may also be concerned to see an increasing population of, say, labor-managed firms, small high technology firms, businesses owned by minority ethnic groups, and so on. The question is whether desired types of entrant are crowded out by other types during market processes, and thus whether (and, if so, how) policy might discriminate by type of entrant.

Geroski (1989a) studied this question with respect to domestic and foreign-based entrants. In an economy with as large a trade deficit and as large an employment problem as the United Kingdom has, it matters whether imports are necessary to help keep markets competitive. Further, many people have voiced concern that imports into the United Kingdom are displacing UK firms at the high value added, high technology end of the market, thus sowing the seeds of further decline in the United Kingdom's comparative advantage. Thus it is of some concern to ascertain whether imports are crowding out domestic entrants. The exercise involved estimating a simple model of both types of entry flow, and looking to see how (if at all) they interacted with each other and, in particular, whether either foreclosed market opportunities that were potentially open to the other. Although domestic UK-based entrants appeared to be quicker to respond to UK market opportunities and had a larger impact on profits than importers into the United Kingdom, the results suggested that, on balance, the two types of entrant were essentially not competing. They evidently operated in quite different market niches, and, by and large, neither appeared to crowd the other out. Thus, however strong one's feeling is about the relative desirability of domestic and foreign-based entry, there may actually be very little need to make a choice between them at all.

Another area where the question of crowding out takes on substantial policy importance is with the apparent paradox associated with labor-managed or participatory firms. The evidence suggests that labor-managed firms are often rather more productive than capitalist firms of equivalent size in the same sector (e.g. Defourney et al., 1985), yet the incidence of labor-managed formation and, more tellingly, their ability to displace apparently less efficient capitalist firms and penetrate markets seems to be distinctly limited. The interesting question is why such firms seem unable to crowd out less efficient but more conventionally organized firms, and why the market does not seem to select strictly on the basis of efficiency.

Finally, it is worth briefly returning to the empirical observation that was discussed in section 3 to ask whether the very small average size of most entrants of all types is the result of interactions between entrants. That is, is small-scale entry a consequence of high entry rates? There are two reasons to think that this might be the case. First, the number of consumers potentially detachable from incumbents in any given period may be limited, and the more entrants that there are trying to attract the attention of these consumers, the less each entrant will obtain, *ceteris paribus*. The most likely reason for such an outcome is that entrants typically compete in niches of limited size that serve customers who are not interested in standardized products or are isolated in particular geographical markets. The second sense in which small-scale entry may be the consequence of high entry rates is that the knowledge that entry rates are and will continue to be high may stampede entrants into entering "too soon," into competing without having fully prepared themselves. As a consequence, they may fail to attract as many consumers as they potentially could and, indeed, they may fail far more frequently than they should.

5 Is Entry Worth It?

The final interesting property of the data that is worth commenting on is the size of the effects on market performance that have been attributed to entry. The general conclusion of, it must be said, a relatively small number of studies seems to be that the effects of entry – like the lives of most entrants – are fairly modest (e.g. Geroski, 1989b).

The most obvious and most important question that this raises is whether there is "too much" entry, whether the benefits of entry are worth the costs involved. On the face of it, these costs seem to be fairly substantial. Although the failure of any particular small firm may not involve a sacrifice of much in the way of nonsalvageable assets, there is no doubt that the planning, setting up, and running of such a firm requires a substantial input of human resources. Again, although the opportunity cost of these human resources is quite modest when reckoned on a per firm basis, the extremely large number of failures in each sector per year generates a total opportunity cost that is not insubstantial. It is worth trying to obtain at least a ballpark estimate of the orders of magnitude involved. If setting up and closing down costs absorb six person-months per firm, then 150 firms exiting per sector per year across 100 sectors (as was observed in the United Kingdom in 1983) adds up to about 7,500 person-years of labor that might have produced saleable output in the form of goods or services in a continuing firm. If these figures are at all accurate, they suggest that entry is indeed a costly process.

Of course, simple calculations like this overstate the costs of entry in numerous ways. If entry is truly hit and run and decisions are made rationally, then many of these costs will be covered by the returns earned by entrepreneurs while the window of opportunity is open. Similarly, if entry is a trial of some sort or another, then the benefits of selection may provide a kind of externality that helps to amortize some of these costs. Certainly, it is clear that "mistakes" are bound to happen, and it is hard to subscribe to any proposal suggesting that serious efforts should be made to eliminate them altogether. The interesting question is the extent to which they can be reduced without sacrificing the benefits of entry. Most studies which have studied the effect of entry have found that it is market penetration which is important, and this indicates that there may be scope for reducing the number of entrants whilst increasing their size without sacrificing the benefits of entry. Indeed, to the extent that this creates stronger competitors more capable of challenging incumbents, then one may actually increase the benefits of entry while reducing its costs. Following the discussion in section 2, one conjectures that this might involve raising entry barriers and lowering mobility barriers.

That it is the market penetration by entrants rather than the number of entrants or the entry rate which seems to matter raises the much broader question of whether market performance depends on the share of sales accounted for by leading incumbents, or on changes in that share. Entry directly causes a change in shares but, as we have seen, it may only be transitory change and it may not involve a net transfer of sales from leading incumbents. The importance of entry may not be that it reduces market concentration at any time so much as that it causes a reshuffling of sales amongst all firms in the market. More generally, it may be that it is the degree of market share mobility rather than the size distribution of market shares at any time which matters in determining how competitive a market is. Entry would be important, then, as one type of market share mobility.

While numerous economists have an intuitive feeling that market share mobility matters, many have some trouble in saying why. One of the simplest rationalizations of the importance of share mobility emerges in a natural way from Stigler's theory of oligopoly (Stigler, 1964). As is well known, if collusion is difficult to detect, then the temptation to free-ride may incline participants in an agreement to cheat on each other. Since it is rather hard to observe directly whether a rival is cheating or not, firms are likely to use indirect indicators, such as whether a rival is getting more than its "fair share" of business. The worth of these indirect indicators depends on the underlying "noisiness" of the market, on the myriad of supply and demand side shocks that affect sales – shocks that include entry by both new buyers and new sellers in the market. The stronger and less systematic these are, the more difficult it is to detect cheating, *ceteris paribus*. Since these shocks are likely to manifest themselves in a continual fluctuation of market shares, one concludes that competitive pricing and market share instability are likely to go hand in hand. The Stigler argument is, in fact, richer than this, since he also shows that, given the degree of instability in market shares, more concentrated markets are more likely to be able to sustain an agreement. This arises because large firms can, in effect, pool information on the shocks that make inferring collusion difficult, and this enhanced ability to detect cheating reduces the incentives of rivals to do so. Still, at bottom, what makes markets competitive in this story is not so much the number of firms present as the fact that market positions are not stable.

The bottom line, then, is that the modest effects of entry on market performance that have been observed may reflect the simple fact that what makes markets competitive is turbulence, manifested in a high enough degree of market share mobility to keep firms a little uncertain about the actions of their rivals. Entry is only one manifestation of this process, and a rather special one at that. Even if this is the case, and even if entry is the source of most of the dynamics of market share changes, it still remains true that entry seems to be a rather expensive way of administering shocks to the markets that need them. Regulation of both the number and types of entrants, and post-entry support given to help sustain entrants through their initial market trials may enhance the effect that entry has on market performance. Whether it can do so without increasing the costs of disciplining markets is an open question.

6 Concluding Remarks

It would be more than foolhardy to draw strong conclusions from a paper that is largely conjecture. What seems clear from the raw data on entry flows is that entry is a rich multi-dimensional phenomenon, a process that is both more interesting and more involved than the mechanical error-correction mechanism that features in most simple textbooks. On the face of it, entry is probably also a much less important determinant of market performance than is frequently asserted. Although this certainly reflects the fact that entrants face real obstacles in trying to penetrate into most markets, it probably reflects the fact that entry is only part of the complex process of market share dynamics which is both an important cause and a major consequence of market performance.

References

Bain, J.S. (1956) *Barriers to New Competition*. Cambridge, MA: Harvard University Press.

Biggadike, E. (1976) Corporate diversification: Entry, strategy and performance. Graduate School of Business Administration, Harvard University, Boston, MA.

Caves, R. and Porter, M. (1977) From entry barriers to mobility barriers: conjectural decisions and contrived deterrence to new competition. *Quarterly Journal of Economics* 97, 247–21.

Defourney, Estrin, J.S. and Jones, D. (1985) The effects of workers participation on enterprise performance. *International Journal of Industrial Organization* 3, 197–217.

Gaskins, D. (1971) Dynamic limit pricing: optimal pricing under threat of entry. *Journal of Economic Theory* 2, 306–22.

Geroski, P. (1989a) The interaction between domestic and foreign based entrants. In D. Audretsch, L. Sleuwaegar, and H. Yamawaki (eds), *The Convergence of Domestic and International Markets*, Amsterdam: North-Holland.

Geroski, P. (1989b) The effects of entry on profit margins in the short and long run. *Annales d'Economie et de Statistique* 15–16, 333–53.

Stigler, G. (1964) A theory of oligopoly. *Journal of Political Economy* 72, 44–61.

Worcester, D. (1959) Why dominant firms decline. *Journal of Political Economy* 65, 338–47.

Index

abrasive products industry 126, 132
adjustment costs 68–9, 80, 249
advertising 9, 24, 268
  in Belgium 115, 117
  in Japan 180–2
  in Korea 161–2
  in Norway 96
  in the UK 71
  in the US 44
asbestos industry 129–30

Basic Organizations of Associated
    Labor (BOALS) 207
Belgium
  advertising 115, 117
  capital requirements for
    entry 115, 117
  domestic entry 113–14
  entry, gross 258–60, 272
  entry, net 259, 274
  entry determinants 257, 267
    international profit
      opportunities 114–17, 263,
      265
  entry distribution 278
  entry model 113–16, 265
  entry rates 113–15, 117–19, 276
  exit 259–61, 274
  exit distribution 280
  exit rates 113–15, 118–19, 276,
    278
  follower strategy 113–14, 120
  foreign entry 113–14

Germany, as trading partner
    116–17, 119–20
  import penetration 112–13
  industry size 115, 118
  minimum efficient scale 115, 118
  open economy 111–12
  product differentiation 115, 117,
    120
  research and development 112,
    115, 117–19
  sunk costs 115, 117, 120
  turnover, in industries 119–20
Bell Laboratories 231
biotechnology industry 235–7
Boyer, Herbert, biotechnology
    industry 235
buildings, as sunk costs 34–5, 37–42,
    94
business groups 146

Canada
  entry, gross 259, 272
  entry, net 259, 274
  entry distribution 278
  entry rates 276
  exit 259, 274
  exit distribution 280
  exit rates 276, 278
  expanding firms, as entrants
    market share 250–1
    productivity 249–50
    turnover 252

Canada *continued*
  market share penetration 244–5
    regression analysis 249–52
  productivity, change due to
    entrants and exits 247–53
  productivity of firms 245–7,
    253–4
  turnover, in industries 245–7
capacity, excess, as entry deterrent
    8–9
capital, as entry barrier 28
capital durability 49, 94
capital markets
  in Korea 150–1
  in Yugoslavia 204, 206
capital requirements for entry 51,
    266
  in Belgium 115, 117
  in Germany 127–30
  in Japan 177–8
  in Korea 146, 156
  in Norway 95, 102–3, 107–8
  in the UK 71
  in the US 41
capital specificity 49
cartels 4–5
cereals industry 5, 7, 12–13
cigarette industry 129–30
clocks and watches industry 172,
    173
cola soft drink industry 10
communications equipment industry
    172, 173
competition *see* market contestability
computer-aided design (CAD)
    industry 237
concentrated industries 3, 51–2, 55
  in Germany
    change due to entrants and
      exits 123–6, 130–41
    regression analysis 126–7
  in Korea
    as cause of exit 161–2
    as entry barriers 147, 157
    influence on profits 158–61
  in Norway 95, 107

  in the UK 71
  in the US 27–8, 38, 42, 268
  in Yugoslavia 218
concrete products industry 125–6,
    132
contestability of markets *see* market
    contestability
costs of adjustment 68–9, 80, 249
credit markets 146
customer loyalty 32

de novo entrants
  data variance due to independent
    variables 99–101
  entry barriers across industry
    103–7
differentiation *see* product
    differentiation
disappearance of firms 150–1, 161–2
diversifying firms 56–7, 100–3, 108
domestic entry 13–14
  in Belgium 113–14
  in Norway 90, 93
  in the UK 75, 291–2
    speed of entry 80–1, 84
  in Yugoslavia 206
durability of capital 49, 94

economies of scale 51, 55–6
  in Germany 127–9
  in Japan 175–6
  in Norway 94–5
  in the UK 71
electronic components industry 172,
    173
entrants
  distinctions between 11, 290–2
  life span 79, 151
entrepreneurs 15–16, 226, 229, 238
  case studies 231, 235, 237
  in Yugoslavia 207–8
entry forestalling level *see* limit
    profits
entry measurement *see* measurement
    of entry
entry models *see* models of entry

entry success and failure
  entry barriers 285
  environmental factors 283, 285
  learning process 283–4, 286
  risk assessment 284, 286
equipment *see* machinery, as sunk
  costs
excess capacity, as entry deterrent
  8–9
expanding firms, as entrants
  in Canada
    market share 250–1
    productivity 249–50
    turnover 252
  in Norway
    data variance due to
      independent variables 100–2
    entry barriers across industry
      103–7
exports
  from Korea 157–60
  from Norway 93

failed entrants *see* entry success and
  failure
Fairchild Semiconductor 231–3
first-movers 9–10, 13
foreign entry
  in Belgium 113–14
  in the UK 75, 291–2
    speed of entry 80–1, 84
  in Yugoslavia 206
Fujitsu 233

General Electric 237
Genetech 235
Germany
  Belgium, as trading partner
    116–17, 119–20
  capital requirements for
    entry 127–30
  concentration change, due to
    entrants and exits 123–6,
    130–41
    regression analysis 126–7
  contestable markets 127–30

economies of scale 127–9
entry, gross 122, 259–61, 272
entry, net 259, 274
entry barriers 129–30
entry determinants 257, 267
entry distribution 278
entry model 123–6, 264
entry rates 122–3, 276
exit 122–3, 259–61, 274
exit distribution 280
exit rates 122–3, 276, 278
incumbent firms 116
industrial finance, bank-based 270
industry size 127, 128, 130
market share penetration 122–3
product differentiation 127–9
research and development 127–9
size of entrants 121–2
Golden Wonder 237
government policy
  in Korea 143–6, 156–7
  in Yugoslavia 205–7, 213–14,
    219–20, 269
growth in productivity *see*
    productivity growth

heterogeneity *see* product
    differentiation
Hitachi 233

IBM 238
imports 230
  to Belgium 112–13
  to Korea 158–60
  to Norway 93
incumbent firms 50–2, 55, 57,
    237–8, 289
  in Germany 116
  in Korea 147
  in Norway 96–7
  in the UK 66–9, 74
  in the US 27–9, 31, 36–44, 268
industry size
  in Belgium 115, 118
  in Germany 127, 128, 130
  in Norway 100, 102

industry size *continued*
  in the UK 74–5
  in the US 190–1, 193–4
  in Yugoslavia 216–18
industry turnover *see* turnover, in
  industries
innovation
  case studies 230–8
  entrepreneurs 229, 235, 238
  in the US 188, 192, 200–1
  industry life cycle 224–7, 230
  market structure, effect on 223
  product differentiation 225
  related to entry 222–3, 224, 226
  related to firm size 223–4
  research and development 225–6
Innoven Corporation 235

Japan
  advertising 180–2
  business cycle 168–70, 177–82
  capital requirements for entry
    177–8
  economies of scale 175–6
  entry, net 170–1, 274
    industry variations 172–5
  entry barriers 181
  entry determinants 268
  entry model 175–7
  industrial groups 270
  product differentiation 175–6
  size of entrants 175–6
  sub-contracting 182

Kellogg's 7, 12
Kodak 8, 10
Korea
  advertising 161–2
  business groups 146, 270
  capital market 150–1
  capital requirements for
    entry 146, 156
  concentrated industries
    as cause of exit 161–2
    as entry barriers 147, 157
    influence on profits 158–61

disappearance of firms 150–1
entry, gross 143, 259–61, 273
entry, net 259–60, 275
entry barriers 156
entry determinants 151–7, 257,
  267
entry distribution 279
entry model 144–5, 265
  independent variables 145–7
  measures of entry 148–50
entry rates 276
exit 143, 259–61, 275
exports 157–60
government policy 143–6, 156–7
imports 158–60
incumbent firms 147
limit pricing 144–5, 160
limit profits 144–5
market share penetration 149, 262
minimum efficient scale 146, 156,
  160
product differentiation 146
productivity growth 143
turnover, in industries 163

labor-management 205–9, 269, 292
life span of entrants 79, 151
limit pricing 2, 8
  in Korea 144–5, 160
  in the UK 71
limit profits 266
  in Korea 144–5
  in the UK 65–6, 70
  in the US 43
linen industry 126, 139
loans, subsidized 146–7, 156–7
loyalty, customer 32
Lubrizol 235

machinery, as sunk costs
  buildings, less sunk than
    machinery 37–9, 41, 94
  irrecoverable entry cost 34–5, 99
market contestability
  cereals industry 12–13
  effect of entrants 160–1

effect on incumbents 51
entry barriers 71, 79
identification 127–30
in Belgium 113
in Germany 127–30
industry concentration 95
industry effect 63, 64
market share penetration 75,
   288–9, 294–5
producer volatility 199
profits 103
related to sunk costs 44
stochastic factors 6–7
technology, influence of 225
market share penetration 288–9,
   293–4
in Canada 244–5
in Germany 122–3
in Korea 149, 262
in Norway 92
in the UK 75–8, 81
in the US 189–95, 198–9
market size *see* industry size
market specification 92–3
measurement of entry
choices in measurement 287–90
in Norway 91–2
in the US 33
medical equipment industry 126,
   135
mergers 150–1, 209–11
minimum efficient scale (MES)
in Belgium 115, 118
in Korea 146, 156, 160
in Norway 95, 99–101, 107
Mitsubishi 233
models of entry 50–2, 261–6
for Belgium 114–16
follower strategy 113–14
international profit
   opportunities 114
for Germany 123–6
for Japan 175–7
for Korea 144–5
independent variables 145–7
measures of entry 148–50

for Norway 91
for the UK 66–8
entry barriers 64–5, 73
incumbent firms 66–9, 74
limit profits 65–6, 70
speed of adjustment 68–9, 72,
   73–4
for the US 24–7, 189–90, 192–3
advertising 31–3, 35
entry measurement 33
growth in demand 30–1
incumbent firms 27–9
price-cost margins 30, 190
scale of entry 35–6
sunk costs 29–30, 34–5
monopolies 5–11, 32, 84
moving firms, as entrants
data variance due to independent
   variables 100–2
entry barriers across
   industry 103–7

Norway
advertising 96
capital requirements for entry 95,
   102–3, 107–8
concentrated industries 95, 107
distinctions between entrants 90
domestic entry 90, 93
economies of scale 94–5
entry, gross 259, 260, 273
entry, net 259, 275
entry barriers 89–90, 94–7, 103–7
entry determinants 257, 267
entry distribution 279
entry measurement 91–2
entry model 91, 264
entry rates 277
exit 259, 260, 275
exit distribution 281
exit rates 277, 279
exports 93
imports 93
incumbent firms 96–7
industry size 100, 102
market share penetration 92

Norway *continued*
  market specification 92–3
  minimum efficient scale 95,
    99–101, 107
  research and development 93,
    95–6, 99–102, 108
  risk of entry 97, 102
  size of entrants 92
  sunk costs 90, 94, 99–102, 107
  turnover, in industries 97

oligopolies, static models 2–5
Orr models 257–8, 261–6

Polaroid 15
Portugal
  entry, gross 258–9, 273
  entry, net 259–60, 275
  entry barriers 263, 265
  entry determinants 257, 267
  entry distribution 279
  entry model 262, 264
  entry rates 277
  exit 259–60, 275
  exit distribution 281
  exit rates 277, 279
  flexibility of firms 58–9
  open economy 54
potato crisp industry 237–8
preferential loans 146–7, 156–7
producer turnover *see* turnover, in
    industries
product differentiation 7, 8, 14, 16,
    52, 56, 255, 266
  in Belgium 115, 117, 120
  in Germany 127–9
  in Japan 175–6
  in Korea 146
  in the UK 71–2
productivity growth 245–7, 253–4
  due to entrants and exits 247–53
  expanding firms, as entrants
    market share 250–1
    productivity 249–50
    turnover 252

market share penetration 244–5
  regression analysis 249–52

radio and television industry 126,
    135
rate of entry 72, 73–4, 84, 128
rental market 35, 38–9, 42–4
(R&D) research and
    development 266
  in Belgium 112, 115, 117–19
  in Germany 127–9
  in Norway 93, 95–6, 99–102, 108
  in the UK 71
  in the US 285
risk of entry 267
  in Norway 97, 102
  in the US 29, 32

scale economies *see* economies of
    scale
second-hand markets 53–4, 57, 94
self-management 205–9, 269, 292
semiconductor industry 231–3
Shockley, William, semiconductor
    industry 231
Signetics 222–3
size, industry *see* industry size
size of entrants
  in Germany 121–2
  in Japan 175–6
  in Norway 92
  in the UK 78
  in the US 190–1, 193–4
Smiths (potato crisp industry) 237–8
social ownership 204, 206
socialist economy *see* Yugoslavia
specificity, capital 49
speed of entry 72, 73–4, 84, 128
stochastic factors in industry 6–7
sub-contracting 182
subsidized loans 146–7, 156–7
successful entrants *see* entry success
    and failure
sunk costs 49–58, 266–8
  in Belgium 115, 117, 120
  in Norway 90, 94, 99–102, 107

in the US 29–30, 34–5, 192, 196, 200–1
Swanson, Robert, biotechnology industry 235

Teal, Gordon, semiconductor industry 231
technology *see* innovation
television and radio industry 126, 135
Texas Instruments 231
Toshiba 233
turnover, in industries
  in Belgium, related to European market 119–20
  in Canada, related to productivity 245–7
  in Korea, related to measurement of entry 163
  in Norway, risk factor 97
  in the US, inter-industry differences 195–9

United Kingdom
  advertising 71
  capital requirements for entry 71
  concentrated industries 71
  domestic entry 75, 291–2
    speed of entry 80–1, 84
  economies of scale 71
  entry, gross 76–9, 259, 266, 273
  entry, net 259–60, 275
  entry barriers 79–84
  entry determinants 257, 267
  entry distribution 279
  entry model 66–8, 264
    entry barriers 64–5, 73
    incumbent firms 66–9, 74
    limit profits 65–6, 70
    regression analysis 70–1
    speed of adjustment 68–9, 72, 73–4
  entry rates 277
  exit 76–9, 259–61, 266, 275
  exit distribution 281
  exit rates 277, 279

foreign entry 75, 291–2
  speed of entry 80–1, 84
future returns 70
imports 291–2
industrial finance, market based 270
industry size 74–5
limit pricing 71
market share penetration 75–8, 81, 266
product differentiation 71–2
profits, expected 72–3, 80–1
research and development 71
size of entrants 78, 260
United States
  advertising 44
  capital requirements for entry 41
  concentrated industries 27–8, 38–42, 268
  entry, gross 259–60, 273
  entry, net 259, 275
  entry determinants 268
  entry distribution 279
  entry models 24–7, 189–90, 192–3
    advertising 31–3, 35
    entry measurement 33
    growth in demand 30–1
    incumbent firms 27–9
    price-cost margin 30, 190
    scale of entry 35–6
    sunk costs 29–30, 34–5
  entry rates 277
  exit 259–61, 275
  exit distribution 281
  exit rates 277, 279
  incumbent firms 31, 36–44, 268
  industrial finance, market based 270
  industry size 190–1, 193–4
  limit profits 43
  markets share penetration 189–95, 198–9
  research and development 285
  risk of entry 29, 32
  size of entrants 190–1, 193–4
  sunk costs 192, 196, 200–1

United States *continued*
  technology 188, 192, 200–1
  turnover, in industries 195–9

video display terminal (VDT)
  industry 234

watches and clocks industry 172,
  173

Yugoslavia
  Basic Organizations of Associated
    Labor 207
  capital markets 204, 206
  concentrated industries 218
  domestic entry 206
  earnings potential 212–15, 268–9

employment, as entry determinant
  213–15
entrepreneurs 207–8
entry, gross 209–13
entry, net 209–10
entry rates 204, 210–12
exit 208, 210
exit rates 204
foreign entry 206
government policy 205–7, 213–14,
  219–20, 269
industry size 216–18
lack of entry,
  consequences 216–18
self-management 205–9
social ownership 204, 206
state ownership 205–6